Fairfax County
Virginia

𝔅irth 𝔕egister

1880–1896

Patricia B. Duncan

HERITAGE BOOKS
2010

HERITAGE BOOKS
AN IMPRINT OF HERITAGE BOOKS, INC.

Books, CDs, and more—Worldwide

For our listing of thousands of titles see our website
at
www.HeritageBooks.com

Published 2010 by
HERITAGE BOOKS, INC.
Publishing Division
100 Railroad Ave. #104
Westminster, Maryland 21157

International Standard Book Numbers
Paperbound: 978-0-7884-5239-0
Clothbound: 978-0-7884-8482-7

TABLE OF CONTENTS

INTRODUCTION

The Virginia Bureau of Vital Records and Health Statistics has records of births from 1853 to present, with the exception of the years between 1896 and June 14, 1912, when there was no law requiring them. These records are based on an act passed by the Virginia General Assembly on April 11, 1853.

This is the second of a two volume series of transcriptions of microfilms reel no. 15 (1871-1896) Bureau of Vital Statistics, Births of Fairfax County, available through the Library of Virginia Interlibrary Loan Service. Some pages gave place of birth and father's residence only as Fairfax. Some pages listed the occupation of every father as farmer. Some pages listed the occupation and residence of the father as farmer and Fairfax on the first line but did not indicate any repeating for the rest of the column. On those pages, as it did not specifically state so, I listed the occupation and residence of father for the remainder of the page as ___. Page 206 ends with number 37 and page 207 begins with number 60.

Volume I of this series contains records from 1853 to 1879. Volume II of this series contains records from 1880 to 1896.

Appendix I contains a listing of additional handwritten information that appeared on each page, such as year, district, and commissioner recording the information.

Entries appear as follows:

SURNAME, given name, race/sex, date of birth, place of birth, father, father's occupation, father's residence, mother, informant, any notation; page:line [page on register].

Abbreviations used:

Ffx – Fairfax
WM – white male
WF – white female
FF – free female
FM – free male
CF – colored female
CM – colored male

SF – slave female
SM – slave male
inf: - informant
occ: - occupation
res: - resides
[ ] author's comment

Special thanks to the Library of Virginia and the Special Collections Library in Albuquerque, New Mexico for their help with this project.

APPENDIX I

Page 124: 1880; North District, R. F. Broadwater Commissioner
Page 125: 1880; North District, R. F. Broadwater Commissioner
Page 126: 1880; North District, R. F. Broadwater Commissioner
Page 127: 1880; South District, F. Wooster Commissioner
Page 128: 1880; South District, F. Wooster Commissioner
Page 129: 1880; South District, F. Wooster Commissioner
Page 130: 1881; North District, R. F. Broadwater Commissioner
Page 131: 1881; North District, R. F. Broadwater Commissioner
Page 132: 1881; South District, Frank Wooster Commissioner
Page 133: 1881; South District, Frank Wooster Commissioner
Page 134: 1882; North District, R. F. Broadwater Commissioner
Page 135: 1882; North District, R. F. Broadwater Commissioner
Page 136: 1882; South District, F. Wooster Commissioner
Page 137: 1882; South District, F. Wooster Commissioner
Page 138: 1882; South District, F. Wooster Commissioner
Page 139: 1883; North District, R. F. Broadwater Commissioner
Page 140: 1883
Page 141: 1883; North District, R. F. Broadwater Commissioner
Page 142: 1883; North District, R. F. Broadwater Commissioner
Page 143: 1883; South District, F. Wooster Commissioner
Page 144: 1883; South District, F. Wooster Commissioner
Page 145: 1883; South District, F. Wooster Commissioner
Page 146: 1884; South District, F. Wooster Commissioner
Page 147: 1884; South District, F. Wooster Commissioner
Page 148: 1884; South District, F. Wooster Commissioner
Page 149: 1884; North District, R. F. Broadwater Commissioner
Page 150: 1884; North District, R. F. Broadwater Commissioner
Page 151: 1884; North District, R. F. Broadwater Commissioner
Page 152: 1885; North District, R. F. Broadwater Commissioner
Page 153: 1885; North District, R. F. Broadwater Commissioner
Page 154: 1885; North District, R. F. Broadwater Commissioner
Page 155: 1886; South District, F. Wooster Commissioner [Note:
    1885 for South Dist. back of 1886 South]
Page 156: 1885; South District, F. Wooster Commissioner
Page 157: 1885; South District, F. Wooster Commissioner
Page 158: 1886; North District, R. F. Broadwater Commissioner
Page 159: 1886; North District, R. F. Broadwater Commissioner
Page 160: 1886; North District, R. F. Broadwater Commissioner
Page 161: 1887; North District, S. A. Wrenn Commissioner
Page 162: 1887; North District, S. A. Wrenn Commissioner
Page 163: 1887; North District, S. A. Wrenn Commissioner
Page 164: 1887; North District, S. A. Wrenn Commissioner
Page 165: 1887; North District, S. A. Wrenn Commissioner
Page 166: 1887; South District, Robt. Wiley Commissioner
Page 167: 1887; South District, Robt. Wiley Commissioner

Page 208: 1892; South District (#1-27 Centreville, #28-32 ???), J. N. Ballard Commissioner

Page 209: 1892; South District (#33-43 Falls Church, #44-59 Lee), J. N. Ballard Commissioner

Page 210: 1893; South District, J. N. Ballard Commissioner

Page 211: 1893; South District, J. N. Ballard Commissioner

Page 212: 1893; South District, J. N. Ballard Commissioner

Page 213: 1893; North District, S. A. Wrenn Commissioner

Page 214: 1893; North District, S. A. Wrenn Commissioner

Page 215: 1893; North District, S. A. Wrenn Commissioner

Page 216: 1893; North District, S. A. Wrenn Commissioner

Page 217: 1894; North District, S. A. Wrenn Commissioner

Page 218: 1894; North District, S. A. Wrenn Commissioner

Page 219: 1894; North District, S. A. Wrenn Commissioner

Page 220: 1894; North District, S. A. Wrenn Commissioner

Page 221: 1896; South District, J. N. Ballard Commissioner [note on top of page: This seems to be 1894. Birth registration for Elmo Cross, line 16, places year of this report as 1894.]

Page 222: 1895 [1894 written above]

Page 223: 1895; South District, J. N. Ballard Commissioner [1895 x out and 1894 written above]

Page 224: 1895; South District, J. N. Ballard Commissioner [1894 written above 1895]

Page 225: 1896; North District, S. A. Wrenn Commissioner

Page 226: 1896; North District, S. A. Wrenn Commissioner

Page 227: 1896; North District, S. A. Wrenn Commissioner

Page 228: 1896; North District, S. A. Wrenn Commissioner

Page 229: 1897; South District, J. N. Ballard Commissioner [1897 x out and 1896 written above]

Page 230: 1897; South District, J. N. Ballard Commissioner [1896 written above 1897]

Page 231: 1896; South District, J. N. Ballard Commissioner

Page 232: 1897; South District, J. N. Ballard Commissioner [1896 written above 1897]

FAIRFAX COUNTY BIRTH REGISTER 1880-1896

ADAMS, Allen; WM; b. 4 Dec 1890, in Ffx; father: Robt. L. ADAMS; occ: farmer; res: Ffx; mother: Letty ADAMS; inf: R. L. ADAMS, father; pg:ln: 189:01

ADAMS, Beulah; WF; b. 6 Oct 1890, in Ffx; father: C. H. ADAMS; occ: telegraph operator; res: Ffx; mother: Blanch ADAMS; inf: C. H. ADAMS, father; pg:ln: 185:01

ADAMS, Clara Lee; WF; b. 15 Sep 1892, in Ffx; father: T. S. ADAMS; occ: farmer; res: Ffx; mother: Idella ADAMS; inf: T. S. ADAMS, father; pg:ln: 202:03

ADAMS, Effie Viola; WF; b. 14 Dec 1891, in Burke Sta.; father: Chas. A. ADAMS; occ: telegraph operator; res: Burke Sta.; mother: Blanche ADAMS; inf: parents; pg:ln: 193:01

ADAMS, Grace; WF; b. 1 Feb 1885, in Gt. Falls; father: Phillip ADAMS; occ: farmer; res: Gt. Falls; mother: Olivia ADAMS; inf: father; pg:ln: 152:01

ADAMS, H. S.; WM; b. 29 Dec 1893, in Ffx; father: R. L. ADAMS; occ: farmer; res: Ffx; mother: Lettie ADAMS; inf: R. L. ADAMS, father; pg:ln: 213:02

ADAMS, Harmonia; WF; b. 21 May 1881, in Hunters Mill; father: Oscar ADAMS; occ: farmer; res: Hunters Mill; mother: Isabella ADAMS; inf: father; pg:ln: 130:01

ADAMS, Oscar; WM; b. 18 Jun 1890, in Ffx; father: Oscar ADAMS; occ: farmer; res: Ffx; mother: Isabella ADAMS; inf: O. ADAMS, father; pg:ln: 189:02

ADAMS, Robt.; CM; b. 15 Apr 1894, in Ffx; father: Jas. ADAMS; occ: farmer; res: Ffx; mother: F. ADAMS; inf: Jas. ADAMS, father; pg:ln: 217:04

ADAMS, Sallie; CF; b. 25 Nov 1892, in Ffx; father: Jas. ADAMS; occ: farmer; res: Ffx; mother: Fannie ADAMS; inf: Jas. ADAMS, father; pg:ln: 202:01

ADAMS, Truman; WM; b. 28 Oct 1888, in ___; father: Oscar ADAMS; occ: farmer; res: Ffx; mother: Isabell ADAMS; inf: O. ADAMS, father; pg:ln: 173:03

ADAMS, W. P.; CM; b. 3 Nov 1894, in Ffx; father: W. ADAMS; occ: farmer; res: Ffx; mother: Lizzie ADAMS; inf: W. ADAMS, father; pg:ln: 217:03

ADDISON, Bland Newton; WM; b. 10 Oct 1889, in Ffx; father: Thos. D. ADDISON; occ: farmer; res: Ffx; mother: Mary ADDISON; inf: T. D. ADDISON, father; pg:ln: 181:01

ADDISON, Jno. D.; WM; b. 19 Jan 1887 in Ffx; father: Thos. D. ADDISON; occ: farmer; res: Ffx; mother: Mary ADDISON; inf: Thos. D. ADDISON, father; pg:ln: 166:01

ALEXANDER, Eugene E.; CM; b. 26 May 1892, in Ffx; father: Eugene ALEXANDER; occ: farmer; res: Ffx; mother: Mary ALEXANDER; inf: E. ALEXANDER, father; pg:ln: 202:02

ALLEN, ___ (dead); CM; b. 1 Jun 1889, in Ffx; father: Fenton ALLEN; occ: laborer; res: Ffx; mother: Alice ALLEN; inf: Fenton ALLEN, father; pg:ln: 181:05

ALLEN, Carl Y.; WM; b. 19 Apr 1889, in Ffx; father: James ALLEN; occ: carpenter; res: Ffx; mother: Laura ALLEN; inf: Jas. ALLEN, father; pg:ln: 177:01

ALLEN, Edward Thos.; WM; b. 22 Jun 1896, in Accotink Sta.; father: E. H. ALLEN; occ: telegraph operator & depot agent; res: Accotink Sta.; mother: Alice ALLEN; inf: father; pg:ln: 229:02

ALLEN, John Fields; CF; b. 2 Aug 1891 nr Alexandria; father: A. ALLEN; occ: laborer; res: nr Alex.; mother: Ella Gaines ALLEN; inf: parent; pg:ln: 196:25

ALLEN, not named; WF; b. 6 Dec 1892 in Huntley; father: Wm. ALLEN; occ: farmer; res: Huntley; mother: Essy ALLEN; inf: father; pg:ln: 207:61

ALLEN, Paul F.; WM; b. 11 Sep 1895 in Ffx; father: F. M. ALLEN; occ: farmer; res: Ffx; mother: J. B. ALLEN; inf: F. M. ALLEN, father; pg:ln: 225:03

ALLNUT, W. P.; WM; b. 6 Apr 1894 in Ffx; father: R. J. ALLNUT; occ: farmer; res: Ffx; mother: J. C. ALLNUTT; inf: R. J. ALLNUT, father; pg:ln: 217:01

ALLNUTT, Raymond; WM; b. 24 Aug 1896 in Ffx; father: Raymond J. ALLNUTT; occ: farmer; res: Ffx; mother: Jennie C. ALLNUTT [originally written as Jane]; inf: R. J. ALLNUTT, father Birth certificate: Raymond Joseph ALLNUTT of 1349 Eastern Dr., Fairlawn NJ, SSN [given but I won't print here], b. 24 Aug 1896, father Richard Joseph Allnutt age 33. Mother Jennie Dedonia Bennett age 31 of 4420 Alton Rd NW Wash. DC. Clerk in Charge of old records: Applicant states that his father's name is Richard and not Raymond as shown on the fact of this certificate.; pg:ln: 225:02

AMBLER, Earle; WM; b. 5 Mar 1889 in Ffx; father: C. F. AMBLER; occ: laborer; res: Ffx; mother: Elmira AMBLER; inf: C. F. AMBLER, father; pg:ln: 181:04

AMBROSE, Henry; CM; b. 20 Oct 1887 in Ffx; father: Thornton AMBROSE; occ: farmer; res: Ffx; mother: Jennie AMBROSE; inf: Thornton AMBROSE, father; pg:ln: 160:01

AMBROSE, Mordica; CM; b. 1 Mar 1888 in ___; father: Thornton AMBROSE; occ: farmer; res: Ffx; mother: Jennie AMBROSE; inf: T. AMBROSE, father; pg:ln: 173:02

ANDERSON, __ _ (stillborn); CM; b. 16 Feb 1880 in Ffx; father: W. ANDERSON; occ: farmer; res: Ffx; mother: Rosa; inf: W. ANDERSON, father; pg:ln: 127:02

ANDERSON, ___; CF; b. 11 Jun 1883 in Ffx; father: W. ANDERSON; occ: farmer; res: Ffx; mother: Rose ANDERSON; inf: Rose ANDERSON, mother; pg:ln: 143:01

ANDERSON, ___; CM; b. 3 Mar 1883 in Ffx; father: Charles ANDERSON; occ: farmer; res: Ffx; mother: Sarah ANDERSON; inf: Chas. ANDERSON, father; pg:ln: 143:02

ANDERSON, Albert; CM; b. 20 Dec 1896 nr Fairfax C. H.; father: Silas ANDERSON; occ: farmer; res: nr C. H.; mother: Pearl ANDERSON; inf: father; pg:ln: 229:04

ANDERSON, Anna Rebecca; CF; b. 2 Apr 1892 nr Clifton Sta.; father: Stephen ANDERSON; occ: laborer; res: nr Clifton; mother: Elizabeth ANDERSON; inf: father; pg:ln: 206:17

ANDERSON, Elizabt.; CF; b. 16 Nov 1880 in Ffx; father: Geo. ANDERSON; occ: farmer; res: Ffx; mother: Matilda; inf: Geo. ANDERSON, father; pg:ln: 127:01

ANDERSON, Frank; CM; b. 9 Nov 1889 in Ffx; father: J. L. ANDERSON; occ: laborer; res: Ffx; mother: Catherine ANDERSON; inf: J. L. ANDERSON, father; pg:ln: 181:06

ANDERSON, Jno. Luther; CM; b. 3 Jun 1887 in Ffx; father: Luther ANDERSON; occ: laborer; res: Ffx; mother: Kate ANDERSON; inf: L. ANDERSON, father; pg:ln: 166:04

ANDERSON, Margt.; WF; b. 12 Nov 1882 in Falls Church; father: Jos. F. ANDERSON; occ: mechanic; res: Falls Church; mother: Mary E. ANDERSON; inf: father; pg:ln: 134:02

ANDERSON, Robert W.; CM; b. 1 Aug 1893 nr Fairfax C. H.; father: Luther ANDERSON; occ: shoemaker; res: nr Fairfax C. H.; mother: Catharine ANDERSON; inf: parent; pg:ln: 212:100

ANDERSON, Sevenia; CF; b. 23 Sep 1887 in Ffx; father: George ANDERSON; occ: laborer; res: Ffx; mother: Amelia ANDERSON; inf: George ANDERSON, father; pg:ln: 166:05

ANKERS, Mary H.; WF; b. 10 Sep 1890 in Ffx; father: Jonothan ANKERS; occ: farmer; res: Ffx; mother: Annie ANKERS; inf: J. ANKERS, father; pg:ln: 189:03

ARCHARD, Harry J.; WM; b. 8 Sep 1893 in Burke Sta.; father: Patrick ARCHARD; occ: farmer; res: nr Burke Sta.; mother: Florince ARCHARD; inf: father; pg:ln: 210:01

ARCHER, Wm. S.; CM; b. 12 Jun 1893 nr Accotink; father: Wm. S. ARCHER; occ: laborer; res: nr Accotink; mother: Charlotte ARCHER; inf: father; pg:ln: 210:02

ARMSTRONG, Frank E.; WM; b. 23 May 1896 in Ffx; father: Chas. ARMSTRONG; occ: farmer; res: Ffx; mother: Josephin[e] ARMSTRONG; inf: C. ARMSTRONG, father; pg:ln: 225:04

ARMSTRONG, Oliver; WM; b. 17 Aug 1894 in Ffx; father: Chas. L. ARMSTRONG; occ: farmer; res: Ffx; mother: Josephine ARMSTRONG; inf: C. L. ARMSTRONG, father; pg:ln: 217:02

ARNOLD, Harry; WM; b. 1 Jan 1887 in Ffx; father: Marshall ARNOLD; occ: laborer; res: Ffx; mother: Jennie ARNOLD; inf: Marshall ARNOLD, father; pg:ln: 166:02

ARNOLD, Willie; WM; b. 12 Oct 1884 in Ffx; father: Marshal ARNOLD; occ: farmer; res: Ffx; mother: Jennie ARNOLD; inf: M. ARNOLD, father; pg:ln: 146:01

ASHBY, Garnet A.; CM; b. 6 May 1896 in Ffx; father: Isaac ASHBY; occ: farmer; res: Ffx; mother: Maria ASHBY; inf: I. ASHBY, father; pg:ln: 225:01

ASHBY, Virginia; CF; b. 10 Jun 1893 in Ffx; father: Saml. ASHBY; occ: farmer; res: Ffx; mother: Lou ASHBY; inf: S. ASHBY, father; pg:ln: 213:03

ASHFORD, ___; WF; b. 9 May 1884 in Falls Church; father: E. S. ASHFORD; occ: merchant; res: Falls Church; mother: Minnie ASHFORD; inf: father; pg:ln: 149:01

ASHFORD, Dorothy [Dora lined thru]; WF; b. 28 Aug 1889 [19 lined thru] in Ffx; father: Geo. S. ASHFORD; occ: laborer; res: Ffx; mother: Cora ASHFORD; inf: Geo. S. ASHFORD, father Note of 28 Mar 1936 Washington DC - I wish to state that the date of birth of Dora Ashford is August 28, 1889 and not August 19, 1889. The name should be corrected to Dorothy instead of Dora. Signed Cora S. ASHFORD, mother.; pg:ln: 181:03

ASHFORD, Edgar B.; WM; b. 11 Oct 1886 in Falls Ch.; father: E. S. ASHFORD; occ: mcht.; res: Falls Ch.; mother: ___ ASHFORD; inf: father; pg:ln: 158:01

ASHFORD, Elizabeth; WF; b. 2 Dec 1881 in Ffx; father: Edgar S. ASHFORD; occ: carpenter; res: Ffx; mother: Fannie ASHFORD; inf: E. S. ASHFORD, father; pg:ln: 132:02

ASHFORD, Mary M.; WF; b. 27 Apr 1881 in Ffx; father: Jas. W. ASHFORD; occ: carpenter; res: Ffx; mother: Melvina ASHFORD; inf: J. W. ASHFORD, father; pg:ln: 132:01

ASHTON, Henry; CM; b. 27 Jun 1885 in Falls Church; father: Armstead ASHTON; occ: laborer; res: Falls Church; mother: Mary ASHTON; inf: father; pg:ln: 152:02

ASHTON, Kattie; CF; b. 29 Aug 1883 in Falls Church; father: Armstead ASHTON; occ: laborer; res: Falls Church; mother: Mary ASHTON; inf: father; pg:ln: 139:01

ASHTON, Lora Barnes; WF; b. 10 Oct 1889 in Ffx; father: Dr. S. T. ASHTON; occ: physician; res: Ffx; mother: Nina ASHTON; inf: Dr. S. T. ASHTON, father; pg:ln: 181:02

ASHTON, Mary E.; CF; b. 11 Oct 1882 in Falls Church; father: Armstead ASHTON; occ: laborer; res: Falls Church; mother: Elizabeth ASHTON; inf: father; pg:ln: 134:01

ASHTON, Mary; CF; b. 27 Oct 1888 in Ffx; father: Armstead ASHTON; occ: farmer; res: Ffx; mother: Mary ASHTON; inf: A. ASHTON, father; pg:ln: 173:01

ASHTON, not named; CF; b. 28 Dec 1885 in Langley; father: Basil ASHTON; occ: laborer; res: Langley; mother: Isabella ASHTON; inf: father; pg:ln: 152:03

ASHTON, Stuart T.; WM; b. 10 Sep 1891 nr Chantilly; father: Dr. S. T. ASHTON; occ: physician; res: nr Chantilly; mother: Nina ASHTON; inf: parents; pg:ln: 194:04

AVERILL, Julia B.; WF; b. 11 Jul 1893 in Ffx; father: F. C. AVERILL; occ: farmer; res: Ffx; mother: Effie AVERILL; inf: F. C. AVERILL, father; pg:ln: 213:01

AYRE, Elmer Thomas; WM; b. 19 Jul 1891 in Clifton; father: Thomas A. AYRE; occ: Dept. Agent; res: Clifton; mother: Rosa L. AYRE; inf: parents; pg:ln: 194:05

AYRE, Samue[l] E.; WM; b. 13 Aug 1880 in Ffx; father: Thos. P. AYRE; occ: farmer; res: Ffx; mother: Ella V.; inf: T. P. AYRE, father; pg:ln: 127:03

AYRES, Annie May; WF; b. 1 Aug 1887 in Ffx; father: Thos. P. AYRES; occ: farmer; res: Ffx; mother: Mary AYRES; inf: Thos. P. AYRES, father; pg:ln: 166:03

AYRES, Columbus; WM; b. 23 Oct 1892 in Hybla Valley; father: Thos. P. AYRES; occ: farmer; res: Hybla Valley; mother: Ella V. AYRES; inf: father; pg:ln: 207:60

AYRES, Etta V.; WF; b. 22 May 1896 nr Alex.; father: W. L. AYRES; occ: farmer; res: nr Alex.; mother: Hellen A. AYRES; inf: father; pg:ln: 229:03

AYRES, Mary; WF; b. 1 Mar 1896 nr Alex.; father: Thos. P. AYRES; occ: farmer; res: nr Alex.; mother: Ellen V. AYRES; inf: father; pg:ln: 229:01

AYRES, Myrtle; WF; b. 3 Apr 1894 nr Alexandria; father: Thos. P. AYRES; occ: farmer; res: nr Alexandria; mother: Ella B. AYRES; inf: father; pg:ln: 221:01

BAGGOTT, Annie Louise; WF; b. 23 Mar 1894 nr Accotink; father: Levi BAGGOTT; occ: R. R. hand; res: nr Accotink; mother: Rebecca Anne BAGGOTT; inf: mother; pg:ln: 221:12

BAGGOTT, Everett; WM; b. 27 Jan 1892 nr Accotink; father: Thomas BAGGOTT; occ: rail roading; res: nr Accotink; mother: Elizabeth BAGGOTT; inf: father; pg:ln: 207:63

[BAGGOT1], not named (dead twin girls); WF; b. 29 Dec 1891 nr Accotink; father: Levi BAGGOTT; occ: farmer; res: nr Accotink; mother: Rebecca A. BAGGOTT; inf: parents; pg:ln: 195:03

BAGGOTT, Thos.; WM; b. 29 Dec 1894 nr Accotink; father: Thomas BAGGOTT; occ: R. R. hand; res: nr Accotink; mother: Elizabeth BAGGOTT; inf: mother; pg:ln: 221:11

BAGGOTT, Willie; WM; b. 23 Nov 1889 in Ffx; father: Thos. BAGGOTT; occ: laborer; res: Ffx; mother: Elizabeth BAGGOTT; inf: Thos. BAGGOT, father; pg:ln: 181:07

BAILEY, ___; CF; b. 10 Nov 1890 in Ffx; father: W. BAILEY; occ: farmer; res: Ffx; mother: Jemima BAILEY; inf: W. BAILEY, father; pg:ln: 189:07

BAILEY, Baby; CF; b. 12 Nov 1889 in Ffx; father: W. BAILEY; occ: farmer; res: Ffx; mother: Jennie BAILEY; inf: W. BAILEY, father; pg:ln: 177:10

BAILEY, Dora A.; WF; b. 28 Feb 1883 in Bailey's X Roads; father: Theodore BAILEY; occ: mechanic; res: Bailey's X Roads; mother: M. O. BAILEY; inf: father; pg:ln: 139:03

BAILEY, Edgar H.; WM; b. 27 Jun 1889 in Ffx; father: Theodore BAILEY; occ: farmer; res: Ffx; mother: M. BAILEY; inf: Theo. BAILEY, father; pg:ln: 177:19

BAILEY, French L.; WM; b. 15 Dec 1886 in Bailey's X Rds; father: Theodore BAILEY; occ: mechanic; res: Bailey's X Rds; mother: M. O. BAILEY; inf: father; pg:ln: 158:05

BAILEY, French; WM; b. 20 Apr 1887 in Ffx; father: Theodore BAILEY; occ: wheelwright; res: Ffx; mother: Mis[s]ouri BAILEY; inf: T. BAILEY, father; pg:ln: 160:23

BAILEY, Grace (twin); WF; b. 1 Aug 1881 in Baileys X Roads; father: Ray T. BAILEY; occ: farmer; res: Baileys X Roads; mother: Mary BAILEY; inf: father; pg:ln: 130:02

BAILEY, Hattie; CF; b. 17 Apr 1896 in Ffx; father: Henson BAILEY; occ: farmer; res: Ffx; mother: Nora BAILEY; inf: H. BAILEY, father; pg:ln: 225:11

BAILEY, Horace C.; WM; b. 8 Apr 1886 in Bailey's X Rds; father: Horace BAILEY; occ: farmer; res: Bailey's X Rds; mother: Eliza BAILEY; inf: father; pg:ln: 158:04

BAILEY, Ida; WF; b. 6 Jul 1884 in Bailey's X Roads; father: Ray T. BAILEY; occ: farmer; res: Bailey's X Roads; mother: Mary BAILEY; inf: father; pg:ln: 149:05

BAILEY, Joseph; WM; b. 10 Oct 1888 in Ffx; father: Dennis BAILEY; occ: R. Rd. employee; res: Ffx; mother: J. H. BAILEY; inf: Dennis BAILEY, father; pg:ln: 170:05

BAILEY, Lewis B.; WM; b. 6 Oct 1885 in Bailey's X Roads; father: Ray T. BAILEY; occ: farmer; res: Bailey's X Roads; mother: Mary B. BAILEY; inf: father; pg:ln: 152:05

BAILEY, Lizzie; WF; b. 10 Feb 1894 in Ffx; father: H. B. BAILEY; occ: farmer; res: Ffx; mother: E. BAILEY; inf: H. B. BAILEY, father; pg:ln: 217:09

BAILEY, Molly; CF; b. 15 Jul 1884 in Falls Church; father: Silas BAILEY; occ: laborer; res: Falls Church; mother: Eliz. BAILEY; inf: father; pg:ln: 149:03

BAILEY, not named; CF; b. 16 Apr 1893 in Ffx; father: W. BAILEY; occ: farmer; res: Ffx; mother: Jane BAILEY; inf: W. BAILEY, father; pg:ln: 213:10

BAILEY, Rosier B.; CM; b. 18 Jun 1881 in Dranesville; father: James BAILEY; occ: laborer; res: Dranesville; mother: Lucy BAILEY; inf: father; pg:ln: 130:04

BAILEY, S. C. N. (twin); WM; b. 17 Feb 1881 in Baileys X Roads; father: Theodore BAILEY; occ: mechanic; res: Baileys X Roads; mother: Missouri BAILEY; inf: father; pg:ln: 130:03

BAILEY, W.; CM; b. 14 Jul 1894 in Ffx; father: W. BAILEY; occ: farmer; res: Ffx; mother: Jane BAILEY; inf: W. BAILEY, father; pg:ln: 217:12

BAILISS, Jennie, WF; b. 30 Sep 1891 nr Alexandria; father: Hilman BAILISS; occ: farmer; res: nr Alexandria; mother: Katie BAILISS; inf: parents; pg:ln: 195:01

BAILISS, Maud; WF; b. 2 Jun 1887 in Ffx; father: Harrison BAILISS; occ: farmer; res: Ffx; mother: Catharine BAILISS; inf: H. BAILISS, father; pg:ln: 160:25

BAKER, Alice; WF; b. 5 Oct 1893 nr Mt. Vernon; father: H. J. BAKER; occ: mechanick; res: nr Mt. Vernon; mother: Ann L. BAKER; inf: mother; pg:ln: 210:11

BAKER, Elizabeth; WF; b. 5 Dec 1889 in Ffx; father: H. Judson BAKER; occ: farmer; res: Ffx; mother: Anna L. BAKER; inf: H. J. BAKER, father; pg:ln: 181:09

BAKER, Mary E.; WF; b. 1 Nov 1887 in Ffx; father: H. Judson BAKER; occ: farmer; res: Ffx; mother: Annie L. BAKER; inf: H. Judson BAKER, father; pg:ln: 166:08

BALL, Carry; CF; b. 3 Jan 1887 in Ffx; father: David BALL; occ: farmer; res: Ffx; mother: Sarah BALL; inf: D. BALL, father; pg:ln: 160:21

BALL, Jane; CF; b. 24 Mar 1888 in ___; father: David BALL; occ: farmer; res: Ffx; mother: Sara BALL; inf: D. BALL, father; pg:ln: 173:08

BALL, Newton; CM; b. 25 Jul 1883 in Falls Church; father: David BALL; occ: laborer; res: Falls Church; mother: Sarah BALL; inf: father; pg:ln: 139:04

BALL, Perry L.; WM; b. 27 Nov 1883 in Vienna; father: Jno. T. BALL; occ: farmer; res: Vienna; mother: Kate BALL; inf: mother; pg:ln: 139:07

BALL, Sarah; CF; b. 24 Feb 1885 in Falls Church; father: David BALL; occ: laborer; res: Falls Church; mother: Sarah BALL; inf: father; pg:ln: 152:06

BALL, W. A.; CM; b. 14 Sep 1892 in Ffx; father: Chas. BALL; occ: farmer; res: Ffx; mother: Sarah BALL; inf: Chas. BALL, father; pg:ln: 202:08

BALLARD, Maggie; WF; b. 1 Jul 1889 in Ffx; father: J. N. BALLARD; occ: farmer; res: Ffx; mother: Mary R. BALLARD; inf: J. N. BALLARD, father; pg:ln: 181:12

BALLARD, Margt.; WF; b. 11 Dec 1888 in ___; father: Lyman BALLARD; occ: farmer; res: Ffx; mother: Mary BALLARD; inf: L. BALLARD, father; pg:ln: 173:05

BALLENGER, Amy B.; WF; b. 20 Sep 1890 in Ffx; father: Jno. W. BALLENGER; occ: farmer; res: Ffx; mother: Margt. BALLENGER; inf: Mgt. BALLENGER, mother; pg:ln: 189:17

BALLENGER, W. H.; WM; b. 10 Mar 1889 in Ffx; father: Jno. W. BALLENGER; occ: farmer; res: Ffx; mother: Margt. F. BALLENGER; inf: J. W. BALLENGER, father; pg:ln: 177:06

BANISTER, Mary E.; WF; b. 16 Feb 1893 in Ffx; father: G. A. BANISTER; occ: farmer; res: Ffx; mother: Jennie E. BANISTER; inf: G. A. BANISTER, father; pg:ln: 213:14

BANKS, ___; CM; b. 2 May 1884 in Falls Church; father: Henry BANKS; occ: farmer; res: Falls Church; mother: Judy BANKS; inf: father; pg:ln: 149:06

BANKS, Beattrice; CF; b. 10 Jan 1893 in Ffx; father: Willis BANKS; occ: farmer; res: Ffx; mother: Annie BANKS; inf: Willis BANKS, father; pg:ln: 213:08

BANKS, Rosa; CF; b. 12 Jul 1887 in Ffx; father: Henry BANKS; occ: farmer; res: Ffx; mother: Julia BANKS; inf: H. BANKS, father; pg:ln: 160:19

BANKS, W. H.; CM; b. 28 Mar 1893 in Ffx; father: not known; occ: farmer; res: Ffx; mother: Lizzie BANKS; inf: L. BANKS, mother; pg:ln: 213:07

BARKER, Walter C.; WM; b. 3 Feb 1894 in Ffx; father: R. C. BARKER; occ: farmer; res: Ffx; mother: Mamie BARKER; inf: R. C. BARKER, father; pg:ln: 217:11

BARKES, Walter Ernest; WM; b. 25 Mar 1894 nr Pender; father: Wm. BARKES; occ: brick layer; res: nr Pender; mother: Annie BARKES; inf: mother; pg:ln: 221:04

BARLEY, Nellie; CF; b. 28 Nov 1887 in Ffx; father: Ruben BARLEY; occ: laborer; res: Ffx; mother: Lucy BARLEY; inf: R. BARLEY, father; pg:ln: 160:13

BARNES, Carroll H.; WM; b. 21 Jul 1893 nr Pender P.O.; father: J. H. BARNES; occ: farmer; res: nr Pender; mother: Eula BARNES; inf: mother; pg:ln: 210:10

BARNES, Helen Ashton; WF; b. 5 Aug 1891 nr Pender P.O.; father: John H. BARNES Jr.; occ: farmer; res: Pender P.O.; mother: Eula BARNES; inf: parents; pg:ln: 194:06

BARNES, Martha; CF; b. 27 Dec 1887 in Ffx; father: Eli BARNES; occ: farmer; res: Ffx; mother: Lizzie BARNES; inf: E. BARNES, father; pg:ln: 160:22

BARROWS, Eva C.; WF; b. 14 May 1885 in Herndon; father: H. A. BARROWS; occ: clerk; res: Herndon; mother: Grace BARROWS; inf: father; pg:ln: 152:09

BASIL, Rachael; CF; b. 18 Oct 1891 in Ffx; father: Peter BASSIL; occ: farmer; res: Ffx; mother: Bell BASSIL; inf: P. BASSIL, father; pg:ln: 198:12

BASSIL, ___; CF; b. 1 Jan 1883 in Falls Church; father: Peter BASSIL; occ: laborer; res: Falls Church; mother: Ball [Bell] BASSIL; inf: father; pg:ln: 139:15

BASTOW, G. L. B.; WF; b. 22 Apr 1896 in Ffx; father: Chas. BASTOW; occ: farmer; res: Ffx; mother: G. BASTOW; inf: Chas. BASTOW, father; pg:ln: 225:07

BAUGHMAN, ___; WF; b. 17 Apr 1890 in Ffx; father: F. V. BAUGHMAN; occ: farmer; res: Ffx; mother: Mary E. BAUGHMAN; inf: F. V. BAUGHMAN, father; pg:ln: 189:10

BAUGHMAN, ___; WM; b. 17 Apr 1891 in Ffx; father: F. V. BAUGHMAN· occ: farmer; res: Ffx; mother: Mary E. BAUGHMAN; inf: F. V. BAUGHMAN, father; pg:ln: 198:05

BAUMIS, Chas. C.; WM; b. 21 Sep 1882 in Ffx; father: Peter BAUMIS; occ: farmer; res: ___; mother: Maria BAUMIS; inf: P. BAUMIS, father; pg:ln: 136:07

BAYLISS, Eleanor; WF; b. 19 Nov 1884 in Ffx; father: Hillman BAYLISS; occ: farmer; res: Ffx; mother: Viola BAYLISS; inf: H. BAYLISS, father; pg:ln: 146:11

BAYLISS, Elsie; WF; b. 30 Aug 1896 in Lorton Sta.; father: Geo. H. BAYLISS; occ: carpenter; res: Lorton Sta.; mother: Emma BAYLISS; inf: father; pg:ln: 229:12

BAYLISS, George Arthur; WM; b. 20 Oct 1891 in Lorton; father: Geo. H. BAYLISS; occ: carpenter; res: Lorton; mother: Emma BAYLISS; inf: parents; pg:ln: 193:02

BAYLISS, Gladden Eugene; WM; b. 28 Jun 1896 in Lorton Sta.; father: Richard H. BAYLISS; occ: carpenter; res: Lorton Sta.; mother: Elizabeth BAYLLISS; inf: mother; pg:ln: 229:13

BAYLISS, Jennie; WF; b. 1 Jun 1890 in Ffx; father: R. H. BAYLISS; occ: farmer; res: Ffx; mother: Elizabeth BAYLISS; inf: R. H. BAYLISS, father; pg:ln: 185:04

BAYLISS, John; WM; b. 30 Dec 1896 nr Alex.; father: Hilman BAYLISS; occ: farmer; res: nr Alex.; mother: Catharine BAYLISS; inf: father; pg:ln: 229:15

BAYLISS, Mary E.; WF; b. 5 Oct 1888 in Ffx; father: R. H. BAYLISS; occ: farmer; res: Ffx; mother: Elizabt. BAYLISS; inf: R. H. BAYLISS, father; pg:ln: 170:02

BAYLISS, Raymond; WM; b. 14 Feb 1887 in Ffx; father: Ezra BAYLISS; occ: laborer; res: Ffx; mother: Jennie BAYLISS; inf: Ezra BAYLISS, father; pg:ln: 166:11

BAYLISS, Rebecca Virginia; WF; b. 5 Dec 1894 nr Lorton Sta.; father: Geo. H. BAYLISS; occ: carpenter; res: nr Lorton; mother: Emma J. BAYLISS; inf: father; pg:ln: 221:10

BAYLISS, Tyson; WM; b. 20 Oct 1894 nr Lorton Sta.; father: R. H. BAYLISS; occ: farmer; res: nr Lorton; mother: Elizabeth BAYLISS; inf: father; pg:ln: 221:09

BAYLISS, Walter; WM; b. 16 Feb 1884 in Ffx; father: Richd. H. BAYLISS; occ: farmer; res: Ffx; mother: Mary V. BAYLISS; inf: R. H. BAYLISS, father; pg:ln: 146:07

BEACH, ___ (stillborn); WM; b. 18 Oct 1880 in Ffx; father: Cornelius BEACH; occ: farmer; res: Ffx; mother: Martha; inf: C. BEACH, father; pg:ln: 127:13

BEACH, ___; WF; b. 6 Apr 1890 in Ffx; father: Chas. W. BEACH; occ: farmer; res: Ffx; mother: Mary BEACH; inf: Chas. W. BEACH, father; pg:ln: 185:10

BEACH, Alice; WF; b. 5 Jan 1883 in Ffx; father: Geo. A. BEACH; occ: farmer; res: Ffx; mother: Sarah J. BEACH; inf: G. A. BEACH, father; pg:ln: 143:03

BEACH, Alta; WF; b. 5 Feb 1890 in Ffx; father: Thos. R. BEACH; occ: farmer; res: Ffx; mother: Mary Ann BEACH; inf: Thos. R. BEACH, father; pg:ln: 185:11

BEACH, Annie Elizabeth; WF; b. 29 Nov 1894 nr Stoneleigh; father: David BEACH; occ: farmer; res: nr Stoneleigh; mother: Maggie BEACH; inf: father; pg:ln: 221:08

BEACH, Annie L.; WF; b. 5 Sep 1881 in Ffx; father: W. T. BEACH; occ: farmer; res: Ffx; mother: Mary F. BEACH; inf: W. T. BEACH, father; pg:ln: 132:03

BEACH, Charles (twin); WM; b. 14 Sep 1887 in Ffx; father: Jno. R.
BEACH; occ: carpenter; res: Ffx; mother: Louisa V. BEACH; inf:
Jno. R. BEACH, father; pg:ln: 166:10

BEACH, Chas.; WM; b. 18 Jan 1884 in Ffx; father: Jno. T. BEACH; occ:
farmer; res: Ffx; mother: Eliza A. BEACH; inf: J. T. BEACH, father;
pg:ln: 146:05

BEACH, Clarence L.; WM; b. 1 Oct 1890 in Ffx; father: Wm. Thos.
BEACH; occ: farmer; res: Ffx; mother: Mary BEACH; inf: W. T.
BEACH, father; pg:ln: 185:08

BEACH, Daisie Alice; WF; b. 16 Nov 1887 in Ffx; father: Chas. BEACH;
occ: laborer; res: Ffx; mother: M. Cath BEACH; inf: Chas. BEACH,
father; pg:ln: 166:06

BEACH, Daniel M.; WM; b. 6 Jan 1892 nr Stoneleigh; father: David M.
BEACH; occ: farmer; res: nr Stoneleigh; mother: Margaret BEACH;
inf: father; pg.ln: 209:44

BEACH, David M.; WM; b. 16 Jan 1893 nr Stoneleigh; father: David
BEACH; occ: farmer; res: nr Stoneleigh; mother: Maggie BEACH;
inf: mother; pg:ln: 210:08

BEACH, Elias; WM; b. 12 Jun 1882 in Falls Church; father: Frank
BEACH; occ: laborer; res: Falls Church; mother: Ellen BEACH; inf:
father; pg:ln: 134:06

BEACH, Etzel; WF; b. 13 Aug 1888 in Ffx; father: J. D. BEACH; occ:
farmer; res: Ffx; mother: Florene BEACH; inf: J. D. BEACH, father;
pg:ln: 170:11

BEACH, Isabella; WF; b. 5 Apr 1890 in Ffx; father: Jas. L. BEACH; occ:
farmer; res: Ffx; mother: Malvina BEACH; inf: Jas. L. BEACH, father;
pg:ln: 185:09

BEACH, Jas. F.; WM; b. 16 Jun 1884 in Ffx; father: Worden BEACH;
occ: farmer; res: Ffx; mother: Sarah E. BEACH; inf: Worden BEACH,
father; pg:ln: 146:06

BEACH, John Sullivan; WM; b. 4 Apr 1890 in Ffx; father: Jno. S.
BEACH; occ: farmer; res: Ffx; mother: Emma BEACH; inf: Jno. S.
BEACH, father; pg:ln: 185:12

BEACH, John T.; WM; b. 4 Mar 1894 nr Pleasant Valley; father:
Clarence BEACH; occ: farmer; res: nr Pleasant Valley; mother:
Maud BEACH; inf: mother; pg:ln: 221:06

BEACH, Katie; WF; b. 30 Dec 1891 in Stoneleigh; father: James L.
BEACH; occ: farmer; res: Stoneleigh; mother: Malvina BEACH; inf:
parents; pg:ln: 193:03

BEACH, Maud; WF; b. 17 Jan 1896 nr Burke Sta.; father: Clarence
BEACH; occ: farmer; res: nr Burke Sta.; mother: Maude BEACH; inf:
father; pg:ln: 229:05

BEACH, Nettie Virginia; WF; b. 9 Sep 1894 nr Stoneleigh; father:
Andrew BEACH; occ: farmer; res: nr Stoneleigh; mother: Hattie
BEACH; inf: mother; pg:ln: 221:07

BEACH, not named; WF; b. 14 Apr 1880 in Ffx; father: Jno. R. BEACH;
occ: farmer; res: Ffx; mother: Louisa; inf: J. R. BEACH, father; pg:ln:
127:11

[BEACH], not named; WF; b. 14 Jul 1891 nr Burke Sta.; father: John T. BEACH; occ: farmer; res: nr Burke Sta.; mother: Eliza BEACH; inf: parents; pg:ln: 193:04

BEACH, not named; WM; b. 10 Dec 1894 nr Burke Sta.; father: Wm. BEACH; occ: farmer; res: nr Burke Sta.; mother: Diana BEACH; inf: father; pg:ln: 221:15

BEACH, Rob. A.; WM; b. 17 Jun 1892 nr Pleasant Valley; father: C. BEACH; occ: farmer; res: nr Pleasant Valley; mother: Maud H. BEACH; inf: father; pg:ln: 208:03

BEACH, Samuel Thos.; WM; b. 5 Dec 1893 nr Stoneleigh; father: Thos. B. BEACH; occ: farmer; res: nr Stoneleigh; mother: Mary Ann BEACH; inf: mother; pg:ln: 210:09

BEACH, Thos. W.; WM; b. 22 Mar 1890 in Ffx; father: Clarence BEACH; occ: farmer; res: Ffx; mother: Maud BEACH; inf: Clarence BEACH, father; pg:ln: 185:13

BEACH, W, H.; WM; b. 3 Jan 1885 in Ffx; father: Mack BEACH; occ: farmer; res: Ffx; mother: Carrie BEACH; inf: M. BEACH, father; pg:ln: 156:05

BEACH, Willie (twin); WM; b. 14 Sep 1887 in Ffx; father: Jno. R. BEACH; occ: carpenter; res: Ffx; mother: Louisa V. BEACH; inf: Jno. R. BEACH, father; pg:ln: 166:10

BEALL, Chas. E.; WM; b. 30 May 1887 in Ffx; father: Chas. E. BEALL; occ: farmer; res: Ffx; mother: Mary E. BEALL; inf: C. E. BEALL, father; pg:ln: 160:06

BEALL, Wm. R.; WM; b. 14 Apr 1887 in Ffx; father: David H. BEALL; occ: laborer; res: Ffx; mother: Mollie BEALL; inf: D. H. BEALL, father; pg:ln: 160:05

BEAN, Merle H.; WM; b. 27 Apr 1889 in Ffx; father: Chaning S. BEAN; occ: farmer; res: Ffx; mother: Minnie BEAN; inf: C. S. BEAN, father; pg:ln: 177:09

BEAN, not named; WM; b. 25 Apr 1886 in Providence; father: Channing S. BEAN; occ: farmer; res: Prov.; mother: Minnie BEAN; inf: father; pg:ln: 158:08

BEAN, Oneal; WM; b. 22 Dec 1892 in Ffx; father: C. S. BEAN; occ: farmer; res: Ffx; mother: M. T. BEAN; inf: C. S. BEAN, father; pg:ln: 202:10

BEAN, Virginia F.; WF; b. 15 Sep 1887 in Ffx; father: Channing BEAN; occ: farmer; res: Ffx; mother: Minnie BEAN; inf: C. BEAN, father; pg:ln: 160:14

BEANS, Blanche D.; WF; b. 5 Mar 1882 in Providence; father: T. A. BEANS; occ: farmer; res: Providence; mother: Margt. V. BEANS; inf: father; pg:ln: 134:10

BEANS, Blanchet; WF; b. 1 Mar 1883 in Providence Dist.; father: T. A. BEANS; occ: farmer; res: Providence Dist.; mother: Margaret BEANS; inf: father; pg:ln: 139:11

BEARD, Pearl; WF; b. 17 Apr 1892 in Ffx; father: Jos. BEARD; occ: farmer; res: Ffx; mother: Mary BEARD; inf: Jos. BEARD, father; pg:ln: 202:05

BEARD, W. F.; WM; b. 5 Apr 1890 in Ffx; father: Jos. BEARD; occ: farmer; res: Ffx; mother: Mary BEARD; inf: J. BEARD, father; pg:ln: 189:15

BEATIE, Winter; WM; b. 20 Jul 1889 in Ffx; father: Fountain BEATIE; occ: farmer; res: Ffx; mother: Fannie BEATIE; inf: F. BEATIE, father; pg:ln: 177:15

BEATTIE, Lilian; WF; b. 5 Dec 1884 in Green Spring; father: Fountaine BEATTIE; occ: farmer; res: Green Spring; mother: Annie E. BEATTIE; inf: father Note: A certificate of baptism viewed in this bureau shows that Lilian Carlin Beattie was born in Fairfax County on December 3, 1884, and was baptised on the 17th day of October 1885.; pg:ln: 149:07

BEAVERS, Bertha O.; WF; b. 14 Mar 1892 in Ffx; father: W. L. BEAVERS; occ: farmer; res: Ffx; mother: Sarah BEAVERS; inf: W. L. BEAVERS, father; pg:ln: 202:06

BEAVERS, Bertie; WF; b. 25 Jun 1894 nr Woodlawn; father: Henry BEAVERS; occ: farmer; res: nr Woodlawn; mother: Mary BEAVERS; inf: father; pg:ln: 221:14

BEAVERS, Evertt; WM; b. 19 Mar 1880 in Dranesville; father: John T. BEAVERS; occ: farmer; res: Dranesville; mother: Ulary BEAVERS; inf: father; pg:ln: 124:02

BEAVERS, Howard; WM; b. 27 Jul 1894 in Ffx; father: J. W. BEAVERS; occ: farmer; res: Ffx; mother: Sarah C. BEAVERS; inf: J. W. BEAVERS, father; pg:ln: 217:05

BEAVERS, Jesse M.; WF; b. 28 Aug 1891 in Ffx; father: J. T. BEAVERS; occ: farmer; res: Ffx; mother: Sarah E. BEAVERS; inf: J. T. BEAVERS, father; pg:ln: 198:10

BEAVERS, Joseph; WM; b. 1 May 1882 in Providence; father: Jno. T. BEAVERS; occ: farmer; res: Providence; mother: Mary BEAVERS; inf: father; pg:ln: 134:09

[BEAVERS], not named; WM; b. 23 Apr 1883 in Dranesville; father: Jno. T. BEAVERS; occ: farmer; res: Dranesville; mother: Mary F. BEAVERS; inf: father; pg:ln: 139:13

BECKWITH, ___ (dead); CM; b. 11 Dec 1888 in Ffx; father: Alfred BECKWITH Sr.; occ: farmer; res: Ffx; mother: Fannie BECKWITH; inf: Alfred BECKWITH, father; pg:ln: 170:06

BECKWITH, Chas. M.; CM; b. 16 Feb 1882 in Ffx; father: Albt. BECKWITH; occ: farmer; res: ___; mother: Sarah BECKWITH; inf: Albt. BECKWITH, father; pg:ln: 136:04

BECKWITH, Chas.; CM; b. 21 Nov 1882 in Ffx; father: Alfred BECKWITH; occ: farmer; res: ___; mother: Fannie BECKWITH; inf: Alfred BECKWITH, father; pg:ln: 136:05

BECKWITH, Ida (twin); CF; b. 13 Aug 1888 in Ffx; father: Alfred BECKWITH Jr.; occ: farmer; res: Ffx; mother: Sarah BECKWITH; inf: Alfred BECKWITH, father; pg:ln: 170:10

BECKWITH, Jno. H.; CM; b. 11 Feb 1884 in Ffx; father: Alfred BECKWITH; occ: farmer; res: Ffx; mother: Fannie BECKWITH; inf: A. BECKWITH, father; pg:ln: 146:03

BECKWITH, John (twin); CM; b. 13 Aug 1888 in Ffx; father: Alfred
    BECKWITH Jr.; occ: farmer; res: Ffx; mother: Sarah BECKWITH;
    inf: Alfred BECKWITH, father; pg:ln: 170:09
BECKWITH, Robert; CM; b. 25 Oct 1891 nr Clifton; father: Albert
    BECKWITH; occ: farmer; res: nr Clifton; mother: Sarah BECKWITH;
    inf: Albert BECKWITH; pg:ln: 197:02
BECKWITH, W.; CM; b. 11 Apr 1880 in Ffx; father: Albt. BECKWITH;
    occ: farmer; res: Ffx; mother: Sarah; inf: Albt. BECKWITH, father;
    pg:ln: 127:08
BELFIELD, Stella; CF; b. 24 Jul 1889 in Ffx; father: L. BELFIELD; occ:
    farmer; res: Ffx; mother: Sarah A. BELFIELD; inf: S. A. BELFIELD,
    mother; pg:ln: 181:15
BELL, Abner J.; CM; b. 1 Dec 1884 in Falls Church; father: John BELL;
    occ: minister; res: Falls Church; mother: Margt. BALL [BELL]; inf:
    mother; pg:ln: 149:04
BELL, Abner; CM; b. 1 Dec 1883 in Falls Church; father: John BELL;
    occ: minister; res: Falls Church; mother: Margaret BELL; inf: father;
    pg:ln: 139:02
BELL, Annah; CF; b. 20 Apr 1886 in Bailey's X Rds; father: John BELL;
    occ: minister; res: Bailey's X Rds; mother: Margt. BELL; inf: father;
    pg:ln: 158:03
BELL, Clarence; CM; b. 22 May 1889 in Ffx; father: Moses BELL; occ:
    farmer; res: Ffx; mother: Eliza BELL; inf: M. BELL, father; pg:ln:
    177:08
BELL, Joseph; CM; b. 17 Mar 1889 in Ffx; father: Frank BELL; occ:
    farmer; res: Ffx; mother: Lavenia BELL; inf: F. BELL, father; pg:ln:
    177:12
BELL, Lawrence; CM; b. 24 Aug 1889 in Ffx; father: John BELL; occ:
    preacher; res: Ffx; mother: not given; inf: Jno. BELL, father; pg:ln:
    177:13
BELL, Maggie; CF; b. 13 Aug 1890 in Ffx; father: Fred. BELL; occ:
    farmer; res: Ffx; mother: Sarah BELL; inf: F. BELL, father; pg:ln:
    189:13
BELL, Rodger; CM; b. 20 Oct 1894 in Ffx; father: Moses BELL; occ:
    farmer; res: Ffx; mother: Eliza BELL; inf: M. BELL, father; pg:ln:
    217:13
BELL, Sarah; CF; b. 25 Dec 1891 in Ffx; father: Fred BELL; occ: farmer;
    res: Ffx; mother: Sarah BELL; inf: F. BELL, father; pg:ln: 198:13
BELL, Thomas; CM; b. 7 Jul 1883 in Falls Church; father: John BELL;
    occ: farmer; res: Falls Church; mother: Susan BELL; inf: father;
    pg:ln: 139:06
BENNET, Lucy; WF; b. 7 Jul 1893 in Ffx; father: Jno. C. BENNET; occ:
    farmer; res: Ffx; mother: Lillie BENNET; inf: J. C. BENNET, father;
    pg:ln: 213:12
BENNETT, Chas. Edward; WM; b. 7 Feb 1896 in Springfield; father:
    John BENNETT; occ: farmer; res: Springfield; mother: Mary
    BENNETT; inf: father; pg:ln: 229:14

BENNETT, George; WM; b. 11 Oct 1887 in Ffx; father: Jno. BENNETT; occ: farmer; res: Ffx; mother: Mary BENNETT; inf: Jno. BENNETT, father; pg:ln: 166:07

BENNETT, Jas. Gordon; WM; b. 2 Jun 1890 in Ffx; father: John BENNETT; occ: farmer; res: Ffx; mother: Mary BENNETT; inf: John BENNETT, father; pg:ln: 185:02

BENNETT, Laura; WF; b. 23 Dec 1889 in Ffx; father: J. C. BENNETT; occ: farmer; res: Ffx; mother: Laura S. BRENT [BENNETT]; inf: J. C. BENNET[T], father; pg:ln: 177:02

[BENNETT], not named; WM; b. 17 Jan 1891 nr Springfield; father: John BENNETT; occ: farmer; res: nr Springfield; mother: Mary BENNETT; inf: parents; pg:ln: 195:02

BENNETT, Robt. L.; WM; b. 18 Jul 1891 in Ffx; father: Jno. C. BENNETT; occ: farmer; res: Ffx; mother: L. S. BENNETT; inf: J. C. BENNETT, father; pg:ln: 198:08

BERKLEY, Edward; CM; b. 17 Jul 1884 in Ffx; father: Armstead BERKLEY; occ: farmer; res: Ffx; mother: Amanda BERKLEY; inf: A. BERKLEY, father; pg:ln: 146:13

BERKLEY, Emily; CF; b. 22 Dec 1886 in Ffx; father: Armstead BERKLEY; occ: farmer; res: Ffx; mother: Mary BERKLEY; inf: A. BERKLEY, father; pg:ln: 155:02

BERKLEY, Henry S.; CM; b. 3 Sep 1885 in Ffx; father: Harrison BERKLEY; occ: farmer; res: Ffx; mother: Mary BERKLEY; inf: H. BERKLEY, father; pg:ln: 156:06

BERKLEY, Lewis; CM; b. 3 Dec 1881 in Ffx; father: A. BERKLEY; occ: farmer; res: Ffx; mother: Ann BERKLEY; inf: A. BERKLEY, father; pg:ln: 132:08

BERKLEY, Lou Gussie; CF; b. 16 Jun 1891 in Masons Neck; father: Harrison BERKLEY; occ: farmer; res: Masons Neck; mother: Susan Ann BERKLEY; inf: parent; pg:ln: 196:02

BERNES, Edith; WF; b. 9 Apr 1887 in Ffx; father: Jno. F. BERNES; occ: farmer; res: Ffx; mother: Ida BERNES; inf: Jno. F. BERNES, father; pg:ln: 166:12

BERRY, not named (dead); WF; b. 9 Oct 1882 in Providence; father: Elisha D. BERRY; occ: farmer; res: Prov.; mother: Prida BERRY; inf: father; pg:ln: 135:74

BESLEY, Harry G.; WM; b. 28 Dec 1886 in Providence; father: W. B. BESLEY; occ: farmer; res: Prov.; mother: N. V. BESLEY; inf: father; pg:ln: 158:07

BIAS, Horace; CM; b. 23 Dec 1882 in Ffx; father: Seldon BIAS; occ: farmer; res: Ffx; mother: Betty BIAS; inf: N. HARRIS, grandfather; pg:ln: 136:31

BICKSLER, Carrie; WF; b. 15 Mar 1882 in Dranesville; father: Henry F. BICKSLER; occ: farmer; res: Dranesville; mother: Sarah BICKSLER; inf: father; pg:ln: 134:05

BINNS, Blanche A.; WF; b. 15 Jan 1882 in On Potomac; father: Jno. A. BINNS; occ: farmer; res: On Potomac; mother: Mary E. BINNS; inf: father; pg:ln: 134:07

BINNS, Chas. A.; WM; b. 1 Oct 1883 in Langley; father: Jno. A. BINNS; occ: farmer; res: Langley; mother: Mary BINNS; inf: father; pg:ln: 139:08

BINNS, Geo.; WM; b. 15 Jun 1890 in Ffx; father: Jno. A. BINNS; occ: farmer; res: Ffx; mother: Mary BINNS; inf: J. A. BINNS, father; pg:ln: 189:11

BINNS, W.; WM; b. 15 Jun 1892 in Ffx; father: Jno. A. BINNS; occ: farmer; res: Ffx; mother: Mary BINNS; inf: J. A. BINNS, father; pg:ln: 202:11

BIRCH, Alvin Ashton; WM; b. 20 Feb 1894 nr Chantilly; father: E. L. BIRCH; occ: farmer; res: nr Chantilly; mother: M. L. BIRCH; inf: father; pg:ln: 221:03

BIRCH, E. F.; WF; b. 4 Jul 1884 in Horse Shoe Hill; father: Frank L. BIRCH; occ: farmer; res: Falls Church Dist.; mother: F. B. [L.] BIRCH; inf: father; pg:ln: 149:02

BIRCH, Frances; WF; b. 20 Jan 1896 nr Chantilly; father: Edwin L. BIRCH; occ: farmer; res: nr Chantilly; mother: Mattie BIRCH; inf: father; pg:ln: 229:07

BIRCH, Isaac; WM; b. 15 Oct 1890 in Ffx; father: Frank L. BIRCH; occ: farmer; res: Ffx; mother: Flora BIRCH; inf: F. L. BIRCH, father; pg:ln: 189:04

BIRCH, not named (dead); WF; b. 22 Mar 1892 nr Chantilly; father: Lee BIRCH; occ: farmer; res: nr Chantilly; mother: Matilda BIRCH; inf: father; pg:ln: 208:05

BIRD, Amply; CM; b. 13 Jan 1882 in Falls Church; father: Amply BIRD; occ: laborer; res: Falls Church; mother: Julia BIRD; inf: father; pg:ln: 134:08

BIRD, Amply; CM; b. 28 Aug 1886 in Falls Ch.; father: Amply BIRD; occ: laborer; res: Falls Ch.; mother: Julia BIRD; inf: father; pg:ln: 158:02

BIRD, Frank; CM; b. 11 May 1887 in Ffx; father: Samuel BIRD; occ: laborer; res: Ffx; mother: Ella BIRD; inf: S. BIRD, father; pg:ln: 160:17

BIRD, Julia A.; CF; b. 30 May 1884 in Falls Ch.; father: Amply BIRD; occ: laborer; res: Falls Ch.; mother: Julia BIRD; inf: father; pg:ln: 149:10

BIRD, not named; CM; b. 5 Mar 1881 in Falls Church; father: Samuel BIRD; occ: laborer; res: Falls Church; mother: ___ BIRD; inf: father; pg:ln: 130:05

BIRKET, Edna; WF; b. 2 Aug 1885 in Ffx; father: Jas. BIRKET; occ: farmer; res: Ffx; mother: Edna V. BIRKIT; inf: Jas. BIRKET, father; pg:ln: 156:02

BIXLER, ___; WM; b. 14 Apr 1886 in Dranesville; father: F. D. BIXLER; occ: mechanic; res: Dranesville; mother: Ida BIXLER; inf: father; pg:ln: 158:10

BIXLER, Delbert; WM; b. 14 Apr 1887 in Ffx; father: F. D. BIXLER; occ: farmer; res: Ffx; mother: Ida BIXLER; inf: F. D. BIXLER, father; pg:ln: 160:11

BIXLER, Harry; WM; b. 15 Aug 1880 in Dranesville; father: John F. BIXLER; occ: farmer; res: Dranesville; mother: Sarah BIXLER; inf: father; pg:ln: 124:01

BIXLER, Leon; WM; b. 6 Oct 1890 in Ffx; father: F. D. BIXLER; occ: farmer; res: Ffx; mother: Ida BIXLER; inf: F. D. BIXLER, father; pg:ln: 189:16

BLACK, Martha E.; WF; b. 28 Oct 1887 in Ffx; father: Wm. BLACK; occ: laborer; res: Ffx; mother: Rosie BLACK; inf: Wm. BLACK, father; pg:ln: 160:04

BLACK, Robt. J.; WM; b. 9 Jul 1891 in Ffx; father: Wm. A. BLACK; occ: farmer; res: Ffx; mother: Rosie BLACK; inf: W. A. BLACK, father; pg:ln: 198:07

BLACKBURN, Ruth; CF; b. 24 Apr 1889 in Ffx; father: H. BLACKBURN; occ: sailor; res: Ffx; mother: Cath. BLACKBURN; inf: C. BLACKBURN, mother; pg:ln: 181:16

BLACKFORD, Anna M.; WF; b. 26 Mar 1891 in Ffx; father: L. M. BLACKFORD; occ: school teacher; res: Ffx; mother: E. C. A. BLACKFORD; inf: L. M. BLACKFORD, father; pg:ln: 198:01

BLACKWELL, Alice; CF; b. 26 Sep 1887 in Ffx; father: Peter BLACKWELL; occ: laborer; res: Ffx; mother: Martha BLACKWELL; inf: P. BLACKWELL, father; pg:ln: 160:12

BLACKWELL, Bertha; CF; b. 24 Apr 1883 in Lincolnville; father: Peter BLACKWELL; occ: laborer; res: Lincolnville; mother: Martha BLACKWELL; inf: father; pg:ln: 139:09

BLACKWELL, Jno. H.; CM; b. 10 Jan 1891 in Ffx; father: Peter BLACKWELL; occ: farmer; res: Ffx; mother: Martha BLACKWELL; inf: P. BLACKWELL, father; pg:ln: 198:11

BLACKWELL, Peter; CM; b. 8 Mar 1885 in Providence; father: Peter BLACKWELL; occ: laborer; res: Providence; mother: Martha BLACKWELL; inf: father; pg:ln: 152:11

BLAND, not named (dead); CF; b. 7 Jul 1881 in Falls Church; father: George BLAND; occ: laborer; res: Falls Church; mother: Lavinia BLAND; inf: father; pg:ln: 131:75

BLINCO, John Gordon; WM; b. 14 Jul 1896 nr Burke Sta.; father: John T. BLINCO; occ: telegraph operator; res: nr Burke Sta.; mother: Mary BLINCO; inf: mother; pg:ln: 229:10

BLUNT, Herbert Oliver; WM; b. 18 Sep 1896 nr Alex.; father: H. H. BLUNT; occ: merchant; res: nr Alex.; mother: Nellie BLUNT; inf: father; pg:ln: 229:17

BOND, W. H.; WM; b. 9 Oct 1896 in Ffx; father: W. H. BOND; occ: farmer; res: Ffx; mother: Ida BOND; inf: W. H. BOND, father; pg:ln: 225:05

BORDEN, not named; WM; b. 24 Oct 1889 in Ffx; father: D. L. BORDEN; occ: merchant; res: Ffx; mother: H. E. BORDEN; inf: D. L. BORDEN, father; pg:ln: 177:04

BOTTS, Bridgett; WF; b. 14 Aug 1880 in Ffx; father: Peter BOTTS; occ: farmer; res: Ffx; mother: Mary; inf: P. BOTTS, father; pg:ln: 127:10

BOTTS, Jas.; CM; b. 15 May 1882 in Ffx; father: Chas. BOTTS; occ: farmer; res: Ffx; mother: Laura BOTTS; inf: Chas. BOTTS, father; pg:ln: 136:03

BOUCHER, Cora F.; WF; b. 24 Jun 1884 in Langley; father: J. E. BOUCHER; occ: farmer; res: Langley; mother: Ann B. BOUCHER; inf: father; pg:ln: 149:12

[BOUCHER], not named; WF; b. 9 Feb 1883 in Balls Hill; father: E. BOUCHER; occ: farmer; res: Balls Hill; mother: Matilda BOUCHER; inf: father; pg:ln: 139:12

BOUTON, E. C. P.; WM; b. 17 Aug 1896 in Ffx; father: E. C. BOUTON; occ: farmer; res: Ffx; mother: M. M. BOUTON; inf: E. C. BOUTON, father; pg:ln: 225:09

BOUTON, Jno. R.; WM; b. 27 May 1892 in Ffx; father: E. C. BOUTON; occ: farmer; res: Ffx; mother: E. BOUTON; inf: E. C. BOUTON, father; pg:ln: 202:13

BOWERS, Nettie B.; WF; b. 5 Jan 1887 in Ffx; father: J. Luther BOWERS; occ: farmer; res: Ffx; mother: Alice BOWERS; inf: J. L. BOWERS, father; pg:ln: 160:02

BOWIE, Francis Virginia; CF; b. 3 Nov 1891 nr Woodlawn; father: Thomas BOWIE; occ: laborer; res: Woodlawn; mother: Anna BOWIE; inf: parent; pg:ln: 196:24

BOWLES, Ida; CF; b. 12 Dec 1880 in Ffx; father: Robt. BOWLES; occ: farmer; res: Ffx; mother: Jane E.; inf: R. BOWLES, father; pg:ln: 127:12

BOWLES, Lottie; CF; b. 16 Jul 1884 in Ffx; father: Danl. BOWLES; occ: farmer; res: Ffx; mother: Mary L. BOWLES; inf: Daniel BOWLES, father; pg:ln: 146:08

BOWMAN, Albert; CM; b. 24 Dec 1883 in Falls Church; father: Albert BOWMAN; occ: laborer; res: Falls Church; mother: Margt. BOWMAN; inf: father; pg:ln: 139:05

BOWMAN, Alva; WF; b. 25 Aug 1893 in Ffx; father: H. A. BOWMAN; occ: farmer; res: Ffx; mother: Ida K. BOWMAN; inf: H. A. BOWMAN, father; pg:ln: 213:11

BOWMAN, Baby; CM; b. 16 Jul 1887 in Ffx; father: Alfred BOWMAN; occ: farmer; res: Ffx; mother: Millie BOWMAN; inf: A. BOWMAN, father; pg:ln: 160:18

BOWMAN, Carrie A.; CF; b. 25 Jan 1890 in Ffx; father: Geo. BOWMAN; occ: farmer; res: Ffx; mother: Elizabt. BOWMAN; inf: Geo. BOWMAN, father; pg:ln: 189:12

BOWMAN, Carrie; CF; b. 8 Feb 1880 in Falls Church; father: Albert BOWMAN; occ: laborer; res: Falls Church; mother: Millie BOWMAN; inf: mother; pg:ln: 124:05

BOWMAN, G. Warner; WM; b. 19 Oct 1891 in Ffx; father: H. A. BOWMAN; occ: post m.; res: Ffx; mother: Ida K. BOWMAN; inf: H. A. BOWMAN, father; pg:ln: 198:04

BOWMAN, James; CM; b. 12 Jan 1882 in Falls Church; father: Albert BOWMAN; occ: laborer; res: Falls Church; mother: Milly BOWMAN; inf: father; pg:ln: 134:03

BOYCE, Edna; WF; b. 17 Jan 1887 in Ffx; father: W. F. BOYCE; occ: farmer; res: Ffx; mother: Roberta BOYCE; inf: W. F. BRYCE, father; pg:ln: 160:03

BOYER, Chas. R.; WM; b. 26 May 1881 in Ffx; father: Danl. BOYER; occ: farmer; res: Ffx; mother: Hariet BOYER; inf: Danl. BOYER, father; pg:ln: 132:05

BRADLEY, Alice; CF; b. 26 Apr 1888 in ___; father: Robt. BRADLEY; occ: farmer; res: Ffx; mother: Virginia BRADLEY; inf: R. BRADLEY, father; pg:ln: 173:11

BRADLEY, Bertram B.; WM; b. 27 Feb 1893 nr Farr P.O.; father: Horace E. BRADLEY; occ: farmer; res: nr Farr P.O.; mother: Lorena BRADLEY; inf: father; pg:ln: 210:07

BRADLEY, Edward; WM; b. 19 Nov 1884 in Ffx; father: Jno. F. BRADLEY; occ: farmer; res: Ffx; mother: Jane BRADLEY; inf: J. F. BRADLEY, father; pg:ln: 146:10

BRADLEY, Eliza; CF; b. 22 Apr 1880 in Falls Church; father: Robert BRADLEY; occ: laborer; res: Falls Church; mother: Virginia BRADLEY; inf: mother; pg:ln: 124:04

BRADLEY, Hurbert; CM; b. 12 Sep 1885 in Merrifield; father: Robt. BRADLEY; occ: laborer; res: Merrifield; mother: Virginia BRADLEY; inf: father; pg:ln: 152:07

BRADLEY, Mamie; CF; b. 9 Jul 1893 in Ffx; father: Robt. BRADLEY; occ: farmer; res: Ffx; mother: Virginia BRADLEY; inf: R. BRADLEY, father; pg:ln: 213:09

BRADLEY, Minnie; CF; b. 10 Apr 1889 in Ffx; father: Robt. BRADLEY; occ: farmer; res: Ffx; mother: Eugenia BRADLEY; inf: R. BRADLEY, father; pg:ln: 177:11

BRADLEY, Minnie; CF; b. 30 Jan 1890 in Ffx; father: Robt. BRADLEY; occ: farmer; res: Ffx; mother: Virginia BRADLEY; inf: R. BRADLEY, father; pg:ln: 189:05

BRADLY, Rulin; WF; b. 11 Jan 1896 nr Farr P.O.; father: Horrace BRADLEY; occ: farmer; res: nr Farr P.O.; mother: Lorena BRADLEY; inf: mother; pg:ln: 229:11

BRADSHAW, Walter; WM; b. 1 Aug 1896 in Ffx; father: R. BRADSHAW; occ: farmer; res: Ffx; mother: J. F. BRADSHAW; inf: R. BRADSHAW, father; pg:ln: 225:15

BRADWAY, Ruth V.; WF; b. 12 May 1896 in Ffx; father: C. W. BRADWAY; occ: farmer; res: Ffx; mother: Maggie BRADWAY; inf: C. W. BRADWAY, father; pg:ln: 225:16

BRADY, Beverley B.; WM; b. 15 Jul 1896 in Ffx; father: Jno. T. BRADY; occ: farmer; res: Ffx; mother: Emma BRADY; inf: J. T. BRADY, father; pg:ln: 225:14

BRADY, Margaret D.; WF; b. 7 Dec 1887 in Ffx; father: Jno. T. BRADY; occ: farmer; res: Ffx; mother: Emma J. BRADY; inf: J. T. BRADY, father; pg:ln: 160:07

BRANIGAN, ___; CF; b. 20 Feb 1883 in Ffx; father: Henry BRANIGAN; occ: farmer; res: Ffx; mother: Lavina BRANIGAN; inf: H. BRANIGAN, father; pg:ln: 143:04

BRANIGAN, Hattie; CF; b. __ Nov 1882 in Ffx; father: Henry
BRANIGAN; occ: farmer; res: Ffx; mother: Lavina BRANIGAN; inf:
H. BRANIGAN, father; pg:ln: 136:02

BRANNOM, Harmon; CM; b. 14 Jul 1891 in Ffx; father: Jeff BRANNOM;
occ: farmer; res: Ffx; mother: Flora BRANNOM; inf: J. BRANNOM,
father; pg:ln: 198:15

BRANNON, not named; CM; b. 10 Jun 1893 in Ffx; father: Jeff.
BRANNON; occ: farmer; res: Ffx; mother: Flora BRANNON; inf: Jeff
BRANNON, father; pg:ln: 213:13

BRAWNER, Edwd. Walter; WM; b. 2 Sep 1889 in Ffx; father: J. P.
BRAWNER; occ: farmer; res: Ffx; mother: Ida BRAWNER; inf: J. P.
BRAWNER, father; pg:ln: 181:08

BRAWNER, Emery Stone; WM; b. 19 Feb 1892 nr Alexandria; father: J.
P. BRAWNER; occ: farmer; res: nr Alex.; mother: Ida BRAWNER;
inf: father; pg:ln: 207:62

BRAWNER, Geo. M.; WM; b. 14 Dec 1890 in Ffx; father: Jno. A.
BRAWNER; occ: farmer; res: Ffx; mother: Mary E. BRAWNER; inf:
Jno. A. BRAWNER, father; pg:ln: 185:03

BRAWNER, Ida; WF; b. 22 Feb 1894 nr Alexandria; father: J. P.
BRAWNER; occ: farmer; res: nr Alexandria; mother: Ida BRAWNER;
inf: father; pg:ln: 221:13

BRAXTON, Edwd. T.; CM; b. 27 Jun 1887 in Ffx; father: Thos. H.
BRAXTON; occ: farmer; res: Ffx; mother: Emma BRAXTON; inf:
Thos. H. BRAXTON, father; pg:ln: 166:09

BRAXTON, Frank Robert; CM; b. 8 Feb 1891 nr Woodlawn; father: T.
H. BRAXTON; occ: laborer; res: nr Woodlawn; mother: Emma
BRAXTON; inf: parent; pg:ln: 196:01

BRENT, Benj.; CM; b. 25 May 1883 in Falls Church; father: Geo.
BRENT; occ: laborer; res: Falls Church; mother: Isabel BRENT; inf:
father; pg:ln: 139:10

BRENT, Lester; CM; b. 10 Aug 1889 in Ffx; father: Richd. BRENT; occ:
farmer; res: Ffx; mother: Rachael BRENT; inf: R. BRENT, father;
pg:ln: 177:14

BRENT, Pauline; CF; b. 1 Apr 1888 in ___; father: Geo. BRENT; occ:
farmer; res: Ffx; mother: Belle BRENT; inf: G. BRENT, father; pg:ln:
173:06

BRENT, Susannah; CF; b. 10 Aug 1888 in ___; father: not known; occ:
___; res: ___; mother: Charlotte BRENT; inf: C. BRENT, mother;
pg:ln: 173:09

BRENT, Wash.; CM; b. 17 Jul 1884 in Ffx; father: Wash. BRENT; occ:
farmer; res: Ffx; mother: Alice BRENT; inf: W. BRENT, father; pg:ln:
146:12

BRICE Jerome; CM; b. 17 Feb 1894 in Ffx; father: Randolph BRICE;
occ: farmer; res: Ffx; mother: Ellen BRICE; inf: R. BRICE, father;
pg:ln: 217:14

BRIGGS, Chas. H.; CM; b. 22 May 1890 in Ffx; father: Nathan BRIGGS;
occ: laborer; res: Ffx; mother: Lucinda BRIGGS; inf: Nathan
BRIGGS, father; pg:ln: 185:17

BRIGGS, Nellie; CF; b. 28 Aug 1892 nr Burnside Sta.; father: Nathan BRIGGS; occ: laborer; res: nr Burnside Sta.; mother: Lucinda BRIGGS; inf: mother; pg:ln: 206:30

BRINKMAN, Conrad; WM; b. 4 Mar 1896 nr Fairfax C. H.; father: Chas. BRINKMAN; occ: farmer; res: nr Clifton Sta.; mother: Susan BRINKMAN; inf: mother; pg:ln: 229:06

BROOKE, Grace; WF; b. 15 Aug 1881 in near Vienna; father: Samuel BROOKE; occ: farmer; res: near Vienna; mother: Mary E. BROOKE; inf: father; pg:ln: 130:07

BROOKS, ___; CM; b. 28 Sep 1888 in Ffx; father: Chas. BROOKS Jr.; occ: farmer; res: Ffx; mother: Francis BROOKS; inf: Chas. BROOKS, father; pg:ln: 170:04

BROOKS, Addie B.; CF; b. 23 Sep 1890 in Ffx; father: Henry BROOKS; occ: farmer; res: Ffx; mother: Annie BROOKS; inf: H. BROOKS, father; pg:ln: 189:09

BROOKS, Benj'n.; CM; b. 18 Aug 1887 in Ffx; father: Melvin BROOKS; occ: laborer; res: Ffx; mother: Catharine BROOKS; inf: M. BROOKS, father; pg:ln: 160:16

BROOKS, Carl; CM; b. 14 May 1890 in Ffx; father: Orlando BROOKS; occ: carpenter; res: Ffx; mother: Alice BROOKS; inf: O. BROOKS, father; pg:ln: 185:15

BROOKS, Earl D.; WM; b. 24 Apr 1896 in Ffx; father: Eppa BROOKS; occ: farmer; res: Ffx; mother: Kate BROOKS; inf: Ep BROOKS, father; pg:ln: 225:10

BROOKS, Eliza; WF; b. 4 May 1892 in West End; father: Olando BROOKS; occ: molder ironworks; res: West End; mother: Alice BROOKS; inf: mother; pg:ln: 209:33

BROOKS, Jas. A.; WM; b. 1 Jul 1890 in Ffx; father: Mason R. BROOKS; occ: farmer; res: Ffx; mother: Mary BROOKS; inf: M. BROOKS, father; pg:ln: 189:18

BROOKS, Jeneva; CF; b. 14 Oct 1893 nr Centreville; father: Chas. W. BROOKS; occ: laborer; res: nr Centreville; mother: Mary Z. BROOKS; inf: mother; pg:ln: 210:12

BROOKS, L. H.; WM; b. 11 May 1884 in Ffx; father: Clark J. BROOKS; occ: farmer; res: Ffx; mother: Susan BROOKS; inf: C. J. BROOKS, father Typed statement posted to record on back of each certified copy issued 7/18/42. The family record viewed in this office shows that Lenard H. Brooks was born May 15, 1884. State Registrar; pg:ln: 146:02

BROOKS, Lizzie E.; WF; b. 16 Aug 1891 in Ffx; father: Mason R. BROOKS; occ: farmer; res: Ffx; mother: Mary M. BROOKS; inf: M. R. BROOKS, father; pg:ln: 198:06

BROOKS, Mary S.; CF; b. 9 Apr 1889 in Ffx; father: Arthur BROOKS; occ: farmer; res: Ffx; mother: Phebe BROOKS; inf: A. BROOKS, father; pg:ln: 177:07

BROOKS, Prissy Granville; CM; b. 28 Feb 1891 nr Centreville; father: Charles BROOKS; occ: farmer; res: nr Centreville; mother: Francis BROOKS; inf: Chs. BROOKS; pg:ln: 197:01

BROOKS, Sadie M.; CF; b. 8 Sep 1893 in Ffx; father: Henry BROOKS; occ: farmer; res: Ffx; mother: Annie BROOKS; inf: H. BROOKS, father; pg:ln: 213:04

BROOKS, Saml; WM; b. 21 Dec 1892 in Ffx; father: S. A. BROOKS; occ: farmer; res: Ffx; mother: Mary E. BROOKS; inf: S. A. BROOKS, father; pg:ln: 202:12

BROOKS, Sanl [Saml.] W.; WM; b. 27 Jul 1894 in Ffx; father: Saml. A. BROOKS; occ: farmer; res: Ffx; mother: M. E. BROOKS; inf: S. A. BROOKS, father; pg:ln: 217:08

BROOKS, Susan; CF; b. 30 Jun 1890 in Ffx; father: Melvin BROOKS; occ: farmer; res: Ffx; mother: Catharine BROOKS; inf: M. BROOKS, father; pg:ln: 189:08

BROOKS, Thos.; CM; b. 28 Jan 1896 nr Centreville; father: Thos. BROOKS; occ: farmer; res: nr Centreville; mother: Elizabeth BROOKS; inf: father; pg:ln: 229:16

BROOKS, Walter; CM; b. 26 Jul 1888 in ___; father: Henry BROOKS; occ: farmer; res: Ffx; mother: Annie BROOKS; inf: H. BROOKS, father; pg:ln: 173:07

BROOKS, Wm. T.; CM; b. 15 Nov 1880 in Providence; father: Henry BROOKS; occ: farmer; res: Providence; mother: Hapy BROOKS; inf: father; pg:ln: 124:03

BROWN, ___ (dead); CM; b. 7 Jun 1883 in Ffx; father: Fred. BROWN; occ: farmer; res: ___; mother: Maria BROWN; inf: F. BROWN, father; pg:ln: 143:05

BROWN, Charity; CF; b. 10 Feb 1887 in Ffx; father: Geo. BROWN; occ: laborer; res: Ffx; mother: Mary BROWN; inf: Geo. BROWN, father; pg:ln: 160:09

BROWN, Chas. A.; WM; b. 17 Dec 1894 in Ffx; father: C. R. BROWN; occ: farmer; res: Ffx; mother: Ann E. BROWN; inf: C. R. BROWN, father; pg:ln: 217:06

BROWN, Chas. Wm.; CM; b. 6 Sep 1888 in Ffx; father: Benjn. BROWN; occ: preacher; res: Ffx; mother: Mary E. BROWN; inf: Benjn. BROWN, father; pg:ln: 170:03

BROWN, Clarence (twin); CM; b. 4 Aug 1885 in Ffx; father: Fred BROWN; occ: farmer; res: Ffx; mother: Maria BROWN; inf: Fred BROWN, father; pg:ln: 156:03

BROWN, Daniel; CM; b. 15 Mar 1889 in Ffx; father: Fred BROWN; occ: farmer; res: Ffx; mother: Maria BROWN; inf: F. BROWN, father; pg:ln: 181:13

BROWN, Earle Evans; WM; b. 10 Oct 1893 nr Lorton Sta.; father: Geo. H. BROWN; occ: fisherman; res: nr Lorton Sta.; mother: Eliza BROWN; inf: father; pg:ln: 210:03

BROWN, Edna; WF; b. 14 Aug 1890 in Ffx; father: Arthur BROWN; occ: carpenter; res: Ffx; mother: Ella BROWN; inf: A. BROWN, father; pg:ln: 185:14

BROWN, Edw'd. R.; WM; b. 28 Jan 1894 in Ffx; father: Edw'd. BROWN; occ: farmer; res: Ffx; mother: Alice BROWN; inf: Edw'd. BROWN, father; pg:ln: 217:07

BROWN, Ernest (twin); CM; b. 4 Aug 1885 in Ffx; father: Fred BROWN; occ: farmer; ies: Ffx; mother: Maria BROWN; inf: Fred BROWN, father; pg:ln: 156:04

BROWN, George W.; WM; b. 20 Mar 1891 nr Alexandria; father: Rezin F. BROWN; occ: clerk; res: nr Alexandria; mother: Emma V. BROWN; inf: parents; pg:ln: 195:26

BROWN, Homer; WM; b. 13 Aug 1896 in Ffx; father: E. S. BROWN; occ: farmer; res: Ffx; mother: Artimesia BROWN; inf: E. S. BROWN, father; pg:ln: 225:08

BROWN, Horace E.; WM; b. 22 Aug 1886 in Providence; father: J. W. BROWN; occ: mcht.; res: Prov.; mother: Lizzie W. BROWN; inf: father; pg:ln: 158:09

BROWN, Jas. H.; WM; b. 2 May 1892 in Ffx; father: J. W. BROWN; occ: farmer; res: Ffx; mother: L. W. BROWN; inf: J. W. BROWN, father; pg:ln: 202:07

BROWN, Jesse; WM; b. 5 Nov 1889 in Ffx; father: Irwin BROWN; occ: farmer; res: Ffx; mother: Mary BROWN; inf: I. BROWN, father; pg:ln: 177:03

BROWN, L. W.; WF; b. 16 Apr 1891 in Ffx; father: J. H. BROWN; occ: farmer; res: Ffx; mother: Louisa BROWN; inf: J. H. BROWN, father; pg:ln: 198:09

BROWN, Lenard; WM; b. 31 May 1887 in Ffx; father: J. H. BROWN; occ: carpenter; res: Ffx; mother: Annie BROWN; inf: J. H. BROWN, father; pg:ln: 160:08

BROWN, Lettie; CF; b. 3 Jun 1889 in Ffx; father: Oliver BROWN; occ: farmer; res: Ffx; mother: Sarah BROWN; inf: Oliver BROWN, father; pg:ln: 181:14

BROWN, Maria; WF; b. 10 Mar 1889 in Ffx; father: Jno. BROWN; occ: farmer; res: Ffx; mother: Anna BROWN; inf: Jno. BROWN, father; pg:ln: 177:17

BROWN, Martha C.; WF; b. 6 Feb 1887 in Ffx; father: David BROWN; occ: farmer; res: Ffx; mother: Roberta BROWN; inf: D. BROWN, father; pg:ln: 160:15

BROWN, Mary C.; WF; b. 31 Aug 1896 in Ffx; father: C. R. BROWN; occ: farmer; res: Ffx; mother: Anna BROWN; inf: C. R. BROWN, father; pg:ln: 225:17

BROWN, Mary E.; WF; b. 14 Jan 1884 in Falls Ch. Dist.; father: J. W. BROWN; occ: mcht.; res: Falls Ch. Dist.; mother: Lizzie W. BROWN; inf: father; pg:ln: 149:08

[BROWN], not named; CM; b. 22 Jun 1886 in Ffx; father: Oliver BROWN; occ: farmer; res: Ffx; mother: Matilda BROWN; inf: O. BROWN, father; pg:ln: 155:03

BROWN, R. A.; WF; b. 26 Mar 1881 in Ffx; father: Esra BROWN; occ: farmer; res: Ffx; mother: Martha BROWN; inf: E. BROWN, father; pg:ln: 132:06

BROWN, Rebecca; WF; b. 11 Mar 1880 in Ffx; father: Ezra BROWN; occ: farmer; res: Ffx; mother: Martha; inf: E. BROWN, father; pg:ln: 127:09

BROWN, Rosier Oneil; WM; b. 14 Apr 1896 nr Alex.; father: Rosier F.
BROWN; occ: miller; res: nr Alex.; mother: Emma BROWN; inf:
mother; pg:ln: 229:09

BROWN, Sadie M.; WF; b. 16 Sep 1896 in Ffx; father: E'd. BROWN;
occ: farmer; res: Ffx; mother: Annie M. BROWN; inf: E'd. BROWN,
father; pg:ln: 225:13

BROWN, Solomon; CM; b. 11 Aug 1884 in Seminary; father: Nimrod
BROWN; occ: laborer; res: Seminary; mother: Margt. BROWN; inf:
father; pg:ln: 149:09

BROWN, Thomas E.; CM; b. 21 Dec 1891 in Germantown; father: Benj.
W. BROWN; occ: minister; res: Germantown; mother: Mary E.
BROWN; inf: parent; pg:ln: 196:26

BROWN, Thos. Earl; CM; b. 21 Dec 1890 in Ffx; father: B. W. BROWN;
occ: minister; res: Ffx; mother: Mary E. BROWN; inf: B. W. BROWN,
father; pg:ln: 185:16

BROWN, Zula E.; WF; b. 1 May 1887 in Ffx; father: Irving BROWN; occ:
farmer; res: Ffx; mother: Mary BROWN; inf: Irving BROWN, father;
pg:ln: 160:10

BRUEN, Mary; WF; b. 29 Jan 1888 in ___; father: Chas. M. BRUEN;
occ: farmer; res: Ffx; mother: Mary BRUEN; inf: C. BRUEN, father;
pg:ln: 173:10

BRUNER, Florence; WF; b. 25 Sep 1891 in Ffx; father: G. A. BRUNER;
occ: carpenter; res: Ffx; mother: C. C. BRUNER; inf: G. A.
BRUNER, father; pg:ln: 198:03

BRUNER, Jos. E.; WM; b. 20 Mar 1893 in Ffx; father: G. A. BRUNER;
occ: farmer; res: Ffx; mother: C. D. BRUNER; inf: G. A. BRUNER,
father; pg:ln: 213:05

BRUNNER, Lester Carlisle; WM; b. 13 Apr 1884 in Falls Ch.; father:
Geo. BRUNNER; occ: mechanic; res: Falls Ch.; mother: Carrie
BRUNNER; inf: father; pg:ln: 149:11

BRUSH, Jannet; WF; b. 3 Sep 1882 in Falls Church; father: Jno. D.
BRUSH; occ: farmer; res: Falls Church; mother: Elizabeth BRUSH;
inf: father; pg:ln: 134:04

BRUSH, Robert D.; WM; b. 10 Jul 1886 in Oakmount; father: Jno. D.
BRUSH; occ: farmer; res: Oak Mount; mother: Elizabeth BRUSH;
inf: father; pg:ln: 158:06

BRYANT, Arthur W.; WM; b. ___ Feb 1882 in Ffx; father: Jas. BRYANT;
occ: farmer; res: Ffx; mother: Rosa BRYANT; inf: Jas. BRYANT,
father; pg:ln: 136:01

BRYANT, Jas. M.; CM; b. 11 Aug 1884 in Ffx; father: Jas. BRYANT;
occ: farmer; res: Ffx; mother: Maria BRYANT; inf: Jas. BRYANT,
father; pg:ln: 146:04

BRYCE, W. M.; WM; b. 24 Aug 1881 in Ffx; father: J. W. BRYCE; occ:
farmer; res: Ffx; mother: F. J. BRYCE; inf: J. W. BRYCE, father;
pg:ln: 132:04

BUCKLEY, ___ (dead); WM; b. 8 Aug 1888 in Ffx; father: Robt. A.
BUCKLEY; occ: farmer; res: Ffx; mother: May BUCKLEY; inf: Robt.
A. BUCKLEY, father; pg:ln: 170:08

BUCKLEY, Alfonzo; WM; b. 17 Mar 1886 in Ffx; father: W. T.
BUCKLEY; occ: farmer; res: Ffx; mother: Anna BUCKLEY; inf: W. T.
BUCKLEY, father; pg:ln: 155:01
BUCKLEY, Annie May; WF; b. 31 Mar 1894 nr Clifton Sta.; father: Robt.
A. BUCKLEY; occ: farmer; res: nr Clifton Sta.; mother: Eugenia M.
BUCKLEY; inf: father; pg:ln: 221:02
BUCKLEY, David; WM; b. 1 Dec 1887 in Ffx; father: Wilton BUCKLEY;
occ: farmer; res: Ffx; mother: Cora L. BUCKLEY; inf: Wilton
BUCKLEY, father; pg:ln: 166:15
BUCKLEY, Earl; WM; b. 26 Dec 1893 nr Farr P.O.; father: Saml. W.
BUCKLEY; occ: farmer; res: nr Farr P.O.; mother: Lucy V.
BUCKLEY; inf: father; pg:ln: 210:04
BUCKLEY, Gertrude; WF; b. 20 Jan 1890 in Ffx; father: Wm. T.
BUCKLEY; occ: farmer; res: Ffx; mother: Annie BUCKLEY; inf: Wm.
T. BUCKLEY, father; pg:ln: 185:07
BUCKLEY, Gertrude; WF; b. 23 Feb 1892 nr Centreville; father: Wm. T.
BUCKLEY; occ: farmer; res: nr Centreville; mother: Annie
BUCKLEY; inf: father; pg:ln: 208:01
BUCKLEY, Hattie; WF; b. 4 Nov 1887 in Ffx; father: Jno. W. BUCKLEY;
occ: farmer; res: Ffx; mother: Worceline BUCKLEY; inf: Jno. W.
BUCKLEY, father; pg:ln: 166:14
BUCKLEY, Jas. F.; WM; b. 21 Sep 1882 in Ffx; father: J. W. BUCKLEY;
occ: farmer; res: Ffx; mother: Wesseleanor BUCKLEY; inf: J. W.
BUCKLEY, father; pg:ln: 136:06
BUCKLEY, Lizzie; WF; b. 3 Nov 1883 in Ffx; father: W. BUCKLEY; occ:
farmer; res: Ffx; mother: Annie BUCKLEY; inf: W. BUCKLEY, father;
pg:ln: 143:06
BUCKLEY, M. P.; WM; b. 30 May 1883 in Ffx; father: Jas. F. BUCKLEY;
occ: farmer; res: Ffx; mother: Lizzie BUCKLEY; inf: J. F. BUCKLEY,
father; pg:ln: 143:07
BUCKLEY, Mamie; WF; b. 4 Apr 1890 in Ffx; father: Jno. W. BUCKLEY;
occ: farmer; res: Ffx; mother: Wessalener BUCKLEY; inf: J. W.
BUCKLEY, father; pg:ln: 185:06
BUCKLEY, Mary A.; WF; b. 25 Jun 1880 in Ffx; father: W. T. BUCKLEY;
occ: farmer; res: Ffx; mother: Annie; inf: W. T. BUCKLEY, father;
pg:ln: 127:06
BUCKLEY, Mary V.; WF; b. 23 Feb 1887 in Ffx; father: Robt. A.
BUCKLEY; occ: farmer; res: Ffx; mother: May BUCKLEY; inf: Robt.
A. BUCKLEY, father; pg:ln: 166:13
BUCKLEY, Milton; WM; b. 4 Nov 1888 in Ffx; father: Jno. W.
BUCKLEY; occ: farmer; res: Ffx; mother: Wessalener BUCKLEY;
inf: Jno. W. BUCKLEY, father; pg:ln: 170:07
BUCKLEY, R. A.; WM; b. 21 Aug 1889 in Ffx; father: R. A. BUCKLEY;
occ: farmer; res: Ffx; mother: E. M. BUCKLEY; inf: R. A. BUCKLEY,
father; pg:ln: 181:11
BUCKLEY, Ralph; WM; b. 2 May 1893 nr Centreville; father: John
BUCKLEY; occ: farmer; res: nr Centreville; mother: Lena BUCKLEY;
inf: father; pg:ln: 210:05

BUCKLEY, Rose; WF; b. 19 Oct 1893 nr Clifton Sta.; father: Wilton
    BUCKLEY; occ: farmer; res: nr Clifton; mother: Cora L. BUCKLEY;
    inf: father; pg:ln: 210:06
BUCKLEY, Ruth; WF; b. 17 Mar 1892 nr Clifton; father: Rob. A.
    BUCKLEY; occ: farmer; res: nr Centreville; mother: Eugenia M.
    BUCKLEY; inf: father; pg:ln: 208:02
BUCKLEY, Thos. L.; WM; b. 26 May 1885 in Ffx; father: Robt. A.
    BUCKLEY; occ: farmer; res: Ffx; mother: Mary BUCKLEY; inf: R. A.
    BUCKLEY, father; pg:ln: 156:01
BUCKLEY, W. W.; WM; b. 29 Feb 1880 in Ffx; father: Jas. F.
    BUCKLEY; occ: farmer; res: Ffx; mother: Lizzie; inf: J. F. BUCKLEY,
    father; pg:ln: 127:05
BUCKLEY, Willie; WM; b. 19 Nov 1884 in Ffx; father: Saml. W.
    BUCKLEY; occ: farmer; res: Ffx; mother: Lucy BUCKLEY; inf: S. W.
    BUCKLEY, father; pg:ln: 146:09
BUCKNER, Betty; CF; b. 20 Oct 1887 in Ffx; father: John BUCKNER;
    occ: farmer; res: Ffx; mother: Bettie BUCKNER; inf: J. BUCKNER,
    father; pg:ln: 160:20
BURCH, Clifton; WM; b. 19 Feb 1885 in Falls Church; father: J. E.
    BURCH; occ: farmer; res: Falls Church; mother: Frances BURCH;
    inf: father; pg:ln: 152:04
BURCH, Mary Simpson; WF; b. 1 Feb 1885 in Falls Ch.; father: E. J.
    BURCH; occ: mcht.; res: Falls Ch.; mother: M. C. BURCH; inf:
    father; pg:ln: 152:08
BURKE, Alice; CF; b. 27 Apr 1888 in ___; father: Geo. BURKE; occ:
    farmer; res: Ffx; mother: Annie BURKE; inf: G. BURKE, father; pg:ln:
    173:04
BURKE, Charlie; WM; b. 22 Feb 1888 in Ffx; father: Geo. H. BURKE;
    occ: merchant; res: Ffx; mother: Dollie BURKE; inf: Geo. H. BURKE,
    father; pg:ln: 170:01
BURKE, Ira E.; WM; b. 17 May 1889 in Ffx; father: R. A. BURKE; occ:
    farmer; res: Ffx; mother: Clementine BURKE; inf: R. A. BURKE,
    father; pg:ln: 181:10
BURKE, Jesse; CM; b. 21 Mar 1891 in Ffx; father: Jesse BURKE; occ:
    farmer; res: Ffx; mother: Maria BURKE; inf: Jesse BURKE, father;
    pg:ln: 198:14
BURKE, John; WM; b. 27 Dec 1894 nr Clifton Sta.; father: Richard A.
    BURKE; occ: farmer; res: nr Clifton Sta.; mother: Clemantine
    BURKE; inf: father; pg:ln: 221:05
BURKE, Loise; WF; b. 18 Oct 1885 in Ffx; father: Geo. H. BURKE; occ:
    farmer; res: Ffx; mother: Dollie BURKE; inf: G. H. BURKE, father;
    pg:ln: 156:07
BURKE, Lula; CF; b. 18 Jan 1885 in Dranes.; father: Jessie BURKE;
    occ: laborer; res: Dranes.; mother: Maria BURKE; inf: father; pg:ln:
    152:10
BURKE, not named; WF; b. 18 Dec 1880 in Ffx; father: Rich'd. BURKE;
    occ: farmer; res: Ffx; mother: Clementine; inf: R. BURKE, father;
    pg:ln: 127:07

BURKE, not named; WM; b. 22 Feb 1892 nr Clifton; father: Alex R. BURKE; occ: farmer; res: nr Clifton; mother: Clementine BURKE; inf: father; pg:ln: 208:04

BURKE, not named; WM; b. 27 Dec 1893 nr Clifton Sta; father: Richard A. BURKE; occ: farmer; res: nr Clifton; mother: Catharine BURKE; inf: parent; pg:ln: 212:101

BURLEIGH, Alice M.; WF; b. 1 Oct 1892 in Ffx; father: J. L. BURLEIGH; occ: farmer; res: Ffx; mother: Emma J. BURLEIGH; inf: J. L. BURLEIGH, father; pg:ln: 202:04

BURLEIGH, Allie; WM; b. 13 Jul 1890 in Ffx; father: J. L. BURLEIGH; occ: farmer; res: Ffx; mother: Annie BURLEIGH; inf: J. L. BURLEIGH, father; pg:ln: 189:14

BURNES, Gertrude; WF; b. 9 Mar 1890 in Ffx; father: Jno. F. BURNES; occ: farmer; res: Ffx; mother: Ida BURNES; inf: J. F. BURNES, father; pg:ln: 185:05

BURNES, Lawrence; WM; b. 11 Sep 1887 in Ffx; father: Wm. BURNES; occ: farmer; res: Ffx; mother: Julia BURNES; inf: W. BURNES, father; pg:ln: 160:24

BURNES, Ollie; WF; b. 24 Jan 1894 in Ffx; father: W. H. BURNES; occ: farmer; res: Ffx; mother: F. BURNES; inf: W. H. BURNES, father; pg:ln: 217:10

BURNES, W.; CM; b. 8 Apr 1896 in Ffx; father: Turner BURNS; occ: farmer; res: Ffx; mother: Mary BURNS; inf: T. BURNS, father; pg:ln: 225:12

BURNETT, Mamie; CF; b. 4 Feb 1881 in Vienna; father: Fred BURNETT; occ: laborer; res: Vienna; mother: Agnes BURNETT; inf: father; pg:ln: 130:06

BURNS, Clintus; WM; b. 19 Jan 1896 in Ffx; father: W. H. BURNES; occ: farmer; res: Ffx; mother: Julia F. BURNS; inf: W. H. BURNS. father; pg:ln: 225:06

BURNS, Oscar H.; WM; b. 25 Feb 1889 in Ffx; father: Wm. BURNS; occ: farmer; res: Ffx; mother: Julia BURNS; inf: W. BURNS, father Clerk in Charge of Old Records: Applicant states that his correct name is Herbert Oscar Burns.; pg:ln: 177:18

BURNSIDE, Sarah; WF; b. 15 Jul 1880 in Ffx; father: Jno. BURNSIDE; occ: farmer; res: Ffx; mother: Josephine; inf: Jno. BURNSIDE, father; pg:ln: 127:04

BURT, Margaret; CF; b. 20 Apr 1881 in Dranesville; father: John G. BURT; occ: laborer; res: Dranesville; mother: Mary E. BURT; inf: father; pg:ln: 130:08

BUSHROD, Viola; CF; b. 23 May 1896 in Masons Neck; father: John BUSHROD; occ: farmer; res: nr Gunston; mother: Sarah BUSHROD; inf: father; pg:ln: 229:18

BUTLER, Emma; CF; b. 10 Feb 1894 nr Gum Spring; father: Henry BUTLER; occ: laborer; res: nr Gum Spring; mother: Martha BUTLER; inf: father; pg:ln: 221:16

BUTLER, Estine; CM; b. 31 Dec 1892 in Ffx; father: Jacob BUTLER; occ: farmer; res: Ffx; mother: Ellen BUTLER; inf: J. BUTLER, father; pg:ln: 202:09

BUTLER, Henrietta; CF; b. 21 Sep 1890 in Ffx; father: Jacob BUTLER; occ: farmer; res: Ffx; mother: Ella BUTLER; inf: J. BUTLER, father; pg:ln: 189:06

BUTLER, Mary; CF; b. 5 Sep 1889 in Ffx; father: Geo. BUTLER; occ: laborer; res: Ffx; mother: Bella BUTLER; inf: Geo. BUTLER, father; pg:ln: 181:17

BUTLER, not named; WM; b. 10 Sep 1889 in Ffx; father: W. H. BUTLER; occ: farmer; res: Ffx; mother: Mollie BUTLER; inf: W. H. BUTLER, father; pg:ln: 177:05

BUTLER, Sadie; CF; b. 2 Aug 1892 nr Mt. Vernon; father: Henry BUTLER; occ: laborer; res: nr Mt. Vernon; mother: Martha BUTLER; inf: mother; pg:ln: 206:01

BYRNE, Annabell; WF; b. 27 Oct 1889 in Ffx; father: Henry M. BYRNE; occ: farmer; res: Ffx; mother: Kate BYRNE; inf: H. M. BYRNE, father; pg:ln: 177:16

BYRNE, Jas. H.; WM; b. 3 Oct 1883 in Chantilly; father: ___ BYRNE; occ: farmer; res: Chantilly; mother: Ida BYRNE; inf: father; pg:ln: 139:14

BYRNE, Louise; WF; b. 26 Feb 1893 in Ffx; father: H. M. BYRNE; occ: farmer; res: Ffx; mother: Kate M. BYRNE; inf: H. M. BYRNE, father; pg:ln: 213:06

BYRNE, not named; WM; b. 29 Mar 1896 nr Annandale; father: W. E. BYRNE; occ: farmer; res: nr Annandale; mother: Minnie BYRNE; inf: father; pg:ln: 229:08

BYRNE, Wm. H.; WM; b. 14 May 1891 in Ffx; father: H. M. BYRNE; occ: farmer; res: Ffx; mother: Kate M. BYRNE; inf: H. M. BYRNE, father; pg:ln: 198:02

CALLAHAN, E. P.; WF; b. 7 Oct 1893 in Ffx; father: G. W. CALLAHAN; occ: farmer; res: Ffx; mother: W. L. CALLAHAN; inf: G. W. CALLAHAN, father; pg:ln: 213:24

CAMPBELL, Dave M.; WM; b. 12 Feb 1893 in Ffx; father: T. J. CAMPBELL; occ: farmer; res: Ffx; mother: Susie CAMPBELL; inf: T. J. CAMPBELL, father; pg:ln: 213:16

CAMPBELL, Les. F.; WM; b. 31 Jan 1892 in Ffx; father: W. H. CAMPBELL; occ: farmer; res: Ffx; mother: Kate CAMPBELL; inf: W. H. CAMPBELL, father; pg:ln: 202:23

CAMPBELL, not named; WF; b. 10 Sep 1893 in Ffx; father: W. P. CAMPBELL; occ: farmer; res: Ffx; mother: E. L. CAMPBELL; inf: W. P. CAMPBELL, father; pg:ln: 213:25

CANFIELD, B.; WM; b. 17 Jul 1880 in Ffx; father: Chas. H. CANFIELD; occ: farmer; res: Ffx; mother: Annie; inf: C. H. CANFIELD, father; pg:ln: 127:21

CARLIN, Fannie; CF; b. 8 Nov 1896 in Ffx; father: Jno. T. CARTER; occ: farmer; res: Ffx; mother: Lydia CARTER; inf: J. T. CARTER, father; pg:ln: 225:25

CARLIN, Frank E.; WM; b. 13 Oct 1884 in Providence; father: James
    CARLIN; occ: farmer; res: Providence; mother: Mary E. CARLIN; inf:
    father; pg:ln: 149:21
CARLISLE, Lola M.; WF; b. 3 Sep 1896 in Ffx; father: W. H. CARLISLE;
    occ: farmer; res: Ffx; mother: Mary H. CARLISLE; inf: W. H.
    CARLISLE, father; pg:ln: 225:20
CARLISLE, Mable A.; WF; b. 15 Mar 1894 in Ffx; father: Jos. A.
    CARLISLE; occ: farmer; res: Ffx; mother: Florence CARLISLE; inf:
    J. A. CARLISLE, father; pg:ln: 217:15
CARLISLE, Myrtle E.; WF; b. 16 Jun 1893 in Ffx; father: W. F.
    CARLISLE; occ: farmer; res: Ffx; mother: Mary H. CARLISLE; inf:
    W. F. CARLISLE, father; pg:ln: 213:19
CARPER, Thos. Y.; WM; b. 20 Oct 1889 in Ffx; father: Thos. S.
    CARPER; occ: farmer; res: Ffx; mother: Laura V. CARPER; inf: T. S.
    CARPER, father; pg:ln: 177:35
CARR, Florence; WF; b. 21 Mar 1894 in Ffx; father: W. E. CARR; occ:
    farmer; res: Ffx; mother: H. A. CARR; inf: W. E. CARR, father; pg:ln:
    217:24
CARR, Magdaline; WF; b. 20 Apr 1893 in Ffx; father: W. E. CARR; occ:
    farmer; res: Ffx; mother: Hellen A. CARR; inf: W. E. CARR, father;
    pg:ln: 213:21
CARROLL, not named; CM; b. 9 Oct 1896 nr Hayfield; father: John
    CARROL; occ: laborer; res: nr Hayfield; mother: Della CARROLL;
    inf: father; pg:ln: 229:25
CARSON, Carl; WM; b. 30 Aug 1888 in ___; father: W. CARSON; occ:
    farmer; res: Ffx; mother: Martha CARSON; inf: W. CARSON, father;
    pg:ln: 173:16
CARTER, ___; CF; b. 3 Jan 1890 in Ffx; father: not known; occ: farmer;
    res: Ffx; mother: Ellen CARTER; inf: Ellen CARTER, mother; pg:ln:
    189:21
CARTER, A. J.; CM; b. 16 Apr 1888 in ___; father: A. J. CARTER; occ:
    farmer; res: Ffx; mother: Sara E. CARTER; inf: A. J. CARTER,
    father; pg:ln: 173:18
CARTER, Alberta; CF; b. 15 May 1896 in Ffx; father: W. H. CARTER;
    occ: farmer; res: Ffx; mother: Lavina CARTER; inf: W. H. CARTER,
    father; pg:ln: 225:24
CARTER, Annie; CM; b. 5 Jun 1892 in Ffx; father: J. T. CARTER; occ:
    farmer; res: Ffx; mother: Lydia CARTER; inf: J. T. CARTER, father;
    pg:ln: 202:22
CARTER, Asbry; WM; b. 1 Nov 1896 in Centreville; father: M. M.
    CARTER; occ: farmer; res: Centreville; mother: Bell CARTER; inf:
    father; pg:ln: 229:19
CARTER, Beatrice; CF; b. 23 Mar 1888 in ___; father: Jno. CARTER;
    occ: farmer; res: Ffx; mother: Maoney CARTER; inf: Jno. CARTER,
    father; pg:ln: 173:19
CARTER, Benjn.; WM; b. 10 Sep 1890 in Ffx; father: M. M. CARTER;
    occ: farmer; res: Ffx; mother: Belle CARTER; inf: M. M. CARTER,
    father; pg:ln: 185:18

CARTER, Bessie; CF; b. 6 Mar 1880 in Vienna; father: R. R. CARTER; occ: laborer; res: Vienna; mother: Fannie CARTER; inf: father; pg:ln: 124:10

CARTER, Charity; CF; b. 7 Dec 1889 in Ffx; father: Isaac CARTER; occ: laborer; res: Ffx; mother: Harriet CARTER; inf: I. CARTER, father; pg:ln: 181:23

CARTER, Charles Cornelius; CM; b. 30 Aug 1892 nr Woodlawn; father: Albert N. CARTER; occ: laborer; res: nr Woodlawn; mother: Laura F. CARTER; inf: mother; pg:ln: 206:02

CARTER, Chas. Saml.; WM; b. 20 Jan 1887 in Ffx; father: Giles CARTER; occ: laborer; res: Ffx; mother: Mary CARTER; inf: Giles CARTER, father; pg:ln: 166:16

CARTER, Clinton; CM; b. 23 Apr 1891 in Ffx; father: R. R. CARTER; occ: farmer; res: Ffx; mother: Fannie CARTER; inf: R. R. CARTER, father; pg:ln: 198:21

CARTER, Cornelius; CM; b. 7 Apr 1885 in Vienna; father: Cyrus CARTER; occ: minister; res: Vienna; mother: Malinda CARTER; inf: father; pg:ln: 152:16

CARTER, Effie; CF; b. 18 Sep 1880 in Providence; father: Andrew CARTER; occ: laborer; res: Providence; mother: Ellen CARTER; inf: father; pg:ln: 124:07

CARTER, Ella; CF; b. 18 Sep 1887 in Ffx; father: J. E. CARTER; occ: laborer; res: Ffx; mother: Minnie CARTER; inf: J. E. CARTER, father; pg:ln: 160:31

CARTER, Etta; CF; b. 18 May 1888 in ___; father: Jno. T. CARTER; occ: farmer; res: Ffx; mother: Lyddia CARTER; inf: J. T. CARTER, father; pg:ln: 173:20

CARTER, Eugene; WM; b. 29 Jul 1887 in Ffx; father: Mason CARTER; occ: farmer; res: Ffx; mother: Belle CARTER; inf: Mason CARTER, father; pg:ln: 166:21

CARTER, Fannie; WF; b. 8 Mar 1890 in Ffx; father: C. C. CARTER; occ: farmer; res: Ffx; mother: Pauline CARTER; inf: C. C. CARTER, father; pg:ln: 185:19

CARTER, Geo. K.; CM; b. 21 Sep 1889 in Ffx; father: Chas. CARTER; occ: farmer; res: Ffx; mother: Martha CARTER; inf: Chas. CARTER, father; pg:ln: 177:31

CARTER, Howard; CM; b. 22 Apr 1883 in Lincolnville; father: Cyrus CARTER; occ: minister; res: Lincolnville; mother: Delilah CARTER; inf: father; pg:ln: 139:16

CARTER, James; CM; b. 4 Jan 1890 in Ffx; father: Joseph CARTER Sr.; occ: laborer; res: Ffx; mother: Elizabeth CARTER; inf: Jos. CARTER Sr., father; pg:ln: 185:22

CARTER, Jas. H.; CM; b. 6 Apr 1894 in Ffx; father: Chas. H. CARTER; occ: farmer; res: Ffx; mother: M. A. CARTER; inf: C. H. CARTER, father; pg:ln: 217:28

CARTER, Jennie B.; CF; b. 1 Dec 1893 nr Woodlawn; father: ___; occ: ___; res: ___; mother: Jennie CARTER; inf: mother; pg:ln: 210:14

CARTER, Jennie; CF; b. 14 Aug 1886 in Prov.; father: C. H. CARTER; occ: laborer; res: Prov.; mother: M. A. CARTER; inf: father; pg:ln: 158:12

CARTER, Julian; WM; b. 12 Apr 1896 in Ffx; father: Luther CARTER; occ: farmer; res: Ffx; mother: Rose CARTER; inf: L. CARTER, father; pg:ln: 225:36

CARTER, Laura; CF; b. 30 Sep 1880 in Vienna; father: Cyrus CARTER; occ: laborer; res: Vienna; mother: Malinda CARTER; inf: father; pg:ln: 124:13

CARTER, Lena (twin); CF; b. 18 Nov 1894 in Ffx; father: L. ODERICK [CARTER?]; occ: farmer; res: Ffx; mother: Kate CARTER; inf: Kate CARTER, mother; pg:ln: 217:30

CARTER, Leonard; CM; b. 4 Apr 1887 in Ffx; father: Cyrus CARTER; occ: laborer; res: Ffx; mother: Milly CARTER; inf: Cyrus CARTER, father; pg:ln: 160:30

CARTER, Leslie; CM; b. 29 Oct 1889 in Ffx; father: Robt. CARTER; occ: farmer; res: Ffx; mother: Fannie CARTER; inf: Robt. CARTER, father; pg:ln: 177:32

CARTER, Mary A.; CF; b. 1 Sep 1884 in Dranes.; father: Jno. T. CARTER; occ: laborer; res: Dranes.; mother: Lydia CARTER; inf: father; pg:ln: 149:23

CARTER, Mary E.; CF; b. 3 Sep 1884 in Providence; father: Alfred CARTER; occ: laborer; res: Providence; mother: Mary CARTER; inf: father; pg:ln: 149:19

CARTER, Mary Essie; CF; b. 5 Mar 1890 in Ffx; father: Jos. CARTER Jr.; occ: laborer; res: Ffx; mother: Annie M. CARTER; inf: Jos. CARTER Jr., father; pg:ln: 185:23

CARTER, not named (twin); WM; b. 13 Nov 1893 nr Centreville; father: M. M. CARTER; occ: farmer; res: nr Centreville; mother: Bell CARTER; inf: parents; pg:ln: 210:21

CARTER, not named (twin); WM; b. 13 Nov 1893 nr Centreville; father: M. M. CARTER; occ: farmer; res: nr Centreville; mother: Bell CARTER; inf: parents; pg:ln: 210:21

CARTER, not named; CF; b. 29 Nov 1886 in Prov.; father: R. R. CARTER; occ: laborer; res: Prov.; mother: F. CARTER; inf: father; pg:ln: 158:13

CARTER, not named; CM; b. 9 Dec 1892 nr Mt. Vernon; father: Alexander CARTER; occ: laborer; res: nr Mt. Vernon; mother: Martha CARTER; inf: mother; pg:ln: 206:04

CARTER, not named; WF; b. 14 Feb 1894 nr Woodlawn; father: Albert H. CARTER; occ: farmer; res: nr Woodlawn; mother: Sarah CARTER; inf: mother; pg:ln: 221:23

CARTER, Robert F.; CM; b. 14 Nov 1893 nr Woodlawn; father: ___; occ: ___; res: ___; mother: Hettie B. CARTER; inf: mother; pg:ln: 210:13

CARTER, Ruby R.; CF; b. 24 Dec 1890 in Ffx; father: Chas. CARTER; occ: farmer; res: Ffx; mother: Martha CARTER; inf: C. CARTER, father; pg:ln: 189:22

CARTER, Sarah Jane; CF; b. 25 Apr 1892 nr Mt. Vernon; father:
Benjamin CARTER; occ: laborer; res: nr Mt. Vernon; mother: Sarah
CARTER; inf: mother; pg:ln: 206:03

CARTER, Sarah; CF; b. 24 Mar 1893 nr Gum Spring; father: Isaac
CARTER [written as Isacc]; occ: laborer; res: nr Gum Spring;
mother: Harriet CARTER; inf: mother; pg:ln: 210:15

CARTER, Tillie F. (twin); CF; b. 18 Nov 1894 in Ffx; father: L. ODERICK
[CARTER?]; occ: farmer; res: Ffx; mother: Kate CARTER; inf: Kate
CARTER, mother; pg:ln: 217:29

CARTER, William; CM; b. 25 May 1884 in Providence; father: William
CARTER; occ: laborer; res: Providence; mother: Louisa CARTER;
inf: father; pg:ln: 149:20

CARTER, Wm. L.; CM; b. 16 Mar 1882 in Providence; father: A. J.
CARTER; occ: laborer; res: Providence; mother: Sarah E. CARTER;
inf: father; pg:ln: 134:11

CARY, Alice; CF; b. 19 Dec 1893 in Ffx; father: Elisha CARY; occ:
farmer; res: Ffx; mother: Mary CARY; inf: E. CARY, father; pg:ln:
213:26

CARY, Nettie; CF; b. 20 Nov 1892 in Ffx; father: Elisha CARY; occ:
farmer; res: Ffx; mother: Mary CARY; inf: E. CARY, father; pg:ln:
202:16

CASSEDY, William; WM; b. 19 Mar 1884 in Providence; father: James
CASSEDY; occ: mechanic; res: Providence; mother: Maggie R.
CASSEDY; inf: father; pg:ln: 149:18

CASSIDY, Laura M.; WF; b. 15 Mar 1888 in ___; father: Jas. CASSIDY;
occ: farmer; res: Ffx; mother: Maggie CASSIDY; inf: J. CASSIDY,
father; pg:ln: 173:13

CASSIDY, Mary L.; WF; b. 30 Mar 1887 in Ffx; father: James CASSIDY;
occ: basketmaker; res: Ffx; mother: Maggie CASSIDY; inf: J.
CASSIDY, father; pg:ln: 161:36

CASTLEMAN, Oliver F.; WM; b. 1 Feb 1894 in Ffx; father: Robt. A.
CASTLEMAN; occ: farmer; res: Ffx; mother: Fannie CASTLEMAN;
inf: R. A. CASTLEMAN, father; pg:ln: 217:17

CATON, Golder Amanda; WF; b. 10 Feb 1891 nr Sudley; father:
Erastus G. CATON; occ: farmer; res: nr Sudley; mother: Allie
CATON; inf: parents; pg:ln: 194:07

CATON, Howard; WM; b. 19 Dec 1896 in Ffx; father: Jno. C. CATON;
occ: farmer; res: Ffx; mother: Sarah CATON; inf: Jno. C. CATON,
father; pg:ln: 225:35

CATON, Lillian; WF; b. 8 Apr 1896 in Ffx; father: E. F. CATON; occ:
farmer; res: Ffx; mother: Irene CATON; inf: E. F. CATON, father;
pg:ln: 225:30

CATON, Lula; WF; b. 4 Sep 1892 in Ffx; father: Enoch CATON; occ:
farmer; res: Ffx; mother: Irene CATON; inf: E. CATON, father; pg:ln:
202:20

CATON, Michael; WM; b. 16 Feb 1883 in Providence Dist.; father: W. H.
CATON; occ: laborer; res: Providence Dist.; mother: Mary CATON;
inf: father; pg:ln: 139:18

CATTS, Oliver; WM; b. 1 Nov 1892 in Ffx; father: J. H. CATTS; occ: farmer; res: Ffx; mother: Grace CATTS; inf: J. H. CATTS, father; pg:ln: 202:21

CATTS, Raymond; WM; b. 25 Jan 1887 in Ffx; father: J. H. CATTS; occ: merchant; res: Ffx; mother: Gracie B. CATTS; inf: J. H. CATTS, father; pg:ln: 166:18

CAWMAN, Victoria; WF; b. 5 Oct 1890 in Ffx; father: J. W. S. CAWMAN; occ: farmer; res: Ffx; mother: Jane E. CAWMAN; inf: J. W. S. CAWMAN, father; pg:ln: 185:24

CHAMBERS, Luther F.; CM; b. 30 Nov 1892 in Fairfax C. H.; father: Luther CHAMBERS; occ: laborer; res: nr C H; mother: Margaret CHAMBERS; inf: mother; pg:ln: 206:36

CHAMBERS, not named; CM; b. 1 Apr 1887 in Ffx; father: Luther CHAMBERS; occ: laborer; res: Ffx; mother: Maggie CHAMBERS; inf: L. CHAMBERS, father; pg:ln: 166:22

CHAPIN, Mary C.; WF; b. 10 Sep 1896 in Ffx; father: Jno. D. CHAPIN; occ: farmer; res: Ffx; mother: N. M. CHAPIN; inf: J. D. CHAPIN, father; pg:ln: 225:34

CHAUNCEY, J. E.; WM; b. 26 Aug 1896 in Ffx; father: Julian CHAUNCEY; occ: butcher; res: Ffx; mother: Leana CHAUNCEY; inf: J. CHAUNCEY, father; pg:ln: 226:37

CHAUNCEY, Mary; WF; b. 9 Dec 1894 in Ffx; father: Julian CHAUNCEY; occ: farmer; res: Ffx; mother: Leana CHAUNCEY; inf: J. CHAUNCEY, father; pg:ln: 217:25

CHEW, Addison; CM; b. 15 Dec 1896 in Ffx; father: Addison CHEW; occ: farmer; res: Ffx; mother: Betsey CHEW; inf: A. CHEW, father; pg:ln: 225:26

CHEW, Jno. H.; CM; b. 18 Oct 1889 in Ffx; father: Addison CHEW; occ: farmer; res: Ffx; mother: Betsey CHEW; inf: Ad[d]ison CHEW, father; pg:ln: 177:36

CHICHESTER, Harry C.; WM; b. 18 May 1881 in Seminary; father: C. C. CHICHESTER; occ: butcher; res: Seminary; mother: Roxanna CHICHESTER; inf: mother; pg:ln: 130:09

CHICHESTER, Peyton Moncure; WM; b. 21 Aug 1880 in Fairfax C. H.; father: D. M. CHICHESTER; occ: atty at law; res: Fairfax C. H.; mother: Agnes R. CHICHESTER; inf: father; pg:ln: 124:06

CHICHESTER, Peyton Moncure; WM; b. 7 Oct 1884 in Fairfax C. H.; father: D. M. CHICHESTER; occ: atty law; res: Fairfax C. H.; mother: A. R. CHICHESTER; inf: father; pg:ln: 149:13

CHURCH, Guy; WM; b. 26 Jul 1889 in Ffx; father: M. E. CHURCH; occ: farmer; res: Ffx; mother: Carrie CHURCH; inf: M. E. CHURCH, father; pg:ln: 177:27

CLAGETT, J. H.; WM; b. 5 Sep 1891 in Pohick Ch.; father: J. H. CLAGETT; occ: farmer; res: Pohick Ch.; mother: Laura CLAGETT; inf: parents; pg:ln: 193:06

CLAGGETT, Virginia; WF; b. 24 Jul 1889 in Ffx; father: Hamett CLAGGETT; occ: farmer; res: Ffx; mother: Laura CLAGGETT; inf: H. CLAGGETT, father; pg:ln: 181:21

CLAIBORN, Edmond; CM; b. 10 Mar 1891 in Sheridan Neck; father: Wm. CLAIBORN; occ: laborer; res: Sheridans Neck; mother: Julia CLAIBORN; inf: parent; pg:ln: 196:04

CLARK, ___; WM; b. 11 Jul 1883 in Ffx; father: Jas. CLARK; occ: farmer; res: Ffx; mother: Hannah CLARK; inf: Jas. CLARK, father; pg:ln: 143:12

CLARK, Elizabt.; WF; b. __ Feb 1892 in Ffx; father: Robt. CLARK; occ: farmer; res: Ffx; mother: Emma CLARK; inf: Robt. CLARK, father; Clerk in change of old records: Applicant states that she was born Feb. 8, 1892.; pg:ln: 202:24

CLARK, J. B.; WM; b. 18 Apr 1892 in Ffx; father: W. A. CLARK; occ: farmer; res: Ffx; mother: Virginia CLARK; inf: W. A. CLARK, father; pg:ln: 202:14

CLARK, Louisa; WF; b. 6 May 1891 in Ffx; father: Thos. J. CLARK; occ: farmer; res: Ffx; mother: Susan CLARK; inf: T. J. CLARK, father; pg:ln: 198:18

CLARK, Maude Irene; WF; b. 7 Dec 1891 nr Lorton; father: Frank CLARK; occ: farmer; res: nr Lorton; mother: Mary Etta CLARK; inf: parents; pg:ln: 193:07

CLARK, Melvin Simpson; WM; b. 25 Nov 1894 nr Lorton Sta.; father: Frank CLARK; occ: farmer; res: nr Lorton; mother: Mary Ella CLARK; inf: father; pg:ln: 221:19

CLARK, Minnie; WF; b. 8 Jun 1889 in Ffx; father: Robt. CLARK; occ: farmer; res: Ffx; mother: Emma CLARK; inf: Rob CLARK, father; pg:ln: 177:23

CLAY, Earle C.; CM; b. 1 Feb 1888 in ___; father: Henry CLAY; occ: farmer; res: Ffx; mother: Eliza CLAY; inf: H. CLAY, father; pg:ln: 173:15

CLAY, Henry; CM; b. 16 Jul 1880 in Providence; father: Henry CLAY; occ: laborer; res: Providence; mother: Eliza CLAY; inf: father; pg:ln: 124:08

CLAYBERGER, Clara A.; WF; b. 12 Sep 1887 in Ffx; father: B. F. CLAYBERGER; occ: R R agnt.; res: Ffx; mother: N. E. CLAYBERGER; inf: B. F. CLAYBERGER, father; pg:ln: 160:32

CLAYBERGER, Elizabt.; WF; b. 14 Aug 1889 in Ffx; father: B. F. CLAYBERGER; occ: farmer; res: Ffx; mother: Nillie CLAYBERGER [Nellie?]; inf: B. F. CLAYBERGER, father; pg:ln: 177:34

CLAYBURGER, B. F. JR.; WM; b. 24 Oct 1883 in Providence Dist.; father: B. F. CLAYBURGER; occ: farmer; res: Providence Dist.; mother: M. E. CLAYBURGER; inf: father; pg:ln: 139:19

CLEARY, Bertha; WF; b. 20 Apr 1896 nr Burke Sta.; father: Michael CLEARY; occ: farmer; res: nr Burke Sta.; mother: Jennie CLEARY; inf: mother; pg:ln: 229:23

CLEAVLAND, Harry; WM; b. 23 Mar 1883 in Seminary; father: Arthur CLEAVLAND; occ: mechanic; res: Seminary; mother: ___ CLEAVLAND; inf: father; pg:ln: 139:17

CLEAVLAND, Mary; WF; b. 23 Mar 1885 in Seminary; father: Arthur
CLEAVLAND; occ: mechanic; res: Seminary; mother: Annie
CLEAVLAND; inf: father; pg:ln: 152:17

CLEAVLAND, Nannie; WF; b. 19 Jan 1884 in Seminary; father: Caleb
CLEAVLAND; occ: laborer; res: Seminary; mother: Emma
CLEAVLAND; inf: father; pg:ln: 149:14

CLEMENTS, Tyler; CM; b. 24 Aug 1888 in ___; father: Jno.
CLEMENTS; occ: farmer; res: Ffx; mother: Rachael CLEMENTS; inf:
J. CLEMENTS, father; pg:ln: 173:12

CLEMMONS, Rachael; CF; b. 1 Oct 1886 in Prov.; father: John
CLEMMONS; occ: laborer; res: Prov.; mother: Rachael
CLEMMONS; inf: father; pg:ln: 158:11

CLEVELAND, ___; WF; b. 18 Jan 1887 in Ffx; father: Arthur
CLEVELAND; occ: farmer; res: Ffx; mother: M. K. CLEVELAND; inf:
A. CLEVELAND, father; pg:ln: 161:37

CLEVELAND, A. A.; WM; b. 30 Aug 1896 in Ffx; father: A. H.
CLEVELAND; occ: farmer; res: Ffx; mother: Mary C. CLEVELAND;
inf: A. H. CLEVELAND, father; pg:ln: 225:33

CLEVELAND, Eliza E.; WF; b. 11 Aug 1896 in Ffx; father: Andrew
CLEVELAND; occ: farmer; res: Ffx; mother: Cath'e. CLEVELAND;
inf: A. CLEVELAND, father; pg:ln: 225:32

CLEVELAND, Nellie; WF; b. 20 May 1889 in Ffx; father: Luther
CLEVELAND; occ: farmer; res: Ffx; mother: Mary CLEVELAND; inf:
L. CLEVELAND, father; pg:ln: 177:28

CLEVELAND, Robt. L.; WM; b. 19 May 1894 in Ffx; father: Andrew
CLEVELAND; occ: farmer; res: Ffx; mother: F. C. CLEVELAND; inf:
A. CLEVELAND, father; pg:ln: 217:26

CLEWS, Rachael; CF; b. 31 Oct 1885 in Merrifield; father: John
CLEWS; occ: laborer; res: Merrifield; mother: Rachael CLEWS; inf:
father; pg:ln: 152:13

CLINKSCALES, Bertha A.; WF; b. 2 Feb 1894 nr Lorton Sta.; father:
Samuel P. CLINKSCALES; occ: farmer; res: nr Lorton; mother:
Florence M. CLINKSCALES; inf: father; pg:ln: 221:18

CLINKSCALES, Bertha Virginia; WF; b. 2 Feb 1893 nr Lorton Sta.;
father: Samuel CLINKSCALES; occ: farmer; res: nr Lorton Sta.;
mother: Florince M. CLINKSCALES; inf: parents; pg:ln: 210:19

CLINKSCALES, Ella V.; WF; b. 22 Sep 1888 in Ffx; father: Saml.
CLINKSCALES; occ: farmer; res: Ffx; mother: Florence
CLINKSCALES; inf: Saml. CLINKSCALES, father; pg:ln: 170:12

CLOE, Mary; CF; b. 1 Sep 1888 in Ffx; father: Wm. H. CLOE; occ:
farmer; res: Ffx; mother: Columbia CHLOE; inf: Wm. H. CLOE,
father; pg:ln: 170:13

[CLOWE], not named (dead); CM; b. ___ Feb 1891 nr Centreville; father:
Wm. CLOWE; occ: farmer; res: nr Centreville; mother: Columbia
CLOWE; inf: parent; pg:ln: 197:03

COATS, Chas. W.; CM; b. 21 Jul 1882 in Providence; father: Jno. E.
COATS; occ: laborer; res: Providence; mother: Lucy J. COATS; inf:
father; pg:ln: 134:12

COATS, Essy; CF; b. 4 Jul 1887 in Ffx; father: John COATS; occ: farmer; res: Ffx; mother: Lucy COATS; inf: J. COATS, father; pg:ln: 160:35

COATS, Hattie; CF; b. 18 Oct 1880 in Falls Church; father: John COATS; occ: laborer; res: Falls Church; mother: Lucy COATS; inf: father; pg:ln: 124:09

COATS, Herbert; CM; b. 5 Nov 1891 in Ffx; father: Jas. COATS; occ: farmer; res: Ffx; mother: Maria COATS; inf: J. COATS, father; pg:ln: 198:23

COATS, Malinda; CF; b. 3 Nov 1889 in Ffx; father: James COATS; occ: farmer; res: Ffx; mother: Maria COATS; inf: Jas. COATS, father; pg:ln: 177:21

COATS, Ulyssis; CM; b. 27 Jun 1892 in Ffx; father: Jno. E. COATS; occ: farmer; res: Ffx; mother: Lucy COATS; inf: J. E. COATS, father; pg:ln: 202:15

COCK, Clay Forrest; WM; b. 15 Dec 1881 in An[n]andale; father: Henry C. COCK; occ: farmer; res: An[n]andale; mother: Caroline S. COCK; inf: father; pg:ln: 130:10

COCKERILL, Addie; WM; b. 13 Nov 1896 in Ffx; father: H. E. COCKERILL; occ: farmer; res: Ffx; mother: S. C. COCKERILL; inf: H. E. COCKRELL, father; pg:ln: 225:27

COCKERILL, Alfred; WM; b. 20 Mar 1890 in Ffx; father: J. C. COCKERILL; occ: farmer; res: Ffx; mother: Laura COCKERILL; inf: J. C. COCKERILL, father; pg:ln: 189:26

COCKERILL, Anna B.; WF; b. 31 Jul 1896 in Ffx; father: Stonewell COCKERILL; occ: farmer; res: Ffx; mother: Sarah COCKERILL; inf: S. COCKRELL, father; pg:ln: 225:21

COCKERILL, C. B.; WM; b. 25 Jul 1894 in Ffx; father: Chas. B. COCKERILL; occ: farmer; res: Ffx; mother: M. A. COCKERILL; inf: C. B. COCKERILL, father; pg:ln: 217:27

COCKERILL, Effie J.; WF; b. 16 Sep 1894 in Ffx; father: Mark COCKERILL; occ: farmer; res: Ffx; mother: Maud COCKERILL; inf: M. COCKERILL, father; pg:ln: 217:19

COCKERILL, Harry C.; WM; b. 13 Feb 1888 in ___; father: J. C. COCKERILL; occ: farmer; res: Ffx; mother: Laura COCKERILL; inf: J. C. COCKERILL, father; pg:ln: 173:21

COCKERILL, Leonard; WM; b. 20 Aug 1894 in Ffx; father: Stonewall COCKERILL; occ: farmer; res: Ffx; mother: Sarah COCKERILL; inf: S. COCKERILL, father; pg:ln: 217:20

COCKERILL, Ola J.; WF; b. 7 Jun 1891 in Ffx; father: Mark COCKERILL; occ: farmer; res: Ffx; mother: Maud COCKERILL; inf: M. COCKERILL, father; pg:ln: 198:19

COCKERILL, Pearl (twin); WF; b. 20 Dec 1890 in Ffx; father: W. G. COCKERILL; occ: farmer; res: Ffx; mother: Ada COCKERELL; inf: W. G. COCKERILL, father; pg:ln: 189:20

COCKERILL, Pearl (twin); WF; b. 6 May 1891 in Ffx; father: Wm. G. COCKERILL; occ: farmer; res: Ffx; mother: A. B. COCKERILL; inf: W. G. COCKERILL, father; pg:ln: 198:24

COCKERILL, Rosa M.; WF; b. 1 May 1891 in Ffx; father: J. C.
COCKERILL; occ: farmer; res: Ffx; mother: May COCKERILL; inf: J.
C. COCKERILL, father; pg:ln: 198:20

COCKERILL, Ruby (twin); WF; b. 20 Dec 1890 in Ffx; father: W. G.
COCKERILL; occ: farmer; res: Ffx; mother: Ada COCKERELL; inf:
W. G. COCKERILL, father; pg:ln: 189:19

COCKERILL, Ruby (twin); WF; b. 6 May 1891 in Ffx; father: Wm. G.
COCKERILL; occ: farmer; res: Ffx; mother: A. B. COCKERIL; inf: W.
G. COCKERILL, father; pg:ln: 198:25

COCKERILL, Ruby; WF; b. 13 Feb 1894 in Ffx; father: J. C.
COCKERILL; occ: farmer; res: Ffx; mother: Laura COCKKERILL; inf:
J. C. COCKERILL, father; pg:ln: 217:18

COCKERILLE, Blanche; WF; b. 1 Feb 1884 in Cloud's. Mill; father:
Chas. B. COCKERILLE; occ: farmer; res: Cloud's. Mill; mother:
Maggie COCKERILLE; inf: father; pg:ln: 149:16

COCKERILLE, Maggie; WF; b. 6 Jun 1884 in Cloud's Mill; father: W. G.
COCKERILLE; occ: farmer; res: Cloud's Mill; mother: Ada
COCKERILLE; inf: father; pg:ln: 149:15

COCKERILLE, Mamie E.; WF; b. 20 Mar 1880 in Falls church; father:
W. G. COCKERILE; occ: farmer; res: Falls church; mother: Ada B.
COCKERILLE; inf: father; pg:ln: 124:12

COCKERILLE, Walter; WM; b. 20 Oct 1881 in Vienna; father: J. W.
COCKERILLE; occ: sewing machine agt.; res: Vienna; mother:
Bennie COCKERILLE; inf: father; pg:ln: 130:13

COFFER, Frank; WM; b. 15 Jun 1891 nr Annandale; father: M. C.
COFFER; occ: farmer; res: nr Annandale; mother: Annie COFFER;
inf: parents; pg:ln: 195:27

COFFEY, Agnes; WF; b. 9 Feb 1889 in Ffx; father: Dennis COFFEY;
occ: farmer; res: Ffx; mother: Annie COFFEY; inf: D. COFFEY,
father; pg:ln: 181:22

COFFEY, Martin; WM; b. 3 Oct 1887 in Ffx; father: Dennis COFFEY;
occ: farmer; res: Ffx; mother: Annie COFFEY; inf: Dennis COFFEY,
father; pg:ln: 166:17

COGAN, Roxie May; WF; b. 29 Jan 1894 nr Alexandria; father: A. H.
COGAN; occ: farmer; res: nr Alex.; mother: Sadie COGAN; inf:
mother; pg:ln: 221:22

COLBERT, Wm. Andrew; CM; b. 20 Oct 1891 in Germantown; father:
Jocb [Jacob] COLBERT; occ: laborer; res: Germantown; mother:
Mollie COLBERT; inf: parent; pg:ln: 196:27

COLE, Bessie; CF; b. __ Nov 1889 in Ffx; father: Jno. COLE; occ:
farmer; res: Ffx; mother: Maria COLE; inf: Jno. COLE, father; pg:ln:
177:29

COLE, James Edward; WM; b. 9 Oct 1896 nr Alex.; father: Frank COLE;
occ: farmer; res: nr Alex.; mother: Mary Ellen COLE; inf: mother;
pg:ln: 229:24

COLE, Mary A.; CF; b. 17 Nov 1891 in Ffx; father: Henry COLE; occ:
farmer; res: Ffx; mother: Martha COLE; inf: H. COLE, father; pg:ln:
198:22

COLEMAN, Frederick; CM; b. 11 Jun 1893 nr Gum Spring; father: John COLEMAN; occ: laborer; res: nr Gum Spring; mother: Hanah COLEMAN; inf: mother; pg:ln: 210:16

COLEMAN, Jno. C.; WM; b. 19 Feb 1884 in Dranes.; father: Chas. W. COLEMAN; occ: farmer; res: Dranes.; mother: Sarah COLEMAN; inf: father; pg:ln: 149:22

COLEMAN, John; WM; b. 3 May 1887 in Ffx; father: C. W. COLEMAN; occ: farmer; res: Ffx; mother: Sarah COLEMAN; inf: C. W. COLEMAN, father; pg:ln: 160:28

COLEMAN, Ralph; WM; b. 16 Jan 1885 in Dranes.; father: Rich'd. COLEMAN; occ: farmer; res: Dranes.; mother: T. COLEMAN; inf: father; pg:ln: 152:14

COLLINS, Chas.; CM; b. 28 Aug 1889 in Ffx; father: Thos. COLLINS; occ: farmer; res: Ffx; mother: Elizabt. COLLINS; inf: Thos. COLLINS, father; pg:ln: 177:33

COLLINS, Chas.; WM; b. 13 Aug 1890 in Ffx; father: Thos. COLLINS; occ: farmer; res: Ffx; mother: Elizabt. COLLINS; inf: T. COLLINS, father; pg:ln: 189:23

COLLINS, John Edward; CM; b. 26 Jun 1891 in Potomac; father: Marshall COLLINS; occ: laborer; res: Potomac; mother: Maria COLLINS; inf: parent; pg:ln: 196:03

COLLINS, Joseph; CM; b. 12 Apr 1887 in Ffx; father: Wm. COLLINS; occ: farmer; res: Ffx; mother: Maria COLLINS; inf: W. COLLINS, father; pg:ln: 160:34

COLLINS, Mason; CM; b. 7 Sep 1893 nr Gunston; father: Marshall COLLINS; occ: laborer; res: nr Gunston; mother: Mary COLLINS; inf: parents; pg:ln: 210:18

COMPHER, Benj. H.; WM; b. 26 May 1889 in Ffx; father: Frank COMPHER; occ: farmer; res: Ffx; mother: Mollie COMPHER; inf: F. COMPHER, father; pg:ln: 177:24

COMPTON, Lucinda; WF; b. 1 Jul 1881 in Ffx; father: Felix COMPTON; occ: farmer; res: Ffx; mother: Eloise COMPTON; inf: F. COMPTON, father; pg:ln: 132:07

COMPTON, Norman; WM; b. 14 Mar 1884 in Ffx; father: Felix COMPTON; occ: farmer; res: Ffx; mother: Eloise COMPTON; inf: F. COMPTON, father; pg:ln: 146:15

CONNELL [CORNELL?], Mirtle; WF; b. 25 Mar 1886 in Forrestville; father: H. O. CORNELL; occ: farmer; res: Forrestville; mother: Julia CORNELL; inf: father; pg:ln: 158:15

COOK, Agnes; WF; b. 11 Jul 1896 nr Pohick Ch.; father: George COOK; occ: rail road hand; res: nr Pohick Ch.; mother: Annie Elizabeth COOK; inf: mother; pg:ln: 229:22

COOK, Alvin; WM; b. 2 Nov 1894 in Ffx; father: Jas. E. COOK; occ: farmer; res: Ffx; mother: Nora COOK; inf: J. E. COOK, father; pg:ln: 217:16

COOK, Annie C.; WF; b. 2 May 1888 in ___; father: M. M. COOK; occ: farmer; res: Ffx; mother: Hannah COOK; inf: M. M. COOK, father; pg:ln: 173:23

COOK, Beckie; CF; b. 20 Sep 1892 nr Burke Sta; father: ___; occ: ___; res: ___; mother: Annie COOK; inf: mother; pg:ln: 206:34

COOK, Grace; WF; b. 20 Sep 1891 in Ffx; father: Israel COOK; occ: farmer; res: Ffx; mother: L. M. COOK; inf: I. COOK, father; pg:ln: 198:16

COOK, Israel; WM; b. 10 Jun 1881 in Near C. H.; father: Israel COOK; occ: laborer; res: Near C. H.; mother: Lucy COOK; inf: father; pg:ln: 130:12

COOK, James Edward; WM; b. 16 Jul 1894 nr Pohick Church; father: George COOK; occ: farmer; res: nr Pohick Ch.; mother: Annie E. COOK; inf: father; pg:ln: 221:20

COOK, John; WM; b. 12 Nov 1882 in Ffx; father: Enoch COOK; occ: farmer; res: Ffx; mother: Martha COOK; inf: E. COOK, father; pg:ln: 136:10

COOK, Lizie; CF; b. 20 Aug 1892 nr Burke Sta; father: ___; occ: ___; res: ___; mother: Mary COOK; inf: mother; pg:ln: 206:33

COOK, Mary C.; CF; b. 5 Dec 1883 in Ffx; father: Jno. COOK; occ: farmer; res: Ffx; mother: Mary J. COOK; inf: Jno. COOK, father; pg:ln: 143:11

COOK, Morris L.; WM; b. 21 Feb 1896 in Ffx; father: Geo. E. COOK; occ: farmer; res: Ffx; mother: Bell COOK; inf: Geo. E. COOK, father; pg:ln: 225:28

COOK, Orbry; WM; b. 26 Jan 1890 in Ffx; father: M. M. COOK; occ: farmer; res: Ffx; mother: Fannie COOK; inf: M. M. COOK, father; pg:ln: 189:27

COOK, Ruth Bell; WF; b. 7 Oct 1892 in Hayfield; father: Geo. W. COOK; occ: farmer; res: Hayfield; mother: Annie COOK; inf: mother; pg:ln: 207:64

COOKSEY, Dora; WF; b. 12 Apr 1885 in Ffx; father: Jas. W. COOKSEY; occ: farmer; res: Ffx; mother: Francis COOKSEY; inf: J. W. COOKSEY, father; pg:ln: 156:09

COOKSEY, Lizzie; WF; b. 10 Apr 1884 in Ffx; father: Jas. W. COOKSEY; occ: farmer; res: Ffx; mother: Francis L. COOKSEY; inf: J. W. COOKSEY, father; pg:ln: 146:14

COOKSEY, not named; WM; b. 11 Jun 1880 in Ffx; father: J. W. COOKSEY; occ: farmer; res: Ffx; mother: Frances L.; inf: J. W. COOKSEY, father; pg:ln: 127:14

COOKSEY, Robt. S.; WM; b. 3 Apr 1883 in Ffx; father: Thos. H. COOKSEY; occ: ___; res: ___; mother: Harriet COOKSEY; inf: T. H. COOKSEY, father; pg:ln: 143:08

COOMBS, Julian S.; WM; b. 18 Jan 1890 in Ffx; father: Thos P. COOMBS; occ: blacksmith; res: Ffx; mother: Annie COOMBS; inf: T. P. COOMBS, father; pg:ln: 185:21

COOPER, ___; CF; b. 4 Feb 1896 in Ffx; father: Herbert COOPER; occ: farmer; res: Ffx; mother: Minnie COOPER; inf: H. COOPER, father; pg:ln: 225:23

COOPER, Geo. W.; WM; b. 22 Jun 1881 in Vienna; father: Thos. J.
COOPER; occ: farmer; res: Vienna; mother: Virginia C. COOPER;
inf: father; pg:ln: 130:11

COOPER, Thos. A.; WM; b. 12 May 1888 in ___; father: Thos. J.
COOPER; occ: farmer; res: Ffx; mother: Virginia COOPER; inf: T. J.
COOPER, father; pg:ln: 173:17

CORNELL, Geo.; WM; b. 14 Nov 1896 in Ffx; father: E. D. CORNELL;
occ: farmer; res: Ffx; mother: J. V. CORNELL; inf: E. D. CORNELL,
father; pg:ln: 225:29

CORNELL, Mable V.; WF; b. 24 Jul 1893 in Ffx; father: Rich'd.
CORNELL; occ: farmer; res: Ffx; mother: Cornelia CORNELL; inf:
Rich'd. CORNELL, father; pg:ln: 213:18

CORNELL, Mirtle see CONNELL, Mirtle

CORNIC, Blanche; WF; b. 5 Sep 1894 nr C. H.; father: Henry CORNIC;
occ: laborer; res: Fairfax C. H.; mother: Carrie CORNIC; inf: mother;
pg:ln: 221:24

CORNICK, Blanche; CF; b. 15 Sep 1893 nr Fairfax C. H.; father: Henry
CORNICK; occ: laborer; res: nr Fairfax C. H.; mother: Carrie
CORNICK; inf: parents; pg:ln: 210:17

CORNING, Stewart P.; WM; b. 18 Feb 1896 in Ffx; father: Albt.
CORNING; occ: farmer; res: Ffx; mother: Annie L. CORNING; inf:
Albt. CORNING, father; pg:ln: 225:31

CORNWELL, Annie B.; WF; b. 15 Dec 1893 in Ffx; father: Jesse A.
CORNWELL; occ: farmer; res: Ffx; mother: Maggie CORNWELL;
inf: J. A. CORNWELL, father; pg:ln: 213:20

CORNWELL, Dallas; WM; b. 2 Aug 1890 in Ffx; father: Dallas
CORNWELL; occ: farmer; res: Ffx; mother: Emma CORNWELL; inf:
D. CORNWELL, father; pg:ln: 185:20

CORNWELL, Edna; WF; b. 12 Jun 1890 in Ffx; father: B. H.
CORNWELL; occ: farmer; res: Ffx; mother: B. G. CORNWELL; inf:
B. G. [H.?] CORNWELL, father; pg:ln: 189:29

CORNWELL, Franklin H.; WM; b. 6 Jun 1896 in Ffx; father: H. B.
CORNWELL; occ: farmer; res: Ffx; mother: Bessie CORNWELL; inf:
H. B. CORNWELL, father Clerk in charge of old records: Applicant
states that his middle name is Benjamin.; pg:ln: 225:19

CORNWELL, Freda May; WF; b. 8 Feb 1892 in Ffx; father: Jesse A.
CORNWELL; occ: farmer; res: Ffx; mother: Maggie CORNWELL;
inf: Jesse A. CORNWELL, father; pg:ln: 202:26

CORNWELL, Louis; WM; b. 7 Mar 1892 in Ffx; father: H. B.
CORNWELL; occ: farmer; res: Ffx; mother: Bernice CORNWELL;
inf: H. B. CORNWELL, father; pg:ln: 202:25

CORNWELL, Ruth; WF; b. 12 Jun 1894 in Ffx; father: H. B.
CORNWELL; occ: farmer; res: Ffx; mother: Fannie CORNWELL; inf:
H. B. CORNWELL, father; pg:ln: 217:21

COWDEN, Jno. G.; WM; b. 22 Apr 1894 in Ffx; father: J. S. COWDON;
occ: farmer; res: Ffx; mother: Marion COWDON; inf: J. S.
COWDON, father; pg:ln: 217:23

COWDON, Jno. S.; WM; b. 22 Apr 1893 in Ffx; father: J. S. COWDON; occ: farmer; res: Ffx; mother: Mariana COWDEN; inf: J. S. COWDON, father; pg:ln: 213:23

COX, Mabel; WF; b. 17 Dec 1882 in Vienna; father: Rob. W. COX; occ: farmer; res: Vienna; mother: Mary L. COX; inf: father; pg:ln: 134:14

COX, Ruby L.; WF; b. 17 Mar 1887 in Ffx; father: Robt. W. COX; occ: farmer; res: Ffx; mother: Mary L. COX; inf: R. W. COX, father; pg:ln: 160:33

CRAIG, Mary Viola; WF; b. 12 Nov 1894 nr Alexandria; father: Wm. CRAIG; occ: farm hand; res: nr Alex.; mother: Emma CRAIG; inf: mother; pg:ln: 221:21

CRANFORD, Gracie; WF; b. 6 Jun 1882 in Ffx; father: Jas. H. CRANFORD; occ: farmer; res: Ffx; mother: Virginia CRANFORD; inf: J. H. CRANFORD, father; pg:ln: 136:09

CRANFORD, S. R.; WM; b. 22 Dec 1880 in Ffx; father: J. W. CRANFORD; occ: farmer; res: Ffx; mother: Sallie F.; inf: J. W. CRANFORD, father; pg:ln: 127:19

CRAVEN, Matthew R.; CM; b. 16 Feb 1894 in Ffx; father: Chas. CRAVEN; occ: farmer; res: Ffx; mother: Hettie CRAVEN; inf: Chas. CRAVEN, father; pg:ln: 217:22

CRAWLE, Thomas E.; WM; b. 3 Dec 1885 in Dranes.; father: Michael CRAWLE; occ: farmer; res: Dranes.; mother: Alice CRAWLE; inf: father; pg:ln: 152:15

CRIDER, Chas. D.; WM; b. 8 Nov 1888 in ___; father: Jno. W. CRIDER; occ: farmer; res: Ffx; mother: Annie CRIDER; inf: J. W. CRIDER, father; pg:ln: 173:22

CRIDLER, Chas. C.; WM; b. 8 Nov 1889 in Ffx; father: Jno. W. CRIDLER; occ: farmer; res: Ffx; mother: Anna CRIDLER; inf: J. W. CRIDLER, father; pg:ln: 177:26

CRIPPEN, Effie J.; WF; b. 25 Oct 1890 in Ffx; father: H. A. CRIPPEN; occ: farmer; res: Ffx; mother: Lavinia CRIPPIN; inf: H. A. CRIPPEN, father; pg:ln: 189:25

CRIPPEN, not named; WF; b. 28 Feb 1889 in Ffx; father: Henry A. CRIPPEN; occ: farmer; res: Ffx; mother: Lavenia CRIPPEN; inf: H. A. CRIPPEN, father; pg:ln: 177:25

CROPPER, ___; WM; b. 15 Mar 1885 in Ffx; father: A. C. CRUPPER; occ: farmer; res: Ffx; mother: Elizbt. CRUPPER; inf: A. C. CRUPPER, father; pg:ln: 156:12

CROSIN, Ewel T.; WM; b. 9 Dec 1888 in Ffx; father: Jas. T. CROSIN; occ: farmer; res: Ffx; mother: Nettie CROSIN; inf: Jas. T. CROSIN, father; pg:ln: 170:14

CROSON, Carrie Ellen; WF; b. 20 Dec 1891 nr Pender; father: Evritt W. CROSON; occ: laborer; res: nr Pender P.O.; mother: Nancy Ellen CROSON; inf: parents; pg:ln: 194:08

CROSON, Ernest W.; WM; b. 28 Oct 1893 in Ffx; father: Ernest R. CROSON; occ: farmer; res: Ffx; mother: Mary P. CROSON; inf: E. R. CROSON, father; pg:ln: 213:15

CROSON, Florence; WF; b. 1 Nov 1891 nr Pender; father: Tobe
CROSON; occ: laborer; res: nr Pender P.O.; mother: Florence
CROSON; inf: parents; pg:ln: 194:09

CROSON, Jno. A.; WM; b. 21 Nov 1896 in ___; father: Ernest R.
CROSON; occ: clerk; res: Ffx; mother: Mary P. CROSON; inf: Mary
CROSON, mother; pg:ln: 226:38

CROSON, Joseph; WM; b. 25 Jun 1885 in Ffx; father: Chas. CROSON;
occ: farmer; res: Ffx; mother: Annie CROSON; inf: C. CROSON,
father; pg:ln: 156:08

CROSON, Lena May; WF; b. 7 Sep 1896 nr Chantilly; father: Everett W.
CROSON; occ: farmer; res: nr Chantilly; mother: Nannie E.
CROSON; inf: mother; pg:ln: 229:21

CROSON, Mamie Elizabeth; WF; b. 7 Dec 1893 nr Centreville; father:
Edward CROSON; occ: farmer; res: nr Centreville; mother: Nancy E.
CROSON; inf: parents; pg:ln: 210:22

CROSON, Myrtle; WF; b. 15 Jun 1893 in Ffx; father: J. T. CROSON;
occ: farmer; res: Ffx; mother: Nettie CROSON; inf: J. T. CROSON,
father; pg:ln: 213:22

CROSON, not named; WM; b. 1 Feb 1889 in Ffx; father: Jas. T.
CROSON; occ: farmer; res: Ffx; mother: Nettie CROSON; inf: J. T.
CROSON, father; pg:ln: 177:30

CROSS, Barbara A.; WF; b. 23 Aug 1889 in Ffx; father: Jas. B. CROSS;
occ: farmer; res: Ffx; mother: Cora L. CROSS; inf: Jas. B. CROSS,
father; pg:ln: 181:18

CROSS, Cecie M.; WF; b. 6 Nov 1889 in Ffx; father: E. W. CROSS;
occ: blacksmith; res: Ffx; mother: Laura A. CROSS; inf: E. W.
CROSS, father; pg:ln: 181:19

CROSS, Cecil Bernard; WM; b. 9 Feb 1887 in Ffx; father: Benjn. F.
CROSS; occ: farmer; res: Ffx; mother: May W. CROSS; inf: B. F.
CROSS, father; pg:ln: 166:19

CROSS, Elmer; WM; b. 4 Feb 1894 nr Centreville; father: Arthur
CROSS; occ: farmer; res: nr Centreville; mother: Ida J. CROSS; inf:
father; pg:ln: 221:17

CROSS, H. M.; WM; b. 22 Mar 1883 in Ffx; father: W. CROSS; occ:
farmer; res: Ffx; mother: Annie CROSS; inf: W. CROSS, father;
pg:ln: 143:09

CROSS, Margaret; WF; b. 6 Dec 182 nr Clifton; father: James B.
CROSS; occ: wheelwright; res: Clifton; mother: Cora L. CROSS; inf:
father; pg:ln: 208:07

CROSS, Rosie Bell; WF; b. 9 Jun 1893 nr Centreville; father: Wm.
CROSS; occ: carpenter; res: nr Centreville; mother: Addie CROSS;
inf: parents; pg:ln: 210:20

CROSS, Selsner; WM; b. 29 Jun 1880 in Falls Church; father: Charles
N. CROSS; occ: overseer; res: Falls Church; mother: Adonia
CROSS; inf: father; pg:ln: 124:14

CROSS, Wm. Wallis; WM; b. 16 Jun 1887 in Ffx; father: Wm. D.
CROSS; occ: carpenter; res: Ffx; mother: Addie CROSS; inf: Wm.
D. CROSS, father; pg:ln: 166:20

CROSSMAN, Betsey; WF; b. 2 Oct 1885 in Maple Lawn; father: J. M.
CROSSMAN; occ: farmer; res: Maple Lawn; mother: Annie C.
CROSSMAN; inf: father; pg:ln: 152:12

CROUCH, Frank; WM; b. 6 Mar 1882 in Ffx; father: Jno. J. CROUCH;
occ: farmer; res: Ffx; mother: Louisa CROUCH; inf: J. J. CROUCH,
father; pg:ln: 136:08

CROUCH, Inez; WF; b. 8 Jun 1880 in Ffx; father: M. C. CROUCH; occ:
farmer; res: Ffx; mother: Elgiva; inf: M. C. CROUCH, father; pg:ln:
127:17

CROUCH, Josephine; WF; b. 27 Jun 1896 nr Clifton Sta.; father: ___;
occ: ___; res: ___; mother: Josephine CROUCH; inf: mother; pg:ln:
229:20

CROUCH, Louisa; WF; b. 21 Aug 1889 in Ffx; father: Jno. T. CROUCH;
occ: farmer; res: Ffx; mother: John CROUCH [??]; inf: J. T.
CROUCH, father; pg:ln: 181:20

CROUCH, Martha; WF; b. 2 May 1883 in ___; father: Jos. CROUCH;
occ: farmer; res: Ffx; mother: Cath. CROUCH; inf: Jos. CROUCH,
father; pg:ln: 143:10

CROUCH, R. T.; WM; b. 19 Jun 1881 in Ffx; father: M. C. CROUCH;
occ: farmer; res: Ffx; mother: Elgiva CROUCH; inf: M. C. CROUCH,
father; pg:ln: 132:09

CROUCH, Rosa; WF; b. 8 Jul 1892 nr Centreville; father: John
CROUCH; occ: farmer; res: nr Centreville; mother: Louisa
CROUCH; inf: father; pg:ln: 208:06

CROUCH, Shelby L.; WM; b. 21 Aug 1880 in Ffx; father: W. CROUCH;
occ: farmer; res: Ffx; mother: Susannah; inf: W. CROUCH, father;
pg:ln: 127:15

CROUNSE, Lucy; WF; b. 4 Jun 1880 in Dranesville; father: Eli
CROUNSE; occ: farmer; res: Dranesville; mother: Elnora
CROUNSE; inf: father; pg:ln: 124:11

CROWDER, F. J.; WM; b. 2 Dec 1880 in Ffx; father: H. G. CROWDER;
occ: farmer; res: Ffx; mother: Salie K.; inf: H. G. CROWDER, father;
pg:ln: 127:16

CROWELL, Isabella; WF; b. 12 Jul 1890 in Ffx; father: Michael
CROWELL; occ: farmer; res: Ffx; mother: Alice CROWELL; inf: M.
CROWELL, father; pg:ln: 189:28

CROWLE, Jos. M.; WM; b. 25 Sep 1887 in Ffx; father: Michael
CROWLE; occ: farmer; res: Ffx; mother: Alice CROWLE; inf: M.
CROWLE, father; pg:ln: 160:26

CRUMBAUGH, Edwina; WF; b. 25 Nov 1892 in Ffx; father: Edwd.
CRUMBAUGH; occ: farmer; res: Ffx; mother: Ella CRUMBAUGH;
inf: E. CRUMBAUGH, father; pg:ln: 202:19

CRUMP, Ethel M.; WF; b. 18 Jan 1880 in Ffx; father: Geo. CRUMP;
occ: farmer; res: Ffx; mother: Emma; inf: E. CRUMP, father [mother];
pg:ln: 127:20

CRUMP, Ethel; WF; b. 12 Feb 1885 in Ffx; father: Geo. CRUMP; occ:
farmer; res: Ffx; mother: Emma CRUMP; inf: G. CRUMP, father;
pg:ln: 156:10

CRUMP, L. V.; WM; b. 30 Nov 1892 in Ffx; father: E. J. CRUMP; occ: farmer; res: Ffx; mother: H. M. CRUMP; inf: E. J. CRUMP, father; pg:ln: 202:17

CRUPPER, Eva; WF; b. 16 Dec 1892 in Ffx; father: Winter CRUPPER; occ: farmer; res: Ffx; mother: Eva CRUPPER; inf: W. CRUPPER, father; pg:ln: 202:18

CRUPPER, L. B.; WM; b. 6 Oct 1881 in Ffx; father: Brook CRUPPER; occ: farmer; res: Ffx; mother: Josephine CRUPPER; inf: J. CRUPFER, father [mother]; pg:ln: 132:10

CRUPPER, no name; WF; b. 30 Mar 1887 in Ffx; father: Henry A. CRUPPER; occ: farmer; res: Ffx; mother: L. V. CRUPPER; inf: H. A. CRUPPER, father; pg:ln: 160:27

[CRUPPER], not named (dead); WF; b. 10 Feb 1891 nr Alexandria; father: A. B. CRUPPER; occ: miller; res: nr Alexandria; mother: Josephine CRUPPER; inf: parents; pg:ln: 195:28

CULLINAN, Bridget; WF; b. 12 May 1885 in Ffx; father: Jno. CULLINAN; occ: farmer; res: Ffx; mother: Mary Ann CULLINAN; inf: J. CULLINAN, father; pg:ln: 156:11

CULLINAN, Bridget; WF; b. 13 Dec 1884 in Ffx; father: Jno. CULLINAAN {sic}; occ: farmer; res: Ffx; mother: Mary A. CULINNAN; inf: J. CULLINNAN, father; pg:ln: 146:17

CULLINAN, Honora; WF; b. 25 Feb 1880 in Ffx; father: Jno. CULLINAN; occ: farmer; res: Ffx; mother: Ann; inf: J. CULLINAN, father; pg:ln: 127:18

CUMINS, Florence; WF; b. 19 Feb 1888 in ___; father: King CUMINS; occ: farmer; res: Ffx; mother: Verlinda CUMINS; inf: K. CUMINS, father; pg:ln: 173:14

CUMINS, Mary L.; WF; b. 27 Nov 1896 in Ffx; father: Geo. W. CUMINS; occ: farmer; res: Ffx; mother: Maggie CUMINS; inf: G. W. CUMINS, father; pg:ln: 225:22

CUMMINGS, ___; WF; b. 6 Jul 1884 nr Falls Ch.; father: E. F. CUMMINGS; occ: farmer; res: nr Falls Ch.; mother: Malinda CUMMINGS; inf: father; pg:ln: 149:17

CUMMINS, not named; WF; b. 30 Jun 1886 in Falls Ch.; father: Frank CUMMINS; occ: farmer; res: Falls Ch.; mother: V. CUMMINS; inf: father; pg:ln: 158:14

CUNNINGHAM, ___; WM; b. 27 Mar 1887 in Ffx; father: R. S. CUNNINGHAM; occ: farmer; res: Ffx; mother: M. L. CUNNINGHAM; inf: R. S. CUNNINGHAM, father; pg:ln: 160:29

CUNNINGHAM, Carl; WM; b. 8 May 1896 in Ffx; father: R. S. CUNNINGHAM; occ: farmer; res: Ffx; mother: Mary L. CUNINHAM; inf: R. S. CUNNINHAM, father; pg:ln: 225:18

CUNNINGHAM, Lester L.; WM; b. 16 Apr 1890 in Ffx; father: Robt. CUNNINGHAM; occ: farmer; res: Ffx; mother: Venice CUNNINGHAM; inf: R. CUNNINGHAM, father; pg:ln: 189:24

CUNNINGHAM, no name; WF; b. 28 Mar 1893 in Ffx; father: Howard CUNNINHAM; occ: farmer; res: Ffx; mother: Vinnie CUNNINHAM; inf: H. CUNNINHAM, father; pg:ln: 213:17

CUNNINGHAM, no name; WM; b. 22 Feb 1889 in Ffx; father: H. C. CUNNINGHAM; occ: farmer; res: Ffx; mother: Virginia CUNNINGHAM; inf: H. CUNNINGHAM, father; pg:ln: 177:22

CUNNINGHAM, Treressa M. [Theressa?]; WF; b. 26 Jun 1891 in Ffx; father: Howard CUNNINGHAM; occ: farmer; res: Ffx; mother: Theressa CUNNINGHAM; inf: H. CUNNINGHAM, father; pg:ln: 198:17

CURRIER, Katie; WF; b. 16 Jul 1891 nr Burke Sta.; father: Thos. J. CURRIER; occ: Rail Road hand; res: nr Burke Sta.; mother: Lucy CURRIER; inf: parents; pg:ln: 193:05

CURRY, Mable; CF; b. 20 Jul 1889 in Ffx; father: Geo. CURRY; occ: farmer; res: Ffx; mother: Alice CURRY; inf: Geo. CURRY, father; pg:ln: 177:20

CURRY, Manny; CM; b. 13 Mar 1882 in Falls Church; father: Leroy CURRY; occ: laborer; res: Falls Church; mother: Pattie CURRY; inf: father; pg:ln: 134:13

DADE, Alfred; CM; b. 20 Sep 1891 in Sheridan Neck; father: Henry DADE; occ: laborer; res: Sheridans Neck; mother: Elizabeth DADE; inf: parent; pg:ln: 196:05

DADE, Bertha; CF; b. 30 Aug 1889 in Ffx; father: Henry DADE; occ: laborer; res: Ffx; mother: Elizabeth DADE; inf: Henry DADE, father; pg:ln: 181:29

DADE, John; CM; b. 11 Feb 1885 in Ffx; father: Henry DADE; occ: farmer; res: Ffx; mother: Jane DADE; inf: H. DADE, father; pg:ln: 156:20

DADE, Julia E.; CF; b. 5 Jul 1890 in Ffx; father: Thos. DADE; occ: farmer; res: Ffx; mother: Minnie DADE; inf: Thos. DADE, father; pg:ln: 189:32

DAILEY, Cecil; WF; b. 13 Nov 1894 in Ffx; father: H. O. DAILEY; occ: farmer; res: Ffx; mother: Annie DAILEY; inf: H. O. DAILEY, father; pg:ln: 217:31

DAILEY, Clarence C.; WM; b. 10 Mar 1884 in Seneca; father: Aaron T. DAILEY; occ: farmer; res: Falls Church; mother: Jane DAILEY; inf: father; pg:ln: 149:30

DAILEY, Ethel M.; WF; b. 9 Nov 1888 in ___; father: Aaron T. DAILEY; occ: farmer; res: Ffx; mother: M. J. DAILEY; inf: A. T. DAILEY, father; pg:ln: 173:25

DAILEY, Goldia J.; WM; b. 26 Feb 1883 in Dranesville; father: Jno. S. DAILEY; occ: farmer; res: Dranesville; mother: ___ DAILEY; inf: father; pg:ln: 139:27

DAILEY, Willie; WM; b. 26 May 1892 in Ffx; father: A. T. DAILEY; occ: farmer; res: Ffx; mother: Jane DAILEY; inf: A. T. DAILEY, father; pg:ln: 202:32

DANIEL, Harry; WM; b. 25 Nov 1892 nr Fairfax C. H.; father: James T. DANIEL; occ: farmer; res: nr Fairfax C. H.; mother: Annie Bell DANIEL; inf: father; pg:ln: 208:28

DANIELS, E. W.; WM; b. 31 Dec 1883 in Falls Church; father: William DANIELS; occ: farmer; res: Falls Church; mother: Isabel DANIELS; inf: father; pg:ln: 139:21

DANIELS, Gracie; WF; b. 29 Sep 1896 in ___; father: Letcher DANIELS; occ: farmer; res: Ffx; mother: Kate DANIELS; inf: L. DANIELS, father; pg:ln: 226:40

DANIELS, Joseph Lee; WM; b. 15 Nov 1887 in Ffx; father: James DANIELS; occ: laborer; res: Ffx; mother: Annie DANIELS; inf: Jos. JERMAN, grandfather; pg:ln: 166:30

DANIELS, Louisa A.; WF; b. 30 Sep 1882 in Ffx; father: Wm. T. DANIELS; occ: farmer; res: ___; mother: Alice DANIELS; inf: W. T. DANIELS, father; pg:ln: 136:12

DANNIEL, Hattie; WF; b. 13 Jan 1884 in Bailey's X Roads; father: James DANIEL; occ: laborer; res: Balls X Roads; mother: Rosanah DANIEL; inf: father; pg:ln: 149:25

DARNE, Beulah; WF; b. 6 Sep 1883 in Langley; father: R. H. DARNE; occ: farmer; res: Langley; mother: Octavia DARNE; inf: father; pg:ln: 139:23

DARNE, Bulah; WF; b. 5 Sep 1886 in Prov.; father: R. H. DARNE; occ: farmer; res: Prov.; mother: ___ DARNE; inf: father; pg:ln: 158:16

DARNE, Elmer F.; WM; b. 5 Nov 1888 in ___; father: R. H. DARNE; occ: farmer; res: Ffx; mother: Octavia DARNE; inf: R. H. DARNE, father; pg:ln: 173:26

DARNES, Leonard L.; WM; b. 13 Feb 1882 in Langley; father: Richd. H. DARNES; occ: farmer; res: Langley; mother: Octavia DARNES; inf: father; pg:ln: 134:16

DARROLL, Martin; WM; b. 1 Aug 1893 nr Hayfield; father: ___; occ: ___; res: nr Hayfield; mother: Grace DARROLL; inf: parent; pg:ln: 212:102

[DAVIS], ___ (dead); WF; b. 14 Jul 1882 in Ffx; father: Henry E. DAVIS; occ: farmer; res: ___; mother: Cath. DAVIS; inf: H. E. DAVIS, father; pg:ln: 136:17

DAVIS, ___ (dead); WF; b. 26 Aug 1893 nr Farr P.O.; father: Persifer F. DAVIS; occ: farmer; res: nr Farr P.O.; mother: Sarah C. DAVIS; inf: parents; pg:ln: 210:26

DAVIS, ___; WM; b. 11 Sep 1880 in Falls Church; father: John C. DAVIS; occ: jail guard D.C.; res: Falls Church; mother: Alice DAVIS; inf: father; pg:ln: 124:17

DAVIS, Aubry Ellis; WM; b. 3 Oct 1888 in Ffx; father: Redman DAVIS; occ: farmer; res: Ffx; mother: Harriet L. DAVIS; inf: Redman DAVIS, father; pg:ln: 170:17

DAVIS, Beaulah; WF; b. 22 Sep 1892 in Ffx; father: Philip A. DAVIS; occ: farmer; res: Ffx; mother: Mary E. DAVIS; inf: Philip DAVIS, father; pg:ln: 202:31

DAVIS, Blanch; WF; b. 26 Jul 1892 in Village adj Alex.; father: Henry DAVIS; occ: miller; res: Village adj Alex.; mother: Annie DAVIS; inf: mother; pg:ln: 207:66

DAVIS, C. W.; WM; b. 27 Oct 1883 in ___; father: Rich'd. M. DAVIS; occ: farmer; res: Ffx; mother: Hulda J. DAVIS; inf: R. M. DAVIS, father; pg:ln: 143:21

DAVIS, Carl B.; WM; b. 3 Aug 1894 nr Lorton Sta; father: J. B. DAVIS; occ: merchant; res: Lorton Sta; mother: Edna DAVIS; inf: father; pg:ln: 221:31

DAVIS, Danl. E.; WM; b. 17 May 1883 in Ffx; father: Henry E. DAVIS; occ: farmer; res: Ffx; mother: Cath. V. DAVIS; inf: H. E. DAVIS, father; pg:ln: 143:16

DAVIS, Dora; WF; b. 10 Jan 1894 nr Burke Sta.; father: M. C. DAVIS; occ: merchant; res: nr Burke Sta.; mother: Katie DAVIS; inf: father; pg:ln: 221:29

DAVIS, Ethel; WF; b. 20 Sep 1891 nr Farr P.O.; father: Persifer F. DAVIS; occ: farmer; res: nr Farr P.O.; mother: Sarah C. DAVIS; inf: parents; pg:ln: 193:09

DAVIS, Geo. Hollis; WM; b. 22 Feb 1894 nr Stoneleigh; father: Calvin H. DAVIS; occ: farmer; res: nr Stoneleigh; mother: Amanda DAVIS; inf: father; pg:ln: 221:30

DAVIS, Grace; WF; b. 23 Dec 1883 in ___; father: Haywood DAVIS; occ: farmer; res: Ffx; mother: Fannie S. DAVIS; inf: H. DAVIS, father; pg:ln: 143:20

DAVIS, H. H.; WM; b. 26 Sep 1882 in Ffx; father: Haywood DAVIS; occ: farmer; res: ___; mother: Fannie DAVIS; inf: H. DAVIS, father; pg:ln: 136:11

DAVIS, Hannah; WF; b. 15 Dec 1882 in Ffx; father: F. C. DAVIS; occ: farmer; res: Ffx; mother: Sarah F. DAVIS; inf: F. C. DAVIS, father; pg:ln: 136:14

DAVIS, Hannah; WF; b. 6 Jan 1883 in ___; father: F. C. DAVIS; occ: farmer; res: Ffx; mother: Hannah DAVIS; inf: F. C. DAVIS, father; pg:ln: 143:17

DAVIS, Henry Lee; WM; b. 18 Jan 1890 in Ffx; father: Henry DAVIS; occ: farmer; res: Ffx; mother: Annie DAVIS; inf: Henry DAVIS, father; pg:ln: 185:25

DAVIS, Jas. E.; CM; b. 19 Nov 1896 in ___; father: Geo. W. DAVIS; occ: farmer; res: Ffx; mother: Manerva DAVIS; inf: G. W. DAVIS, father; pg:ln: 226:42

DAVIS, Jessie; WM; b. 27 Apr 1888 in ___; father: Philip A. DAVIS; occ: farmer; res: Ffx; mother: Ella DAVIS; inf: P. A. DAVIS, father; pg:ln: 173:24

DAVIS, Maggie; WF; b. 25 Jul 1884 in Ffx; father: Frank E. DAVIS; occ: farmer; res: Ffx; mother: Mary DAVIS; inf: M. DAVIS, mother; pg:ln: 146:21

DAVIS, Manly; WM; b. 18 Feb 1888 in Ffx; father: F. C. DAVIS; occ: farmer; res: Ffx; mother: Sarah DAVIS; inf: F. C. DAVIS, father; pg:ln: 170:19

DAVIS, Maud C.; WF; b. 11 Dec 1893 in Ffx; father: Arthur DAVIS; occ: farmer; res: Ffx; mother: Sallie D. DAVIS; inf: A. DAVIS, father; pg:ln: 213:27

DAVIS, not known; WM; b. 27 May 1880 in Ffx; father: F. C. DAVIS; occ: farmer; res: Ffx; mother: Sallie F.; inf: F. C. DAVIS, father; pg:ln: 127:26

DAVIS, Persifer; WM; b. 17 Jul 1894 nr Farr P.O.; father: Persifer F. DAVIS; occ: farmer; res: nr Farr P.O.; mother: Sarah C. DAVIS; inf: father; ρg:ln: 221:32

DAVIS, Ramona; CF; b. 21 Mar 1894 nr Woodlawn; father: Humphrey DAVIS; occ: laborer; res: nr Woodlawn; mother: Sarah DAVIS; inf: mother; pg:ln: 222:01

DAVIS, Reginald Fairfax; WM; b. 19 Jun 1888 in Ffx; father: Chas. F. DAVIS; occ: farmer; res: Ffx; mother: Ellen DAVIS; inf: Chas. F. DAVIS, father; pg:ln: 170:20

DAVIS, Rosena; WF; b. 7 Nov 1888 in Ffx; father: Haywood DAVIS; occ: farmer; res: Ffx; mother: Fannie DAVIS; inf: Haywood DAVIS, father; pg:ln: 170:18

DAVIS, Ruby Jane; WF; b. 8 Mar 1896 nr Clifton Sta.; father: Henry E. DAVIS; occ: farmer; res: nr Clifton Sta.; mother: Sophia C. DAVIS; inf: mother; pg:ln: 229:27

DAVIS, Susie; WF; b. 6 Jan 1880 in Ffx; father: not known; occ: farmer; res: Ffx; mother: Mary; inf: T. T. BURKE, Co. Supt. Poor; pg:ln: 127:27

DAVIS, W. W.; WM; b. 17 Mar 1887 in Ffx; father: F. C. DAVIS; occ: farmer; res: Ffx; mother: Sallie F. DAVIS; inf: F. C. DAVIS, father; pg:ln: 166:28

DAVIS, W.; WM; b. 13 Jan 1896 in ___; father: Arthur DAVIS; occ: mcht.; res: Ffx; mother: Sallie DAVIS; inf: A. DAVIS, father; pg:ln: 226:39

DAVIS, Walter W.; WM; b. 17 Jan 1890 in Ffx; father: Henry L. DAVIS; occ: farmer; res: Ffx; mother: Lillie DAVIS; inf: H. L. DAVIS, father; pg:ln: 189:33

DAVIS, Willard; WM; b. 1 Sep 1894 in Ffx; father: Henry L. DAVIS; occ: farmer; res: Ffx; mother: Bertie DAVIS; inf: H. L. DAVIS, father; pg:ln: 217:32

DAVIS, Willie C.; WM; b. 24 Jul 1882 in Ffx; father: F. E. DAVIS; occ: farmer; res: Ffx; mother: Mary A. DAVIS; inf: F. E. DAVIS, father; pg:ln: 136:13

DAVIS, Wilton; WM; b. 18 Jan 1889 in Ffx; father: F. C. DAVIS; occ: farmer; res: Ffx; mother: Sallie DAVIS; inf: F. C. DAVIS, father; pg:ln: 181:24

DAVIS,, E. S.; WM; b. 6 May 1882 in Ffx; father: Geo. E. DAVIS; occ: farmer; res: ___; mother: M. DAVIS; inf: G. E. DAVIS, father; pg:ln: 136:18

DAWSON, Chas. W.; WM; b. 20 Jan 1884 in Ffx; father: Jno. W. DAWSON; occ: farmer; res: Ffx; mother: Annie DAWSON; inf: J. W. DAWSON, father; pg:ln: 146:22

DAWSON, Emma V.; WF; b. 19 Apr 1888 in Ffx; father: H. C. DAWSON; occ: farmer; res: Ffx; mother: Margt. DAWSON; inf: H. C. DAWSON, father; pg:ln: 170:15

DAWSON, George Mileken?; WM; b. 16 Aug 1891 in Ox Road; father: H. C. DAWSON; occ: mechanic; res: Ox Road; mother: Margaret Ellen DAWSON; inf: parents; pg:ln: 193:08

DAWSON, Maggie M.; WF; b. 13 Dec 1882 in Ffx; father: Jno. W. DAWSON; occ: farmer; res: Ffx; mother: Addie M. DAWSON; inf: J. W. DAWSON, father; pg:ln: 136:15

DAWSON, Roberta; WF; b. 15 Oct 1886 in Ffx; father: Jas. T. DAWSON; occ: farmer; res: Ffx; mother: Dora E. DAWSON; inf: J. T. DAWSON, father; pg:ln: 155:04

DAWSON, W. B.; WM; b. 16 Dec 1880 in Ffx; father: Jno. W. DAWSON; occ: farmer; res: Ffx; mother: Addie M.; inf: J. W. DAWSON, father; pg:ln: 127:23

DAWSON, W. H.; WM; b. 12 Jul 1880 in Ffx; father: H. C. DAWSON; occ: farmer; res: Ffx; mother: Margt.; inf: H. C. DAWSON, father; pg:ln: 127:24

DAY, Emma E.; WF; b. 30 May 1880 in Providence; father: William B. DAY; occ: farmer; res: Providence; mother: Sarah H. DAY; inf: father; pg:ln: 124:16

DAY, Jno. W.; WM; b. 13 Dec 1894 in Ffx; father: W. B. DAY; occ: farmer; res: Ffx; mother: Sarah DAY; inf: W. B. DAY, father; pg:ln: 217:35

DAY, Martha L.; WF; b. 3 Sep 1890 in Ffx; father: W. B. DAY; occ: farmer; res: Ffx; mother: Sarah DAY; inf: W. B. DAY, father; pg:ln: 189:31

DAZIELL, Elizabeth; WF; b. 4 Apr 1884 in Dranes.; father: James DAZIELL; occ: farmer; res: Falls Church; mother: Mary DAZIELL; inf: father; pg:ln: 149:31

DEAN, Bessie A.; WF; b. 3 Apr 1892 in Ffx; father: Isaac R. DEAN; occ: farmer; res: Ffx; mother: Virginia DEAN; inf: I. R. DEAN, father; pg:ln: 202:29

DEAN, Chas. Lorence; WM; b. 15 Jun 1893 nr Annandale; father: Wm. E. DEAN; occ: brick layer; res: nr Annandale; mother: Ann C. DEAN; inf: parents; pg:ln: 210:27

DEAN, Clarence; WM; b. 14 Feb 1889 in Ffx; father: W. DEAN; occ: farmer; res: Ffx; mother: Anna DEAN; inf: W. DEAN, father; pg:ln: 178:37

DEAN, Harry Joseph; WM; b. 18 Apr 1896 nr Springfield; father: Wm. E. DEAN; occ: plaster & bricklayer; res: nr Springfield; mother: Annie C. DEAN; inf: mother; pg:ln: 229:32

DEAN, Harvey; WM; b. 21 Aug 1884 in Falls Church; father: Isaac R. DEAN; occ: farmer; res: Falls Church; mother: James DEAN [??]; inf: father; pg:ln: 149:28

DEAN, Mary; WF; b. 14 Jun 1891 nr Springfield; father: Wm. Elwood DEAN; occ: farmer; res: nr Springfield; mother: Annie C. DEAN; inf: parents; pg:ln: 195:29

DEAN, not named; WF; b. 12 Mar 1896 nr Woodlawn; father: Wm. DEAN; occ: laborer; res: nr Woodlawn; mother: Susan DEAN; inf: mother; pg:ln: 229:33

DEAN, Phillippi; WF; b. 27 Jun 1882 in Ffx; father: A. C. DEAN; occ: farmer; res: ___; mother: Susie DEAN; inf: A. C. DEAN, father; pg:ln: 136:20

DEAN, Raymond; WM; b. 16 Jun 1894 nr Woodlawn; father: Wm. DEAN; occ: laborer; res: nr Woodlawn; mother: Susie DEAN; inf: father; pg:ln: 221:33

DEAN, Thomas; WM; b. 13 Nov 1889 in Ffx; father: Isaac DEAN; occ: farmer; res: Ffx; mother: Virginia DEAN; inf: I. DEAN, father; pg:ln: 178:40

DEAN, Wm.; WM; b. 14 Jul 1887 in Ffx; father: Wm. DEAN; occ: mason; res: Ffx; mother: Annie DEAN; inf: Wm. DEAN, father; pg:ln: 161:40

DEAVERS, Emma; WF; b. 20 Jul 1894 in Hayfield; father: H. E. DEAVERS; occ: farmer; res: nr Hayfield; mother: Sabina DEAVERS; inf: mother; pg:ln: 221:36

DEAVERS, Virgie; WF; b. 16 Jun 1896 nr Springfield; father: Lambert DEAVERS; occ: farmer; res: nr Springfield; mother: Emma DEAVERS; inf: mother; pg:ln: 229:31

DEBELL, R. E. L.; WM; b. 27 Mar 1882 in Ffx; father. John DEBELL; occ: farmer; res: ___; mother: Ann W. DEBELL; inf: J. D. DEBELL, father; pg:ln: 136:19

DECOSS, Katie; WF; b. 14 Oct 1882 in Ffx; father: Jesse DECOSS; occ: farmer; res: Ffx; mother: Elgiva DECOSS; inf: J. DECOSS, father; pg:ln: 136:16

DECOSS, Willie; WM; b. 20 Nov 1884 in Ffx; father: Jesse DECOSS; occ: farmer; res: Ffx; mother: Virginia DECOSS; inf: J. DECOSS, father; pg:ln: 146:20

DEEVERS, Amanda (twin); WF; b. 3 May 1883 in ___; father: Red. DEEVERS; occ: farmer; res: Ffx; mother: Betsey DEEVERS; inf: Red DEEVERS, father; pg:ln: 143:23

DEEVERS, Calvin; WM; b. 1 Apr 1887 in Ffx; father: Barney DEEVERS; occ: laborer; res: Ffx; mother: Mary Jane DEEVERS; inf: Barney DEEVERS, father; pg:ln: 166:23

DEEVERS, Edna; WF; b. 17 Aug 1892 in Accotink; father: Lewis DEEVERS; occ: miller; res: Accotink; mother: Jane DEEVERS; inf: mother; pg:ln: 207:65

DEEVERS, Effie; WF; b. 6 Jun 1881 in Ffx; father: Barney DEEVERS; occ: farmer; res: Ffx; mother: Mary J. DEEVERS; inf: B. DEEVERS, father; pg:ln: 132:11

DEEVERS, Frank; WM; b. 12 Sep 1884 in Ffx; father: Red. DEEVERS; occ: farmer; res: Ffx; mother: Elizbt. DEEVERS; inf: Red. DEEVERS, father; pg:ln: 146:24

DEEVERS, M. E.; WF; b. 31 May 1880 in Ffx; father: Red DEEVERS; occ: farmer; res: Ffx; mother: Elizabt.; inf: R. DEEVERS, father; pg:ln: 127:22

DEEVERS, Ritta; WF; b. 13 Aug 1882 in Ffx; father: Horace DEEVERS; occ: farmer; res: Ffx; mother: Albina DEEVERS; inf: H. DEEVERS, father; pg:ln: 136:21

DEEVERS, Sarah (twin); WF; b. 3 May 1883 in ___; father: Red.
DEEVERS; occ: farmer; res: Ffx; mother: Betsey DEEVERS; inf:
Red DEEVERS, father; pg:ln: 143:22

DEEVERS, Timothy; WM; b. 21 May 1882 in Ffx; father: Wm.
DEEVERS; occ: farmer; res: ___; mother: Sabina DEEVERS; inf:
Wm. DEEVERS, father; pg:ln: 136:22

DENNISON, Arch. M.; WM; b. 12 Sep 1884 in Vienna; father: C. A.
DENNISON; occ: farmer; res: Falls Church; mother: S. DENNISON;
inf: father; pg:ln: 149:29

DENNISON, Hellen A.; WF; b. 29 Aug 1891 in Ffx; father: Chas. A.
DENNISON; occ: farmer; res: Ffx; mother: Simie DENNISON; inf: C.
A. DENNISON, father; pg:ln: 198:26

DENNISON, Mary J.; WF; b. 29 May 1888 in ___; father: Chas. A.
DENNISON; occ: farmer; res: Ffx; mother: Simmine DENISON; inf:
C. A. DENISON, father; pg:ln: 173:27

DENTY, Ann Elizabeth; WF; b. 7 Mar 1893 nr Pohick Ch.; father: Simon
DENTY; occ: farmer; res: nr Pohick Ch.; mother: Sophia DENTY; inf:
parents; pg:ln: 210:23

DENTY, Annie Elizabeth; WF; b. 23 Jan 1892 nr Pohick Ch.; father:
Simon DENTY; occ: farmer; res: nr Pohick Ch.; mother: Josephine
DENTY; inf: father; pg:ln: 209:46

DENTY, Mary Elizabeth; WF; b. 7 Jun 1894 nr Pohick Church; father:
Napoleon DENTY; occ: farmer; res: Pohick Church; mother:
Catharine DENTY; inf: mother; pg:ln: 221:35

DENTY, Richd. Rotchford; WM; b. 2 Apr 1889 in Ffx; father: Simeon
DENTY; occ: farmer; res: Ffx; mother: Janepher DENTY; inf: S.
DENTY, father; pg:ln: 181:25

DePUTRON, ___; WF; b. 23 Dec 1881 in Falls Church; father: J. C.
DePUTRON; occ: atty law; res: Falls Church; mother: Mary E.
DePUTRON; inf: father; pg:ln: 130:15

DETWILER, Beulah; WF; b. 25 Jan 1894 in Ffx; father: Benj.
DETWILER; occ: farmer; res: Ffx; mother: Roberta DETWILER; inf:
B. DETWILER, father; pg:ln: 217:34

DETWILER, Blanch; WF; b. 24 Aug 1891 in Ffx; father: B. B.
DETWILER; occ: farmer; res: Ffx; mother: B. L. DETWILER; inf: B.
B. DETWILER, father; pg:ln: 198:29

DETWILER, not named (dead); WM; b. 4 Aug 1893 in Ffx; father: E. L.
DETWILER; occ: farmer; res: Ffx; mother: E. T. DETWILER; inf: E.
L. DETWILER, father; pg:ln: 213:29

DEWEY, Esther; WF; b. 23 Aug 1890 in Ffx; father: Alton DEWEY; occ:
farmer; res: Ffx; mother: Sarah F. DEWEY; inf: Alton DEWEY,
father; pg:ln: 185:28

DEWEY, Robt.; WM; b. 1 Dec 1885 in Ffx; father: Alton DEWEY; occ:
farmer; res: Ffx; mother: Sallie DEWEY; inf: A. DEWEY, father;
pg:ln: 156:15

DEY, Ellis C.; WM; b. 4 Jan 1885 in Herndon; father: Chas. W. DEY;
occ: farmer; res: Herndon; mother: Hattie E. DEY; inf: father; pg:ln:
152:20

DEY, Ruby; WF; b. 3 Nov 1880 in Dranesville; father: Charles W. DEY; occ: farmer; res: Dranesville; mother: Hattie E. DEY; inf: father; pg:ln: 124:15

DICKERSON, Ella; CF; b. 4 Mar 1885 in Ffx; father: Henry DICKERSON; occ: farmer; res: Ffx; mother: Ella V. DICKERSON; inf: Henry DICKERSON, father; pg:ln: 156:19

DICKEY, Maria E.; WF; b. 14 Oct 1894 in Ffx; father: Jas. N. DICKEY; occ: farmer; res: Ffx; mother: Sarah DICKEY; inf: J. N. DICKEY, father; pg:ln: 217:33

DILLEY, Jane; WF; b. 4 Aug 1891 in Ffx; father: Chas. DILLEY; occ: farmer; res: Ffx; mother: Susan DILLEY; inf: C. DILLEY, father; pg:ln: 198:28

DIMSEY, Alice B.; WF; b. 4 Feb 1891 in Ffx; father: C. W. DIMSEY; occ: farmer; res: Ffx; mother: Eva DIMSEY; inf: C. W. DIMSEY, father; pg:ln: 198:27

DIMSEY, Edward; WM; b. 11 Nov 1885 in Vienna; father: J. E. DIMSEY; occ: mechanic; res: Vienna; mother: Sarah V. DIMSEY; inf: father; pg:ln: 152:19

DIMSEY, Jno. V.; WM; b. 7 Nov 1883 in Dranesville; father: Chas. W. DIMSEY; occ: farmer; res: Dranesville; mother: Eva J. DIMSEY; inf: father; pg:ln: 139:26

DIMSEY, John; WM; b. 23 Dec 1892 in Ffx; father: Geo. DIMSEY; occ: farmer; res: Ffx; mother: Susan DIMSEY; inf: Geo. DIMSEY, father; pg:ln: 202:30

DIMSEY, Verlinda; WF; b. 2 Feb 1893 in Ffx; father: Jno. E. DIMSEY; occ: farmer; res: Ffx; mother: S. V. DIMSEY; inf: J. E. DIMSEY, father; pg:ln: 213:28

DIMSEY, W. R.; WM; b. 25 Jun 1888 in ___; father: C. W. DIMSEY; occ: farmer; res: Ffx; mother: Eva J. DIMSEY; inf: C. W. DIMSEY, father; pg:ln: 173:33

DIMSEY, W. W.; WM; b. 19 May 1885 in Dranes.; father: Chas. W. DIMSEY; occ: laborer; res: Dranes.; mother: Jane DIMSEY; inf: father; pg:ln: 152:21

DINDLEBECK, Archie; WM; b. 20 Mar 1887 in Ffx; father: Louis DINDLEBECK; occ: farmer; res: Ffx; mother: Mary DINDLEBECK; inf: L. DINDLEBECK, father; pg:ln: 166:29

DINDLEBECK, Grace; WF; b. 28 Sep 1893 nr Fairfax Sta.; father: Lewis DINDLEBECK; occ: farmer; res: nr Fairfax Sta.; mother: Mary DINDLEBECK; inf: parents; pg:ln: 210:28

DINDLEBECK, Jos.; WM; b. 11 Jul 1890 in Ffx; father: J. L. DINDLEBECK; occ: farmer; res: Ffx; mother: Mary DINDLEBECK; inf: J. L DINDLEBECK, father; pg:ln: 185:29

DINDLEBECK, Moses McKinley; WM; b. 3 Nov 1896 nr Fairfax C. H.; father: J. L. DINDLEBECK; occ: farmer; res: nr C. H.; mother: Mary V. DINDLEBECK; inf: father; pg:ln: 229:26

DINDLEBECK, Walter; WM; b. 20 Dec 1888 in Ffx; father: J. L. DINDLEBECK; occ: farmer; res: Ffx; mother: Mary V. DINDLEBECK; inf: J. L. DINDLEBECK, father; pg:ln: 170:21

DINDLEBECK, Wesley; WM; b. 20 Jul 1892 nr Fairfax C. H.; father: J.
L. DINDLEBECK; occ: farmer; res: nr Fairfax C. H.; mother: Mary V.
DINDLEBECK; inf: father; pg:ln: 208:29

DIXON, Allie; CF; b. 10 Mar 1889 in Ffx; father: Henry DIXON; occ:
laborer; res: Ffx; mother: Ella DIXON; inf: Henry DIXON, father;
pg:ln: 181:30

DIXON, Arthur; CM; b. 15 Nov 1890 in Ffx; father: Jackson DIXON; occ:
farmer; res: Ffx; mother: Josephine DIXON; inf: J. DIXON, father;
pg:ln: 189:30

DIXON, Blanche; CF; b. 30 Jun 1893 nr Clifton; father: Henry DIXON;
occ: farmer; res: nr Clifton Sta.; mother: Ella DIXON; inf: parents;
pg:ln: 211:37

DIXON, Chas. L.; WM; b. 13 Nov 1883 in ___; father: Jno. T. DIXON;
occ: farmer; res: Ffx; mother: Delia DIXON; inf: J. T. DIXON, father;
pg:ln: 143:24

DIXON, Henry; CM; b. 3 Apr 1883 in Falls Church; father: Jno. DIXON;
occ: laborer; res: Falls Church; mother: Louisa DIXON; inf: father;
pg:ln: 139:22

DIXON, Julian; CM; b. 15 Jun 1887 in Ffx; father: Henry DIXON; occ:
laborer; res: Ffx; mother: Ella DIXON; inf: Henry DIXON, father;
pg:ln: 166:33

DIXON, Rebecca; CF; b. 26 Apr 1888 in ___; father: Jas. DIXON; occ:
farmer; res: Ffx; mother: Fannie DIXON; inf: Jas. DIXON, father;
pg:ln: 173:29

DOBSON, Elmira; WF; b. 28 Jan 1889 in Ffx; father: Wm. M. DOBSON;
occ: mechanic; res: Ffx; mother: Phoebe DOBSON; inf: Wm.
DOBSON, father; pg:ln: 181:27

DOBSON, Virginia; WF; b. 12 Sep 1884 in Ffx; father: J. F. DOBSON;
occ: farmer; res: Ffx; mother: Deborah DOBSON; inf: J. F.
DOBSON, father; pg:ln: 146:23

DODSON, Alice; WF; b. 30 Jun 1893 nr Bone Mill; father: M. A.
DODSON; occ: farmer; res: nr Bone Mill; mother: Alice DODSON;
inf: parents; pg:ln: 210:32

DODSON, Blanche; WF; b. 7 Sep 1896 nr Ravensworth; father:
Americus DODSON; occ: farmer; res: nr Ravensworth; mother:
Sarah DODSON; inf: mother; pg:ln: 229:30

DODSON, Cinthia; CF; b. 20 Oct 1893 nr Fairfax C. H.; father: John
DODSON; occ: laborer; res: nr Fairfax C. H.; mother: Vida
DODSON; inf: parents; pg:ln: 210:36

DODSON, Florence; CF; b. 21 Aug 1890 in Ffx; father: Samuel
DODSON; occ: laborer; res: Ffx; mother: Melvina DODSON; inf:
Saml. DODSON, father; pg:ln: 185:30

DODSON, Frank; WM; b. 30 Jun 1894 nr Bone Mill; father: M. A.
DODSON; occ: farmer; res: nr Bone Mill; mother: Alice DODSON;
inf: father; pg:ln: 221:34

DODSON, Jno. Maurice; CM; b. 25 Oct 1890 in Ffx; father: John
DODSON; occ: laborer; res: Ffx; mother: Nida DODSON; inf: John
DODSON, father; pg:ln: 185:31

DODSON, Mary Magdalen; WF; b. 4 Mar 1891 nr Burke Sta.; father: C. C. DODSON; occ: farmer; res: nr Burke Sta.; mother: Lavina? DODSON; inf: parents; pg:ln: 193:10

DONALDSON, Edna H.; WF; b. 25 Sep 1884 in Falls Church; father: A. M. DONALDSON; occ: farmer; res: Falls Church; mother: M. G. DONALDSON; inf: father; pg:ln: 149:26

DONALDSON, Estel V.; WF; b. 19 Nov 1881 in Langley; father: Naman DONALDSON; occ: farmer; res: Langley; mother: Fannie DONALDSON; inf: father; pg:ln: 130:14

DONALDSON, Estell V.; WF; b. 6 Jul 1882 in Langley; father: Naman DONALDSON; occ: farmer; res: Langley; mother: ___ DONALDSON; inf: father; pg:ln: 134:15

DONALDSON, Florence B.; WF; b. 25 Nov 1883 in Providence Dist.; father: Naman DONALDSON; occ: farmer; res: Providence Dist.; mother: Frances DONALDSON; inf: father; pg:ln: 139:25

DONALDSON, Wilber T.; WM; b. 17 Feb 1881 in Falls Church; father: A. DONALDSON; occ: farmer; res: Falls Church; mother: Mildred G. DONALDSON; inf: mother; pg:ln: 130:17

DONALSON, Wm. ; WM; b. 23 Jun 1888 in ___; father: Naaman DONALSON; occ: farmer; res: Ffx; mother: M. DONALSON; inf: N. DONALSON, father; pg:ln: 173:28

DONOHOE, Fenton Elmor; WM; b. 12 Jan 1891 nr Alexandria; father: W. S. DONOHOE; occ: farmer; res: nr Alexandria; mother: Lula DONOHOE; inf: parents; pg:ln: 195:06

DONOHOE, Wilie May; WF; b. 20 May 1893 nr Alex; father: Wilbur DONOHOE; occ: farmer; res: nr Alex; mother: Lula DONOHOE; inf: parents; pg:ln: 210:30

DOOLEY, James Mitchell; WM; b. 18 Nov 1892 nr Burke Sta.; father: Joseph W. DOOLEY; occ: rail roading; res: nr Burke Sta.; mother: Jane M. DOOLEY; inf: father; pg:ln: 209:45

DOOLEY, Timothy Leo; WM; b. 29 Jan 1894 nr Burke Sta.; father: Joseph DOOLEY; occ: R. R. boss; res: nr Burke Sta.; mother: Jane DOOLEY; inf: mother; pg:ln: 221:28

DORSEY, ___; WM; b. 8 Jun 1885 in Ffx; father: R. B. DORSEY; occ: farmer; res: Ffx; mother: Lucretia DORSEY; inf: R. B. DORSEY, father; pg:ln: 156:13

DORSEY, Edw'd. (twin); CM; b. 6 Aug 1892 in Ffx; father: Nicholas DORSEY; occ: farmer; res: Ffx; mother: Martha DORSEY; inf: N. DORSEY, father; pg:ln: 202:27

DORSEY, Fre'd. (twin); CM; b. 6 Aug 1892 in Ffx; father: Nicholas DORSEY; occ: farmer; res: Ffx; mother: Martha DORSEY; inf: N. DORSEY, father; pg:ln: 202:28

DORSEY, Mable; WF; b. 13 Jun 1883 in ___; father: R. B. DORSEY; occ: farmer; res: Ffx; mother: Lucretia DORSEY; inf: R. B. DORSEY, father; pg:ln: 143:14

DORSEY, Rebecca; CF; b. 7 Sep 1896 in ___; father: Chas. DORSEY; occ: farmer; res: Ffx; mother: Mary DORSEY; inf: Chas. DORSEY, father; pg:ln: 226:43

DORSEY, Sadie; CF; b. 1 Nov 1893 nr Alex; father: Jarrett DORSEY; occ: laborer; res: nr Alex; mother: Anne DORSEY; inf: parents; pg:ln: 210:35

DORSON, Ellis W.; WM; b. 19 Sep 1894 nr Lorton Sta.; father: James F. DORSON; occ: farmer; res: nr Lorton; mother: Roberta L. DORSON; inf: mother; pg:ln: 221:25

DORSON, Mary G.; WF; b. 10 Jan 1893 nr Stoneleigh; father: H. C. DORSON; occ: farmer; res: nr Stoneleigh; mother: Maye E. DORSON; inf: parents; pg:ln: 210:24

DOTSON, Annie May; WF; b. 1 May 1888 in Ffx; father: M. A. DOTSON; occ: laborer; res: Ffx; mother: Annie DOTSON; inf: M. A. DOTSON, father; pg:ln: 170:16

DOTSON, Annie; WF; b. 8 Oct 1884 in Ffx; father: W. H. DOTSON; occ: farmer; res: Ffx; mother: Annie V. DOTSON; inf: W. H. DOTSON, father; pg:ln: 146:26

DOTSON, Chas. C.; WM; b. 16 Sep 1883 in ___; father: Ferd. DOTSON; occ: farmer; res: Ffx; mother: Mary E. DOTSON; inf: F. DOTSON, father; pg:ln: 143:19

DOTSON, Frank; WM; b. 29 May 1887 in Ffx; father: W. W. DOTSON; occ: laborer; res: Ffx; mother: Annie DOTSON; inf: W. W. DOTSON, father; pg:ln: 166:24

DOTSON, Lucy; WF; b. 15 Jul 1883 in Ffx; father: Lem DOTSON; occ: farmer; res: Ffx; mother: Mary DOTSON; inf: L. DOTSON, father; pg:ln: 143:18

DOTSON, not named; WM; b. 1 Aug 1887 in Ffx; father: Christopher DOTSON; occ: laborer; res: Ffx; mother: Albina DOTSON; inf: Christopher DOTSON, father; pg:ln: 166:25

DOVE, ___; WM; b. 26 Dec 1884 in Bailey's X Roads; father: Wm. F. DOVE; occ: laborer; res: Bailey's X Roads; mother: Mary E. DOVE; inf: father; pg:ln: 149:24

DOVE, Abby; WM; b. 21 May 1886 in Ffx; father: Levi DOVE; occ: farmer; res: Ffx; mother: Emma DOVE; inf: L. DOVE, father; pg:ln: 155:05

DOVE, Annie L.; WF; b. 27 Apr 1889 in Ffx; father: Geo. W. DOVE; occ: laborer; res: Ffx; mother: Rosetta DOVE; inf: G. W. DOVE, father; pg:ln: 181:28

DOVE, Chas. L.; WM; b. 12 Mar 1880 in Ffx; father: Jno. R. DOVE; occ: farmer; res: Ffx; mother: Lydia; inf: J. R. DOVE, father; pg:ln: 127:25

DOVE, Ethel; WF; b. 22 Feb 1893 nr Newington; father: Norman DOVE; occ: farmer; res: nr Newington; mother: Alice DOVE; inf: parents; pg:ln: 210:31

DOVE, Etta; WF; b. 15 Nov 1891 nr Accotink; father: Wm. DOVE; occ: merchant; res: Accotink; mother: Rebecca DOVE; inf: parents; pg:ln: 195:05

DOVE, George Leroy; WM; b. 4 Sep 1891 nr Accotink; father: George W. DOVE; occ: farmer; res: nr Accotink; mother: Rosetta DOVE; inf: parents; pg:ln: 195:04

DOVE, Grace E.; WF; b. 6 Oct 1881 in Ffx; father: Levi DOVE; occ: farmer; res: Ffx; mother: Rebecca DOVE; inf: L. DOVE, father; pg:ln: 132:12

DOVE, Harry Edward; WM; b. 29 May 1891 nr Fairfax C. H.; father: Albert DOVE; occ: farmer; res: nr Fairfax C. H.; mother: Lizzie DOVE; inf: parents; pg:ln: 194:01

DOVE, Havrie; WM; b. 12 Feb 1896 nr Fairfax C. H.; father: John DOVE; occ: farmer; res: nr Fairfax C. H.; mother: Maggie DOVE; inf: father; pg:ln: 229:28

DOVE, Jane; WF; b. 31 Mar 1896 nr Accotink; father: Warrenton DOVE; occ: farmer; res: nr Accotink; mother: Cora DOVE; inf: father; pg:ln: 229:36

DOVE, Jennie V.; WF; b. 30 May 1887 in Ffx; father: Gilman DOVE; occ: carpenter; res: Ffx; mother: Catharine DOVE; inf: Gilman DOVE, father; pg:ln: 166:26

DOVE, Kelley; WM; b. 9 Oct 1890 in Ffx; father: Andrew K. DOVE; occ: farmer; res: Ffx; mother: Elizabeth DOVE; inf: A. K. DOVE, father; pg:ln: 185:26

DOVE, Mary; WF; b. 12 Aug 1885 in Ffx; father: Thos. DOVE; occ: farmer; res: Ffx; mother: Lydia DOVE; inf: T. DOVE, father; pg:ln: 156:16

DOVE, Minnie; WF; b. 23 Oct 1883 in Falls Church; father: Edward DOVE; occ: farmer; res: Falls Church; mother: Elizabeth DOVE; inf: father; pg:ln: 139:20

DOVE, Nettie E. (twin); WF; b. 21 May 1885 in Ffx; father: Samuel DOVE; occ: farmer; res: Ffx; mother: Mary DOVE; inf: S. DOVE, father; pg:ln: 156:18

DOVE, not named; WF; b. 24 Dec 1893 nr Fairfax C. H.; father: John H. DOVE; occ: farmer; res: nr Fairfax C. H.; mother: Maggie DOVE; inf: parents; pg:ln: 210:29

DOVE, Richard; WM; b. 15 Dec 1885 in Seminary; father: W. F. DOVE; occ: laborer; res: Seminary; mother: Mary DOVE; inf: father; pg:ln: 152:18

DOVE, Viola; WF; b. 21 Apr 1896 nr Accotink; father: George DOVE; occ: farmer; res: nr Accotink; mother: Rosetta DOVE; inf: father; pg:ln: 229:37

DOVE, Wilfred E. (twin); WM; b. 21 May 1885 in Ffx; father: Samuel DOVE; occ: farmer; res: Ffx; mother: Mary DOVE; inf: S. DOVE, father; pg:ln: 156:17

DOWNEY, Bruce; WM; b. 20 Dec 1887 in Ffx; father: J. J. DOWNEY; occ: farmer; res: Ffx; mother: Rose DOWNEY; inf: J. J. DOWNEY, father; pg:ln: 166:27

DOWNS, Welby; WM; b. 29 Feb 1896 in ___; father: Geo. F. DOWNS; occ: farmer; res: Ffx; mother: Eva DOWNS; inf: G. F. DOWNS, father; pg:ln: 226:44

DRAKE, Nellie; WF; b. 15 Oct 1887 in Ffx; father: ___; occ: ___; res: Ffx; mother: Alice DRAKE; inf: Luther DRAKE, grandfather; pg:ln: 166:32

DRIVER, Elizabeth Viola; CF; b. 8 Apr 1896 nr Cedar Grove; father:
Henson DRIVER; occ: fisherman; res: nr Accotink; mother: Beckey
DRIVER; inf: father; pg:ln: 229:29

DROWNS, Harvie; WM; b. 16 Dec 1884 in Ffx; father: Jno. T.
DROWNS; occ: farmer; res: Ffx; mother: Ida V. DROWNS; inf: J. T.
DROWNS, father; pg:ln: 146:25

DUDLEY, Joseph J.; CM; b. 7 May 1893 nr Alex; father: Lewis
DUDLEY; occ: laborer; res: nr Alex; mother: Martha DUDLEY; inf:
parents; pg:ln: 210:34

DULANY, Fred S.; CM; b. 16 Aug 1881 in Dranesville; father: Rufus
DULANY; occ: laborer; res: Dranesville; mother: Laura DULANY; inf:
father; pg:ln: 130:16

DULEY, Philip; WM; b. 13 Nov 1884 in Ffx; father: Joseph DULEY; occ:
farmer; res: Ffx; mother: Jane DULEY; inf: Jos. DULEY, father;
pg:ln: 146:16

DULIN, Paul; WM; b. 14 Mar 1889 in Ffx; father: L. E. DULIN; occ:
farmer; res: Ffx; mother: Ella DULIN; inf: L. E. DULIN, father; pg:ln:
178:38

DULY, Joseph W.; WM; b. 14 Feb 1887 in Ffx; father: Joseph DULY;
occ: R. R. laborer; res: Ffx; mother: Jane DULY; inf: Jane DULY,
mother; pg:ln: 166:31

DUNCAN, Christina; WF; b. 18 Jul 1887 in Ffx; father: James DUNCAN;
occ: farmer; res: Ffx; mother: Jennett DUNCAN; inf: J. DUNCAN,
father; pg:ln: 161:38

DUNCAN, Dora J.; CF; b. 28 Oct 1888 in Ffx; father: Cain DUNCAN;
occ: farmer; res: Ffx; mother: Matilda DUNCAN; inf: Cain DUNCAN,
father; pg:ln: 170:22

DUNCAN, Eugene; CM; b. 18 Apr 1880 in Falls Church; father: William
DUNCAN; occ: laborer; res: Falls Church; mother: Casey DUNCAN;
inf: father; pg:ln: 124:18

DUNCAN, John; CM; b. 12 Jul 1885 in Ffx; father: Cain DUNCAN; occ:
farmer; res: Ffx; mother: Matilda DUNCAN; inf: C. DUNCAN, father;
pg:ln: 156:14

DUNCAN, Sylvester; CM; b. 3 Sep 1883 in Ffx; father: Cain DUNCAN;
occ: farmer; res: Ffx; mother: Matilda DUNCAN; inf: C. DUNCAN,
father; pg:ln: 143:15

DUNCAN, Sylvester; CM; b. 5 Jun 1884 in Ffx; father: Cain DUNCAN;
occ: farmer; res: Ffx; mother: Matilda DUNCAN; inf: C. DUNCAN,
father; pg:ln: 146:19

DUNCAN, W. E.; WM; b. 10 Jun 1889 in Ffx; father: Jas. DUNCAN; occ:
farmer; res: Ffx; mother: Mary DUNCAN; inf: J. DUNCAN, father;
pg:ln: 178:39

DUNN, Austin; WM; b. 21 Sep 1896 nr Alex.; father: Dennis DUNN; occ:
farmer; res: nr Alex.; mother: Mable DUNN; inf: mother; pg:ln:
229:34

DURYEE, D. D.; WM; b. 21 Oct 1884 in Falls Church; father: Schuyler
DURYEE; occ: gov. clerk; res: Falls Church; mother: Margt.
DURYEE; inf: father; pg:ln: 149:27

DUTROW, Dora May; WF; b. 20 Apr 1887 in Ffx; father: J. H.
DUTROW; occ: farmer; res: Ffx; mother: Virginia DUTROW; inf: J.
H. DUTROW, father; pg:ln: 161:39

DUTROW, Mary B.; WF; b. 10 Feb 1883 in Lewinsville; father: J. H.
DUTROW; occ: mechanic; res: Langley; mother: Virginia DUTROW;
inf: father; pg:ln: 139:24

DUVALL, Eva; WF; b. 20 Feb 1889 in Ffx; father: A. L. DUVALL; occ:
farmer; res: Ffx; mother: Laura DUVALL; inf: A. L. DUVALL, father;
pg:ln: 181:26

DUVALL, Helen; WF; b. 20 Dec 1891 nr Lorton; father: A. L. DUVALL;
occ: farmer; res: nr Lorton; mother: Lavina DUVALL; inf: parents;
pg:ln: 193:11

DUVALL, James E.; WM; b. 21 Dec 1893 nr Pohick Ch.; father: James
DUVALL; occ: farmer; res: nr Pohick Ch.; mother: Albertha DUVALL;
inf: parents; pg:ln: 210:33

DUVALL, not named; WM; b. 1 Jul 1896 nr Gumspring; father: Wm.
DUVALL; occ: farmer; res: nr Gumspring; mother: Henrietta
DUVALL; inf: father; pg:ln: 229:35

DUVALL, Paul Kingston; WM; b. 6 Apr 1894 nr Lorton Sta.; father: A. L.
DUVALL; occ: farmer; res: nr Lorton Sta.; mother: Laura V.
DUVALL; inf: father; pg:ln: 221:27

DYER, Annie; WF; b. 5 Sep 1892 in Ffx; father: H. M. DYER; occ:
farmer; res: Ffx; mother: Ann DYER; inf: H. M. DYER, father; pg:ln:
202:33

DYER, Beulah; WF; b. 1 Aug 1884 in Ffx; father: Jno. F. DYER; occ:
farmer; res: Ffx; mother: Sallie DYER; inf: J. F. DYER, father; pg:ln:
146:18

DYER, Charlie; WM; b. 25 Aug 1894 nr Burke Sta.; father: John F.
DYER; occ: miller; res: nr Burke Sta.; mother: Sallie DYER; inf:
father; pg:ln: 221:26

DYER, Elgin; WM; b. 17 Nov 1890 in Ffx; father: J. F. DYER; occ: miller;
res: Ffx; mother: Sallie DYER; inf: J. F. DYER, father; pg:ln: 185:27

DYER, Harry; WM; b. 20 Oct 1894 in Ffx; father: Herbert DYER; occ:
farmer; res: Ffx; mother: Annie E. DYER; inf: H. DYER, father; pg:ln:
217:36

DYER, Herbert; WM; b. 15 Nov 1896 in ___; father: Herbert DYER; occ:
farmer; res: Ffx; mother: Annie DYER; inf: H. DYER, father; pg:ln:
226:41

DYER, Mary V.; WF; b. 2 Jan 1883 in Ffx; father: Jno. F. DYER; occ:
farmer; res: Ffx; mother: Sallie DYER; inf: J. F. DYER, father; pg:ln:
143:13

DYER, Ross; WM; b. 9 Feb 1893 in Burke Sta.; father: John F. DYER;
occ: miller; res: Burke Sta.; mother: Sallie DYER; inf: parents; pg:ln:
210:25

EARLE, Pauline; WF; b. 10 Jun 1884 in Vienna; father: Charles EARLE;
occ: farmer; res: Vienna; mother: Margt. EARLE; inf: father; pg:ln:
149:35

EDWARDS, Abram; CM; b. 4 Jul 1890 in Ffx; father: Abram
EDWARDS; occ: farmer; res: Ffx; mother: Hannah EDWARDS; inf:
A. EDWARDS, father; pg:ln: 185:35

EDWARDS, Eva; CF; b. 15 Sep 1887 in Ffx; father: Abram EDWARDS;
occ: laborer; res: Ffx; mother: Hannah EDWARDS; inf: Abram
EDWARDS, father; pg:ln: 167:34

EELLS, Ernest; WM; b. 28 Nov 1892 in Ffx; father: E. EELLS; occ:
farmer; res: Ffx; mother: A. E. EELLS; inf: E. EELLS, father; pg:ln:
202:34

ELGIN, Chas.; WM; b. 10 Aug 1889 in Ffx; father: Jno. O. ELGIN; occ:
farmer; res: Ffx; mother: Martha ELGIN; inf: J. O. ELGIN, father;
pg:ln: 181:31

ELGIN, Ethel; WF; b. 15 Sep 1887 in Ffx; father: T. J. ELGIN; occ:
huxter; res: Ffx; mother: Mary E. ELGIN; inf: T. J. ELGIN, father;
pg:ln: 167:37

ELLIOT, Flowrine; WF; b. 10 Nov 1888 in ___; father: Jas. C. ELLIOT;
occ: farmer; res: Ffx; mother: Martha ELLIOT; inf: J. ELLIOT, father;
pg:ln: 173:30

ELLIOTT, E.; WM; b. 16 Apr 1882 in Langley; father: Perry ELLIOTT;
occ: farmer; res: Langley; mother: Annie M. ELLIOTT; inf: father;
pg:ln: 134:17

ELLIOTT, Joseph H.; WM; b. 22 Oct 1881 in Langley; father: Joseph
ELLIOTT; occ: farmer; res: Langley; mother: Martha E. ELLIOTT; inf:
mother; pg:ln: 130:18

ELLIOTT, Mary Lorietta; WF; b. 28 Sep 1896 nr Centreville; father: A. A.
ELLIOTT; occ: farmer; res: nr Centreville; mother: Martha Va
ELLIOTT; inf: father; pg:ln: 229:38

ELLIOTT, Mary; WF; b. 16 Nov 1884 in Langley; father: J. C. ELLIOTT;
occ: gardener; res: Langley; mother: M. E. ELLIOTT; inf: father;
pg:ln: 149:34

ELLIOTT, Matilda F.; WF; b. 27 Jun 1890 in Ffx; father: J. C. ELLIOTT;
occ: farmer; res: Ffx; mother: Martha E. ELLIOTT; inf: J. C.
ELLIOTT, father; pg:ln: 190:34

ELLIOTT, Pearl L.; WF; b. 14 May 1884 in Langley; father: Perry
ELLIOTT; occ: farmer; res: Langley; mother: Ann M. ELLIOTT; inf:
father; pg:ln: 149:33

ELLIOTT, Virginia; WF; b. 12 Mar 1893 nr Clifton; father: A. H.
ELLIOTT; occ: farmer; res: nr Clifton Sta.; mother: Martha V.
ELLIOTT; inf: parents; pg:ln: 211:38

ELLIS, Nellie; CF; b. 10 Apr 1894 in Ffx; father: Solomon ELLIS; occ:
farmer; res: Ffx; mother: Eliza ELLIS; inf: S. ELLIS, father; pg:ln:
217:38

ELLISON, Ella E.; WF; b. 7 Dec 1884 in Providence; father: Wm. M.
ELLISON; occ: farmer; res: Falls Church; mother: Lillian B.
ELLISON; inf: father; pg:ln: 149:32

ELLISON, Fannie M.; WF; b. 4 Jun 1886 in Falls Ch.; father: Wm. M.
ELLISON; occ: farmer; res: Falls Ch.; mother: C. B. ELLISON; inf:
father; pg:ln: 158:17

ELLISON, Minnie D.; WF; b. 28 Sep 1888 in ___; father: W. M.
ELLISON; occ: farmer; res: Ffx; mother: L. B. ELLISON; inf: W. M.
ELLISON, father; pg:ln: 173:31

ELLZEY, Carrie Eliza; CF; b. 10 Mar 1892 nr Clifton Sta.; father: Filmore
ELZEY; occ: laborer; res: nr Clifton; mother: Carrie ELZEY; inf:
father; pg:ln: 206:19

ELLZEY, John; CM; b. 5 Sep 1889 in Ffx; father: Elias ELLZEY; occ:
farmer; res: Ffx; mother: Lovist ELLZEY; inf: E. ELLZEY, father;
pg:ln: 181:32

ELZEY, Ada; CM; b. 13 Sep 1883 in Ffx; father: Filmore ELLZEY; occ:
farmer; res: Ffx; mother: Jenne ELLZEY; inf: F. ELLZEY, father;
pg:ln: 143:25

ELZEY, Daniel; CM; b. 22 Dec 1892 nr Clifton Sta.; father: Elijah
ELLZEY; occ: laborer; res: nr Clifton; mother: Fannie ELLZEY; inf:
father; pg:ln: 206:18

ELZEY, Edman; CM; b. 14 Oct 1887 in Ffx; father: Elias ELZEY; occ:
laborer; res: Ffx; mother: Lovist ELZEY; inf: Elias ELZEY, father;
pg:ln: 137:35

ENGLISH, Grover C.; WM; b. 28 Dec 1884 in Ffx; father: Chas.
ENGLISH; occ: farmer; res: Ffx; mother: Mary ENGLISH; inf: C.
ENGLISH, father; pg:ln: 146:27

ENGLISH, Julia; WF; b. 1 May 1890 in Ffx; father: Chas. ENGLISH;
occ: R Road man; res: Ffx; mother: Sarah A. ENGLISH; inf: Chas.
ENGLISH, father; pg:ln: 185:32

ENGLISH, Mary E.; WF; b. 21 Jul 1882 in Ffx; father: Chas. ENGLISH;
occ: farmer; res: Ffx; mother: Sarah ENGLISH; inf: Chas. ENGLISH,
father; pg:ln: 136:23

ENGLISH, Raymond; WM; b. 30 Jun 1892 nr Lorton Sta.; father: Chas.
E. ENGLISH; occ: rail roading; res: Lorton Sta.; mother: Sarah Alice
ENGLISH; inf: father; pg:ln: 209:47

ENNIS, John Owen; WM; b. 21 Sep 1893 nr Pohick Ch.; father: Chos.
[Chas.] ENNIS; occ: farmer; res: nr Pohick Ch.; mother: Lillie ENNIS;
inf: parents; pg:ln: 211:39

ENNIS, Mary Edna; WF; b. 15 Nov 1895 in Mason's Neck; father: Chas.
ENNIS; occ: farmer; res: Mason's Neck; mother: Lillie ENNIS; inf:
mother; pg:ln: 222:02

[ENNIS], not named; CF; b. 7 Sep 1891 nr Accotink; father: Lewis
ENNIS; occ: laborer; res: nr Accotink; mother: Martha ENNIS; inf:
parent; pg:ln: 196:06

ENNIS, Robt. Claud; WM; b. 30 May 1890 in Ffx; father: R. P. ENNIS;
occ: farmer; res: Ffx; mother: Mary C. ENNIS; inf: R. P. ENNIS,
father; pg:ln: 185:33

ERSKINE, Matilda Anna L.; WF; b. 20 Jan 1887 in Ffx; father: George
ERSKINE; occ: farmer; res: Ffx; mother: Jane Ann ERSKINE; inf:
Geo. ERSKINE, father; pg:ln: 167:36

ESKRIDGE, Clara V.; CF; b. 14 Aug 1881 in Lewinsville; father: Sam.
ESKRIDGE; occ: laborer; res: Lewinsville; mother: Sarah E.
ESKRIDGE; inf: father; pg:ln: 130:19

ESKRIDGE, Clara V.; CF; b. 14 Aug 1882 in Providence; father: Samuel ESKRIDGE; occ: laborer; res: Providence; mother: Sarah E. ESKRIDGE; inf: mother; pg:ln: 134:18

EVANS, Sumner; WM; b. 22 Dec 1890 in Ffx; father: Chas. S. EVANS; occ: carpenter; res: Ffx; mother: Phoebe A. EVANS; inf: C. S. EVANS, father; pg:ln: 185:34

EVERETT, Hazle; WF; b. 27 May 1894 in Ffx; father: Peyton EVERETT; occ: farmer; res: Ffx; mother: Lavinia EVERETT; inf: P. EVERET[T], father; pg:ln: 217:37

FADELEY, Jas. M.; WM; b. 2 May 1894 in Ffx; father: Geo. B. FADELEY; occ: farmer; res: Ffx; mother: M. R. FADELEY; inf: G. B. FADELEY, father; pg:ln: 218:41

FAIRFAX, ___ (dead); WM; b. 8 May 1880 in Ffx; father: T. M. FAIRFAX; occ: farmer; res: Ffx; mother: Susan; inf: T. M. FAIRFAX, father; pg:ln: 127:32

FAIRFAX, ___ (twin); WF; b. 14 Dec 1882 in Ffx; father: E. S. FAIRFAX; occ: farmer; res: Ffx; mother: Mattie FAIRFAX; inf: E. S. FAIRFAX, twins [father]; pg:ln: 136:27

FAIRFAX, ___ (twin); WM; b. 14 Dec 1882 in Ffx; father: E. S. FAIRFAX; occ: farmer; res: Ffx; mother: Mattie FAIRFAX; inf: E. S. FAIRFAX, twins [father]; pg:ln: 136:26

FAIRFAX, ___; CM; b. 20 Sep 1881 in Providence; father: Frank FAIRFAX; occ: laborer; res: Providence; mother: Martha FAIRFAX; inf: father; pg:ln: 130:20

FAIRFAX, C. F.; CM; b. 18 Dec 1885 in Prov.; father: W. F. FAIRFAX; occ: laborer; res: Prov.; mother: Ida FAIRFAX; inf: father; pg:ln: 152:24

FAIRFAX, Ernest W.; WM; b. 4 Aug 1890 in Ffx; father: Wellington FAIRFAX; occ: farmer; res: Ffx; mother: Viney FAIRFAX; inf: W. FAIRFAX, father; pg:ln: 186:36

FAIRFAX, Geo. Enos; WM; b. ___ Dec 1891 nr Farr P.O.; father: Geo. FAIRFAX; occ: farmer; res: nr Farr P.O.; mother: Martha G. FAIRFAX; inf: parents; pg:ln: 193:12

FAIRFAX, Hanna; WM; b. 9 Sep 1880 in Ffx; father: Luther FAIRFAX; occ: farmer; res: Ffx; mother: Annie; inf: L. FAIRFAX, father; pg:ln: 127:30

FAIRFAX, Hartley; CM; b. 13 Jul 1893 in Ffx; father: J. H. FAIRFAX; occ: farmer; res: Ffx; mother: Ann FAIRFAX; inf: J. H. FAIRFAX, father; pg:ln: 213:35

FAIRFAX, Jas.; CM; b. 20 May 1894 in Ffx; father: W. T. FAIRFAX; occ: farmer; res: Ffx; mother: Ida FAIRFAX; inf: W. T. FAIRFAX, father; pg:ln: 218:45

FAIRFAX, Laura; WF; b. 6 Nov 1885 in Ffx; father: Luther FAIRFAX; occ: farmer; res: Ffx; mother: Anna FAIRFAX; inf: L. FAIRFAX, father; pg:ln: 156:22

FAIRFAX, Lillian L.; WF; b. 5 Jun 1885 in Ffx; father: Wellington FAIRFAX; occ: farmer; res: Ffx; mother: V. FAIRFAX; inf: W. FAIRFAX, father; pg:ln: 156:21

FAIRFAX, Lucy; CF; b. 1 Jul 1883 in Providence Dist.; father: William
FAIRFAX; occ: laborer; res: Providence Dist.; mother: Ida FAIRFAX;
inf: father; pg:ln: 139:30

FAIRFAX, Lurene; WF; b. 23 Dec 1883 in ___; father: Ferd. FAIRFAX;
occ: farmer; res: Ffx; mother: Ann FAIRFAX; inf: F. FAIRFAX, father;
pg:ln: 143:27

FAIRFAX, Mary; CF; b. 10 May 1892 in Ffx; father: W. FAIRFAX; occ:
farmer; res: Ffx; mother: Ida FAIRFAX; inf: W. FAIRFAX, father;
pg:ln: 202:35

FAIRFAX, Norman Brooks; WM; b. 23 Jan 1893 nr Farr P.O.; father:
Wm. Smith FAIRFAX; occ: farmer; res: nr Farr P.O.; mother: Sarah
Virginia FAIRFAX; inf: parents; pg:ln: 211:43

FAIRFAX, Norman; WM; b. 23 Jan 1895 nr Farr P.O.; father: Wm. Smith
FAIRFAX; occ: farmer; res: nr Farr; mother: Sarah Virginia
FAIRFAX; inf: father; pg:ln: 222:05

[FAIRFAX], not named (dead); WM; b. 4 Mar 1891 in Wolf Run; father:
Luther FAIRFAX; occ: farmer; res: Wolf Run; mother: Annie
FAIRFAX; inf: parents; pg:ln: 194:10

FAIRFAX, Not named; WF; b. 10 Dec 1896 nr Farr P.O.; father: Wm. S.
FAIRFAX; occ: farmer; res: nr Farr P.O.; mother: Sarah V.
FAIRFAX; inf: mother; pg:ln: 230:40

[FAIRFAX], not named; WM; b. 10 Dec 1891 in Wolf Run Shoals; father:
Wellington FAIRFAX; occ: farmer; res: Wolf Run Shoals; mother:
Vianna FAIRFAX; inf: parents; pg:ln: 193:13

FAIRFAX, Rose Ethel; WF; b. 9 Dec 1888 in Ffx; father: Wellington
FAIRFAX; occ: farmer; res: Ffx; mother: Viena FAIRFAX; inf:
Wellington FAIRFAX, father; pg:ln: 170:23

FAIRFAX, Ruth; WF; b. 25 Oct 1893 nr Farr P.O.; father: A. T.
FAIRFAX; occ: farmer; res: nr Farr P.O.; mother: Lou E. FAIRFAX;
inf: parents; pg:ln: 211:41

FAIRFAX, Simpson; WM; b. 1 Aug 1893 nr Burke Sta.; father: Herbert
FAIRFAX; occ: farmer; res: nr Burke Sta.; mother: Annie FAIRFAX;
inf: parents; pg:ln: 211:44

FAIRFAX, Wm. Randolph; WM; b. 24 Jun 1893 nr Farr P.O.; father:
John H. FAIRFAX,; occ: farmer; res: nr Farr P.O.; mother: Mary A.
FAIRFAX; inf: parents; pg:ln: 211:42

FARR, Carrie D.; WF; b. 15 Nov 1888 in ___; father: J. D. FARR; occ:
farmer; res: Ffx; mother: Sara FARR; inf: J. D. FARR, father; pg:ln:
173:34

FARR, Clem; WM; b. 9 Jul 1892 in Ffx; father: J. D. FARR; occ: farmer;
res: Ffx; mother: Sarah FARR; inf: J. D. FARR, father; pg:ln: 203:38

FARR, Margt. H.; WF; b. 13 Mar 1888 in ___; father: R. R. FARR; occ:
farmer; res: Ffx; mother: Maggie E. FARR; inf: R. R. FARR, father;
pg:ln: 173:32

FARR, not named; CF; b. 25 Jul 1896 nr Bull Run P.O.; father: John
FARR; occ: farmer; res: nr Bull Run; mother: Julia FARR; inf: father;
pg:ln: 230:43

FARR, Sarah; CF; b. 8 Jul 1892 in Bull Run; father: John FARR; occ: farmer; res: Bull Run; mother: Julia FARR; inf: mother; pg:ln: 206:20

FAULKNER, Eva; WF; b. 13 Mar 1896 in ___; father: W. L. FAULKNER; occ: farmer; res: Ffx; mother: Janie FAULKNER; inf: W. L. FAULKNER, father; pg:ln: 226:51

FEER, ___; CF; b. 10 Feb 1885 in Kenmore; father: Elias FEER; occ: laborer; res: Kenmore; mother: Lucy FEER; inf: father; pg:ln: 152:23

FENNESEY, Kate; WF; b. 25 May 1892 in Ffx; father: J. W. FENNESEY; occ: farmer; res: Ffx; mother: Frances FINNESEY; inf: J. W. FINNESEY, father; pg:ln: 203:37

FERGUSON, Ada Bell; CF; b. 22 Mar 1892 in Gum Spring; father: Isaac FERGUSON; occ: laborer; res: Gum Spring; mother: Anna M. FERGUSON; inf: mother; pg:ln: 206:05

FERGUSON, Eugene B.; WM; b. 21 Jul 1893 in Ffx; father: W. FERGUSON; occ: farmer; res: Ffx; mother: Ida FERGUSON; inf: W. FERGUSON, father; pg:ln: 213:30

FERGUSON, Geneva; CF; b. 1 Jul 1887 in Ffx; father: C. T. FERGUSON; occ: farmer; res: Ffx; mother: Richard FERGUSON; inf: C. T. FERGUSON, father; pg:ln: 161:45

FERGUSON, Isaac; CM; b. 9 Mar 1895 in Gum Spring; father: J. FERGUSON; occ: laborer; res: Gum Spring; mother: Annie FERGUSON; inf: father; pg:ln: 222:08

FERGUSON, Lemuel; CM; b. 28 Jul 1891 in Ffx; father: Lemuel FERGUSON; occ: farmer; res: Ffx; mother: Emaline FERGUSON; inf: L. FERGUSON, father; pg:ln: 198:32

FERGUSON, Willie D.; CM; b. 28 Feb 1889 in Ffx; father: Isaac FERGUSON; occ: laborer; res: Ffx; mother: Annie FERGUSON; inf: I. FERGUSON, father; pg:ln: 181:36

FERLONG, Chas. H.; WM; b. 2 Aug 1882 in Providence; father: Irwin FERLONG; occ: farmer; res: Prov.; mother: Julia T. FERLONG; inf: father; pg:ln: 135:73

FIGGINS, Ruth; WF; b. 2 Aug 1894 in Ffx; father: J. F. FIGGINS; occ: farmer; res: Ffx; mother: L. A. FIGGINS; inf: J. F. FIGGINS, father; pg:ln: 218:40

FINN, Annie C.; WF; b. 25 Jun 1887 in Ffx; father: M. J. FINN; occ: blacksmith; res: Ffx; mother: Elvira FINN; inf: M. J. FINN, father; pg:ln: 167:38

FINN, Annie E.; WF; b. 23 Jun 1884 in Ffx; father: Jno. FINN; occ: farmer; res: Ffx; mother: Anna FINN; inf: Jno. FINN, father; pg:ln: 146:29

FISHER, Harry Elmore; WM; b. 1 Dec 1892 in West End; father: Albert FISHER; occ: carpenter; res: West End; mother: Ada FISHER; inf: mother; pg:ln: 209:34

FISHER, Jessie May; CF; b. 14 Mar 1895 nr Alexandria; father: Beverly FISHER; occ: laborer; res: nr Franconia; mother: Willie Alice FISHER; inf: father; pg:ln: 222:07

FISHER, Jno. A.; WM; b. 15 Jul 1881 in Ffx; father: A. N. FISHER; occ: farmer; res: Ffx; mother: Roxanne FISHER; inf: A. N. FISHER, father; pg:ln: 132:15

FISHER, Kate Va; CF; b. 25 Mar 1896 nr Alex.; father: Beverly FISHER; occ: laborer; res: nr Alex.; mother: Ella FISHER; inf: mother; pg:ln: 229:39

FISHER, Pricilla; CF; b. 24 Jul 1893 nr Lincolnia; father: Beverly FISHER; occ: farmer; res: nr Alex.; mother: Ella FISHER; inf: parents; pg:ln: 211:46

FITZHUGH, Harry H.; WM; b. 1 Feb 1889 in Ffx; father: S. M. FITZHU'GH; occ: farmer; res: Ffx; mother: Margt. FITZHUGH; inf: S. M. FITZHUGH, father. Birth certificate: Harry Herbert Fitzhugh, b. 1 Feb 1889, father Samuel Mark Fitzhugh of Burke Va, b. Louisville KY, clerk in grocery store; mother Margaret E. Marshall of Burke, b. Fairfax Co., housewife. Filed 6/29/38.; pg:ln: 178:42

FITZHUGH, James Marshall (twin) (Harry R. lined thru); WM; b. 7 Jun 1881 in Ffx; father: S. M. FITZHUGH; occ: farmer; res: Ffx; mother: Mgt. M. FITZHUGH; inf: S. M. FITZHUGH, father. Note: of 7/5/38. Twins born June 7, 1881, father Samuel Mark FITZHUGH, mother Margaret E. Marshall. First twin W. Mahone FITZHUGH. Second twin James Marshall FITZHUGH. Signed Margaret M. FITZHUGH mother. Second note: statement of 27 Jun 1938 by Margaret M. FITZHUGH of Burke gives marriage date as Feb 1, 1876 in Burke. Birth certificate of James Marshall FITZHUGH: b. Jun 7, 1881 to Samuel Mark FITZHUGH of Burke, 29 years old, b. Louisville KY, farmer and Margaret E. Marshall, 25 years old, b. Fairfax Co., housewife; 3rd child for mother.; pg:ln: 132:14

FITZHUGH, Richard Henry; CM; b. 16 Mar 1895 in Clifton Station; father: R. B. FITZHUGH; occ: shoemaker; res: Clifton Sta.; mother: Fannie FITZHUGH; inf: father; pg:ln: 222:06

FITZHUGH, V. D.; WF; b. 6 Jul 1880 in Ffx; father: H. C. FITZHUGH; occ: farmer; res: Ffx; mother: Katie; inf: H. C. FITZHUGH, father; pg:ln: 127:29

FITZHUGH, W. Mahone (twin); WM; b. 7 Jun 1881 in Ffx; father: S. M. FITZHUGH; occ: farmer; res: Ffx; mother: Mgt. M. FITZHUGH; inf: S. M. FITZHUGH, father Note: of 7/5/38. Twins born June 7, 1881, father Samuel Mark FITZHUGH, mother Margaret E. Marshall. First twin W. Mahone FITZHUGH. Second twin James Marshall FITZHUGH. Signed Margaret M. FITZHUGH mother. Second note: statement of 27 Jun 1938 by Margaret M. FITZHUGH of Burke gives marriage date as Feb 1, 1876 in Burke. Birth certificate of James Marshall FITZHUGH: b. Jun 7, 1881 to Samuel Mark FITZHUGH of Burke, 29 years old, b. Louisville KY, farmer and Margaret E. Marshall, 25 years old, b. Fairfax Co., housewife; 3rd child for mother.; pg:ln: 132:13

FLETCHER, Addie; CF; b. 6 Oct 1892 in Ffx; father: Arch FLETCHER; occ: farmer; res: Ffx; mother: Cressa FLETCHER; inf: Arch FLETCHER, father; pg:ln: 203:36

FLETCHER, Addie; CF; b. 6 Oct 1893 in Ffx; father: Arch. FLETCHER; occ: farmer; res: Ffx; mother: Teresa FLETCHER; inf: Arch FLETCHER, father; pg:ln: 213:33

FLETCHER, Chas.; CM; b. 11 Oct 1880 in Ffx; father: not known; occ: farmer; res: Ffx; mother: Fannie; inf: T. T. BURKE, Co. Supt. POOR; pg:ln: 127:33

FLETCHER, Elcon; CM; b. 19 Feb 1887 in Ffx; father: Arch FLETCHER; occ: farmer; res: Ffx; mother: Hanna FLETCHER; inf: A. FLETCHER, father; pg:ln: 161:43

FLETCHER, Elvira L.; WF; b. 12 Jul 1888 in Ffx; father: Geo. B. FLETCHER; occ: farmer; res: Ffx; mother: Lucy V. FLETCHER; inf: Geo. B. FLETCHER, father; pg:ln: 170:25

FLETCHER, Everna; CF; b. 8 Oct 1894 in Ffx; father: Arch FLETCHER; occ: farmer; res: Ffx; mother: Fannie FLETCHER; inf: A. FLETCHER, father; pg:ln: 218:44

FLETCHER, Jas.; CM; b. 17 Aug 1883 in ___; father: not known; occ: ___; res: ___; mother: Mary FLETCHER; inf: T. T. BURK, Supt. Poor; pg:ln: 143:28

FLETCHER, Nellie; CF; b. 20 Mar 1893 in Ffx; father: Robt. FLETCHER; occ: farmer; res: Ffx; mother: Frances FLETCHER; inf: Robt. FLETCHER, father; pg:ln: 213:32

FLETCHER, Robt.; CM; b. 6 Apr 1883 in Falls Church; father: Robt. FLETCHER; occ: laborer; res: Falls Church; mother: Fanny FLETCHER; inf: father; pg:ln: 139:28

FOARD, Frank; CM; b. 14 Sep 1882 in Ffx; father: Robt. FOARD; occ: farmer; res: Ffx; mother: Georgianna FORD; inf: Robt. FOARD, father; pg:ln: 136:28

FOLEY, Willie E.; WM; b. 29 Apr 1882 in Ffx; father: B. R. FOLEY; occ: farmer; res: Ffx; mother: Edna FOLEY; inf: B. E. [R.?] FOLEY, father; pg:ln: 136:25

FOLLIN, Alma; WF; b. 1 Jul 1885 in Dranes.; father: Jno. N. FOLLIN; occ: farmer; res: Dranes.; mother: Mary E. FOLLIN; inf: father; pg:ln: 152:22

FOLLIN, Bessie; WF; b. 29 Jan 1887 in Ffx; father: Rich'd. H. FOLLIN; occ: farmer; res: Ffx; mother: Jane FOLLIN; inf: R. H. FOLLIN, father; pg:ln: 161:41

FOLLIN, Drucilla; WF; b. 28 Jul 1886 in Hunters Mill; father: R. J. FOLLIN; occ: farmer; res: Hunters Mill; mother: Alise FOLLIN; inf: father; pg:ln: 158:19

FOLLIN, Earnest R.; WM; b. 29 Aug 1881 in Spring Vale; father: Albert F. FOLLIN; occ: farmer; res: Spring Vale; mother: Catharine C. FOLLIN; inf: father; pg:ln: 130:22

FOLLIN, Howard E.; WM; b. 27 Sep 1880 in Springvale; father: Richard J. FOLLIN; occ: farmer; res: Springvale; mother: Mary F. FOLLIN; inf: father; pg:ln: 124:19

FOLLIN, L. F.; WF; b. 26 Jun 1886 in Hunters Mill; father: Richard FOLLIN; occ: farmer; res: Hunters Mill; mother: Jone FOLLIN; inf: father; pg:ln: 158:18

FOLLIN, Mark H.; WM; b. 2 Dec 1896 in ___; father: Walter FOLLIN; occ: farmer; res: Ffx; mother: Kate FOLLIN; inf: W. FOLLIN, father; pg:ln: 226:45

FOLLIN, Myrtle; WF; b. 15 Apr 1896 in ___; father: Andrew FOLLIN; occ: farmer; res: Ffx; mother: Idella FOLLIN; inf: A. FOLLIN, father; pg:ln: 226:47

FOLLIN, Winter L.; WM; b. 20 Feb 1892 in Ffx; father: Walter L. FOLLIN; occ: farmer; res: Ffx; mother: Kate FOLLIN; inf: W. FOLLIN, father; pg:ln: 203:39

FOOTE, Joseph; CM; b. 21 Aug 1884 in Falls Ch.; father: Frederick FOOTE; occ: farmer; res: Falls Ch.; mother: Margt. FOOTE; inf: father; pg:ln: 149:36

FOOTE, Margaret J.; CF; b. 29 Aug 1881 in Falls Church; father: Fred L. FOOTE; occ: farmer; res: Falls Church; mother: Margaret V. FOOTE; inf: father; pg:ln: 130:23

FORD, ___ (dead); WF; b. 15 Feb 1884 in Providence; father: Clark FORD; occ: farmer; res: Providence; mother: Lydia FORD; inf: father; pg:ln: 150:37

FORD, C. F.; WM; b. 1 May 1883 in ___; father: Fred. FORD; occ: farmer; res: Ffx; mother: Fannie FORD; inf: F. FORD, father; pg:ln: 143:26

FORD, Charles; CM; b. 30 Mar 1888 in Ffx; father: Robt. FORD; occ: laborer; res: Ffx; mother: Georgiana FORD; inf: Robt. FORD, father; pg:ln: 170:24

FORD, Elizabeth; CF; b. 15 Oct 1887 in Ffx; father: Jno. B. FORD; occ: farmer; res: Ffx; mother: Charlotte A. FORD; inf: Jno. B. FORD, father; pg:ln: 167:40

FORD, H.; CF; b. 15 Sep 1880 in Ffx; father: J. B. FORD; occ: ___; res: Ffx; mother: Sarah; inf: J. B. FORD, father; pg:ln: 127:34

FORD, John Wallace; CM; b. 18 Oct 1889 in Ffx; father: Jno. B. FORD; occ: laborer; res: Ffx; mother: Charlotte FORD; inf: J. B. FORD, father; pg:ln: 181:35

FORD, Joseph; CM; b. 20 Jul 1892 in Fairfax C. H.; father: ___; occ: ___; res: ___; mother: Georg Anna FORD; inf: mother; pg:ln: 206:37

FORD, Julia; WF; b. 12 May 1889 in Ffx; father: Wm. F. FORD; occ: merchant; res: Ffx; mother: Annie A. FORD; inf: Wm. F. FORD, father; pg:ln: 181:34

FORD, Martha; CF; b. 27 Oct 1891 nr Gum Spring; father: John FORD; occ: laborer; res: nr Gum Spring; mother: Charlotte FORD; inf: parent; pg:ln: 196:07

FORD, Mildred Mary; CF; b. 16 May 1895 in Gum Spring; father: John D. FORD; occ: laborer; res: Gum Spring; mother: Charlotte FORD; inf: mother; pg:ln: 222:09

FORD, R. A.; WM; b. 1 May 1890 in ___; father: Wm. F. FORD; occ: clerk; res: Ffx; mother: Annie M. FORD; inf: Wm. F. FORD, father; pg:ln: 186:38

FORD, W. E.; WM; b. 23 Nov 1880 in Ffx; father: W. E. FORD; occ: merchant; res: Ffx; mother: Kadura; inf: W. E. FORD, father; pg:ln: 127:28

FORD, W. F.; WM; b. 11 Jul 1887 in Ffx; father: Wm. F. FORD; occ: farmer; res: Ffx; mother: Annie M. FORD; inf: Wm. F. FORD, father; pg:ln: 167:41

FOSSETT, Peter; CM; b. 14 Feb 1884 in Providence; father: David FOSSETT; occ: laborer; res: Providence; mother: Catharine FOSSETT; inf: father; pg:ln: 150:38

FOSTER, Emma Jane; CF; b. 10 Oct 1891 in Occoquan River; father: Thomas FOSTER; occ: laborer; res: Occoquan River; mother: Lillie Ann FOSTER; inf: parent; pg:ln: 197:06

FOULKS, M.; CF; b. __ Aug 1880 in Ffx; father: M. FOULKS; occ: farmer; res: Ffx; mother: Hester; inf: M. FOULKS, father; pg:ln: 127:31

FOULKS, Willie; CM; b. 15 Aug 1884 in Ffx; father: Moses FOULKS; occ: farmer; res: Ffx; mother: Hester FOULKS; inf: M. FOULKS, father; pg:ln: 146:28

FOWLER, Walter Edwin; WM; b. 8 Mar 1896 nr Clifton; father: C. L. FOWLER; occ: farmer; res: nr Clifton Sta.; mother: Olevia FOWLER; inf: father; pg:ln: 230:41

FOX, Ashton T.; WM; b. 26 Aug 1890 in ___; father: Zack FOX; occ: farmer; res: Ffx; mother: Lucy A. FOX; inf: Z. FOX, father; pg:ln: 186:37

FOX, Bernard J.; WM; b. 29 Apr 1881 in Fox's Mill; father: Wm. H. FOX; occ: farmer; res: Fox's Mill; mother: C. M. FOX; inf: father; pg:ln: 130:21

FOX, Carlos; WM; b. 13 Sep 1890 in Ffx; father: Montgomery FOX; occ: farmer; res: Ffx; mother: Fannie FOX; inf: M. FOX, father; pg:ln: 190:36

FOX, Jas. M.; WM; b. 14 Mar 1889 in Ffx; father: Jacob FOX Jr.; occ: farmer; res: Ffx; mother: Janie FOX; inf: Jacob FOX, father; pg:ln: 181:33

FOX, Mary E.; WF; b. 25 Jun 1894 in Ffx; father: Mon[t]gomery FOX; occ: farmer; res: Ffx; mother: Fannie FOX; inf: M. FOX, father; pg:ln: 217:39

FOX, Morris Fits-Wm.; WM; b. 27 Jun 1887 in Ffx; father: Wm. H. FOX; occ: farmer; res: Ffx; mother: C. M. FOX; inf: W. H. FOX, father; pg:ln: 161:42

FOX, Nora; WF; b. 15 Dec 1895 nr Pender P.O.; father: Sylvester FOX; occ: farmer; res: nr Pender; mother: Emma FOX; inf: mother; pg:ln: 222:04

FOX, not named (twin); WM; b. 9 Oct 1892 nr Chantilly; father: Silvester Fox; occ: farmer; res: nr Chantilly; mother: Emma FOX; inf: mother; pg:ln: 208:09

FOX, not named (twin, born dead); WM; b. 9 Oct 1892 nr Chantilly; father: Silvester Fox; occ: farmer; res: nr Chantilly; mother: Emma FOX; inf: mother; pg:ln: 208:09

FOX, Ruth; WF; b. 10 Nov 1892 nr Pleasant Valley; father: Zac FOX; occ: farmer; res: nr Pleasant Valley; mother: Lucy A. FOX; inf: mother; pg:ln: 208:08

FOX, Walter Irving; WM; b. 24 Dec 1887 in Ffx; father: Montgomery FOX; occ: farmer; res: Ffx; mother: Fannie FOX; inf: Montgomery FOX, father; pg:ln: 161:44

FRANCIS, Rich'd.; CM; b. 1 May 1896 in ___; father: not known; occ: ___; res: Ffx; mother: Lula FRANCIS; inf: Lula FRANCIS, mother; pg:ln: 226:52

FRANKS, Alga E.; WM; b. 10 Oct 1896 in ___; father: T. B. FRANKS; occ: farmer; res: Ffx; mother: Ida FRANKS; inf: T. B. FRANKS, father; pg:ln: 226:46

FRANKS, Hazel; WF; b. 14 Jul 1893 in Ffx; father: T. B. FRANKS; occ: farmer; res: Ffx; mother: Ida FRANKS; inf: T. B. FRANKS, father; pg:ln: 213:31

FREEMAN, Dorris L.; WF; b. 26 Dec 1896 in ___; father: L. L. FREEMAN; occ: mcht.; res: Ffx; mother: H. B. FREEMAN; inf: L. L. FREEMAN, father; pg:ln: 226:50

FREEMAN, Edward; CM; b. 24 Mar 1883 in Falls Church; father: Wm. FREEMAN; occ: laborer; res: Falls Church; mother: Martha FREEMAN; inf: father; pg:ln: 139:29

FREEMAN, Robt.; CM; b. 2 Aug 1886 in Ffx; father: W. S. FREEMAN; occ: farmer; res: Ffx; mother: Amanda FREEMAN; inf: W. S. FREEMAN, father; pg:ln: 155:06

FREEMAN, Samuel Alleson?; CM; b. 9 Nov 1893 in Masons Neck; father: W. S. FREEMAN; occ: laborer; res: nr Gunston; mother: Mary F. FREEMAN; inf: parents; pg:ln: 211:40

FREEMAN, Sarah J.; WF; b. 15 Nov 1887 in Ffx; father: W. S. FREEMAN; occ: farmer; res: Ffx; mother: Mary F. FREEMAN; inf: W. S. FREEMAN, father; pg:ln: 167:39

FRENCH, Bessie C.; WF; b. 28 Oct 1891 in Ffx; father: W. J. FRENCH; occ: farmer; res: Ffx; mother: Minnie FRENCH; inf: W. J. FRENCH, father; pg:ln: 198:31

FRENCH, Bessie; CF; b. 28 Nov 1892 in Ffx; father: Edw'd. FRENCH; occ: farmer; res: Ffx; mother: A. FRENCH; inf: Ed'd. FRENCH, father; pg:ln: 203:40

FRENCH, Frances; CF; b. 13 Oct 1890 in Ffx; father: Edw'd. FRENCH; occ: farmer; res: Ffx; mother: Albina FRENCH; inf: E. FRENCH, father; pg:ln: 190:35

FRENCH, Joshua; CF; b. 4 Jun 1896 in ___; father: Fre'd. FRENCH; occ: farmer; res: Ffx; mother: Henrietta FRENCH; inf: Fre'd. FRENCH, father; pg:ln: 226:49

FRENCH, Maggie; CF; b. 30 Jun 1893 in Ffx; father: Fre'd. FRENCH; occ: farmer; res: Ffx; mother: Henrietta FRENCH; inf: F. FRENCH, father; pg:ln: 213:34

FRENCH, Mary J.; CF; b. 1 Sep 1896 in ___; father: Edw'd. FRENCH; occ: farmer; res: Ffx; mother: Elmira FRENCH; inf: E'd. FRENCH, father; pg:ln: 226:48

FRENCH, Thos. B.; CM; b. 17 Jul 1889 in Ffx; father: Fred. FRENCH;
    occ: farmer; res: Ffx; mother: Henrietta FRENCH; inf: F. FRENCH,
    father; pg:ln: 178:41
FRENZELL, Charlotte; WF; b. 24 Dec 1892 nr Fairfax C. H.; father: W.
    FRENZELL; occ: farmer; res: nr Fairfax C. H.; mother: Delia
    FRENZELL; inf: father; pg:ln: 208:30
FRENZELL, Donald; WM; b. 20 Oct 1896 nr Fairfax C. H.; father:
    Edward W. FRENZELL; occ: farmer; res: nr C. H.; mother: Mary
    Elizabeth FRENZELL; inf: father; pg:ln: 230:42
FRENZELL, Joseph M.; WM; b. 1 Sep 1893 nr Fairfax C. H.; father:
    Edward FRENZELL; occ: farmer; res: nr Fairfax C. H.; mother: Mary
    E. FRENZELL; inf: parents; pg:ln: 211:45
FRENZELL, Lottie Jennette; WF; b. 29 Dec 1895 nr Fairfax C. H.;
    father: L. H. FRENZELL; occ: photographer; res: nr Fairfax C. H.;
    mother: Lizzie FRENZELL; inf: mother; pg:ln: 222:03
FRIDELL, Geo. W.; WM; b. 21 Jun 1883 in Dranesville; father: John
    FRIDELL; occ: laborer; res: Dranesville; mother: ____; inf: father;
    pg:ln: 139:31
FULLER, Albt.; CM; b. 20 May 1894 in Ffx; father: Abram FULLER; occ:
    farmer; res: Ffx; mother: Mary FULLER; inf: A. FULLER, father;
    pg:ln: 218:42
FURLONG, Patrick; WM; b. 17 Mar 1882 in Ffx; father: Ewd.
    FURLONG; occ: farmer; res: Ffx; mother: Isabelle FURLONG; inf: E.
    FURLONG, father; pg:ln: 136:24
FURR, Clara; CF; b. 15 Jun 1894 in Ffx; father: Eli FURR; occ: farmer;
    res: Ffx; mother: Lucy FURR; inf: E. FURR, father; pg:ln: 218:43
GAINES, Geo. Raymond; WM; b. 18 Dec 1887 in Ffx; father: J. W.
    GAINES; occ: farmer; res: Ffx; mother: Della GAINES; inf: J. W.
    GAINES, father; pg:ln: 167:43
GAINES, Goldia; WF; b. 30 Jul 1895 in Fairfax Sta.; father: James
    GAINES; occ: Rail Rd. boss; res: Fairfax Sta.; mother: Mary
    GAINES; inf: mother; pg:ln: 222:12
GAINES, James Edward; CM; b. 17 Apr 1893 nr Alex.; father: John E.
    GAINES; occ: laborer; res: nr Alex; mother: Ellen GAINES; inf:
    parents; pg:ln: 211:58
GAINES, Viola; CF; b. 17 Dec 1896 nr Alex.; father: John E. GAINES;
    occ: laborer; res: nr Alex.; mother: Ellen GAINES; inf: mother; pg:ln:
    230:49
GAINES, Wm. Aarcher [Archer]; CM; b. 18 Mar 1893 nr Alex.; father: W.
    E. GAINES; occ: laborer; res: nr Alex.; mother: Charlotte GAINES;
    inf: parents; pg:ln: 211:57
GANT, Chas.; WM; b. 8 Jun 1894 in Ffx; father: Geo. GANTT; occ:
    farmer; res: Ffx; mother: Sada GANTT; inf: Geo. GANTT, father;
    pg:ln: 218:46
GANTT, ____ (dead); CF; b. 9 Oct 1881 in Ffx; father: Geo. GANTT; occ:
    farmer; res: Ffx; mother: Ann GANTT; inf: G. GANTT, father; pg:ln:
    132:17

GANTT, August; CM; b. 13 Aug 1880 in Ffx; father: Geo. GANTT; occ: farmer; res: Ffx; mother: Rose; inf: Geo. GANT, father; pg:ln: 127:37

GANTT, Basil O.; WM; b. 7 May 1892 in Ffx; father: J. O. GANTT; occ: farmer; res: Ffx; mother: Charlotte E. GANTT; inf: J. O. GANTT, father; pg:ln: 203:43

GANTT, Davy; CM; b. 5 Jan 1892 in Masons Neck; father: Geo. GANTT; occ: laborer; res: Masons Neck; mother: Margaret GANTT; inf: mother; pg:ln: 206:06

GANTT, Effie; WF; b. 19 Oct 1890 in Ffx; father: Frank GANTT; occ: farmer; res: Ffx; mother: Mary GANTT; inf: F. GANTT, father; pg:ln: 190:39

GANTT, Geo.; WM; b. 13 Oct 1890 in Ffx; father: Geo. A. GANTT; occ: farmer; res: Ffx; mother: Sada GANTT; inf: G. GANTT, father; pg:ln: 190:41

GANTT, Lula V.; WF; b. 1 Oct 1887 in Ffx; father: Geo. A. GANTT; occ: farmer; res: Ffx; mother: Sada GANTT; inf: G. A. GANTT, father; pg:ln: 161:51

GARNER, Chas. Raymond; WM; b. 18 Jun 1896 nr Farr P.O.; father: J. H. GARNER; occ: farmer; res: nr Farr P.O.; mother: A. Virginia GARNER; inf: father; pg:ln: 230:47

GARNER, Henry H.; WM; b. 25 Feb 1886 in Falls Ch.; father: J. W. GARNER; occ: attorney; res: Falls Ch.; mother: ___ GARNER; inf: father; pg:ln: 158:20

GARNER, J. H.; WM; b. 1 Mar 1883 in ___; father: Henry GARNER; occ: farmer; res: Ffx; mother: Judy GARNER; inf: H. GARNER, father; pg:ln: 143:32

GARNER, Ruth; WF; b. 18 Dec 1887 in Ffx; father: J. W. GARNER; occ: farmer; res: Ffx; mother: Lilly GARNER; inf: J. W. GARNER, father; pg:ln: 161:47

GARNER, Virgie N.; WF; b. 24 Dec 1888 in Ffx; father: Newton GARNER; occ: laborer; res: Ffx; mother: Harriet A. GARNER; inf: Newton GARNER, father; pg:ln: 170:28

GARRET, Ninna; WF; b. 5 Mar 1888 in ___; father: Albt. GARRETT; occ: farmer; res: Ffx; mother: Emma F. GARRETT; inf: A. GARRETT, father; pg:ln: 173:36

GARRETT, Allen D.; WM; b. 11 Dec 1890 in Ffx; father: W. M. GARRETT; occ: farmer; res: Ffx; mother: Sadie GARRETT; inf: W. M. GARRETT, father; pg:ln: 190:38

GARRETT, Chas. G.; WM; b. 20 Nov 1884 in Langley; father: Jno. F. GARRETT; occ: farmer; res: Langley; mother: Harriet GARRETT; inf: father; pg:ln: 150:41

GARRETT, Clarence; WM; b. 1 Oct 1889 in Ffx; father: W. M. GARRETT; occ: farmer; res: Ffx; mother: S. D. GARRETT; inf: W. M. GARRETT, father; pg:ln: 178:46

GARRETT, Jno. F. Jr.; WM; b. 9 Sep 1882 in Langley; father: Jno. F. GARRETT; occ: shoemaker; res: Langley; mother: Harriett GARRETT; inf: father; pg:ln: 134:21

GARRETT, Mable C.; WF; b. 27 Jan 1887 in Ffx; father: W. M.
GARRETT; occ: farmer; res: Ffx; mother: Sarah E. GARRETT; inf:
W. M. GARRETT, father; pg:ln: 161:49

GARRISON, C. M.; WM; b. 11 Jun 1881 in Seminary; father: Wm. E.
GARRISON; occ: laborer; res: Seminary; mother: Annie A.
GARRISON; inf: father; pg:ln: 130:26

GARRISON, Edgar McCarty; WM; b. 11 Feb 1895 nr Burke Station;
father: W. E. GARRISON; occ: farmer; res: nr Burke Sta.; mother:
Annie A. GARRISON; inf: mother; pg:ln: 222:10

GARRISON, Jno. H.; WM; b. 28 Dec 1889 in Ffx; father: W. E.
GARRISON; occ: farmer; res: Ffx; mother: Annie A. GARRISON; inf:
W. E. GARRISON, father; pg:ln: 182:38

GASKINS, Bertha A.; CF; b. 4 Mar 1891 nr Clifton; father: Tasco
GASKINS; occ: laborer; res: nr Clifton; mother: Catharine GASKINS;
inf: parent; pg:ln: 197:04

GASKINS, Catharine; CF; b. 9 Mar 1893 nr Centreville; father: Sam
GASKINS; occ: laborer; res: nr Centreville; mother: Nannie
GASKINS; inf: parents; pg:ln: 211:59

GASKINS, Catherine; CF; b. 5 May 1884 in Ffx; father: Tasco
GASKINS; occ: farmer; res: Ffx; mother: Catherine GASKINS; inf: T.
GASKINS, father; pg:ln: 146:30

GASKINS, Mattie Dorey; CF; b. 20 Oct 1895 nr Centreville; father:
Joseph GASKINS; occ: laborer; res: Centreville; mother: Maggie
GASKINS; inf: father; pg:ln: 222:17

GASKINS, Nellie; CF; b. 29 Oct 1890 in Ffx; father: F. W. GASKINS;
occ: farmer; res: Ffx; mother: Cath'n. GASKINS; inf: F. GASKINS,
father; pg:ln: 190:40

GASKINS, Theresa H.; CF; b. 31 Oct 1887 in Ffx; father: Jas. W.
GASKINS; occ: laborer; res: Ffx; mother: Mary GASKINS; inf: Jas.
W. GASKINS, father; pg:ln: 167:42

GENELLA Jos. M.; WM; b. 9 Apr 1892 in Ffx; father: W. B. GENELLA;
occ: farmer; res: Ffx; mother: E. T. GENELLA; inf: W. B. GENELLA,
father; pg:ln: 203:44

GETSON, Charlotte; CF; b. 2 Mar 1888 in ___; father: Wesley
GETSON; occ: farmer; res: Ffx; mother: Betty GETSON; inf: W.
GETSON, father; pg:ln: 173:35

GHEEN, Annie; WF; b. 22 Nov 1892 nr Fairfax C. H.; father: Jackson
GHEEN; occ: farmer; res: nr Fairfax C. H.; mother: Alice GHEEN;
inf: mother; pg:ln: 208:10

GHEEN, Chas.; WM; b. 19 Jun 1886 in Ffx; father: J. R. M. GHEEN;
occ: farmer; res: Ffx; mother: Harriet GHEEN; inf: J. R. M. GHEEN,
father; pg:ln: 155:07

GHEEN, Ernest Wilmer; WM; b. 4 Jan 1891 in Bull Run; father: Thom J.
G[H]EEN; occ: farmer; res: Bull Run; mother: Alice GHEEN; inf:
parents; pg:ln: 194:12

GHEEN, Evaline May; WF; b. 8 Nov 1895 nr Bull Run; father: Wm.
GHEEN; occ: laborer; res: nr Bull Run; mother: Laura L. GHEEN;
inf: mother; pg:ln: 222:11

GHEEN, Magt. E.; WF; b. 15 Jun 1882 in Ffx; father: Geo. GHEEN; occ: farmer; res: ___; mother: Emma GHEEN; inf: Geo. GHEEN, father; pg:ln: 136:29

GHEEN, Paul Elton; WM; b. 9 Nov 1896 nr Bull Run P.O.; father: D. W. GHEEN; occ: farmer; res: nr Bull Run; mother: Lizzie GHEEN; inf: father; pg:ln: 230:44

GHEEN, Stuart Ashton; WM; b. 1 Nov 1891 in Bull Run; father: J. R. M. GHEEN; occ: farmer; res: Bull Run; mother: E. H. GHEEN; inf: parents; pg:ln: 194:11

GHEEN, Thad.; WM; b. 25 Jun 1885 in Ffx; father: Geo. F. GHEEN; occ: farmer; res: Ffx; mother: Jennie GHEEN; inf: G. F. GHEEN, father; pg:ln: 156:24

GHEEN, Wm. T.; WM; b. 26 Oct 1887 in Ffx; father: Thos. J. GHEEN; occ: farmer; res: Ffx; mother: Alice GHEEN; inf: Thos. J. GHEEN, father; pg:ln: 167:45

GHOROM, Epelona; WF; b. 29 Jun 1896 nr Franconia Sta.; father: Wm. GHOROM; occ: laborer; res: Franconia; mother: Epelona GHOROM; inf: father; pg:ln: 230:45

GHORUM, Bertha Virginia; WF; b. 16 Sep 1895 nr Franconia; father: Beauregard GHORUM; occ: laborer; res: Franconia; mother: Ada GHORUM; inf: mother; pg:ln: 222:15

GIBSON, ___; CM; b. 14 Nov 1890 in Ffx; father: Albert GIBSON; occ: farmer; res: Ffx; mother: Rose E. GIBSON; inf: A. GIBSON, father; pg:ln: 190:37

GIBSON, Allen; CM; b. 7 Jun 1882 in Providence; father: Wesley GIBSON; occ: laborer; res: Providence; mother: Betty GIBSON; inf: father; pg:ln: 134:19

GIBSON, Alonzo; CM; b. 11 Apr 1893 in ___; father: Albt. GIBSON; occ: ___; res: ___; mother: Rose GIBSON; inf: Albt. GIBSON, father; pg:ln: 214:38

GIBSON, Charlie; CM; b. 5 Mar 1887 in Ffx; father: Wesley GIBSON; occ: farmer; res: Ffx; mother: Mary GIBSON; inf: Wesley GIBSON, father; pg:ln: 161:48

GIBSON, Cora E.; CF; b. 4 Apr 1896 in ___; father: Allen GIBSON; occ: farmer; res: Ffx; mother: Virginia GIBSON; inf: Allen GIBSON, father; pg:ln: 226:54

GIBSON, Eddie; CM; b. 1 Mar 1882 in Ffx; father: Sam GIBSON; occ: farmer; res: Ffx; mother: Lizzie GIBSON; inf: S. GIBSON, father; pg:ln: 136:30

GIBSON, Edgar R.; CM; b. 26 May 1891 in Ffx; father: Albt. GIBSON; occ: farmer; res: Ffx; mother: Rose GIBSON; inf: A. GIBSON, father; pg:ln: 198:33

GIBSON, Emaline; CF; b. 3 Jul 1885 in Ffx; father: Strother GIBSON; occ: farmer; res: Ffx; mother: Martha GIBSON; inf: S. GIBSON, father; pg:ln: 156:27

GIBSON, Grace; WF; b. 25 Sep 1881 in Kenmore; father: Henry H. GIBSON; occ: farmer; res: Kenmore; mother: Elizabeth GIBSON; inf: father; pg:ln: 130:25

GIBSON, Irene; WF; b. 4 Apr 1885 in Prov.; father: Henry GIBSON; occ: farmer; res: Prov.; mother: Lizzie GIBSON; inf: father; pg:ln: 152:25

GIBSON, Lucy; CF; b. 8 Jan 1880 in Providence; father: Peter GIBSON; occ: laborer; res: Providence; mother: Ellen GIBSON; inf: father; pg:ln: 124:22

GIBSON, Margt.; CF; b. 26 Aug 1881 in Ffx; father: Strother GIBSON; occ: farmer; res: Ffx; mother: Martha GIBSON; inf: S. GIBSON, father; pg:ln: 132:19

GIBSON, Mary A.; WF; b. 10 Mar 1884 in Providence; father: Henry GIBSON; occ: farmer; res: Providence; mother: Frances GIBSON; inf: father; pg:ln: 150:39

GIBSON, Norman; CM; b. 14 Feb 1894 in Ffx; father: A. GIBSON; occ: farmer; res: Ffx; mother: V. E. GIBSON; inf: A. GIBSON, father; pg:ln: 218:48

GIBSON, Rena F.; CF; b. 10 Oct 1889 in Ffx; father: Saml. GIBSON; occ: farmer; res: Ffx; mother: Fannie GIBSON; inf: Saml. GIBSON, father; pg:ln: 182:40

GILLINHAM, Geo. C.; WM; b. 14 Oct 1881 in Ffx; father: Lewis GILLINHAM; occ: farmer; res: Ffx; mother: Esther GILLINHAM; inf: L. GINNINHAM, father; pg:ln: 132:16

GILROY, Joseph Henry; WM; b. 24 Jan 1896 nr Alex.; father: John A. GILROY; occ: brick layer; res: nr Alex.; mother: Elizabeth GILROY; inf: father; pg:ln: 230:48

GOCHNAUER, Fairfax L.; WM; b. 10 Dec 1896 in ___; father: P. B. GOCHNAUER; occ: farmer; res: Ffx; mother: Annie GOCHNAUER; inf: P. B. GOCHNAUER, father; pg:ln: 226:53

GOODING, Estella; WF; b. 16 Sep 1884 in Masons Hill; father: Chas. F. GOODING; occ: farmer; res: Masons Hill; mother: Alice M. GOODING; inf: father; pg:ln: 150:40

GOODING, Nettie; WF; b. 6 Oct 1881 in Court House; father: Jno. J. GOODING; occ: farmer; res: Court House; mother: Oliva J. GOODING; inf: father; pg:ln: 130:27

GOODING, Ray P.; WM; b. 26 Apr 1890 in ___; father: A. W. GOODING; occ: farmer; res: Ffx; mother: Sybilia GOODING; inf: A. W. GOODING, father; pg:ln: 186:40

GOODWIN, Edith May; WF; b. 25 Oct 1891 in Lorton; father: John H. GOODWIN; occ: farmer; res: Lorton; mother: Rachel J. GOODWIN; inf: parents; pg:ln: 193:14

GORAM, Jno. R.; WM; b. 30 May 1889 in Ffx; father: Chas. GORAM; occ: farmer; res: Ffx; mother: Abby GORAM; inf: C. GORAM, father; pg:ln: 178:43

GORDON, ___; CF; b. 28 Dec 1883 in Falls Church; father: Abraham GORDON; occ: laborer; res: Falls Church; mother: Bettie GORDON; inf: father; pg:ln: 139:32

GORDON, Ruth; WF; b. 3 Apr 1894 in Ffx; father: W. L. GORDON; occ: farmer; res: Ffx; mother: L. R. JORDON; inf: W. L. GORDON, father; pg:ln: 218:47

GORRUM, Samuel; WM; b. 8 Dec 1889 in Ffx; father: Thos.
GOR[R]UM; occ: farmer; res: Ffx; mother: Sarah GOR[R]UM; inf: T.
GORRUM, father; pg:ln: 182:37

GOSSAGE, Howard; WM; b. 24 Mar 1896 nr Fairfax Sta.; father: Harry
C. GOSSAGE; occ: painter; res: nr Fairfax Sta.; mother: Mollie F.
GOSSAGE; inf: father; pg:ln: 230:46

GOSSAGE, not named; WM; b. 24 May 1895 nr Fairfax Sta.; father:
Harry GOSSAGE; occ: printer; res: Fairfax Sta.; mother: Mollie
GOSSAGE; inf: mother; pg:ln: 222:13

GRAHAM, Ashby Mc.; WM; b. 18 Aug 1888 in Ffx; father: Wm. E.
GRAHAM; occ: Clerk Ct. Court; res: Ffx; mother: Fannie C.
GRAHAM; inf: Wm. E. GRAHAM, father; pg:ln: 170:29

GRAHAM, Bell; WF; b. 12 Aug 1890 in ___; father: Wm. E. GRAHAM;
occ: Clerk Ct. Court; res: Ffx; mother: Fannie C. GRAHAM; inf: Wm.
E. GRAHAM, father; pg:ln: 186:39

GRAHAM, H. C.; WM; b. 20 Oct 1882 in Falls Church; father: Neil F.
GRAHAM; occ: phy.; res: Falls Church; mother: H. A. GRAHAM; inf:
father; pg:ln: 134:20

GRAHAM, Harriet F.; WF; b. 27 Jun 1880 in Falls Church; father: N. F.
GRAHAM; occ: office holder D.C.; res: Falls Church; mother: Harriet
A. GRAHAM; inf: mother; pg:ln: 124:23

GRAHAM, M.; WM; b. 9 Sep 1883 in ___; father: T. B. GRAHAM; occ:
farmer; res: Ffx; mother: Elizab. A. GRAHAM; inf: T. B. GRAHAM,
father; pg:ln: 143:29

GRAHAM, Montrose; WM; b. 7 Sep 1885 in Ffx; father: Thos. B.
GRAHAM; occ: farmer; res: Ffx; mother: Elizbt. GRAHAM; inf: T. B.
GRAHAM, father; pg:ln: 156:23

GRAMER, Mary Page; WF; b. 11 Oct 1893 in Ffx; father: Carl E.
GRAMER; occ: farmer; res: Ffx; mother: Mary P. GRAMER; inf: C.
E. GRAMER, father; pg:ln: 213:36

GRAMER, Virginia N.; WF; b. 7 May 1892 in Ffx; father: C. E.
GRAMER; occ: Professor The. Seminary; res: Ffx; mother: M. P.
GRAMER; inf: C. E. GRAMER, father; pg:ln: 203:45

GRAY, Bertha; CF; b. 24 Nov 1896 nr Gumspring; father: Hamilton
GRAY; occ: laborer; res: nr Gumspring; mother: Cora GRAY; inf:
father; pg:ln: 230:50

GRAY, Ira S.; CM; b. 3 Jun 1886 in Ffx; father: Hamilton GRAY; occ:
farmer; res: Ffx; mother: Edith GRAY; inf: H. GRAY, father; pg:ln:
155:08

GRAY, Isaiah; CM; b. 15 Jul 1887 in Ffx; father: Hamilton GRAY; occ:
laborer; res: Ffx; mother: Mary GRAY; inf: Hamilton GRAY, father;
pg:ln: 167:44

GRAY, John Henry; CM; b. 20 Oct 1891 nr Gum Spring; father:
Hamilton GRAY; occ: laborer; res: nr Gum Spring; mother: Cassie
GRAY; inf: parent; pg:ln: 196:08

GRAY, Mary A.; WF; b. 29 Jun 1884 in Prov.; father: J. H. GRAY; occ:
laborer; res: Prov.; mother: Sarah GRAY; inf: father; pg:ln: 150:42

GRAY, Sarah Elizabeth; CF; b. 6 Mar 1895 in Gum Spring; father: Hamilton GRAY; occ: farmer; res: Gum Spring; mother: Carrie E. GRAY; inf: father; pg:ln: 222:18

GRAY, Spillman; CM; b. 4 Jul 1885 in Ffx; father: Hamilton GRAY; occ: farmer; res: Ffx; mother: Jennie GRAY; inf: H. GRAY, father; pg:ln: 156:26

GRAY, Wm. Henry; CM; b. 9 Sep 1890 in ___; father: Hamilton GRAY; occ: farmer; res: Ffx; mother: Carrie GRAY; inf: Hamilton GRAY, father; pg:ln: 186:41

GRAYSON, Dolly; CF; b. 30 May 1889 in Ffx; father: W. GRAYSON; occ: farmer; ies: Ffx; mother: Mary GRAYSON; inf: W. GRAYSON, father; pg:ln: 178:45

GREEHAN, E.; WM; b. 10 Nov 1880 in Ffx; father: J. I. GREEHAN; occ: farmer; res: Ffx; mother: Hannah; inf: J. I. GREEHAN, father; pg:ln: 127:35

GREEN, John C.; WM; b. 23 Jul 1881 in Dranesville; father: H. W. GREEN; occ: farmer; res: Dranesville; mother: M. E. GREEN; inf: father; pg:ln: 130:24

GREEN, John; CM; b. 7 Mar 1883 in ___; father: Wilson GREENE; occ: farmer; res: Ffx; mother: Betsey GREEN; inf: W. GREEN, father; pg:ln: 143:33

GREEN, Martha; CF; b. 21 Feb 1895 nr Clifton Sta.; father: Andrew GREEN; occ: laborer; res: Clifton Sta.; mother: Mary GREEN; inf: father; pg:ln: 222:16

GREEN, Nathan; CM; b. 7 Nov 1896 nr Fairfax C. H.; father: Washington GREEN; occ: laborer; res: nr C. H.; mother: Leanna GREEN; inf: father; pg:ln: 230:51

GREEN, not named; CF; b. 10 Jul 1896 nr Clifton Sta.; father: Andrew GREEN; occ: laborer; res: nr Clifton Sta.; mother: Mary GREEN; inf: mother; pg:ln: 230:53

GREEN, Robt.; CM; b. 13 Jul 1889 in Ffx; father: Henry GREEN; occ: farmer; res: Ffx; mother: Mary GREEN; inf: H. GREEN, father; pg:ln: 178:47

GREEN, Wilber; CM; b. 13 Aug 1880 in Ffx; father: Albt. GREEN; occ: farmer; res: Ffx; mother: Mary; inf: Albt. GREEN, father; pg:ln: 127:36

GREENE, Lucy; CF; b. 8 Apr 1883 in ___; father: Andrew GREEN; occ: farmer; res: Ffx; mother: Mary L. GREEN; inf: A. GREEN, father; pg:ln: 143:31

GREENE, Martin; WM; b. 31 Oct 1883 in Ffx; father: W. GREEN; occ: farmer; res: Ffx; mother: Kate H. GREEN; inf: W. GREEN, father; pg:ln: 143:30

GRIFFITH, C. E.; WM; b. 9 Oct 1889 in Ffx; father: B. T. GRIFFETH; occ: farmer; res: Ffx; mother: M. B. GRIFFETH; inf: B. T. GRIFFETH, father; pg:ln: 182:39

GRIFFITH, Harry B.; WM; b. 12 May 1892 nr Clifton; father: B. L. GRIFFITH; occ: farmer; res: nr Clifton; mother: Mary B. GRIFFITH; inf: father; pg:ln: 208:11

GRIMSLEY, Jas.; WM; b. 9 Sep 1881 in Ffx; father: Thos. GRIMSLEY; occ: farmer; res: Ffx; mother: Rebecca GRIMSLEY; inf: T. GRIMSLEY, father; pg:ln: 132:18

GRIMSLEY, Levi; WM; b. 13 Feb 1895 nr Woodlawn; father: Wm. GRIMSLEY; occ: fisherman; res: Woodlawn; mother: Lydia GRIMSLEY; inf: mother; pg:ln: 222:14

GRIMSLEY, Maggie T.; WF; b. 28 Aug 1888 in Ffx; father: F. M. GRIMSLEY; occ: farmer; res: Ffx; mother: Emma J. GRIMSLEY; inf: F. M. GRIMSLEY, father; pg:ln: 170:27

GRIMSLEY, Norman; WM; b. 28 Mar 1892 nr Accotink; father: Wm. GRIMSLEY; occ: farmer; res: nr Accotink; mother: Lillie GRIMSLEY; inf: mother; pg:ln: 207:67

GROFF, Margaret Lucretia; WF; b. 18 Apr 1892 nr Burnside Sta.; father: Harry GROFF; occ: farmer; res: nr Burnside Sta.; mother: Freda GROFF; inf: mother; pg:ln: 209:48

GROOM, Lillian; CF; b. 4 Nov 1885 in Ffx; father: Nelson GROOM; occ: farmer; res: Ffx; mother: Anna GROOM; inf: N. GROOM, father; pg:ln: 156:25

GROOME, James; CM; b. __ Oct 1891 nr Lorton; father: Nilson GROOME; occ: laborer; res: nr Lorton; mother: Annie GROOME; inf: parent; pg:ln: 197:07

GROOMS, Allie; CF; b. 15 Aug 1888 in Ffx; father: Nelson GROOMS; occ: laborer; res: Ffx; mother: Annie GROOMS; inf: Nelson GROOMS, father; pg:ln: 170:26

GROOMS, Rosa May; CF; b. 10 Sep 1896 nr Lorton Sta.; father: Nelson GROOMS; occ: laborer; res: nr Lorton Sta.; mother: Annie GROOMS; inf: father; pg:ln: 230:52

GUN, S. V.; WF; b. 28 Feb 1893 in ___; father: W. T. GUN; occ: ___; res: ___; mother: Lawa [Laura?] GUN; inf: W. T. GUN, father; pg:ln: 214:39

GUNNELL, ___; WF; b. 15 Jun 1887 in Ffx; father: Geo. GUNNELL; occ: farmer; res: Ffx; mother: E. G. GUNNELL; inf: Geo. GUNNELL, father; pg:ln: 161:50

GUNNELL, Albt.; WM; b. 30 Dec 1892 in Ffx; father: Jno. H. GUNNELL; occ: farmer; res: Ffx; mother: Annie GUNNELL; inf: J. H. GUNNELL, father; pg:ln: 203:41

GUNNELL, Annie; WF; b. 14 Nov 1891 in Ffx; father: Hugh W. GUNNELL; occ: farmer; res: Ffx; mother: Mary F. GUNNELL; inf: H. W. GUNNELL, father; pg:ln: 198:30

GUNNELL, Carl F.; WM; b. 11 Nov 1893 in ___; father: Amos GUNNELL; occ: ___; res: ___; mother: Martha GUNNELL; inf: A. GUNNELL, father; pg:ln: 214:41

GUNNELL, Chas. A.; WM; b. 5 Oct 1885 in Dranes; father: Geo. W. GUNNELL; occ: farmer; res: Dranes; mother: Emma G. GUNNELL; inf: father; pg:ln: 152:26

GUNNELL, Eugene; WM; b. 15 Sep 1889 in Ffx; father: Hugh GUNNELL; occ: farmer; res: Ffx; mother: Mary GUNNELL; inf: H. GUNNELL, father; pg:ln: 178:44

GUNNELL, Gibert S. [Gilbert?]; WM; b. 9 Jun 1893 in ___; father: G. W.
GUNNELL; occ: ___; res: ___; mother: Alice GUNNELL; inf: G. W.
GUNNELL, father; pg:ln: 214:40

GUNNELL, Grover C.; WM; b. 10 Sep 1887 in Ffx; father: J. H.
GUNNELL; occ: farmer; res: Ffx; mother: Annie GUNNELL; inf: J. H.
GUNNELL, father; pg:ln: 161:46

GUNNELL, Jno. A.; WM; b. 26 Feb 1893 in Ffx; father: Jno. H.
GUNNELL; occ: farmer; res: Ffx; mother: Annie GUNNELL; inf: J. H.
GUNNELL, father; pg:ln: 214:37

GUNNELL, not named (twin); WF; b. 9 May 1880 in Providence; father:
D. P. GUNNELL; occ: farmer; res: Providence; mother: Blanche
GUNNELL; inf: father; pg:ln: 124:20

GUNNELL, not named (twin); WF; b. 9 May 1880 in Providence; father:
D. P. GUNNELL; occ: farmer; res: Providence; mother: Blanche
GUNNELL; inf: father; pg:ln: 124:21

GUNNELL, Paul B.; WM; b. 15 Jun 1896 in ___; father: Amos
GUNNELL; occ: farmer; res: Ffx; mother: Mattie GUNNELL; inf: A.
GUNNELL, father; pg:ln: 226:55

GUNNELL, W. H.; WM; b. 8 Nov 1892 in Ffx; father: Hugh W.
GUNNELL; occ: farmer; res: Ffx; mother: Fannie GUNNELL; inf: H.
W. GUNNELL, father; pg:ln: 203:42

HAGAR, Carl A.; WM; b. 25 Jun 1880 in Dranesville; father: John F.
HAGAR; occ: farmer; res: Dranesville; mother: Ophelia E. HAGAR;
inf: father; pg:ln: 124:24

HAIGHT, Alexr.; WM; b. 9 Dec 1891 in Ffx; father: H. C. HAIGHT; occ:
farmer; res: Ffx; mother: Emma HAIGHT; inf: H. C. HAIGHT, father;
pg:ln: 199:40

HAIGHT, Bessie; WF; b. 15 Jan 1889 in Ffx; father: Henry C. HAIGHT;
occ: farmer; res: Ffx; mother: Emma HAIGHT; inf: H. C. HAIGHT,
father; pg:ln: 178:54

HAIGHT, Charlotte H.; WF; b. 6 Oct 1888 in Ffx; father: Henry C.
HAIGHT; occ: farmer; res: Ffx; mother: Emma J. HAIGHT; inf: H. C.
HAIGHT, father; pg:ln: 174:43

HAINES, Clarence; WM; b. 13 Sep 1891 in Ffx; father: R. D. HAINES;
occ: farmer; res: Ffx; mother: Rosa HAINES; inf: R. D. HAINES,
father; pg:ln: 199:43

HAINES, Clarica V.; WF; b. 8 Sep 1893 in ___; father: R. D. HAINES;
occ: ___; res: ___; mother: R. M. HAINES; inf: R. D. HAINES, father;
pg:ln: 214:46

HAINES, Leo. F.; WM; b. 25 Aug 1888 in Ffx; father: R. D. HAINES;
occ: farmer; res: Ffx; mother: Rose M. HAINES; inf: R. D. HAINES,
father; pg:ln: 174:40

HAINES, Robt. R.; WM; b. 5 Mar 1890 in Ffx; father: R. D. HAINES;
occ: farmer; res: Ffx; mother: Rose M. HAINES; inf: R. D. HAINES,
father; pg:ln: 190:45

HAINEY, ___; CM; b. 1 Jul 1881 in Vienna; father: Fleming HAINEY;
occ: mechanic; res: Vienna; mother: Mary HAINEY; inf: father; pg:ln:
130:29

HAISLIP, Julian M.; WM; b. 18 Aug 1891 in Masons Neck; father: J. A. HAISLIP; occ: farmer; res: Masons Neck; mother: Keziah E. HAISLIP; inf: parents; pg:ln: 195:08

HAISLIP, Robert; WM; b. 1 Mar 1890 in ___; father: Chas. L. HAISLIP; occ: carpenter; res: Ffx; mother: Mary HAISLIP; inf: C. L. HAISLIP, father; pg:ln: 186:46

HALL,)___ (dead); CF; b. 19 Jun 1889 in Ffx; father: Columbus HALL; occ: farmer; res: Ffx; mother: Maria HALL; inf: C. HALL, father; pg:ln: 178:48

HALL, Alpheus; CM; b. 17 Dec 1894 in Ffx; father: W. HALL; occ: farmer; res: Ffx; mother: Mattie HALL; inf: W. HALL, father; pg:ln: 218:50

HALL, Annie E.; WF; b. 13 May 1890 in ___; father: John Q. HALL; occ: farmer; res: Ffx; mother: Emaline HALL; inf: Jno. Q. HALL, father; pg:ln: 186:55

HALL, Annie May; CF; b. 15 Nov 1896 nr Alex.; father: Moses HALL; occ: laborer; res: nr Alex.; mother: Mary HALL; inf: mother; pg:ln: 230:64

HALL, Benjamin; CM; b. 24 Feb 1884 in Prov.; father: Columbus HALL; occ: laborer; res: Prov.; mother: Martha HALL; inf: father; pg:ln: 150:51

HALL, Bessie Lee; WF; b. 4 Oct 1896 nr Pohick Ch.; father: Elihugh HALL; occ: farmer; res: nr Pohick Ch.; mother: Georgeannah HALL; inf: father; pg:ln: 230:61

HALL, Effie; WF; b. 3 May 1880 in Ffx; father: J. R. HALL; occ: farmer; res: Ffx; mother: Emaline; inf: J. R. HALL, father; pg:ln: 128:42

HALL, Jane; WF; b. 6 Jul 1884 in Ffx; father: Jno. Q. HALL; occ: farmer; res: Ffx; mother: Emaline HALL; inf: Jno. HALL, father; pg:ln: 147:36

HALL, Jas. H.; CM; b. 2 Mar 1892 in Ffx; father: W. HALL; occ: laborer; res: Ffx; mother: Susan HALL; inf: W. HALL, father; pg:ln: 203:46

HALL, Jno. W.; WM; b. 4 Aug 1883 in Ffx; father: Elihu HALL; occ: farmer; res: Ffx; mother: Georgian HALL; inf: E. HALL, father; pg:ln: 144:36

HALL, John L.; WM; b. 4 Jul 1895 nr Burke Sta.; father: John L. HALL; occ: farmer; res: nr Burke Sta.; mother: Emmaline HALL; inf: father; pg:ln: 222:25

HALL, John; CM; b. 8 Sep 1880 in Providence; father: Columbus HALL; occ: farmer; res: Providence; mother: Maria HALL; inf: father; pg:ln: 124:27

HALL, Julia (twin); CF; b. 7 Jun 1890 in ___; father: Oscar HALL; occ: laborer; res: Ffx; mother: Jennie HALL; inf: Oscar HALL, father; pg:ln: 186:56

HALL, Kate; WF; b. 3 Aug 1896 nr Burke Sta.; father: James HALL; occ: farmer; res: nr Burke Sta.; mother: Rosie HALL; inf: father; pg:ln: 230:60

HALL, Lewis E.; CM; b. 29 Jul 1894 in Ffx; father: W. H. HALL; occ: farmer; res: Ffx; mother: Susan HALL; inf: W. H. HALL, father; pg:ln: 218:57

HALL, Lizzie; CF; b. 15 Mar 1893 in ___; father: Vincent HALL; occ: ___; res: ___; mother: Maggie HALL; inf: V. HALL, father; pg:ln: 214:45

HALL, Lovell Lee; WM; b. 30 Jan 1891 nr Lorton Sta.; father: Geo. W. HALL; occ: farmer; res: nr Lorton Sta.; mother: Florence O. HALL; inf: parents; pg:ln: 193:18

HALL, Mable V.; WF; b. 5 Aug 1890 in Ffx; father: W. E. HALL; occ: farmer; res: Ffx; mother: Mary V. HALL; inf: W. HALL, father; pg:ln: 190:44

HALL, Milton D.; WM; b. 8 Jul 1888 in Ffx; father: Jno. Q. HALL; occ: farmer; res: Ffx; mother: Emaline HALL; inf: Jno. Q. HALL, father; pg:ln: 170:34

HALL, Nannie C.; WF; b. 8 Aug 1887 in Ffx; father: M. D. HALL; occ: farmer; res: Ffx; mother: Ella A. HALL; inf: M. D. HALL, father; pg:ln: 167:52

HALL, Nettie Lee; WF; b. 9 Mar 1893 nr Pohick Ch.; father: R. HALL; occ: farmer; res: nr Pohick Ch.; mother: Georgea A. HALL; inf: parents; pg:ln: 211:49

HALL, not named (twin); CF; b. 28 Jul 1884 in Seminary; father: Vincent HALL; occ: laborer; res: Seminary; mother: Maggie HALL; inf: father; pg:ln: 150:45

HALL, not named (twin); CM; b. 28 Jul 1884 in Seminary; father: Vincent HALL; occ: laborer; res: Seminary; mother: Maggie HALL; inf: father; pg:ln: 150:44

HALL, Oliver; CM; b. 25 Jul 1882 in Providence; father: Columbus HALL; occ: laborer; res: Providence; mother: Maria H. HALL; inf: father; pg:ln: 134:27

HALL, Perle; CF; b. 17 Feb 1896 in ___; father: W. HALL; occ: farmer; res: Ffx; mother: Martha HALL; inf: W. HALL, father; pg:ln: 226:58

HALL, William Kye Jr.; WM; b. 3 Mar 1895 nr Burke Sta.; father: M. D. HALL; occ: farmer; res: nr Burke Sta.; mother: Ella HALL; inf: father; pg:ln: 222:24

HALL, Willie; WM; b. 15 May 1884 in Ffx; father: Arch HALL; occ: farmer; res: Ffx; mother: Amanda HALL; inf: A. HALL, father; pg:ln: 147:35

HALL, Wm. (twin); CM; b. 7 Jun 1890 in ___; father: Oscar HALL; occ: laborer; res: Ffx; mother: Jennie HALL; inf: Oscar HALL, father; pg:ln: 186:57

HALLEY, Roberta E.; WF; b. 28 Jun 1887 in Ffx; father: Richd. N. HALLEY; occ: farmer; res: Ffx; mother: Emaline V. HALLEY; inf: Richd. N. HALLEY, father; pg:ln: 167:57

HAMILL, B. T.; WM; b. 31 Dec 1883 in Ffx; father: Jno. HAMILL; occ: farmer; res: Ffx; mother: Alice HAMILL; inf: Jno. HAMILL, father; pg:ln: 144:40

HAMILL, Thos.; WM; b. 14 Aug 1890 in ___; father: Jno. J. HAMILL; occ: farmer; res: Ffx; mother: Alice HAMILL; inf: J. J. HAMILL, father; pg:ln: 186:45

HAMILTON, Mary E.; WF; b. 20 Nov 1884 in Ffx; father: Andrew
    HAMILTON; occ: farmer; res: Ffx; mother: S. A. HAMILTON; inf: A.
    HAMILTON, father; pg:ln: 147:39
HAMILTON, Rufus Henry; CM; b. 1 Jun 1887 in Ffx; father: Wm. T.
    HAMILTON; occ: laborer; res: Ffx; mother: Rosa HAMILTON; inf:
    Wm. T. HAMILTON, father; pg:ln: 167:46
HAMILTON, Walter; CM; b. 25 Apr 1880 in Ffx; father: W. T.
    HAMILTON; occ: farmer; res: Ffx; mother: Rosa; inf: W. T.
    HAMILTON, father; pg:ln: 128:45
HAMMELL, Alice; WF; b. 26 Jan 1892 nr Fairfax Sta.; father: J. J.
    HAMMELL; occ: farmer; res: nr Fairfax Sta.; mother: Alice
    HAMMELL; inf: mother; pg:ln: 209:49
[HAMMOND], not named (dead); CM; b. __ Apr 1891 in Masons Neck;
    father: George HAMMOND; occ: laborer; res: Masons Neck; mother:
    Sarah HAMMOND; inf: parent; pg:ln: 196:10
HAMMOND, not named; CF; b. 1 May 1887 in Ffx; father: Geo.
    HAMMOND; occ: laborer; res: Ffx; mother: Sarah HAMMOND; inf:
    Geo. HAMMOND, father; pg:ln: 167:59
HAMMONTREE, Gertrude; CF; b. 13 Dec 1883 in Providence; father:
    Jere HAMMONTREE; occ: laborer; res: Providence; mother:
    Georgia HAMMONTREE; inf: father; pg:ln: 140:38
HAMPTON, N. B.; WM; b. 30 May 1882 in Ffx; father: Wm. H.
    HAMPTON; occ: farmer; res: Ffx; mother: Annie HAMPTON; inf: W.
    H. HAMPTON, father; pg:ln: 136:33
HAMPTON, Naomi; CF; b. 7 Nov 1883 in Ffx; father: not known; occ:
    farmer; res: Ffx; mother: Harriet HAMPTON; inf: J. HAMPTON,
    grandfather; pg:ln: 144:38
HAMPTON, Rose; WF; b. 19 Oct 1883 in Ffx; father: W. H. HAMPTON;
    occ: farmer; res: Ffx; mother: Ann HAMPTON; inf: W. H. HAMPTON,
    father; pg:ln: 144:39
HARDBOWER see HAUTBOWER, HOUTBOWER
HARDBOWER, David S.; WM; b. 7 Nov 1889 in Ffx; father: Jos.
    HARDBOWER; occ: farmer; res: Ffx; mother: Mary HARDBOWER;
    inf: Jos. HARDBOWER, father; pg:ln: 182:41
HARDBOWER, M. E.; WF; b. 9 May 1880 in Ffx; father: Jos.
    HARDBOWER; occ: farmer; res: Ffx; mother: Mary; inf: J.
    HARDBOWER, father; pg:ln: 128:50
HARDBOWER, not named; WM; b. 14 Mar 1895 nr Alexandria; father:
    Joseph HARDBOWER; occ: gardener and farmer; res: ___; mother:
    Mary HARDBOWER; inf: mother [originally written as
    HARDBOWER, noted to see line 50 page 128 Fairfax Co.]; pg:ln:
    222:28
HARDIN, O.; WF; b. 4 Jun 1883 in Falls Church; father: Anthony
    HARDIN; occ: farmer; res: Falls Church; mother: Sarah HARDIN; inf:
    father; pg:ln: 139:33
HARLEY, Berta Dernia?; WF; b. 11 May 1896 in Masons Neck; father:
    Columbus HARLEY; occ: fisherman; res: Masons Neck; mother:
    Irene HARLEY; inf: mother; pg:ln: 230:54

HARLEY, L.; WF; b. 15 May 1880 in Ffx; father: Isaiah HARLEY; occ: farmer; res: Ffx; mother: Louisa; inf: I. HARLEY, father; pg:ln: 128:48

HARLEY, Nellie; WF; b. 18 Jan 1892 in Masons Neck; father: Harry HARLEY; occ: farmer; res: Masons Neck; mother: Mamie HARLEY; inf: father; pg:ln: 207:69

HARMAN, Basil; CF; b. 29 Jan 1895 in Centreville; father: ___; occ: ___; res: Centreville; mother: Fannie HARMAN; inf: mother; pg:ln: 222:30

HARMAN, Maggie; WF; b. 1 Nov 1891 nr Burke Sta.; father: Charles HARMAN; occ: farmer; res: nr Burke Sta.; mother: Effie HARMON; inf: parents; pg:ln: 193:15

HARMAN, Walter; WM; b. 5 Sep 1881 in Ffx; father: Jno. HARMAN; occ: farmer; res: Ffx; mother: Mary HARMAN; inf: Jno. HARMAN, father; pg:ln: 132:22

HARMON, ___; WM; b. 7 Nov 1890 in ___; father: John HARMON; occ: farmer; res: Ffx; mother: Mary HARMON; inf: John HARMON, father; pg:ln: 186:50

HARMON, Annie; WF; b. 5 Sep 1888 in Ffx; father: Chas. HARMON; occ: farmer; res: Ffx; mother: Effie HARMON; inf: Chas. HARMON, father; pg:ln: 170:32

HARMON, Elizabeth; WF; b. 13 Mar 1887 in Ffx; father: Charles HARMON; occ: laborer; res: Ffx; mother: Ella HARMON; inf: Charles HARMON, father; pg:ln: 167:48

HARMON, Katie; WF; b. 6 Jun 1890 in ___; father: Charles HARMON; occ: farmer; res: Ffx; mother: Eppa HARMON; inf: Chas. HARMON, father; pg:ln: 186:51

HARMON, Laura E.; WF; b. 13 May 1887 in Ffx; father: Jno. R. HARMON; occ: laborer; res: Ffx; mother: Mary HARMON; inf: Jno. R. HARMON, father; pg:ln: 167:47

HARMON, Mary; WF; b. 10 Nov 1888 in Ffx; father: John HARMON; occ: farmer; res: Ffx; mother: Mary HARMON; inf: John HARMON, father; pg:ln: 170:33

HARMON, not named (dead); WM; b. 23 Jan 1892 nr Burke Sta.; father: John HARMON; occ: farmer; res: nr Burke Sta.; mother: Mary HARMON; inf: mother; pg:ln: 209:50

HAROVER, George; WM; b. 10 Oct 1896 nr Lorton Sta.; father: R. L. HAROVER; occ: farmer; res: Lorton Sta.; mother: Alice HAROVER; inf: father; pg:ln: 230:58

HARPER, Cath'e. L.; CF; b. 30 Jan 1893 in ___; father: Jas. HARPER; occ: ___; res: ___; mother: Fannie HARPER; inf: Jas. HARPER, father; pg:ln: 214:49

HARPER, Walter; WM; b. 22 Apr 1893 nr Franconia; father: Wm. HARPER; occ: R. Road hand; res: nr Franconia; mother: Ida HARPER; inf: parents; pg:ln: 211:55

HARRING, Chister W.; WM; b. 30 Jul 1894 in Ffx; father: Chas. R. HARRING; occ: farmer; res: Ffx; mother: E. M. HARRING; inf: C. R. HARRING, father; pg:ln: 218:55

HARRIS, Albert C.; CM; b. 14 Apr 1893 nr Clifton Sta.; father: John
HARRIS; occ: farmer; res: nr Clifton; mother: Ella HARRIS; inf:
parents; pg:ln: 211:56

HARRIS, Albert; CM; b. 15 Aug 1888 in Ffx; father: Levi HARRIS; occ:
laborer; res: Ffx; mother: Matilda HARRIS; inf: Levi HARRIS, father;
pg:ln: 171:37

HARRIS, Alfred Lewis; CM; b. 14 May 1895 in Bull Run; father: Geo. W.
HARRIS; occ: farmer; res: Bull Run; mother: Narcissa HARRIS; inf:
mother; pg:ln: 222:19

HARRIS, Alice; CF; b. 10 Apr 1896 nr Centreville; father: Jessie
HARRIS; occ: farmer; res: nr Centreville; mother: Lucy HARRIS; inf:
father; pg:ln: 230:69

HARRIS, Annie; CF; b. 10 Apr 1896 nr Bull Run P.O.; father: Joseph
HARRIS; occ: farmer; res: nr Bull Run; mother: Annie HARRIS; inf:
father; pg:ln: 230:67

HARRIS, Bernice [Bernard]; CM; b. 2 Apr 1892 in Bull Run; father:
Joseph HARRIS; occ: farmer; res: Bull Run; mother: Annie HARRIS;
inf: mother; pg:ln: 206:22

HARRIS, Bessie; CF; b. 24 Jul 1885 in Ffx; father: Obed HARRIS; occ:
farmer; res: Ffx; mother: Margt. HARRIS; inf: Obed HARRIS, father;
pg:ln: 156:31

HARRIS, Geo.; CM; b. 1 Oct 1889 in Ffx; father: Alfred HARRIS; occ:
farmer; res: Ffx; mother: Martha HARRIS; inf: Alfred HARRIS, father;
pg:ln: 182:46

HARRIS, Harriet; CF; b. 14 Jan 1889 in Ffx; father: Chas. HARRIS; occ:
farmer; res: Ffx; mother: Alice HARRIS; inf: C. HARRIS, father;
pg:ln: 178:49

HARRIS, Henry; CM; b. 14 Apr 1889 in Ffx; father: Joseph HARRIS;
occ: farmer; res: Ffx; mother: Annie HARRIS; inf: Joseph HARRIS,
father; pg:ln: 182:47

HARRIS, Herman; CM; b. 23 Dec 1891 nr Chantilly; father: Obid
HARRIS Jr.; occ: laborer; res: nr Bull Run; mother: Minnie HARRIS;
inf: parent; pg:ln: 197:05

HARRIS, Jane E.; CF; b. 15 Jul 1889 in Ffx; father: W. HARRIS; occ:
farmer; res: Ffx; mother: Florence HARRIS; inf: Wm. HARRIS,
father; pg:ln: 182:45

HARRIS, Jas. A.; WM; b. 6 Dec 1890 in ___; father: Jas. HARRIS; occ:
carpenter; res: Ffx; mother: Carrie HARRIS; inf: Jas. HARRIS,
father; pg:ln: 186:52

HARRIS, John; CM; b. 1 Jun 1893 in ___; father: C. B. HARRIS; occ:
___; res: ___; mother: M. L. HARRIS; inf: C. B. HARRIS, father;
pg:ln: 214:51

HARRIS, Laura; CF; b. 6 May 1884 in Ffx; father: not known; occ:
farmer; res: Ffx; mother: Laura HARRIS; inf: Nimrod HARRIS,
grandfather; pg:ln: 147:34

HARRIS, Lester; CM; b. 14 Feb 1893 in ___; father: W. HARRIS; occ:
___; res: ___; mother: Cora HARRIS; inf: W. HARRIS, father; pg:ln:
214:50

HARRIS, Luther; CM; b. 10 May 1895 nr Chantilly; father: Levi HARRIS; occ: farmer; res: nr Chantilly; mother: Matilda HARRIS; inf: mother; pg:ln: 222:21

HARRIS, Mary Ellen; CF; b. 9 Oct 1896 nr Clifton Sta.; father: Henry HARRIS; occ: rail roading; res: nr Clifton Sta.; mother: Lillie HARRIS; inf: father; pg:ln: 230:62

HARRIS, not named; CF; b. 1 May 1896 nr Hayfield; father: Edward HARRIS; occ: laborer; res: nr Hayfield; mother: Sarah HARRIS; inf: mother; pg:ln: 230:65

HARRIS, not named; CM; b. 10 Nov 1882 in Providence; father: J. B. HARRIS; occ: laborer; res: Providence; mother: Maria V. HARRIS; inf: father; pg:ln: 134:29

HARRIS, Sterling Rufus; CM; b. 9 Mar 1895 in Bull Run; father: William HARRIS; occ: farmer; res: Bull Run; mother: Florence HARRIS; inf: mother; pg:ln: 222:29

HARRIS, Virginia; CF; b. 5 Jun 1892 in Ffx; father: Chas. HARRIS; occ: laborer; res: Ffx; mother: Maggie HARRIS; inf: Chas. HARRIS, father; pg:ln: 203:49

HARRIS, Walter; CM; b. 10 Jul 1895 in Bull Run; father: Alfred HARRIS; occ: farmer; res: Bull Run; mother: Martha HARRIS; inf: mother; pg:ln: 222:20

HARRIS, Walter; CM; b. 14 Sep 1883 in Falls Church; father: Jno. H. HARRIS; occ: laborer; res: Falls Church; mother: Maria HARRIS; inf: father; pg:ln: 140:40

HARRISON, ___; WF; b. 30 Aug 1885 in Ffx; father: Jas. M. HARRISON; occ: farmer; res: Ffx; mother: Hannah HARRISON; inf: J. M. HARRISON, father; pg:ln: 156:32

HARRISON, ___; WM; b. 10 Nov 1882 in Ffx; father: Wm. HARRISON; occ: farmer; res: Ffx; mother: Julia HARRISON; inf: Wm. HARRISON, father; pg:ln: 136:36

HARRISON, Albert; WM; b. 16 Jun 1892 in Washington DC; father: Chs. M. HARRISON; occ: fisherman; res: Masons Neck; mother: Fannie HARRISON; inf: father; pg:ln: 207:72

HARRISON, Albt.; CM; b. 3 Sep 1893 in ___; father: Peter HARRISON; occ: ___; res: ___; mother: Ida HARRISON; inf: P. HARRISON, father; pg:ln: 214:48

HARRISON, Alma; WF; b. 4 Mar 1887 in Ffx; father: J. M. HARRISON; occ: farmer; res: Ffx; mother: Hannah HARRISON; inf: J. M. HARRISON, father; pg:ln: 167:51

HARRISON, Amos; WM; b. 7 Jul 1883 in Ffx; father: J. M. HARRISON; occ: farmer; res: Ffx; mother: Hannah HARRISON; inf: J. M. HARRISON, father; pg:ln: 144:37

HARRISON, Amy; WF; b. 29 Nov 1888 in Ffx; father: John HARRISON; occ: farmer; res: Ffx; mother: Laura HARRISON; inf: J. HARRISON, father; pg:ln: 174:39

HARRISON, Atta Virginia; WF; b. 6 Aug 1892 nr Centreville; father: Wm. H. HARRISON; occ: farmer; res: nr Centreville; mother: Annah HARRISON; inf: father; pg:ln: 208:12

HARRISON, Bertha Rena; WF; b. 25 Aug 1893 nr Burke Sta.; father: W. H. HARRISON; occ: farmer; res: nr Burke Sa.; mother: Mary J. HARRISON; inf: parents; pg:ln: 211:48

HARRISON, Bessie; WF; b. 19 Mar 1882 in West End; father: Wm. H. HARRISON; occ: laborer; res: West End; mother: Cora HARRISON; inf: father; pg:ln: 134:25

HARRISON, Franklin; WM; b. 22 Jul 1884 in Seminary; father: Wm. H. HARRISON; occ: laborer; res: Seminary; mother: Cora HARRISON; inf: father; pg:ln: 150:47

HARRISON, George; WM; b. 1 May 1890 in ___; father: Wm. HARRISON; occ: farmer; res: Ffx; mother: Mary HARRISON; inf: Wm. HARRISON, father; pg:ln: 186:42

HARRISON, Grace A.; WF; b. 22 Mar 1889 in Ffx; father: C. M. HARRISON; occ: farmer; res: Ffx; mother: Fannie HARRISON; inf: C. M. HARRISON, father; pg:ln: 182:42

HARRISON, Grace Virginia; WF; b. 3 Jan 1892 in Colchester; father: Frank HARRISON; occ: fisherman; res: Colchester; mother: Ella HARRISON; inf: mother; pg:ln: 209:51

HARRISON, Hannah T.; WF; b. 6 Nov 1888 in Ffx; father: J. M. HARRISON; occ: farmer; res: Ffx; mother: Hannah HARRISON; inf: J. M. HARRISON, father; pg:ln: 170:30

HARRISON, Henry McKinley; WM; b. 13 May 1896 nr Sideburn Sta.; father: J. M. HARRISON; occ: farmer; res: nr Sideburn Sta.; mother: Hannah HARRISON; inf: father; pg:ln: 230:56

HARRISON, Jas. Lewis; WM; b. 6 Nov 1887 in Ffx; father: Arthur HARRISON; occ: farmer; res: Ffx; mother: Carry HARRISON; inf: A. HARRISON, father; pg:ln: 161:57

HARRISON, Jas. W.; WM; b. 15 Jul 1883 in Providence; father: James W. HARRISON; occ: laborer; res: Providence; mother: Laura HARRISON; inf: father; pg:ln: 140:39

HARRISON, Jas. W.; WM; b. 24 Jun 1882 in Providence; father: J. W. HARRISON; occ: laborer; res: Providence; mother: Laura V. HARRISON; inf: father; pg:ln: 134:28

HARRISON, Julian (twin); WM; b. 27 Feb 1895 nr Burnside Sta.; father: J. M. HARRISON; occ: farmer; res: nr Burnside Sta.; mother: Hannah HARRISON; inf: father; pg:ln: 222:22

HARRISON, Kenneth (twin); WM; b. 27 Feb 1895 nr Burnside Sta.; father: J. M. HARRISON; occ: farmer; res: nr Burnside Sta.; mother: Hannah HARRISON; inf: father; pg:ln: 222:22

HARRISON, Lucy; WF; b. 5 Mar 1881 in Ffx; father: Geo. H. HARRISON; occ: farmer; res: Ffx; mother: Mary HARRISON; inf: G. H. HARRISON, father; pg:ln: 132:21

HARRISON, Luther C.; WM; b. 26 Jan 1889 in Ffx; father: W. HARRISON; occ: farmer; res: Ffx; mother: Emiley HARRISON; inf: W. HARRISON, father; pg:ln: 178:56

HARRISON, M.; WF; b. 25 Nov 1880 in Ffx; father: W. G. HARRISON; occ: farmer; res: Ffx; mother: Johannah; inf: W. G. HARRISON, father; pg:ln: 127:39

HARRISON, Maggie; WF; b. 30 Jun 1895 in Mason's Neck; father: Chas. HARRISON; occ: fisherman; res: Mason's Neck; mother: Fannie HARRISON; inf: mother; pg:ln: 222:27

HARRISON, Mary E.; WF; b. 1 Jun 1885 in Lincolnville; father: J. W. HARRISON; occ: laborer; res: Lincolnville; mother: Laura V. HARRISON; inf: father; pg:ln: 152:31

HARRISON, Mary; WF; b. 15 Aug 1887 in Ffx; father: Wm. H. HARRISON; occ: laborer; res: Ffx; mother: Mary J. HARRISON; inf: W. H. HARRISON, father; pg:ln: 167:49

[HARRISON], not named (dead); WM; b. __ Dec 1891 nr Burke Sta.; father: Wm. HARRISON; occ: farmer; res: nr Burke Sta.; mother: M. HARRISON; inf: parents; pg:ln: 193:17

HARRISON, not named; WF; b. 1 Dec 1880 in Ffx; father: G. H. HARRISON; occ: farmer; res: Ffx; mother: Mary; inf: G. H. HARRISON, father; pg:ln: 128:44

HARRISON, not named; WM; b. 11 May 1883 in Dranesville; father: Randolph HARRISON; occ: farmer; res: Dranesville; mother: M. HARRISON; inf: father; pg:ln: 140:44

HARRISON, Rebecca; WF; b. 20 Jan 1884 in Ffx; father: Frank HARRISON; occ: farmer; res: Ffx; mother: Ella HARRISON; inf: Frank HARRISON, father; pg:ln: 147:38

HARRISON, Russell; WM; b. 1 Jun 1890 in ___; father: J. M. HARRISON; occ: farmer; res: Ffx; mother: Hannah E. HARRISON; inf: J. M. HARRISON, father; pg:ln: 186:43

HARRISON, W. C.; WM; b. 19 Apr 1883 in Dranesville; father: E. M. HARRISON; occ: farmer; res: Dranesville; mother: Elizabeth HARRISON; inf: father; pg:ln: 140:43

HARRISON, Walter; WM; b. 26 Oct 1890 in ___; father: Charles HARRISON; occ: farmer; res: Ffx; mother: Fannie HARRISON; inf: Chas. HARRISON, father; pg:ln: 186:44

HARRISON, William ; WM; b. 15 Dec 1886 in Bailey's X Rds.; father: W. H. HARRISON; occ: gardener; res: Bailey's X Rds; mother: C. F. HARRISON; inf: father; pg:ln: 158:22

HARRISON, Wilmer; WM; b. 6 Jan 1884 in Ffx; father: Jas. A. HARRISON; occ: farmer; res: Ffx; mother: Martha C. HARRISON; inf: J. A. HARRISON, father; pg:ln: 147:37

HARRISON, Wm. Clayton; WM; b. 2 Nov 1895 nr Centreville; father: W. G. HARRISON; occ: farmer; res: nr Centreville; mother: G. W. HARRISON; inf: father; pg:ln: 222:23

HARRISON, Wm. Edward; WM; b. 28 Feb 1887 in Ffx; father: Charles HARRISON; occ: laborer; res: Ffx; mother: Martha HARRISON; inf: Charles HARRISON, father; pg:ln: 167:50

HARRISON, Wm. I.; WM; b. 9 Mar 1889 in Ffx; father: W. H. HARRISON; occ: farmer; res: Ffx; mother: Mary HARRISON; inf: W. H. HARRISON, father; pg:ln: 182:43

HARROD, Chas.; CM; b. 5 Jan 1891 in Ffx; father: Chas. HARROD; occ: farmer; res: Ffx; mother: Alice HARROD; inf: C. HARROD, father; pg:ln: 198:35

HARROLD, Geo. L.; CM; b. 26 Aug 1883 in Providence Dist.; father: Chas. W. HARROLD; occ: laborer; res: Providence Dist.; mother: Alice HARROLD; inf: father; pg:ln: 140:41

HARROLD, Robt. A.; CM; b. 2 Sep 1884 in Seminary; father: Robt. A. HARROLD; occ: laborer; res: Seminary; mother: Maggie HARROLD; inf: father; pg:ln: 150:49

HATCHER, Henrietta; CF; b. 24 Nov 1880 in Providence; father: William HATCHER; occ: laborer; res: Providence; mother: Sallie HATCHER; inf: father; pg:ln: 124:29

HATCHER, Jennie E.; CF; b. 4 Jun 1891 in Ffx; father: Wm. HATCHER; occ: farmer; res: Ffx; mother: Sallie HATCHER; inf: Wm. HATCHER, father; pg:ln: 199:45

HATCHER, Rebecca; CF; b. 28 Aug 1883 in Providence Dist.; father: William HATCHER; occ: laborer; res: Providence Dist.; mother: Sallie HATCHER; inf: father; pg:ln: 140:42

HATCHER, Sallie; CF; b. 29 Nov 1889 in Ffx; father: W. HATCHER; occ: farmer; res: Ffx; mother: Sallie HATCHER; inf: W. HATCHER, father; pg:ln: 178:51

HAUTBOWER see HARDBOWER, HOUTBOWER

HAUTBOWER, Elizbt.; WM [WF]; b. 7 Dec 1882 in Ffx; father: Wm. HAUTBOWER; occ: farmer; res: Ffx; mother: Virginia HAUTBOWER; inf: Wm. HAUTBOWER, father; pg:ln: 136:35

HAUTBOWER, Emma; WF; b. 27 Dec 1891 nr Alexandria; father: Joseph HAUTBOWER; occ: farmer; res: nr Alexandria; mother: Mary HAUTBOWER; inf: parents; pg:ln: 195:07

HAUTBOWER, Francis; WF; b. 5 Aug 1890 in ___; father: Wm. HAUTBOWER; occ: farmer; res: Ffx; mother: Virginia HAUTBOWER; inf: Wm. HAUTBOWER, father; pg:ln: 186:49

HAUXHURST, Adrian; WM; b. 14 Jul 1891 in Ffx; father: E. E. HAUXHURST; occ: farmer; res: Ffx; mother: E. O. HAUXHURST; inf: E. E. HAUXHURST, father; pg:ln: 199:44

HAUXHURST, Bertha; WF; b. 14 Aug 1887 in Ffx; father: E. E. HAUXHURST; occ: merchant; res: Ffx; mother: Emma HAUXHURST; inf: E. E. HAUXHURST, father; pg:ln: 167:53

HAWLEY, Geo. W.; WM; b. 10 Oct 1884 in Ffx; father: Gordon HAWLEY; occ: farmer; res: Ffx; mother: Lora HAWLEY; inf: G. HAWLEY, father; pg:ln: 147:32

HAWLEY, Mollie; WF; b. 5 Jan 1891 in Ffx; father: Richd. N. HAWLEY; occ: farmer; res: Ffx; mother: Virginia HAWLEY; inf: R. N. HAWLEY, father; pg:ln: 199:42

HAYNES, Chas. Wm.; WM; b. 20 Jan 1888 in Ffx; father: James HAYNES; occ: farmer; res: Ffx; mother: Mary C. HAYNES; inf: Jas. HAYNES, father; pg:ln: 170:31

HAYNES, James Edward; WM; b. 19 Feb 1891 nr Ravensworth; father: James HAYNES; occ: carpenter; res: nr Ravensworth; mother: Mary P. HAYNES; inf: parents; pg:ln: 193:16

HAYWOOD, Catharine; WF; b. 11 May 1893 nr Alex.; father: Frank
HAYWOOD; occ: laborer; res: nr Alex.; mother: Lena HAYWOOD;
inf: parents; pg:ln: 211:52

HEAD, A. S.; WM; b. 9 Dec 1884 in Bailey's X Roads; father: Geo. J.
HEAD; occ: mechanic; res: Bailey's X Roads; mother: Mary HEAD;
inf: father; pg:ln: 150:46

HEAD, Andrew S.; WM; b. 1 Feb 1883 in Falls Church; father: Geo. J.
HEAD; occ: mechanic; res: Falls Church; mother: Mary HEAD; inf:
father; pg:ln: 139:34

HEAD, Geo. F.; WM; b. 16 Dec 1885 in Bailey's X Roads; father: Geo.
HEAD; occ: mechanic; res: Bailey's X Roads; mother: Mary A.
HEAD; inf: father; pg:ln: 152:28

HEAD, Henry M.; WM; b. 6 Nov 1880 in Vienna; father: William HEAD;
occ: farmer; res: Vienna; mother: Margaret HEAD; inf: father; pg:ln:
124:26

HEAD, John; WM; b. 19 Jul 1888 in Ffx; father: Jas. M. HEAD; occ:
farmer; res: Ffx; mother: Annie HEAD; inf: J. M. HEAD, father; pg:ln:
174:41

HEARNS, Jas. A.; CM; b. 26 Jul 1894 in Ffx; father: Rich'd. HEARN;
occ: farmer; res: Ffx; mother: Dolly HEARNS; inf: Rich'd. HEARN,
father; pg:ln: 218:51

HEATH, ___; WM; b. 17 Sep 1882 in Langley; father: Isaac N. HEATH;
occ: farmer; res: Langley; mother: ___ HEATH; inf: father; pg:ln:
134:22

HEATH, Bertha; WF; b. 29 Jan 1883 in Providence; father: Isaac N.
HEATH; occ: farmer; res: Providence; mother: Almeda HEATH; inf:
father; pg:ln: 140:37

HEATH, Blanche; WF; b. 8 Nov 1887 in Ffx; father: Isaac N. HEATH;
occ: farmer; res: Ffx; mother: Armenia HEATH; inf: I. N. HEATH,
father; pg:ln: 161:52

HEATH, Isaac; WM; b. 7 Jun 1885 in Lincolnville; father: I. N. HEATH;
occ: farmer; res: Lincolnville; mother: Alice HEATH; inf: father; pg:ln:
152:32

[HEDGMAN], not named; CF; b. 10 Jan 1891 nr Alexandria; father:
Henry HEDGMAN; occ: laborer; res: nr Alexandria; mother: Annie
HEDGMAN; inf: parent; pg:ln: 196:09

HENDERSON, ___ (dead); CF; b. 1 Jul 1888 in Ffx; father: John
HENDERSON; occ: laborer; res: Ffx; mother: Jennie HENDERSON;
inf: Jno. HENDERSON, father; pg:ln: 170:36

HENDERSON, Chas.; WM; b. 6 Feb 1894 in Ffx; father: Chas. F.
HENDERSON; occ: farmer; res: Ffx; mother: E. V. HENDERSON;
inf: C. F. HENDERSON, father; pg:ln: 218:53

HENDERSON, Elizabt.; CF; b. 15 Dec 1884 in Ffx; father: Jno.
HENDERSON; occ: farmer; res: Ffx; mother: Jennie HENDERSON;
inf: Jno. HENDERSON, father; pg:ln: 147:33

HENDERSON, Elmer L.; WM; b. 12 Jul 1889 in Ffx; father: Jno. R.
HENDERSON; occ: farmer; res: Ffx; mother: Emiley HENDERSON;
inf: J. R. HENDERSON, father; pg:ln: 178:55

HENDERSON, Garland R.; WM; b. 1 Aug 1891 in Ffx; father: Wm. H.
HENDERSON; occ: farmer; res: Ffx; mother: Mary E.
HENDERSON; inf: Wm. H. HENDERSON, father; pg:ln: 199:38
HENDERSON, Ira L.; WM; b. 12 Nov 1888 in Ffx; father: Chas. F.
HENDERSON; occ: farmer; res: Ffx; mother: Emma B.
HENDERSON; inf: C. F. HENDERSON, father; pg:ln: 174:44
HENDERSON, Jessie; CM; b. 28 Mar 1886 in Falls Ch.; father: Henry
HENDERSON; occ: farmer; res: Falls Ch.; mother: Sarah
HENDERSON; inf: father; pg:ln: 158:23
HENDERSON, Jos. E.; CM; b. 12 Nov 1883 in Providence Dist.; father:
Albert HENDERSON; occ: farmer; res: Providence; mother: Emma
HENDERSON; inf: father; pg:ln: 139:35
HENDERSON, Joseph; WM; b. 25 Nov 1890 in ___; father: Luther
HENDERSON; occ: blacksmith; res: Ffx; mother: Elizabt.
HENDERSON; inf: L. HENDERSON, father; pg:ln: 186:48
HENDERSON, Lucinda; CF; b. 1 Aug 1892 in Prince Wm. Co.; father:
John HENDERSON; occ: laborer; res: nr Centreville; mother: Lottie
HENDERSON; inf: mother; pg:ln: 206:24
HENDERSON, Mary; CF; b. 1 May 1888 in Ffx; father: Jas.
HENDERSON; occ: farmer; res: Ffx; mother: Martha HENDERSON;
inf: J. HENDERSON, father; pg:ln: 174:42
HENDERSON, Mattie; CF; b. 9 Jan 1887 in Ffx; father: Jas. H.
HENDERSON; occ: farmer; res: Ffx; mother: M. HENDERSON; inf:
J. H. HENDERSON, father; pg:ln: 161:53
HENDERSON, Nellie; CF; b. 8 Jun 1891 in Ffx; father: Frank
HENDERSON; occ: farmer; res: Ffx; mother: Bertie HENDERSON;
inf: F. HENDERSON, father; pg:ln: 198:34
HENDERSON, not named (dead); CM; b. 2 Sep 1882 in Falls Church;
father: Henry HENDERSON; occ: laborer; res: Falls Ch; mother:
Sarah HENDERSON; inf: father; pg:ln: 135:76
HENDERSON, not named (dead); CM; b. 25 Dec 1892 nr Centreville;
father: Sam HENDERSON; occ: laborer; res: nr Centreville; mother:
Emma HENDERSON; inf: mother; pg:ln: 206:23
HENDERSON, not named; CF; b. 11 Apr 1883 in Dranesville; father:
Chas. W. HENDERSON; occ: farmer; res: Dranesville; mother: Mary
E. HENDERSON; inf: father; pg:ln: 140:45
HENDERSON, Ora M.; WF; b. 12 Nov 1887 in Ffx; father: J. R.
HENDERSON; occ: farmer; res: Ffx; mother: Emma HENDERSON;
inf: J. R. HENDERSON, father; pg:ln: 161:59
HENDERSON, Peachey; WM; b. 14 Jun 1896 nr Riverside Park; father:
Wm. P. HENDERSON; occ: farmer; res: nr Riverside Park; mother:
Hester HENDERSON; inf: mother; pg:ln: 230:55
HENDERSON, Philip; CM; b. 16 Mar 1889 in Ffx; father: Saml.
HENDERSON; occ: farmer; res: Ffx; mother: Emma HENDERSON;
inf: S. HEND[ER]SON, father; pg:ln: 182:44
HENDERSON, Sallie; WF; b. 31 Dec 1892 in Ffx; father: Henry
HENDERSON; occ: farmer; res: Ffx; mother: Sallie HENDERSON;
inf: H. HENDERSON, father; pg:ln: 203:53

HENDERSON, Viola; CF; b. 12 Oct 1894 in Ffx; father: Willie
HENDERSON; occ: farmer; res: Ffx; mother: Florence WEST [?]; inf:
Jno. CARTER, friend; pg:ln: 218:58

HENDERSON, William; CM; b. 10 Sep 1884 in Prov.; father: Henry
HENDERSON; occ: laborer; res: Prov.; mother: Sarah
HENDERSON; inf: father; pg:ln: 150:50

HICKS, Joseph Earnest; WM; b. 10 Oct 1893 nr Colchester; father:
Ruben HICKS; occ: fisherman; res: nr Colchester; mother: Martha
HICKS; inf: parents; pg:ln: 211:47

HICKS, Philip P.; WM; b. 25 Jul 1896 in ___; father: Chas. E. HICKS;
occ: farmer; res: Ffx; mother: May HICKS; inf: C. E. HICKS, father;
pg:ln: 226:57

HINSCH, Henrietta; WF; b. 7 Jun 1893 in ___; father: Geo. A. HINSCH;
occ: ___; res: ___; mother: Sadie HINSCH; inf: G. A. HINSCH,
father; pg:ln: 214:42

HINSON, W. Roy; WM; b. 9 Jun 1896 nr Burke Sta.; father: A. J.
HINSON; occ: farmer; res: nr Burke Sta.; mother: Annie May
HINSON; inf: mother; pg:ln: 230:59

HIRST, Lucy Mildred; WF; b. 15 Sep 1892 nr Alexandria; father: T. M. F.
HIRST; occ: farmer; res: Evergreen; mother: Emma H. HIRST; inf:
father; pg:ln: 207:70

HODGKINS, Sophia; WF; b. 29 May 1887 in Ffx; father: J. B.
HODGKINS; occ: farmer; res: Ffx; mother: M. G. HODGKINS; inf: J.
B. HODGKINS, father; pg:ln: 161:55

HOGELAND, Laurence; WM; b. 13 Jul 1886 in Falls Ch.; father: J. B.
HOGELAND; occ: carpenter; res: Falls Ch.; mother: Virginia
HOGELAND; inf: father; pg:ln: 158:24

HOHTELIN, Wm. C.; WM; b. 3 Jul 1880 in Falls Church; father: W. H.
HOHTELIN; occ: farmer; res: Falls Church; mother: Ada M.
HOHTELIN; inf: father; pg:ln: 124:28

HOLDEN, ___; WF; b. 23 Jul 1885 in Ffx; father: Thos. HOLDEN; occ:
farmer; res: Ffx; mother: Bell HOLDEN; inf: T. HOLDEN, father;
pg:ln: 156:28

HOLDEN, Geo. R.; WM; b. 21 Nov 1888 in Ffx; father: Thos. HOLDEN;
occ: farmer; res: Ffx; mother: Bell J. HOLDEN; inf: Thos. HOLDEN,
father; pg:ln: 171:39

HOLDEN, Josephine; WF; b. 30 Jun 1882 in Ffx; father: Thos.
HOLDEN; occ: farmer; res: Ffx; mother: Belle HOLDEN; inf: T.
HOLDEN, father; pg:ln: 136:32

HOLDEN, Josephine; WF; b. 30 Jun 1883 in Ffx; father: Thos.
HOLDEN; occ: farmer; res: Ffx; mother: Bell J. HOLDEN; inf: Thos.
HOLDEN, father; pg:ln: 144:34

HOLDEN, Phebe; WF; b. 29 Oct 1880 in Ffx; father: Thos. HOLDEN;
occ: farmer; res: Ffx; mother: Phebe; inf: T. HOLDEN, father; pg:ln:
128:41

HOLLAND, Edna; CF; b. 30 Apr 1896 nr Woodlawn; father: Robert
HOLLAND; occ: laborer; res: nr Woodburn; mother: Grace
HOLLAND; inf: father; pg:ln: 230:66

HOLLAND, Essie Roberta; CF; b. 29 Sep 1895 nr Woodlawn; father: W. W. HOLLAND; occ: farmer; res: Woodlawn; mother: Elizabeth HOLLAND; inf: mother; pg:ln: 222:31

HOLLAND, Fannie; CF; b. 11 May 1890 in ___; father: Robt. HOLLAND; occ: farmer; res: Ffx; mother: Gracie HOLLAND; inf: R. HOLLAND, father; pg:ln: 186:58

HOLLAND, Geo. Tilman; CM; b. 23 Apr 1895 nr Woodlawn; father: Robert rHOLLAND; occ: farmer; res: Woodlawn; mother: Grace HOLLAND; inf: mother; pg:ln: 222:32

HOLLAND, Idelia; CF; b. 5 Mar 1881 in Ffx; father: Robt. L. HOLLAND; occ: farmer; res: Ffx; mother: Grace HOLLAND; inf: R. L. HOLLAND, father; pg:ln: 132:23

HOLLAND, William; CM; b. 5 Jun 1887 in Ffx; father: Wm. W. HOLLAND; occ: farmer; res: Ffx; mother: Elizabt. HOLLAND; inf: W. W. HOLLAND, father; pg:ln: 167:55

HOLLINS, Hampton; CM; b. 30 Apr 1884 in Prov.; father: Chesley HOLLINS; occ: labor; res: Prov.; mother: Emily HOLLINS; inf: father; pg:ln: 150:53

HOLLINS, Loid; CM; b. 1 Aug 1882 in Falls Church; father: Chesly HOLLINS; occ: laborer; res: Falls Church; mother: Martha HOLLINS; inf: father; pg:ln: 134:26

HOLMES, ___; CM; b. 10 May 1883 in Ffx; father: Taliver HOLMS; occ: farmer; res: Ffx; mother: Cora HOLMS; inf: T. HOLMES, father; pg:ln: 144:42

HOLMES, Jesse B.; CM; b. 30 Mar 1885 in Ffx; father: Taliver HOLMES; occ: farmer; res: Ffx; mother: Cora HOLMES; inf: T. HOLMES, father; pg:ln: 156:33

HONESTY, B. L.; CF; b. 23 Nov 1892 in Ffx; father: C. C. HONESTY; occ: laborer; res: Ffx; mother: Laura V. HONESTY; inf: C. C. HONESTY, father; pg:ln: 203:50

HONESTY, Blanch; CF; b. 23 Nov 1893 in ___; father: C. C. HONESTY; occ: ___; res: ___; mother: Virginia HONESTY; inf: C. C. HONESTY, father; pg:ln: 214:47

HONESTY, Columbus; CM; b. 23 Dec 1894 in Ffx; father: Columb's. HONESTY; occ: farmer; res: Ffx; mother: Laura HONESTY; inf: C. HONESTY, father; pg:ln: 218:59

HONESTY, Morris; CM; b. 13 Dec 1884 in Falls Church; father: Asbury HONESTY; occ: farmer; res: Falls Church; mother: Amanda HONESTY; inf: father; pg:ln: 150:48

HONESTY, Rosa; CF; b. 5 Dec 1892 in Ffx; father: W. HONESTY; occ: laborer; res: Ffx; mother: Martha HONESTY; inf: W. HONESTY, father; pg:ln: 203:48

HONESTY. Henry H.; CM; b. 5 Jun 1891 in Ffx; father: C. C. HONESTY; occ: farmer; res: Ffx; mother: Laura HONESTY; inf: C. C. HONESTY, father; pg:ln: 199:46

HOOF, Asberry Fairfax; WM; b. 6 Sep 1893 nr Clifton Sta.; father: E. L. HOOF; occ: farmer; res: nr Clifton Sta.; mother: Victoria HOOF; inf: parents; pg:ln: 211:50

HOOFF, Annie L.; WF; b. 26 Oct 1890 in ___; father: E. L. HOOFF; occ:
R. Rd. conductor; res: Ffx; mother: Victoria HOOFF; inf: E. L.
HOOFF, father; pg:ln: 186:53

HORN, Elsey; WF; b. 24 Aug 1888 in Ffx; father: Theodore HORN; occ:
farmer; res: Ffx; mother: Minnie HORN; inf: T. HORN, father; pg:ln:
174:37

HORNBECK, Sarah M.; WF; b. 1 Mar 1887 in Ffx; father: Chas.
HORNBECK; occ: farmer; res: Ffx; mother: Sarah HORNBECK; inf:
C. HORNBECK, father; pg:ln: 161:54

HORSEMAN, not named; WF; b. 17 Jul 1883 in Vienna; father: Thos.
HORSEMAN; occ: farmer; res: Vienna; mother: Emma HORSEMAN;
inf: father; pg:ln: 139:36

HORSMAN, Milton; WM; b. 13 Nov 1894 in Ffx; father: Jas. T.
HORSMAN; occ: farmer; res: Ffx; mother: Emma HORSMAN; inf: J.
T. HORSMAN, father; pg:ln: 218:52

HORTON, Emma; CF; b. 3 Oct 1892 nr Centreville; father: Buck
HORTON; occ: farmer; res: nr Centreville; mother: Esther HORTON;
inf: mother; pg:ln: 206:21

HORTON, Ether Rebecca; WF; b. 9 Mar 1896 nr Mt. Vernon; father:
Samuel H. HORTON; occ: farmer; res: nr Mt. Vernon; mother:
Adeline HORTON; inf: father; pg:ln: 230:57

HORTON, George; CM; b. 16 Jul 1887 in Ffx; father: Jas. C. HORTON;
occ: laborer; res: Ffx; mother: Lucy HORTON; inf: J. C. HORTON,
father; pg:ln: 167:56

HORTON, James Leslie; CM; b. 19 Jun 1896 nr Centreville; father: Wm.
HORTON; occ: farmer; res: nr Centreville; mother: Hester HORTON;
inf: father; pg:ln: 230:68

HORTON, Lucy; CF; b. 29 Jun 1880 in Ffx; father: Tobe HORTON; occ:
farmer; res: Ffx; mother: Lucy; inf: T. HORTON, father; pg:ln: 128:40

HORTON, Wm.; WM; b. 14 Apr 1893 nr Mt. Vernon; father: Samuel D.
HORTON; occ: farmer; res: nr Mt. Vernon; mother: Adelade
HORTON; inf: parents; pg:ln: 211:54

HOUTBOWER see HAUTBOWER, HARDBOWER

HOUTBOWER, Annie M.; WF; b. 5 Jan 1892 nr Alexandria; father: Wm.
H. HOUTBOWER; occ: farmer; res: nr Alex.; mother: Virginia
HOUTBOWER; inf: father; pg:ln: 207:71

HOWARD, ___; WM; b. 13 Nov 1890 in Ffx; father: Ernest L. HOWARD;
occ: farmer; res: Ffx; mother: Mary HOWARD; inf: E. L. HOWARD,
father; pg:ln: 190:47

HOWARD, ____ (dead); WF; b. 1 Dec 1887 in Ffx; father: E. L.
HOWARD; occ: farmer; res: Ffx; mother: M. F. HOWARD; inf: E. L.
HOWARD, father; pg:ln: 161:60

HOWARD, Annie J.; WF; b. 15 Jul 1884 in Bailey's X Roads; father:
Wm. J. HOWARD; occ: laborer; res: Bailey's X Roads; mother:
Lizzie HOWARD; inf: father; pg:ln: 150:43

HOWARD, Fannie; WF; b. 23 Nov 1883 in Ffx; father: W. HOWARD;
occ: farmer; res: Ffx; mother: Sarah HOWARD; inf: W. HOWARD,
father; pg:ln: 144:41

HOWARD, Jno. M.; WM; b. 27 Oct 1892 in Ffx; father: Ernest L.
HOWARD; occ: farmer; res: Ffx; mother: Minnie HOWARD; inf: E. L.
HOWARD, father; pg:ln: 203:52

HOWARD, Maud; CF; b. 15 Oct 1888 in Ffx; father: Wm. HOWARD;
occ: laborer; res: Ffx; mother: Ellen HOWARD; inf: Ellen HOWARD,
mother; pg:ln: 170:35

HUGHES, Leonard; CM; b. 17 Feb 1896 nr Alex.; father: Geo. L.
HUGHES; occ: laborer; res: nr Alex.; mother: Mary F. HUGHES; inf:
mother; pg:ln: 230:63

HUGHES, Viola; WF; b. 12 Jun 1890 in ___; father: Geo. T. HUGHES;
occ: farmer; res: Ffx; mother: Florence HUGHES; inf: Geo. T.
HUGHES, father; pg:ln: 186:47

HUGHS. W. H.; WM; b. 14 Sep 1880 in Ffx; father: G. T. HUGHS; occ:
farmer; res: Ffx; mother: Florence; inf: G. T. HUGHS, father; pg:ln:
128:43

HUMER, Geo. W.; WM; b. 25 Feb 1893 in ___; father: Jno. W.
HUMMER; occ: ___; res: ___; mother: Mary E. HUMER; inf: J. W.
HUMMER, father; pg:ln: 214:43

HUMER, Martha; WF; b. 9 May 1888 in Ffx; father: Joseph HUMER;
occ: farmer; res: Ffx; mother: Kate HUMER; inf: J. HUMMER, father;
pg:ln: 174:49

HUMER, Mary A. ; WF; b. 24 Jul 1891 in Ffx; father: Jno. W. HUMER;
occ: farmer; res: Ffx; mother: M. E. HUMER; inf: J. W. HUMER,
father; pg:ln: 199:37

HUMMER, Beverly T.; WM; b. 26 Dec 1886 in Falls Ch.; father: B. A.
HUMMER; occ: farmer; res: Falls Ch.; mother: I. M. HUMMER; inf:
father; pg:ln: 158:25

HUMMER, Daisey F.; WF; b. 18 Aug 1894 in Ffx; father: Jno. W.
HUM[M]ER; occ: farmer; res: Ffx; mother: Mary E. HUM[M]ER; inf:
J. W. HUMER, father; pg:ln: 218:54

HUMMER, Geo. L.; WM; b. 18 Feb 1881 in Munsons Hill; father: Joseph
HUMMER; occ: farmer; res: Munsons Hill; mother: Annie C.
HUMMER; inf: father; pg:ln: 130:28

HUMMER, Jas. H.; WM; b. 30 Dec 1885 in Falls Church; father: B. A.
HUMMER; occ: farmer; res: Falls Church; mother: Ida M. HUMMER;
inf: father; pg:ln: 152:30

HUMMER, Joseph H.; WM; b. 6 Aug 1890 in Ffx; father: Jos. HUMMER;
occ: farmer; res: Ffx; mother: Annie HUMMER; inf: Jos. HUMMER,
father; pg:ln: 190:43

HUMMER, Norman L. [HUMER lined thru]; WM; b. 6 Dec 1891 in Ffx;
father: J. F. HUMMER [Humer lined thru]; occ: farmer; res: Ffx;
mother: Annie C. HUMMER [HUMER lined thru]; inf: J. F. HUMMER,
father; pg:ln: 199:36

HUMMER, not named; WM; b. 9 Nov 1882 in Falls Church; father: Jno.
W. HUMMER; occ: farmer; res: Falls Church; mother: M. E.
HUMMER; inf: father; pg:ln: 134:24

HUMMER, W. A.; WM; b. 28 Apr 1890 in Ffx; father: B. A. HUMMER;
    occ: farmer; res: Ffx; mother: Ida M. HUMMER; inf: B. A. HUMMER,
    father; pg:ln: 190:42

HUMMER, William; WM; b. 1 May 1882 nr Vienna; father: Levi M.
    HUMMER; occ: farmer; res: nr Vienna; mother: Annie R. HUMMER;
    inf: father; pg:ln: 134:23

HUNTER, Bertha; WF; b. 19 May 1892 nr Mt. Vernon; father: John C.
    HUNTER; occ: farmer; res: nr Mt. Vernon; mother: Mary E.
    HUNTER; inf: father; pg:ln: 207:68

HUNTER, Dora; CF; b. 10 Mar 1891 in Germantown; father: James
    HUNTER; occ: laborer; res: Germantown; mother: Sarah Jane
    HUNTER; inf: parent; pg:ln: 196:28

HUNTER, G. W.; CM; b. 1 Feb 1884 in Ffx; father: Robt. HUNTER; occ:
    farmer; res: Ffx; mother: May HUNTER; inf: R. HUNTER, father;
    pg:ln: 147:40

HUNTER, Herbert C.; WM; b. 15 Aug 1886 in Seminary; father: N. C.
    HUNTER; occ: farmer; res: Seminary; mother: Alida HUNTER; inf:
    father; pg:ln: 158:21

HUNTER, Jas.; WM; b. 8 Nov 1882 in Ffx; father: Jas. HUNTER; occ:
    farmer; res: Ffx; mother: Rebecca HUNTER; inf: Jas. HUNTER,
    father; pg:ln: 136:37

HUNTER, Jno. C.; WM; b. 26 Feb 1892 in Ffx; father: Jno. C. HUNTER;
    occ: farmer; res: Ffx; mother: Mary HUNTER; inf: J. C. HUNTER,
    father; pg:ln: 203:54

HUNTER, M. E.; WF; b. 26 Mar 1880 in Ffx; father: W. HUNTER Jr.;
    occ: farmer; res: Ffx; mother: Mary W.; inf: W. HUNTER, father;
    pg:ln: 128:46

HUNTER, Mable; WF; b. 7 Jul 1886 in Ffx; father: Jno. C. HUNTER;
    occ: farmer; res: Ffx; mother: Mable HUNTER; inf: J. C. HUNTER,
    father; pg:ln: 155:09

HUNTER, Melville; WM; b. 15 Aug 1888 in Ffx; father: N. C. HUNTER;
    occ: farmer; res: Ffx; mother: Lida HUNTER; inf: N. C. HUNTER,
    father For correct spelling of mother's name see registration of child
    Nathaniel B. HUNTER.; pg:ln: 174:38

HUNTER, Nathaniel B.; WM; b. 21 Jun 1885 in Bailey's X Roads; father:
    N. C. HUNTER; occ: farmer; res: Bailey's X Roads; mother: Lida
    HUNTER; inf: father; pg:ln: 152:27

HUNTER, not named (dead); CM; b. 10 Apr 1882 in Falls Church;
    father: Washington HUNTER; occ: laborer; res: Falls Ch; mother:
    Betty HUNTER; inf: father; pg:ln: 135:75

HUNTER, Ruth; WF; b. 20 Jan 1880 in Ffx; father: Benj. P. HUNTER;
    occ: farmer; res: Ffx; mother: Mary A.; inf: B. P. HUNTER, father;
    pg:ln: 128:47

HUNTER, Thos.; CM; b. 16 Feb 1880 in Ffx; father: Jas. HUNTER; occ:
    farmer; res: Ffx; mother: Mary J.; inf: Jas. HUNTER, father; pg:ln:
    127:38

HUNTER, W. H.; WM; b. 16 Jun 1885 in Ffx; father: Jas. B. HUNTER; occ: farmer; res: Ffx; mother: Annie HUNTER; inf: J. B. HUNTER, father; pg:ln: 156:30

HUNTINGDON, Elzey; WF; b. 10 Mar 1887 in Ffx; father: Peter HUNTINGDON; occ: farmer; res: Ffx; mother: Eleanor HUNTINGDON; inf: P. HUNTINGDON, father; pg:ln: 167:54

HUNTINGTON, Robert; WM; b. 4 Nov 1895 nr Newington; father: Robert HUNTINGTON; occ: farmer; res: nr Newington; mother: Emma HUNTINGTON; inf: father; pg:ln: 222:26

HUNTINGTON, Wm.; WM; b. 20 Feb 1893 nr Newington; father: Robert HUNTINGTON; occ: farmer; res: nr Newington; mother: Emma HUNTINGTON; inf: parents; pg:ln: 211:53

HUNTT, ___; WF; b. 20 Jun 1887 in Ffx; father: Lewis HUNTT; occ: farmer; res: Ffx; mother: Emma HUNTT; inf: Lewis HUNTT, father; pg:ln: 161:58

HUNTT, Carrie; CF; b. 7 Jan 1880 in Ffx; father: J. H. HUNTT; occ: farmer; res: Ffx; mother: Sarah; inf: J. H. HUNTT, father; pg:ln: 128:49

HUNTT, Florence; WF; b. 30 Nov 1887 in Ffx; father: Jno. S. HUNTT; occ: farmer; res: Ffx; mother: Florence HUNTT; inf: J. S. HUNTT, father; pg:ln: 161:56

HUNTT, Lottie; WF; b. 9 Jun 1884 in Prov.; father: Louis HUNTT; occ: farmer; res: Prov.; mother: Eliza HUNTT; inf: father; pg:ln: 150:52

HUNTT, Milton B.; WM; b. 1 May 1891 in Ffx; father: Thos. E. HUNTT; occ: farmer; res: Ffx; mother: Nora HUNTT; inf: T. E. HUNTT, father; pg:ln: 199:39

HUNTT, Norman; CM; b. 30 Mar 1885 in Ffx; father: Jas. H. HUNTT; occ: farmer; res: Ffx; mother: Dinah HUNTT; inf: J. H. HUNTT, father; pg:ln: 156:29

HUNTT, not named (dead); CF; b. 5 Nov 1887 in Ffx; father: Jas. H. HUNTT; occ: farmer; res: Ffx; mother: Emma HUNTT; inf: J. H. HUNTT, father; pg:ln: 167:58

HUNTT, not named; WF; b. 19 Jan 1889 in Ffx; father: J. N. HUNTT; occ: farmer; res: Ffx; mother: Flora HUNTT; inf: J. N. HUNT[T], father; pg:ln: 178:50

HUNTT, not named; WM; b. 4 Nov 1880 in Providence; father: Lewis H. HUNTT; occ: farmer; res: Providence; mother: Eliz. H. HUNTT; inf: father; pg:ln: 124:25

HUTCHENSON, not named; WM; b. 1 Aug 1885 in Pleasant Valley; father: Philip HUTCHENSON; occ: farmer; res: Pleasant Valley; mother: Ellen HUTCHENSON; inf: father; pg:ln: 152:29

HUTCHINSON, Silas; WM; b. 26 Feb 1893 nr Pleasant Valley; father: Joshua HUTCHINSON; occ: farmer; res: Pleasant Valley; mother: Mattie HUTCHINSON; inf: parents; pg:ln: 211:51

HUTCHISON, Champ; WM; b. 20 Jun 1890 in ___; father: S. M. HUTCHISON; occ: farmer; res: Ffx; mother: Bettie HUTCHISON; inf: S. M. HUTCHISON, father; pg:ln: 186:54

HUTCHISON, Eugene Philip; WM; b. 8 Mar 1891 in Mt. Rocky; father: Wm. H. HUTCHISON; occ: farmer; res: Mt. Rocky; mother: Mary HUTCHISON; inf: parents; pg:ln: 194:13

HUTCHISON, G. H.; WM; b. 13 Jan 1888 in Ffx; father: J. M. HUTCHISON; occ: farmer; res: Ffx; mother: M. M. HUTCHISON; inf: J. M. HUTCHISON, father; pg:ln: 174:47

HUTCHISON, Grace; WF; b. 9 Aug 1891 in Ffx; father: J. M. HUTCHISON; occ: farmer; res: Ffx; mother: Mattie HUTCHISON; inf: J. M. HUTCHISON, father; pg:ln: 199:41

HUTCHISON, Harrie; WM; b. 11 Nov 1889 in Ffx; father: L. E. HUTCHISON; occ: farmer; res: Ffx; mother: not given; inf: L. E. HUTCHISON, father; pg:ln: 178:53

HUTCHISON, Hugh; WM; b. 1 Jun 1888 in Ffx; father: Philip HUTCHISON; occ: farmer; res: Ffx; mother: Ellen HUTCHISON; inf: P. HUTCHISON, father; pg:ln: 174:46

HUTCHISON, Lula; WF; b. 31 Mar 1888 in Ffx; father: L. E. HUTCHISON; occ: farmer; res: Ffx; mother: Sarah E. HUTCHISON; inf: L. E. HUTCHISON, father; pg:ln: 174:48

HUTCHISON, Margt. L.; WF; b. 28 May 1896 in ___; father: Philip HUTCHISON; occ: farmer; res: Ffx; mother: Araminta HUTCHISON; inf: P. HUTCHISON, father; pg:ln: 226:56

HUTCHISON, Mary E.; WF; b. 29 Sep 1894 in Ffx; father: C. T. HUTCHISON; occ: farmer; res: Ffx; mother: Lelia V. HUTCHISON; inf: C. T. HUTCHISON, father; pg:ln: 218:49

HUTCHISON, Olive; WF; b. 22 Feb 1888 in Ffx; father: E. G. HUTCHISON; occ: farmer; res: Ffx; mother: Ella HUTCHISON; inf: E. G. HUTCHISON, father; pg:ln: 174:45

HUTCHISON, Owen H.; WM; b. 8 Jun 1881 in Ffx; father: W. H. HUTCHISON; occ: farmer; res: Ffx; mother: Tomicia HUTCHISON; inf: W. H. HUTCHISON, father; pg:ln: 132:20

HUTCHISON, P. L.; WM; b. 9 Nov 1888 in Ffx; father: Wm. H. HUTCHISON; occ: farmer; res: Ffx; mother: Tomasia HUTCHISON; inf: Wm. H. HUTCHISON, father; pg:ln: 171:38

HUTCHISON, Paul C.; WM; b. 27 Nov 1889 in Ffx; father: J. M. HUTCHISON; occ: farmer; res: Ffx; mother: Mattie HUTCHISON; inf: J. M. HUTCHISON, father; pg:ln: 178:52

HUTCHISON, R. P.; WM; b. 24 Jan 1883 in Ffx; father: Luther D. HUTCHISON; occ: farmer; res: Ffx; mother: A. M. HUTCHISON; inf: L. D. HUTCHISON, father; pg:ln: 144:35

HUTCHISON, Ralph W.; WM; b. 9 Sep 1890 in Ffx; father: E. S. HUTCHISON; occ: farmer; res: Ffx; mother: C. P. HUTCHISON; inf: E. S. HUTCHISON, father; pg:ln: 190:49

HUTCHISON, Robt. E.; WM; b. 29 Mar 1892 in Ffx; father: C. T. HUTCHISON; occ: farmer; res: Ffx; mother: L. V. HUTCHISON; inf: C. T. HUTCHISON, father; pg:ln: 203:51

HUTCHISON, Virginia; WF; b. 15 Mar 1890 in Ffx; father: C. T. HUTCHISON; occ: farmer; res: Ffx; mother: Lelia V. HUTCHISON; inf: C. T. HUTCHISON, father; pg:ln: 190:48

HUTCHISON, W. A. C.; WM; b. 17 Dec 1884 in Ffx; father: W. H.
HUTCHISON; occ: farmer; res: Ffx; mother: Tomacia HUTCHISON;
inf: W. H. HUTCHISON, father; pg:ln: 146:31

HYMAN, Frank B.; CM; b. 11 Nov 1893 in ___; father: Jno. HYMAN;
occ: ___; res: ___; mother: Kate HYMAN; inf: J. HYMAN, father;
pg:ln: 214:44

HYMAN, Frank; CM; b. 20 Jan 1894 in Ffx; father: Jno. B. HYMAN; occ:
farmer; res: Ffx; mother: Hattie HYMAN; inf: J. B. HYMAN, father;
pg:ln: 218:56

HYSON, Viola P.; CF; b. 10 Sep 1892 in Ffx; father: T. W. HYSON; occ:
laborer; res: Ffx; mother: Sarah HYSON; inf: T. W. HYSON, father;
pg:ln: 203:47

HYSON, Walter R.; CM; b. 25 Nov 1890 in Ffx; father: T. W. HYSON;
occ: farmer; res: Ffx; mother: Sarah HYSON; inf: T. W. HYSON,
father; pg:ln: 190:46

IDEN, Bertie; WF; b. 12 May 1886 in Prov.; father: John IDEN; occ:
farmer; res: Prov.; mother: ___ IDEN; inf: father; pg:ln: 158:26

IDEN, James; WM; b. 12 May 1887 in Ffx; father: J. N. IDEN; occ:
farmer; res: Ffx; mother: Mary V. IDEN; inf: J. N. IDEN, father; pg:ln:
161:61

IVES, Ann H.; WF; b. 28 Apr 1885 in Lewinsville; father: Willis C. IVES;
occ: farmer; res: Lewinsville; mother: Alice IVES; inf: father; pg:ln:
152:33

IVES, Mary Alice; WF; b. 16 Oct 1883 in Falls Church; father: Willis C.
IVES [Willie lined thru]; occ: farmer; res: Falls Church; mother: Alice
V. IVES; inf: father. Note: for father's name see marriage of parents
Sept. 15, 1882 Fairfax 105; pg:ln: 140:51

JACKSON, ___; CM; b. 17 Aug 1891 in Ffx; father: Dallas JACKSON;
occ: farmer; res: Ffx; mother: Rachael JACKSON; inf: D. JACKSON,
father; pg:ln: 199:51

JACKSON, Arena; CF; b. 15 Mar 1894 in Ffx; father: Rich'd. JACKSON;
occ: farmer; res: Ffx; mother: Eugene JACKSON; inf: R. JACKSON,
father; pg:ln: 218:66

JACKSON, Arthur Novall?; CM; b. 19 Apr 1896 nr Sideburn Sta.; father:
Minnie [Mannie?] JACKSON; occ: farmer; res: nr Sideburn Sta.;
mother: Daisy Beatrice JACKSON; inf: father; pg:ln: 230:72

JACKSON, Clayton; CM; b. 30 Aug 1896 in ___; father: T. H.
JACKSON; occ: farmer; res: Ffx; mother: Agnes JACKSON; inf: T.
H. JACKSON, father; pg:ln: 226:65

JACKSON, Cora F.; CF; b. 13 Apr 1890 in Ffx; father: W. JACKSON;
occ: farmer; res: Ffx; mother: Amanda JACKSON; inf: W.
JACKSON, father; pg:ln: 190:52

JACKSON, Della; CF; b. 23 Jan 1892 in Ffx; father: Thos. H.
JACKSON; occ: farmer; res: Ffx; mother: Ann JACKSON; inf: T. H.
JACKSON, father; pg:ln: 203:56

JACKSON, Emily May; CF; b. 13 May 1895 nr Centreville; father: Chas.
T. JACKSON; occ: laborer; res: Centreville; mother: C. M.
JACKSON; inf: father; pg:ln: 222:34

JACKSON, Florence; CF; b. 10 Sep 1883 in Bailey's X Road; father: Oscar JACKSON; occ: carpenter; res: Bailey's X Road; mother: Mary JACKSON; inf: father; pg:ln: 140:50

JACKSON, Grace; CF; b. 6 Oct 1896 in ___; father: not known; occ: ___; res: Ffx; mother: Ella JACKSON; inf: Ella JACKSON, mother; pg:ln: 226:62

JACKSON, Hazzell; CF; b. 27 Aug 1896 nr Sideburn Sta; father: Chas. JACKSON; occ: Rail Road hand; res: nr Sideburn Sta; mother: Nellie JACKSON; inf: mother; pg:ln: 230:74

JACKSON, Henry; CM; b. 3 Apr 1893 in ___; father: Dallas JACKSON; occ: ___; res· ___; mother: Rachael JACKSON; inf: D. JACKSON, father; pg:ln: 214:62

JACKSON, Janie; CF; b. 5 Aug 1896 in ___; father: W. A. JACKSON; occ: farmer; res: Ffx; mother: Amanda JACKSON; inf: W. A. JOHNSON, father; pg:ln: 226:61

JACKSON, Jno. B.; WM; b. 11 Aug 1887 in Ffx; father: J. T. JACKSON; occ: farmer; res: Ffx; mother: Francis JACKSON; inf: J. T. JACKSON, father; pg:ln: 161:62

JACKSON, Jno. S.; CM; b. 16 Sep 1891 in Ffx; father: Richd. JACKSON; occ: farmer; res: Ffx; mother: Jennie JACKSON; inf: R. JACKSON, father; pg:ln: 199:50

JACKSON, John T.; WM; b. 15 Sep 1880 in Providence; father: Jno. T. JACKSON; occ: farmer; res: Providence; mother: Elizabeth JACKSON; inf: father; pg:ln: 124:30

JACKSON, Jos.; CM; b. 15 Jun 1888 in Ffx; father: Dallas JACKSON; occ: farmer; res: Ffx; mother: Rachael JACKSON; inf: D. JACKSON, father; pg:ln: 174:56

JACKSON, Joshua; CM; b. 29 Aug 1889 in Ffx; father: Richd. T. JACKSON; occ: farmer; res: Ffx; mother: Virginia JACKSON; inf: R. T. JACKSON, father; pg:ln: 178:58

JACKSON, Kate; CF; b. 3 Dec 1888 in Ffx; father: Jas. F. JACKSON; occ: farmer; res: Ffx; mother: Kitty JACKSON; inf: J. F. JACKSON, father; pg:ln: 174:50

JACKSON, Lotta M.; CF; b. 8 Aug 1896 in ___; father: Saml. JACKSON; occ: farmer; res: Ffx; mother: Bessie JACKSON; inf: Saml. JACKSON, father; pg:ln: 226:63

JACKSON, Lucy, CF; b. 7 Aug 1894 in Ffx; father: Jno. S. JACKSON; occ: farmer; res: Ffx; mother: Lucy JACKSON; inf: J. S. JACKSON, father; pg:ln: 218:67

JACKSON, M. D.; CM; b. 21 Aug 1893 in ___; father: R. T. JACKSON; occ: ___; res: ___; mother: Virginia JACKSON; inf: R. T. JACKSON, father; pg:ln: 214:54

JACKSON, Mary; CF; b. 15 Dec 1887 in Ffx; father: John JACKSON; occ: farmer; res: Ffx; mother: Mary JACKSON; inf: Jno. JACKSON, father; pg:ln: 161:63

JACKSON, Melvina; CF; b. 25 Dec 1896 in ___; father: Rich'd. JACKSON; occ: farmer; res: Ffx; mother: Emma JACKSON; inf: Rich'd. JACKSON, father; pg:ln: 226:64

JACKSON, Peyton S.; CM; b. 10 Jan 1893 in ___; father: Jno. T.
JACKSON; occ: ___; res: ___; mother: Fannie JACKSON; inf: J. T.
JACKSON, father; pg:ln: 214:61

JACKSON, Philip; CM; b. 10 Jun 1885 in Falls Ch.; father: J. M.
JACKSON; occ: laborer; res: Falls Church; mother: ___ JACKSON;
inf: father; pg:ln: 152:34

JACKSON, Randolph; CM; b. 12 Sep 1889 in Ffx; father: Thos.
JACKSON; occ: farmer; res: Ffx; mother: Agnes JACKSON; inf:
Thos. JACKSON, father; pg:ln: 178:62

JACKSON, Sophronia; CF; b. 25 Sep 1886 in Dranes.; father: J. M.
JACKSON; occ: mechanic; res: Dranes.; mother: Mary JACKSON;
inf: father; pg:ln: 158:27

JACKSON, W. H.; CM; b. 1 May 1893 in ___; father: Thos. H.
JACKSON; occ: ___; res: ___; mother: Agnis JACKSON; inf: T. H.
JACKSON, father; pg:ln: 214:56

JACKSON, W.; CM; b. 10 May 1888 in Ffx; father: Jno. JACKSON; occ:
farmer; res: Ffx; mother: Eliza JACKSON; inf: J. JACKSON, father;
pg:ln: 174:51

JACKSON, Willie A.; WM; b. 8 Jun 1882 in Ffx; father: A. JACKSON;
occ: farmer; res: Ffx; mother: Maria JACKSON; inf: A. JACKSON,
father; pg:ln: 136:38

JACOBS, H. C.; WM; b. 18 Apr 1890 in Ffx; father: H. C. JACOBS; occ:
farmer; res: Ffx; mother: Maria JACOBS; inf: H. C. JACOBS, father;
pg:ln: 190:51

JACOBS, Harry; WM; b. 8 Jan 1888 in Ffx; father: H. C. JACOBS; occ:
farmer; res: Ffx; mother: May JACOBS; inf: H. C. JACOBS, father;
pg:ln: 174:52

JACOBS, Jas. R.; WM; b. 1 Apr 1882 in Ffx; father: Jas. JACOBS; occ:
farmer; res: Ffx; mother: Lydia A. JACOBS; inf: J. JACOBS, father;
pg:ln: 136:39

JACOBS, John W.; WM; b. 29 Jul 1896 nr Hayfield; father: John W.
JACOBS; occ: farmer; res: nr Hayfield; mother: Rachael JACOBS;
inf: mother; pg:ln: 230:70

JACOBS, Luther; WM; b. 18 Oct 1893 in ___; father: H. C. JACOBS;
occ: ___; res: ___; mother: M. F. JACOBS; inf: H. C. JACOBS,
father; pg:ln: 214:58

JACOBS, not named; WM; b. 6 Oct 1895 nr Hayfield; father: John W.
JACOBS; occ: laborer; res: Hayfield; mother: Rachael JACOBS; inf:
father; pg:ln: 222:35

JAMES, E. Jane; CF; b. 30 Jul 1887 in Ffx; father: Sandy JAMES; occ:
laborer; res: Ffx; mother: Birtie JAMES; inf: Sandy JAMES, father;
pg:ln: 167:65

JAMES, Estella; CF; b. 28 Jul 1886 in Falls Ch.; father: James
PHILLIPS; occ: laborer; res: Falls Ch.; mother: Ida JAMES; inf:
father; pg:ln: 158:32

JAMES, Rufus; WM; b. 4 Sep 1887 in Ffx; father: J. R. JAMES; occ:
farmer; res: Ffx; mother: Susan J. JAMES; inf: J. R. JAMES, father;
pg:ln: 161:65

JAMES, Wm. McKinley; CM; b. 26 Apr 1896 in ___; father: Philip
    JAMES; occ: farmer; res: Ffx; mother: Ada JAMES; inf: Philip
    JAMES, father; pg:ln: 226:68

JARBOE, Gertrude; WF; b. 22 Nov 1894 in Ffx; father: An'd. J.
    JARBOE; occ: farmer; res: Ffx; mother: G. M. JARBOE; inf: A. J.
    JARBOE, father; pg:ln: 218:65

JASPER, Clarence Edward; CM; b. 8 Dec 1892 nr Mt. Vernon; father:
    Daniel JASPER; occ: laborer; res: nr Mt. Vernon; mother: Martha
    JASPER; inf: father; pg:ln: 206:08

JASPER, Dollie; CF; b. 13 Jun 1893 nr Hayfield; father: Austin T.
    JASPER; occ: laborer; res: nr Hayfield; mother: Mary JASPER; inf:
    mother; pg:ln: 211:62

JASPER, James; CM; b. 1 Jul 1887 in Ffx; father: John JASPER; occ:
    laborer; res: Ffx; mother: Caroline JASPER; inf: Jno. JASPER,
    father; pg:ln: 167:63

JASPER, Mike; CM; b. 6 Dec 1892 nr Mt. Vernon; father: John
    JASPER; occ: laborer; res: nr Mt. Vernon; mother: Caroline
    JASPER; inf: mother; pg:ln: 206:07

JAVINS, Ada; CF; b. 24 Dec 1889 in Ffx; father: Saml. JAVINS; occ:
    farmer; res: Ffx; mother: Florence JAVINS; inf: S. JAVINS, father;
    pg:ln: 178:57

JAVINS, Austin; CM; b. 5 Apr 1887 in Ffx; father: Saml. JAVINS; occ:
    farmer; res: Ffx; mother: Florence JAVINS; inf: Saml. JAVINS,
    father; pg:ln: 161:67

JAVINS, Florence; WF; b. 5 Sep 1887 in Ffx; father: Andrew JAVINS;
    occ: farmer; res: Ffx; mother: Sarah E. JAVINS; inf: And. JAVINS,
    father; pg:ln: 167:62

JAVINS, Noble Lee; WM; b. 23 Oct 1893 nr Bone Mill; father: Geo.
    JAVINS; occ: farmer; res: nr Bone Mill; mother: Ida V. JAVINS; inf:
    mother; pg:ln: 211:60

JEFFERSON, Geo.; CM; b. 6 May 1889 in Ffx; father: Geo.
    JEFFERSON; occ: farmer; res: Ffx; mother: Martha JACKSON [?];
    inf: Geo. JEFFERSON, father; pg:ln: 182:49

JEFFRIES, Frank B.; WM; b. 17 Sep 1894 in Ffx; father: J. W.
    JEFFRIES; occ: farmer; res: Ffx; mother: Gertrude JEFFRIES; inf: J.
    W. JEFFRIES, father; pg:ln: 218:63

JENKINS, Albert; WM; b. 10 Aug 1885 in Dranes.; father: Samuel
    JENKINS; occ: farmer; res: Dranes.; mother: Mary C. JENKINS; inf:
    father; pg:ln: 152:35

JENKINS, Benj. H.; WM; b. 2 Nov 1889 in Ffx; father: Sampson
    JENKINS; occ: farmer; res: Ffx; mother: Zada JENKINS; inf: S.
    JENKINS, father; pg:ln: 178:61

JENKINS, Bertie (twin); WF; b. 4 Jan 1886 in Dranes.; father: Saml.
    JENKINS; occ: farmer; res: Dranes.; mother: ___JENKINS; inf:
    father; pg:ln: 158:30

JENKINS, Clara; WF; b. 14 Jan 1888 in Ffx; father: Sampson JENKINS;
    occ: farmer; res: Ffx; mother: Zada JENKINS; inf: S. JENKINS,
    father; pg:ln: 174:57

JENKINS, Cornelius; WM; b. 22 Aug 1888 in Ffx; father: Cornelius
JENKINS; occ: farmer; res: Ffx; mother: Olivia JENKINS; inf: C.
JENKINS, father; pg:ln: 174:55

JENKINS, Effa; WF; b. 20 Mar 1890 in Ffx; father: Jno. W. JENKINS;
occ: farmer; res: Ffx; mother: Mary L. JENKINS; inf: J. W. JENKINS,
father; pg:ln: 190:54

JENKINS, Ellen; WF; b. 8 Nov 1892 nr Franconia Sta.; father: Norman
JENKINS; occ: carpenter; res: nr Franconia; mother: Ellen
JENKINS; inf: mother; pg:ln: 207:73

JENKINS, Farley; WM; b. 10 Oct 1894 in Ffx; father: Sampson
JENKINS; occ: farmer; res: Ffx; mother: Zada JENKINS; inf: S.
JENKINS, father; pg:ln: 218:62

JENKINS, Franklin; WM; b. 11 Jun 1896 in ___; father: Geo. W.
JENKINS; occ: farmer; res: Ffx; mother: Josephine JENKINS; inf: G.
W. JENKINS, father; pg:ln: 226:69

JENKINS, Ida (twin); WF; b. 4 Jan 1886 in Dranes.; father: Saml.
JENKINS; occ: farmer; res: Dranes.; mother: ___JENKINS; inf:
father; pg:ln: 158:31

JENKINS, Inez; WF; b. 20 Nov 1890 in ___; father: Norman B.
JENKINS; occ: farmer; res: Ffx; mother: Ella JENKINS; inf: N. B.
JENKINS, father; pg:ln: 186:59

JENKINS, Jennie; WF; b. 18 Nov 1881 in Dranesville; father: William
JENKINS; occ: farmer; res: Dranesville; mother: Laura JENKINS; inf:
father; pg:ln: 130:30

JENKINS, Jno.; WM; b. 2 Sep 1891 in Ffx; father: Sampson JENKINS;
occ: farmer; res: Ffx; mother: Zada JENKINS; inf: S. JENKINS,
father; pg:ln: 199:47

JENKINS, Maggie D.; WF; b. 5 Aug 1893 in ___; father: S. JENKINS;
occ: ___; res: ___; mother: Zada JENKINS; inf: S. JENKINS, father;
pg:ln: 214:55

JENKINS, Mary; WF; b. 21 Apr 1888 in Ffx; father: J. W. JENKINS; occ:
farmer; res: Ffx; mother: Mary JENKINS; inf: J. W. JENKINS, father;
pg:ln: 174:54

JERMAN, Benjamin; WM; b. 1 Aug 1895 nr Fairfax C. H.; father: John
JERMAN; occ: farmer; res: nr Fairfax C. H.; mother: Martha J.
JERMAN; inf: father; pg:ln: 223:72

JERMAN, Bernice; WF; b. 9 Sep 1890 in ___; father: M. G. JERMAN;
occ: butcher; res: Ffx; mother: Ida JERMAN; inf: M. G. JERMAN,
father; pg:ln: 186:60

JERMAN, Edna R.; WF; b. 16 Aug 1888 in Ffx; father: M. G. JERMAN;
occ: butcher; res: Ffx; mother: Ida M. JERMAN; inf: M. G. JERMAN,
father; pg:ln: 171:40

JERMAN, Ella; WF; b. 18 Jan 1890 in ___; father: Jno. F. JERMAN;
occ: farmer; res: Ffx; mother: Josephine JERMAN; inf: J. F.
JERMAN, father; pg:ln: 186:61

JERMAN, M.; WF; b. 17 Jul 1880 in Ffx; father: Jos. JERMAN; occ:
farmer; res: Ffx; mother: Sarah; inf: J. JERMAN, father; pg:ln:
128:51

JERMAN, Mabel; WF; b. 10 Jun 1888 in Ffx; father: Jno. F. JERMAN;
occ: farmer; res: Ffx; mother: Marcie J. JERMAN; inf: Jno. F.
JERMAN, father; pg:ln: 171:41

JERMAN, Maud E.; WF; b. 5 Jul 1886 in Ffx; father: M. G. JERMAN;
occ: farmer; res: Ffx; mother: Ida M. JERMAN; inf: M. G. JERMAN,
father; pg:ln: 155:12

JERMAN, W. E.; WM; b. 11 Jun 1883 in Ffx; father: Smith JERMAN;
occ: farmer; res: Ffx; mother: Anna JERMAN; inf: Smith JERMAN,
father; pg:ln: 144:47

JEWELL, Ashton; WM; b. 11 Jan 1889 in Ffx; father: Jno. H. JEWELL;
occ: farmer; res: Ffx; mother: Laura JEWELL; inf: J. H. JEWELL,
father; pg:ln: 178:59

JEWELL, Earl Visbrook?; WM; b. 8 Jul 1892 nr Chantilly; father: John H.
JEWELL; occ: farmer; res: nr Chantilly; mother: Elizabeth JEWELL;
inf: mother; pg:ln: 208:13

JEWELL, Garland; WM; b. 18 Jun 1890 in Ffx; father: Jno. H. JEWELL;
occ: farmer; res: Ffx; mother: Elizabt. JEWELL; inf: J. H. JEWELL,
father; pg:ln: 190:55

JEWELL, Leolia; WF; b. 31 Oct 1889 in Ffx; father: Elijah JEWELL; occ:
farmer; res: Ffx; mother: Ellin JEWELL; inf: E. JEWELL, father;
pg:ln: 178:60

JOHNSON, ___ (dead); WM; b. 10 May 1881 in Vienna; father:
Nathanniel JOHNSON; occ: farmer; res: Vienna; mother: Alberta
JOHNSON; inf: father; pg:ln: 130:31

JOHNSON, ___; CF; b. 3 Oct 1888 in Ffx; father: W. JOHNSON; occ:
farmer; res: Ffx; mother: Martha JOHNSON; inf: W. JOHNSON,
father; pg:ln: 174:53

JOHNSON, ___; WF; b. 15 Feb 1885 in Ffx; father: Greenbery
JOHNSON; occ: farmer; res: Ffx; mother: Lavina JOHNSON; inf: G.
JOHNSON, father; pg:ln: 156:34

JOHNSON, ___; WM; b. 3 Apr 1883 in Dranesville; father: Jas. E.
JOHNSON; occ: farmer; res: Dranesville; mother: Mary JOHNSON;
inf: father; pg:ln: 140:46

JOHNSON, Bertna; CF; b. 15 May 1891 in Ffx; father: Jos. JOHNSON;
occ: farmer; res: Ffx; mother: Carrie JOHNSON; inf: J. JOHNSON,
father; pg:ln: 199:49

JOHNSON, Chas.; CM; b. 10 Jan 1887 in Ffx; father: John JOHNSON;
occ: laborer; res: Ffx; mother: Mary JOHNSON; inf: Jno. JOHNSON,
father; pg:ln: 167:64

JOHNSON, Clarence; CM; b. 1 Feb 1883 in Dranesville; father: Dennis
JOHNSON; occ: laborer; res: Dranesville; mother: Julia JOHNSON;
inf: father; pg:ln: 140:47

JOHNSON, Edgar Davis; CM; b. 2 Dec 1893 nr Centreville; father: Wm.
JOHNSON; occ: laborer; res: nr Centreville; mother: Lottie Davis
JOHNSON; inf: mother; pg:ln: 211:61

JOHNSON, Emma; CF; b. 29 Mar 1883 in Ffx; father: Delvin
JOHNSON; occ: farmer; res: Ffx; mother: Emma JOHNSON; inf: D.
JOHNSON, father; pg:ln: 144:45

JOHNSON, Eva; CF; b. 3 Jul 1893 in ___; father: Ciff [Cliff?]
JOHNSON; occ: ___; res: ___; mother: Harriet JOHNSON; inf: C.
JOHNSON, father; pg:ln: 214:52

JOHNSON, Flora; CF; b. 20 May 1890 in Ffx; father: Cliff JOHNSON;
occ: farmer; res: Ffx; mother: Susan JOHNSON; inf: C. JOHNSON,
father; pg:ln: 190:50

JOHNSON, Florence; CF; b. 9 Nov 1884 in Dranes.; father: Sandy
JOHNSON; occ: laborer; res: Dranes.; mother: Mary JOHNSON; inf:
father; pg:ln: 150:54

JOHNSON, Florence; WF; b. 9 Jul 1894 in Ffx; father: Geo. A.
JOHNSON; occ: farmer; res: Ffx; mother: Annie E. JOHNSON; inf:
Geo. JOHNSON, father; pg:ln: 218:64

JOHNSON, Geo. W.; WM; b. 11 Mar 1883 in Ffx; father: Greenberry
JOHNSON; occ: farmer; res: Ffx; mother: Lavina JOHNSON; inf: G.
JOHNSON, father; pg:ln: 144:46

JOHNSON, H.; CM; b. 17 Dec 1883 in Providence Dist.; father: Clift
JOHNSON; occ: laborer; res: Providence Dist.; mother: Susan
JOHNSON; inf: father; pg:ln: 140:49

JOHNSON, Howard E.; WM; b. 22 Dec 1882 in Lewinsville; father: B. F.
JOHNSTON; occ: farmer; res: Lewinsville; mother: Mary E.
JOHNSON; inf: father; pg:ln: 134:31

JOHNSON, Lawson; WM; b. 28 Jun 1888 in Ffx; father: L. E.
JOHNSON; occ: farmer; res: Ffx; mother: L. A. JOHNSON; inf: L. E.
JOHNSON, father; pg:ln: 174:58

JOHNSON, Mary A.; WF; b. 22 Sep 1884 in Prov.; father: J. H.
JOHNSON; occ: farmer; res: Prov.; mother: Carrie J. JOHNSON; inf:
father; pg:ln: 150:55

JOHNSON, Mary B.; CF; b. 4 Jul 1896 in ___; father: Sidney
JOHNSON; occ: farmer; res: Ffx; mother: Annie JOHNSON; inf: S.
JOHNSON, father; pg:ln: 226:60

JOHNSON, Mary; WF; b. 5 Nov 1882 in Vienna; father: Nathaniel
JOHNSTON; occ: farmer; res: Vienna; mother: Alberta JOHNSON;
inf: father; pg:ln: 134:30

JOHNSON, Morton; CM; b. 30 Aug 1885 in Ffx; father: Delvin
JOHNSON; occ: farmer; res: Ffx; mother: Emaline JOHNSON; inf:
D. JOHNSON, father; pg:ln: 156:35

JOHNSON, not named (dead); CM; b. 4 Jun 1882 in Falls Church;
father: David JOHNSON; occ: laborer; res: Falls Ch; mother:
Caroline JOHNSON; inf: father; pg:ln: 135:77

JOHNSON, Susan; CF; b. 30 Mar 1892 in Ffx; father: Cliff JOHNSON;
occ: farmer; res: Ffx; mother: Susan JOHNSON; inf: C. JOHNSON,
father; pg:ln: 203:55

JOHNSON, Thomas; CM; b. 6 Oct 1890 in ___; father: Gabriel
JOHNSON; occ: laborer; res: Ffx; mother: Francis JOHNSON; inf:
G. JOHNSON, father; pg:ln: 186:62

JOHNSON, W.; CM; b. 17 Sep 1893 in ___; father: J. H. JOHNSON;
occ: ___; res: ___; mother: Carrie JOHNSON; inf: J. H. JOHNSON,
father; pg:ln: 214:60

JOHNSTON, Geo.; WM; b. __ Aug 1882 in Ffx; father: S. S. JOHNSTON; occ: ___; res: ___; mother: Katie JOHNSTON; inf: S. JOHNSTON, father; pg:ln: 137:41

JONES, Albert; WM; b. 16 Dec 1887 in Ffx; father: Jas. JONES; occ: farmer; res: Ffx; mother: M. E. JONES; inf: Jas. JONES, father; pg:ln: 161:66

JONES, Annie M.; WF; b. 27 Sep 1887 in Ffx; father: O. W. JONES; occ: farmer; res: Ffx; mother: Mary E. JONES; inf: O. W. JONES, father; pg:ln: 161:64

JONES, B. H.; WF; b. 11 Feb 1896 in ___; father: J. R. JONES; occ: farmer; res: Ffx; mother: S. J. JONES; inf: J. R. JONES, father; pg:ln: 226:59

JONES, Benj.; WM; b. 17 Apr 1880 in Ffx; father: E. H. JONES; occ: farmer; res: Ffx; mother: Ella; inf: E. H. JONES, father; pg:ln: 128:52

JONES, Bertha May; WF; b. 15 Jun 1887 in Ffx; father: Jas. E. JONES; occ: farmer; res: Ffx; mother: Mary J. JONES; inf: Jas. E. JONES, father; pg:ln: 167:60

JONES, Bessie; WF; b. 1 Jul 1891 in Ravensworth; father: Owen W. JONES; occ: farmer; res: Ravensworth; mother: Mary E. JONES; inf: parents; pg:ln: 195:30

JONES, Bowling Barton; WM; b. 15 Jun 1896 nr Ravensworth; father: Owen W. JONES; occ: farmer; res: Ravensworth; mother: Mary E. JONES; inf: father; pg:ln: 230:71

JONES, Caroline; CF; b. __ Nov 1891 nr Halls X Rds; father: Dennis JONES; occ: laborer; res: nr Halls X Rds; mother: Francis JONES; inf: parent; pg:ln: 197:08

JONES, Carolline; CF; b. 10 Dec 1888 in Ffx; father: Dennis JONES; occ: laborer; res: Ffx; mother: Francis JONES; inf: Dennis JONES, father; pg:ln: 171:42

JONES, Chas. H.; WM; b. 21 Aug 1883 in Fairfax c. H.; father: J. R. JONES; occ: farmer; res: Fairfax C. H.; mother: Susan J. JONES; inf: father; pg:ln: 140:48

JONES, Clinton; WM; b. 15 Feb 1889 in Ffx; father: E. H. JONES; occ: farmer; res: Ffx; mother: E. S. JONES; inf: E. H. JONES, father; pg:ln: 182:48

JONES, Curent; WM; b. 10 Jul 1881 in Dranesville; father: Ben. L. JONES; occ: farmer; res: Dranesville; mother: A. JONES; inf: father; pg:ln: 130:32

JONES, Dennis; CM; b. 18 Sep 1896 in ___; father: Emory JONES; occ: farmer; res: Ffx; mother: Nannie JONES; inf: Emory JONES, father; pg:ln: 226:67

JONES, Douglas; CM; b. 21 Nov 1896 in ___; father: Robt. JONES; occ: farmer; res: Ffx; mother: Jane JONES; inf: Robt. JONES, father; pg:ln: 226:66

JONES, Elizabeth; CF; b. 17 Sep 1887 in Ffx; father: Wm. JONES; occ: farmer; res: Ffx; mother: Mary JONES; inf: Wm. JONES, father; pg:ln: 167:61

JONES, Garrison; CM; b. 13 Feb 1890 in Ffx; father: Garrison JONES; occ: farmer; res: Ffx; mother: Gertrude JONES; inf: G. JONES, father; pg:ln: 190:53

JONES, Howard; WM; b. 1 Oct 1881 in Ffx; father: E. H. JONES; occ: farmer; res: Ffx; mother: Ella JONES; inf: E. H. JONES, father; pg:ln: 132:24

JONES, Jno. E.; CM; b. 5 Dec 1893 in ___; father: Jno. E. JONES; occ: ___; res: ___; mother: Nancy JONES; inf: J. E. JONES, father; pg:ln: 214:53

JONES, John Thos.; WM; b. 30 Jun 1895 in Ravensworth; father: Owen W. JONES; occ: farmer; res: Ravensworth; mother: Mary E. JONES; inf: father; pg:ln: 222:33

JONES, Josiah; WM; b. 8 Apr 1883 in Ffx; father: not known; occ: farmer; res: Ffx; mother: Jennie JONES; inf: T. T. BURK, Supt. Poor; pg:ln: 144:43

JONES, Katie; CF; b. __ Apr 1882 in Ffx; father: Wm. JONES; occ: farmer; res: Ffx; mother: Charlotte JONES; inf: Wm. JONES, father; pg:ln: 137:40

JONES, Nannie; CF; b. 20 Feb 1896 nr Barkers X Rds; father: ___; occ: ___; res: ___; mother: Mollie JONES; inf: mother; pg:ln: 230:73

JONES, Nellie P.; WF; b. 7 Oct 1883 in Ffx; father: E. H. JONES; occ: farmer; res: Ffx; mother: Ella JONES; inf: E. H. JONES, father; pg:ln: 144:44

JONES, not named; CM; b. 30 Aug 1884 in Ffx; father: Jesse JONES; occ: ___; res: ___; mother: Adeline JONES; inf: J. JONES, father; pg:ln: 147:41

JONES, Robert; WM; b. 7 Oct 1892 in Ravensworth; father: Orion JONES; occ: foreman farm; res: Ravensworth; mother: Mary E. JONES; inf: father; pg:ln: 209:35

JONES, Robt. L.; WM; b. 14 Nov 1894 in Ffx; father: Jas. E. JONES; occ: farmer; res: Ffx; mother: Harriet JONES; inf: J. JONES, father; pg:ln: 218:60

JONES, Rufus; CM; b. 8 Jun 1892 nr Halls X Rds; father: Henry JONES; occ: laborer; res: nr Burke; mother: Josephine JONES; inf: mother; pg:ln: 206:35

JONES, Sidney; WM; b. 7Mar 1893 in ___; father: Jas. E. JONES; occ: ___; res: ___; mother: Harriet JONES; inf: J. E. JONES, father; pg:ln: 214:59

JONES, Virginia; WF; b. 29 Oct 1893 in ___; father: J. W. JONES; occ: ___; res: ___; mother: Mary JONES; inf: J. W. JONES, father; pg:ln: 214:57

JONES, Walter; WM; b. 20 Dec 1894 in Ffx; father: Jas. W. JONES; occ: farmer; res: Ffx; mother: Mary JONES; inf: J. W. JONES, father; pg:ln: 218:61

JONES, Wm. M.; WM; b. 20 Dec 1891 in Ffx; father: Jas. R. JONES; occ: farmer; res: Ffx; mother: Susan JONES; inf: J. R. JONES, father; pg:ln: 199:48

JOSPER, Mary Virginia; CF; b. 17 Aug 1891 nr Woodlawn; father:
Daniel W. JOSPER; occ: laborer; res: nr Woodlawn; mother: Martha
E. JOSPER; inf: parent; pg:ln: 196:11

KEARNES, Eva M.; WF; b. 10 Oct 1881 in Ffx; father: Edras KEARNS;
occ: farmer; res: Ffx; mother: M. E. KEARNES; inf: E. KEARNS,
father; pg:ln: 132:25

KEARNES, Philip L.; WM; b. 22 Sep 1889 in Ffx; father: Edras
KEARNES; occ: farmer; res: Ffx; mother: M. E. KEARNES; inf: E.
KEARNES, father; pg:ln: 182:54

KEARNS, Archie; WM; b. 17 Nov 1892 nr Fairfax Sta.; father: Eddris
KEARNS; occ: farmer; res: nr Fairfax Sta.; mother: Martha E.
KEARNS; inf: mother; pg:ln: 208:14

KEEN, Harry; WM; b. 24 Feb 1889 in Ffx; father: Jas. O. KEEN; occ:
farmer; res: Ffx; mother: Elizabt. KEEN; inf: J. O. KEENE, father;
pg:ln: 182:50

KEENE, Lucy; WF; b. 27 Aug 1884 in Ffx; father: Jas. O. KEENE; occ:
___; res: ___; mother: Betty KEENE; inf: J. O. KEENE, father; pg:ln:
147:45

KEENE, Robt.; WM; b. 1 Oct 1886 in Ffx; father: Jas. O. KEEN; occ:
farmer; res: Ffx; mother: Elizabt. KEEN; inf: J. O. KEENE, father;
pg:ln: 155:10

KEER, Milton; WM; b. 29 Aug 1892 [15 Sep lined thru] in Ffx; father: V.
E. KEER [KEERR lined thru]; occ: farmer; res: Ffx; mother: V. KEER
[KEERR lined thru]; inf: V. E. KEER, father; pg:ln: 203:60

KEER, Milton; WM; b. 29 Aug 1893 in ___; father: V. E. KEER; occ:
___; res: ___; mother: Dora V. KEER; inf: V. E. KEER, father See
registration of this child in Fairfax on page 203, line 60.; pg:ln:
214:63

KEER, Walter; WM; b. 10 Feb 1887 in Ffx; father: Virgil E. KEER; occ:
mec[h]anic; res: Ffx; mother: Dora KEER; inf: V. E. KEER, father;
pg:ln: 162:68

KEHLIN, Ruth; WF; b. 26 Jun 1891 nr Alexandria; father: Richard
KEHLIN; occ: farmer; res: nr Alexandria; mother: B. KEHLIN; inf:
parents; pg:ln: 195:09

KELLEY, Louis; CM; b. 17 May 1892 in Ffx; father: Chas. KELLEY; occ:
farmer; res: Ffx; mother: Ada KELLEY; inf: Chas. KELLEY, father;
pg:ln: 203:59

KENYON, A. G.; WM; b. 17 Mar 1885 in Vienna; father: Geo. L.
KENYON; occ: farmer; res: Vienna; mother: Lottie M. KENYON; inf:
father; pg:ln: 153:38

KENYON, Marion; WF; b. 21 Jul 1881 in Vienna; father: Geo. L.
KENYON; occ: farmer; res: Vienna; mother: Lotta M. KENYON; inf:
father; pg:ln: 130:34

KEPHART, ___; WM; b. 19 Apr 1890 in Ffx; father: J. W. KEPHART;
occ: farmer; res: Ffx; mother: C. A. KEPHART; inf: J. W. KEPHART,
father; pg:ln: 190:58

KEPHART, Vergie; WF; b. 5 Nov 1892 in Ffx; father: M. W. KEPHART; occ: farmer; res: Ffx; mother: Jennie KEPHART; inf: M. W. KEPHART, father; pg:ln: 203:58

KERBY, ___; WM; b. 15 Jun 1881 in Lewinsville; father: Francis A. KERBY; occ: farmer; res: Lewinsville; mother: Henrietta C. KERBY; inf: father; pg:ln: 130:36

KERFOOT, Nannie (dead); CF; b. 15 Feb 1883 in Providence Dist.; father: James KERFOOT; occ: laborer; res: Providence Dist.; mother: Caroline KERFOOT; inf: father; pg:ln: 140:54

KERNS, Annie E.; WF; b. 14 Aug 1883 in Dranesville; father: Jno. W. KERNS; occ: farmer; res: Dranesville; mother: Martha V. KERNS; inf: father; pg:ln: 140:57

KESTERSON, Chas.; WM; b. 8 Feb 1885 in Falls Church; father: Geo. KESTERSON; occ: mechanic; res: Falls Church; mother: Margt. KESTERSON; inf: father; pg:ln: 152:36

KESTERSON, Joseph; WM; b. 12 Oct 1886 in Falls Ch.; father: Geo. W. KESTERSON; occ: mechanic; res: Falls Ch.; mother: ___ KESTERSON; inf: father; pg:ln: 158:28

KESTERSON, Oliver; WM; b. 20 Apr 1892 in Ffx; father: Geo. W. KESTERSON; occ: farmer; res: Ffx; mother: Mgt. KESTERSON; inf: G. W. KESTERSON, father; pg:ln: 203:61

KEYES, Benj. Ashton; WM; b. 17 Aug 1892 nr Chantilly; father: Philip KEYES; occ: farmer; res: nr Chantilly; mother: Molly KEYES; inf: father; pg:ln: 208:15

KEYES, Daisy; WF; b. 30 Jun 1882 in Ffx; father: Shirley KEYES; occ: ___; res: ___; mother: America KEYES; inf: S. KEYES, father; pg:ln: 137:42

KEYES, Lurena L.; WF; b. 27 Aug 1884 in Ffx; father: Geo. W. KEYES; occ: ___; res: ___; mother: Elgivia KEYES; inf: G. W. KEYES, father; pg:ln: 147:46

KEYS, Georgianna; WF; b. 20 Dec 1887 in Ffx; father: Geo. W. KEYS; occ: farmer; res: Ffx; mother: Elgiva V. KEYS; inf: Elgiva V. KEYS, mother; pg:ln: 168:68

KEYS, Roberta; WF; b. 7 Dec 1889 in Ffx; father: Philip KEYS; occ: farmer; res: Ffx; mother: Mollie KEYS; inf: Philip KEYS, father; pg:ln: 182:52

KEYS, Silas W.; WM; b. 16 Dec 1890 in ___; father: Geo. W. KEYS; occ: farmer; res: Ffx; mother: Algiva V. KEYS; inf: G. W. KEYS, father; pg:ln: 186:63

KIDWELL, ___; WF; b. 2 May 1883 in Dranesville; father: Jno. T. KIDWELL; occ: farmer; res: Dranesville; mother: Mary J. KIDWELL; inf: father; pg:ln: 140:60

KIDWELL, ___; WF; b. 28 Nov 1881 in near C. H.; father: Albert KIDWELL; occ: farmer; res: near C. H.; mother: Callista V. KIDWELL; inf: father; pg:ln: 130:33

KIDWELL, A. W.; WM; b. 1 Feb 1881 in near C. H.; father: Geo. W. KIDWELL; occ: farmer; res: near C. H.; mother: Margaret KIDWELL; inf: father; pg:ln: 130:35

KIDWELL, Arthur; WM; b. 14 Jul 1885 in Ffx; father: Silas KIDWELL;
occ: farmer; res: Ffx; mother: Mary C. KIDWELL; inf: S. KIDWELL,
father; pg:ln: 156:36

KIDWELL, Augustus; WM; b. 13 Mar 1891 in Ffx; father: Geo. W.
KIDWELL; occ: farmer; res: Ffx; mother: Margt. M. KIDWELL; inf: G.
W. KIDWELL, father; pg:ln: 199:52

KIDWELL, Bessie; WF; b. 23 Apr 1893 in ___; father: Jno. R. KIDWELL;
occ: ___; res: ___; mother: Mary KIDWELL; inf: J. R. KIDWELL,
father; pg:ln: 214:65

KIDWELL, Birt Emerson; WM; b. 4 Jun 1890 in ___; father: Winthrop
KIDWELL; occ: stone mason; res: Ffx; mother: Josephine
KIDWELL; inf: W. KIDWELL, father; pg:ln: 186:65

KIDWELL, Carl; WM; b. 29 Aug 1891 in Ffx; father: Jas. L. KIDWELL;
occ: farmer; res: Ffx; mother: Elizabt. KIDWELL; inf: J. L. KIDWELL,
father; pg:ln: 199:54

KIDWELL, Clarence; WM; b. 1 Nov 1887 in Ffx; father: Silas W.
KIDWELL; occ: laborer; res: Ffx; mother: Mary C. KIDWELL; inf: S.
W. KIDWELL, father; pg:ln: 167:66

KIDWELL, Edward B.; WM; b. 16 Feb 1887 in Ffx; father: Edward
KIDWELL; occ: laborer; res: Ffx; mother: Clara KIDWELL; inf: E.
KIDWELL, father; pg:ln: 162:70

KIDWELL, Ernest E.; WM; b. 23 Dec 1887 in Ffx; father: L. B.
KIDWELL; occ: laborer; res: Ffx; mother: Laura A. KIDWELL; inf: L.
B. KIDWELL, father; pg:ln: 162:73

KIDWELL, Ernest L.; WM; b. 3 Feb 1883 in Dranesville; father: Lemuel
KIDWELL; occ: farmer; res: Dranesville; mother: Elizabeth
KIDWELL; inf: father; pg:ln: 140:56

KIDWELL, Ethel; WF; b. 10 Jul 1896 in ___; father: Geo. W. KIDWELL;
occ: farmer; res: Ffx; mother: M. A. KIDWELL; inf: G. W. KIDWELL,
father; pg:ln: 226:70

KIDWELL, Fannie; WF; b. 12 Jan 1885 in Ffx; father: Jno. KIDWELL;
occ: farmer; res: Ffx; mother: Laura KIDWELL; inf: Jno. KIDWELL,
father; pg:ln: 157:37

KIDWELL, Flora Victoria; WF; b. 29 Dec 1893 nr Clifton Sta.; father:
Earnest KIDWELL; occ: farmer; res: nr Clifton Sta.; mother: Kate
KIDWELL; inf: mother; pg:ln: 211:63

KIDWELL, Floyd; WM; b. 24 Jul 1892 in Ffx; father: Geo. W. KIDWELL;
occ: farmer; res: Ffx; mother: Martha KIDWELL; inf: G. W.
KIDWELL, father; pg:ln: 203:57

KIDWELL, Geo. H.; WM; b. 3 Nov 1893 in ___; father: G. H. KIDWELL;
occ: ___; res: ___; mother: Rose KIDWELL; inf: G. H. KIDWELL,
father; pg:ln: 214:64

KIDWELL, Gertrude; WF; b. 10 Jul 1888 in Ffx; father: Andrew
KIDWELL; occ: farmer; res: Ffx; mother: Elizabt. KIDWELL; inf: A.
KIDWELL, father; pg:ln: 174:61

KIDWELL, Gilbert M.; WM; b. 27 Oct 1887 in Ffx; father: Andrew
KIDWELL; occ: laborer; res: Ffx; mother: Mary E. KIDWELL; inf:
Andrew KIDWELL, father; pg:ln: 162:71

KIDWELL, Gracie; WF; b. 2 Jul 1887 in Ffx; father: Jas. KIDWELL; occ: laborer; res: Ffx; mother: Emma KIDWELL; inf: Emma KIDWELL, mother; pg:ln: 167:67

KIDWELL, Hattie B.; CF; b. 1 Nov 1896 in ___; father: Saml. KIDWELL; occ: farmer; res: Ffx; mother: Annie KIDWELL; inf: Saml. KIDWELL, father; pg:ln: 226:71

KIDWELL, Hattie R.; WF; b. 15 Jun 1883 in Ffx; father: Silas KIDWELL; occ: farmer; res: Ffx; mother: Mary C. KIDWELL; inf: S. KIDWELL, father; pg:ln: 144:49

KIDWELL, Hulda; WF; b. 10 Jul 1884 in Ffx; father: Silas KIDWELL; occ: ___; res: ___; mother: Mary L. KIDWELL; inf: Silas KIDWELL, father; pg:ln: 147:43

KIDWELL, Irene; WF; b. 13 May 1880 in Ffx; father: Jas. H. KIDWELL; occ: farmer; res: Ffx; mother: Jane; inf: J. H. KIDWELL, father; pg:ln: 128:53

KIDWELL, Jno. W.; WM; b. 1 Feb 1888 in Ffx; father: Jno. F. KIDWELL; occ: farmer; res: Ffx; mother: Jennie KIDWELL; inf: J. F. KIDWELL, father; pg:ln: 174:59

KIDWELL, Kate B.; WF; b. 16 Sep 1889 in Ffx; father: Melvin KIDWELL; occ: farmer; res: Ffx; mother: Kate KIDWELL; inf: M. KIDWELL, father; pg:ln: 178:63

KIDWELL, Laurence W.; WM; b. 4 May 1884 in Prov.; father: Edward KIDWELL; occ: mechanic; res: Prov.; mother: Clara KIDWELL; inf: father; pg:ln: 150:56

KIDWELL, Leroy; WM; b. 29 Jul 1894 in Ffx; father: Geo. W. KIDWELL; occ: farmer; res: Ffx; mother: Mary A. KIDWELL; inf: Geo. W. KIDWELL, father; pg:ln: 218:69

KIDWELL, Lester; WM; b. 15 Jul 1890 in ___; father: A. T. KIDWELL; occ: laborer; res: Ffx; mother: Colesta KIDWELL; inf: A. T. KIDWELL, father; pg:ln: 186:64

KIDWELL, Lloyd L.; WM; b. 18 Feb 1889 in Ffx; father: Jos. KIDWELL; occ: farmer; res: Ffx; mother: Della E. KIDWELL; inf: Jos. KIDWELL, father; pg:ln: 178:64

KIDWELL, Lula Lee; WF; b. 3 Jan 1891 nr Fairfax Sta.; father: ___; occ: ___; res: ___; mother: Jane E. KIDWELL; inf: parents; pg:ln: 193:19

KIDWELL, Lula M.; WF; b. 14 Jun 1890 in Ffx; father: Chas. L. KIDWELL; occ: farmer; res: Ffx; mother: Sarah V. KIDWELL; inf: C. L. KIDWELL, father; pg:ln: 190:56

KIDWELL, Martha E.; WF; b. 10 Jan 1887 in Ffx; father: Geo. M. KIDWELL; occ: laborer; res: Ffx; mother: Louisa KIDWELL; inf: Geo. M. KIDWELL, father; pg:ln: 162:72

KIDWELL, Mary E.; WF; b. 7 Oct 1894 in Ffx; father: Saml. C. KIDWELL; occ: farmer; res: Ffx; mother: Annie KIDWELL; inf: S. C. KIDWELL, father; pg:ln: 218:68

KIDWELL, Mary F.; WF; b. 13 Jun 1890 in Ffx; father: Jno. T. KIDWELL; occ: farmer; res: Ffx; mother: Mary KIDWELL; inf: J. T. KIDWELL, father; pg:ln: 190:57

KIDWELL, Maud; WF; b. 12 Jan 1883 in Falls Church; father: Edward
KIDWELL; occ: mechanic; res: Falls Church; mother: Clara
KIDWELL; inf: father; pg:ln: 140:52

KIDWELL, May; WF; b. 9 Jul 1887 in Ffx; father: Albert R. KIDWELL;
occ: laborer; res: Ffx; mother: Collista KIDWELL; inf: A. R.
KIDWELL, father; pg:ln: 162:75

KIDWELL, not named; WF; b. 1 Nov 1880 in Providence; father: Albert
KIDWELL; occ: farmer; res: Providence; mother: Calista KIDWELL;
inf: father; pg:ln: 124:32

KIDWELL, not named; WF; b. 15 Oct 1884 in Ffx; father: Winthrop
KIDWELL; occ: ___; res: ___; mother: Josephine KIDWELL; inf: W.
KIDWELL, father; pg:ln: 147:44

KIDWELL, not named; WM; b. 12 Oct 1880 in Dranesville; father: Jno.
T. KIDWELL; occ: farmer; res: Dranesville; mother: Mary J.
KIDWELL; inf: father; pg:ln: 124:31

KIDWELL, not named; WM; b. 7 Dec 1882 in Dranesville; father: Geo.
M. KIDWELL; occ: farmer; res: Dranesville; mother: ___ KIDWELL;
inf: father; pg:ln: 134:32

KIDWELL, Rose Nell; WF; b. 23 Jan 1887 in Ffx; father: Jno. H.
KIDWELL; occ: laborer; res: Ffx; mother: Laura F. KIDWELL; inf: J.
H. KIDWELL, father; pg:ln: 162:74

KIDWELL, Walter L.; WM; b. 20 May 1888 in Ffx; father: J. L. KIDWELL;
occ: farmer; res: Ffx; mother: Rebecca KIDWELL; inf: J. L.
KIDWELL, father; pg:ln: 174:60

KINCHELOE, ___; WF; b. 4 Sep 1883 in Ffx; father: W. S.
KINCHELOE; occ: farmer; res: Ffx; mother: Anna M. KINCHELOE;
inf: W. S. KINCHELOE, father; pg:ln: 144:48

KINCHELOE, Jennie P.; WF; b. 29 Jan 1889 in Ffx; father: Danl.
KINCHELOE; occ: mechanic; res: Ffx; mother: Florence
KINCHELOE; inf: Danl. KINCHELOE, father; pg:ln: 182:53

KINCHELOE, Nannie T.; WF; b. 18 Dec 1889 in Ffx; father: W. S.
KINCHELOE; occ: farmer; res: Ffx; mother: Annie KINCHELOE; inf:
W. S. KINCHELOE, father; pg:ln: 182:51

KINCHELOE, Robt. Lee; WM; b. 30 Nov 1884 in Ffx; father: J. C.
KINCHELOE; occ: ___; res: ___; mother: Susan T. KINCHELOE;
inf: J. C. KINCHELOE, father; pg:ln: 147:42

KING, John Alexander; WM; b. 1 Oct 1891 in Wolf Run; father: Charles
A. KING; occ: farmer; res: Wolf Run; mother: Eddie Lee KING; inf:
parents; pg:ln: 194:14

KING, Mary Ellen; CF; b. 10 Sep 1890 in ___; father: Robt. KING; occ:
laborer; res: Ffx; mother: Fannie KING; inf: Robt. KING, father;
pg:ln: 186:66

KING, not named; WM; b. 11 May 1885 in Lewinsville; father: Thos. A.
KING; occ: farmer; res: Lewinsville; mother: Martha KING; inf: father;
pg:ln: 153:39

KINNER, Lewis E.; CM; b. 25 Nov 1883 in Providence Dist.; father:
Hiram KINNER; occ: laborer; res: Providence Dist.; mother: Mary
KINNER; inf: father; pg:ln: 140:55

KIRBY, Frank B.; WM; b. 29 Sep 1891 in Ffx; father: E. F. KIRBY; occ: farmer; res: Ffx; mother: Florence KIRBY; inf: E. F. KIRBY, father; pg:ln: 199:53

KISENDOFFER, Herbert; WM; b. 12 Oct 1885 in West End; father: Henry KISENDOFFER; occ: clerk; res: West End; mother: Louisa KISENDOFFER; inf: father; pg:ln: 153:37

KITCHEN, Alfr'd. M.; WM; b. 2 Mar 1896 in ___; father: W. KITCHEN; occ: farmer; res: Ffx; mother: Mary KITCHEN; inf: W. KITCHEN, father; pg:ln: 226:72

KITCHEN, Chas.; WM; b. 14 Sep 1893 in ___; father: W. KITCHEN; occ: ___; res: ___; mother: Mary KITCHEN; inf: W. KITCHEN, father; pg:ln: 214:66

KITCHEN, John; WM; b. 23 Aug 1890 in Ffx; father: W. KITCHEN; occ: farmer; res: Ffx; mother: Mary KITCHEN; inf: W. KITCHEN, father; pg:ln: 190:59

KITSON, Essie; WF; b. 23 Mar 1891 in nr. Seminary; father: Geo. Wm. KITSON; occ: rail road hand; res: nr Alexandria; mother: Lillian KITSON; inf: parents; pg:ln: 195:31

KITSON, Geo.; WM; b. 28 Dec 1883 in Ffx; father: Elihu KITSON; occ: farmer; res: Ffx; mother: Mary E. KITSON; inf: E. KITSON, father; pg:ln: 144:52

KITSON, Minnie; WF; b. 17 Aug 1883 in Ffx; father: Saml. KITSON; occ: farmer; res: Ffx; mother: Sarah M. KITSON; inf: Saml. KITSON, father; pg:ln: 144:51

KLOCK, Edmunda; WF; b. 17 Nov 1883 in Providence Dist.; father: Jonathan KLOCK; occ: farmer; res: Providence Dist.; mother: S. A. KLOCK; inf: father; pg:ln: 140:53

KLOCK, Herbert; WM; b. 8 Dec 1884 in Prov.; father: Webster K[L]OCK; occ: farmer; res: Prov.; mother: Elizabeth KLOCK; inf: father; pg:ln: 150:57

KLOCK, Sarah C.; WF; b. 11 Jul 1880 in Providence; father: Jonathan KLOCK; occ: farmer; res: Providence; mother: Sarah J. KLOCK; inf: father; pg:ln: 124:33

KNIGHT, Annie; CF; b. 9 Oct 1883 in Ffx; father: Jas. KNIGHT; occ: farmer; res: Ffx; mother: Sarah KNIGHT; inf: Jas. KNIGHT, father; pg:ln: 144:50

KNIGHT, Gertrude; CF; b. 15 Apr 1887 in Ffx; father: Robt. M. KNIGHT; occ: laborer; res: Ffx; mother: Mary KNIGHT; inf: R. M. KNIGHT, father; pg:ln: 162:69

LACY, Augustus; WM; b. 20 Aug 1893 nr Accotink; father: John R. LACY; occ: farmer; res: nr Accotink; mother: Rosa LACY; inf: mother; pg:ln: 211:67

LACY, Charles; WM; b. 17 Jan 1885 in Bailey's X Rds; father: B. J. LACY; occ: farmer; res: Bailey's X Rds; mother: Rebecca LACY; inf: father; pg:ln: 153:44

LACY, Charley (twin); WM; b. 10 Dec 1896 nr Woodlawn; father: John R. LACY; occ: farmer; res: nr Woodlawn; mother: Rosa LACY; inf: mother; pg:ln: 230:77

LACY, Elizabt.; WF; b. 10 May 1889 in Ffx; father: R. A. LACY; occ: farmer; res: Ffx; mother: Mary E. LACY; inf: R. A. LACY, father; pg:ln: 182:56

LACY, Fred (twin); WM; b. 10 Dec 1896 nr Woodlawn; father: John R. LACY; occ: farmer; res: nr Woodlawn; mother: Rosa LACY; inf: mother; pg:ln: 230:77

LACY, James; WM; b. 16 Jan 1892 nr Alexandria; father: Richard A. LACY; occ: farmer; res: nr Alex.; mother: Mary LACY; inf: mother; pg:ln: 207:74

LACY, John; WM; b. 8 Sep 1885 in Bailey's X Rds; father: W. B. LACY; occ: farmer; res: Bailey's X Rds; mother: Martha LACY; inf: father; pg:ln: 153:45

LACY, Maud; WF; b. 17 Aug 1888 in Ffx; father: Judas LACY; occ: farmer; res: Ffx; mother: Martha LACY; inf: J. LACY, father; pg:ln: 174:62

LACY, May; WF; b. 14 Jul 1891 in Ffx; father: Hunter LACY; occ: farmer; res: Ffx; mother: Rose LACY; inf: H. LACY, father; pg:ln: 199:57

LACY, Nellie; WF; b. 5 Mar 1891 in Ffx; father: Edgar LACY; occ: farmer; res: Ffx; mother: L. LACY; inf: E. LACY, father; pg:ln: 199:56

LADUE, Robert; WM; b. 15 Nov 1889 in Ffx; father: Geo. W. LADUE; occ: farmer; res: Ffx; mother: Virginia LADUE; inf: G. W. LADUE, father; pg:ln: 182:58

LADUE, Sadie; WF; b. 25 Sep 1893 nr Fairfax Sta; father: Geo. LADUE; occ: farmer; res: nr Fairfax; mother: Virginia E. LADUE; inf: mother; pg:ln: 211:66

LAMBERT, Geo. C.; WM; b. 6 Nov 1887 in Ffx; father: C. H. LAMBERT; occ: physician; res: Ffx; mother: Laura LAMBERT; inf: C. H. LAMBERT, father; pg:ln: 168:69

LANDSTREET, John Leon; WM; b. 26 Nov 1895 nr Accotink; father: John LANDSTREET; occ: farmer; res: nr Accotink; mother: May Elizabeth LANDSTREET; inf: father; pg:ln: 223:79

LANDSTREET, Joseph C.; WM; b. 30 Oct 1882 in Ffx; father: Chas. LANDSTREET; occ: ___; res: ___; mother: Laura LANDSTREET; inf: C. LANDSTREET, father; pg:ln: 137:43

LANDSTREET, May Margaret; WF; b. 31 Jun 1896 nr Accotink Sta; father: John LANDSTREET; occ: farmer; res: nr Accotink Sta; mother: May Elizabeth LANDSTREET; inf: father; pg:ln: 230:75

LANE, Hattie; WF; b. 24 Aug 1880 in Dranesville; father: David LANE; occ: farmer; res: Dranesville; mother: Elizabeth LANE; inf: father; pg:ln: 124:38

LANE, Mary L.; WF; b. 2 Jul 1894 in Ffx; father: Frank LANE; occ: farmer; res: Ffx; mother: Elizabt. LANE; inf: F. LANE, father; pg:ln: 218:70

LANE, O. W.; WM; b. 27 Aug 1883 in Ffx; father: Luther A. LANE; occ: farmer; res: Ffx; mother: Eudora P. LANE; inf: L. LANE, father; pg:ln: 144:53

LANE, Thos. A.; WM; b. 3 Apr 1887 in Ffx; father: Luther A. LANE; occ: farmer; res: Ffx; mother: Uda P. LANE; inf: L. A. LANE, father; pg:ln: 162:85

LANG, Walter N.; WM; b. 6 Feb 1880 in Falls Church; father: James LANG; occ: farmer; res: Falls Church; mother: Ada LANG; inf: mother; pg:ln: 124:35

LANHAM, Chas. P.; WM; b. 13 Aug 1886 in Spring Vale; father: Benj. LANHAM; occ: farmer; res: Spring Vale; mother: E. S. LANHAM; inf: father; pg:ln: 158:36

LANHAM, James; WM; b. 7 Aug 1891 in Ffx; father: Jas. LANHAM; occ: farmer; res: Ffx; mother: Mary LANHAM; inf: J. LANHAM, father; pg:ln: 199:55

LANHAM, not named; WM; b. 16 Oct 1883 in Dranesville; father: Jno. C. LANHAM; occ: farmer; res: Dranesville; mother: Annie LANHAM; inf: father; pg:ln: 140:61

LANHAM, not named; WM; b. 5 Mar 1885 in Dranes.; father: R. B. LANHAM; occ: farmer; res: Dranes.; mother: Minnie LANHAM; inf: father; pg:ln: 153:46

LANHAM, Wm. H.; WM; b. 2 May 1880 in Dranesville; father: Jno. C. LANHAM; occ: farmer; res: Dranesville; mother: Annie E. LANHAM; inf: father; pg:ln: 124:39

LEE, ___ (triplet); CM; b. 5 Mar 1882 in Ffx; father: Andrew LEE; occ: ___; res: ___; mother: Mariah LEE; inf: A. LEE, father; pg:ln: 137:47

LEE, ___ (triplet); CM; b. 5 Mar 1882 in Ffx; father: Andrew LEE; occ: ___; res: ___; mother: Mariah LEE; inf: A. LEE, father; pg:ln: 137:48

LEE, ___ (triplet); CM; b. 5 Mar 1882 in Ffx; father: Andrew LEE; occ: ___; res: ___; mother: Mariah LEE; inf: A. LEE, father; pg:ln: 137:49

LEE, ___ (triplet); CM; b. 5 Mar 1883 in Ffx; father: Andrew LEE; occ: farmer; res: Ffx; mother: Maria LEE; inf: A. LEE, father; pg:ln: 144:55

LEE, ___ (triplet); CM; b. 5 Mar 1883 in Ffx; father: Andrew LEE; occ: farmer; res: Ffx; mother: Maria LEE; inf: A. LEE, father; pg:ln: 144:56

LEE, ___ (triplet); CM; b. 5 Mar 1883 in Ffx; father: Andrew LEE; occ: farmer; res: Ffx; mother: Maria LEE; inf: A. LEE, father; pg:ln: 144:57

LEE, ___ (twin); WF; b. 10 Jun 1890 in Ffx; father: Thos. W. LEE; occ: farmer; res: Ffx; mother: Mag A. LEE; inf: T. W. LEE, father; pg:ln: 190:61

LEE, ___ (twin); WF; b. 10 Jun 1890 in Ffx; father: Thos. W. LEE; occ: farmer; res: Ffx; mother: Mag A. LEE; inf: T. W. LEE, father; pg:ln: 190:62

LEE, Aaron; WM; b. 15 Feb 1886 in Falls Ch.; father: J. W. LEE; occ: farmer; res: Falls Ch.; mother: G. LEE; inf: father; pg:ln: 158:34

LEE, Alfred; CM; b. 19 Jun 1890 in Ffx; father: Henry LEE; occ: farmer; res: Ffx; mother: Dilsie LEE; inf: H. LEE, father; pg:ln: 191:69

LEE, Alice E.; WF; b. 10 Sep 1889 in Ffx; father: E. A. LEE; occ: farmer; res: Ffx; mother: Lola A. LEE; inf: E. A. LEE, father; pg:ln: 178:69

LEE, Alice; CF; b. 8 Jan 1892 nr Clifton; father: Geo. LEE; occ: laborer; res: nr Clifton; mother: Judy LEE; inf: mother; pg:ln: 206:25

LEE, Arthur C.; CM; b. 19 Jul 1893 in ___; father: Henry LEE; occ: ___; res: ___; mother: Dollie LEE; inf: H. LEE, father; pg:ln: 214:68

LEE, Arthur T.; WM; b. 19 Jul 1887 in Ffx; father: Randolph LEE; occ: farmer; res: Ffx; mother: Martha LEE; inf: Randolph LEE, father; pg:ln: 162:80

LEE, Belle; CF; b. 31 May 1895 nr Clifton; father: George LEE; occ: laborer; res: nr Clifton; mother: Judia LEE; inf: father; pg:ln: 223:80

LEE, Bertie V.; WF; b. 28 Aug 1891 in Ffx; father: Reubin R. LEE; occ: farmer; res: Ffx; mother: Martha LEE; inf: R. R. LEE, father; pg:ln: 199:61

LEE, Carl L.; CM; b. 15 Jul 1890 in Ffx; father: Edw'd. LEE; occ: farmer; res: Ffx; mother: Fannie LEE; inf: E'd. LEWIS, father; pg:ln: 191:67

LEE, Carrene; CF; b. 13 Aug 1890 in Ffx; father: W. LEE; occ: farmer; res: Ffx; mother: Emma LEE; inf: W. LEE, father; pg:ln: 191:68

LEE, Chas. Andrew; CM; b. 21 Oct 1896 in Gumspring; father: Henry LEE; occ: laborer; res: Gumspring; mother: Rachael G. LEE; inf: mother; pg:ln: 231:78

LEE, Chloe; CF; b. 11 May 1896 in Ffx; father: Sidney LEE; occ: farmer; res: Ffx; mother: Dora LEE; inf: Sidney LEE, father; pg:ln: 227:75

LEE, Dallas D.; CM; b. 24 May 1896 in Ffx; father: Ernest LEE; occ: farmer; res: Ffx; mother: Ella LEE; inf: E. LEE, father; pg:ln: 227:74

LEE, Dullie; CF; b. 1 Apr 1896 in Masons Neck; father: no father; occ: ___; res: ___; mother: Hattee LEE; inf: mother; pg:ln: 231:79

LEE, E. A.; CM; b. 21? Jan 1889 [written over] in Ffx; father: Ernest LEE; occ: farmer; res: Ffx; mother: Ella LEE; inf: E. LEE, father; pg:ln: 178:66

LEE, E. Lewis; CM; b. 2 Feb 1884 in Falls Church; father: Chas. LEE; occ: farmer; res: Falls Church; mother: Louisa LEE; inf: father; pg:ln: 150:60

LEE, Etna A.; CF; b. 21 Jan 1890 in Ffx; father: Ernest LEE; occ: farmer; res: Ffx; mother: Ella LEE; inf: E. LEE, father; pg:ln: 191:70

LEE, Ezekiel; CM; b. 31 Jul 1884 in Falls Church; father: James E. LEE; occ: farmer; res: Falls Church; mother: Mary LEE; inf: father; pg:ln: 150:61

LEE, F. D.; WM; b. 8 Jan 1881 in Seminary; father: F. D. LEE; occ: farmer; res: Seminary; mother: Annie Taylor LEE; inf: father; pg:ln: 130:37

LEE, Floyd; CM; b. 7 Sep 1892 in Ffx; father: E'd. LEE; occ: farmer; res: Ffx; mother: Fannie LEE; inf: E'd. LEE, father; pg:ln: 203:62

LEE, Grafton Fitzhugh; WM; b. 6 Mar 1895 nr Bull Run; father: Thos. LEE; occ: farmer; res: nr Bull Run; mother: Cornelia LEE; inf: father; pg:ln: 223:76

LEE, Harriet; CF; b. 19 Jun 1880 in Ffx; father: Isaac LEE; occ: farmer; res: Ffx; mother: Matilda; inf: I. LEE, father; pg:ln: 128:58

LEE, Ida; CF; b. 8 Jun 1887 in Ffx; father: Henry LEE; occ: farmer; res: Ffx; mother: Ida LEE; inf: Henry LEE, father; pg:ln: 162:82

LEE, Jas. (twin); WM; b. 28 Feb 1887 in Ffx; father: Washington LEE;
    occ: farmer; res: Ffx; mother: Liizzie LEE; inf: Washington LEE,
    father; pg:ln: 162:79

LEE, Jno.; CM; b. 13 Dec 1891 in Ffx; father: Jas. LEE; occ: farmer; res:
    Ffx; mother: Rose LEE; inf: Jas. LEE, father; pg:ln: 199:59

LEE, John H.; CM; b. 14 Oct 1895 in Gum Spring; father: Henry LEE;
    occ: laborer; res: Gum Spring; mother: Rachael G. LEE; inf: father;
    pg:ln: 224:127

LEE, Jos. (twin); WM; b. 28 Feb 1887 in Ffx; father: Washington LEE;
    occ: farmer; res: Ffx; mother: Liizzie LEE; inf: Washington LEE,
    father; pg:ln: 162:79

LEE, Laura V.; WF; b. 20 Sep 1880 in Ffx; father: J. F. LEE; occ:
    farmer; res: Ffx; mother: Sarah C.; inf: J. F. LEE, father; pg:ln:
    128:55

LEE, Lewis; CM; b. 8 Jul 1887 in Ffx; father: James LEE; occ: laborer;
    res: Ffx; mother: Lilly LEE; inf: J. LEE, father; pg:ln: 162:89

LEE, Lucinda; CF; b. 18 Feb 1895 nr Gum Spring; father: Jarvis LEE;
    occ: laborer; res: nr Gum Spring; mother: Maria LEE; inf: father;
    pg:ln: 223:81

LEE, Lynnie; WF; b. 3 Dec 1889 in Ffx; father: Thos. A. LEE; occ:
    farmer; res: Ffx; mother: Cornelia LEE; inf: Thos. A. LEE, father;
    pg:ln: 182:59

LEE, Mamie; CF; b. 28 Mar 1891 nr Gum Spring; father: Jarvis LEE;
    occ: laborer; res: nr Gum Spring; mother: Maria LEE; inf: parent;
    pg:ln: 196:12

LEE, Maria· CF; b. 20 Aug 1892 in Gum Spring; father: Jarvis LEE; occ:
    laborer; res: nr Gum Spring; mother: Maria LEE; inf: father; pg:ln:
    206:09

LEE, Mason T.; CM; b. 20 Jul 1888 in Ffx; father: Ernest LEE; occ:
    farmer; res: Ffx; mother: Ella LEE; inf: E. LEE, father; pg:ln: 174:65

LEE, Nellie; WF; b. 21 Aug 1895 nr Chantilly; father: Philip LEE; occ:
    farmer; res: nr Chantilly; mother: Rebecca LEE; inf: father; pg:ln:
    223:75

LEE, not named (twin); WM; b. 18 Dec 1892 nr Centreville; father: Wm.
    D. LEE; occ: farmer; res: nr Centreville; mother: Emma E. LEE; inf:
    father; pg:ln: 208:18

LEE, not named (twin); WM; b. 18 Dec 1892 nr Centreville; father: Wm.
    D. LEE; occ: farmer; res: nr Centreville; mother: Emma E. LEE; inf:
    father; pg:ln: 208:18

LEE, not named; CM; b. 15 Dec 1886 in Seminary; father: Samuel LEE;
    occ: farmer; res: Seminary; mother: Mary LEE; inf: father; pg:ln:
    158:35

LEE, not named; CM; b. 20 Apr 1880 in Falls Church; father: James
    LEE; occ: laborer; res: Falls Church; mother: Mary LEE; inf: father;
    pg:ln: 124:34

LEE, not named; WM; b. 1 Dec 1893 nr Centreville; father: Mathew R.
    LEE; occ: farmer; res: nr Centreville; mother: Martha LEE; inf:
    mother; pg:ln: 211:65

LEE, Oxoda A.; CF; b. 17 Apr 1887 in Ffx; father: Ed. LEE; occ: farmer; res: Ffx; mother: Fanny LEE; inf: Ed. LEE, father; pg:ln: 162:78

LEE, Robt. W.; WM; b. 1 Sep 1887 in Ffx; father: T. W. LEE; occ: farmer; res: Ffx; mother: Margaret LEE; inf: T. W. LEE, father; pg:ln: 162:81

LEE, Robt.; WM; b. ___ Jun 1882 in Ffx; father: Thos. H. LEE; occ: ___; res: ___; mother: Mary LEE; inf: T. LEE, father; pg:ln: 137:45

LEE, Sarah A.; WF; b. 13 Sep 1887 in Ffx; father: Ludwell LEE; occ: farmer; res: Ffx; mother: Mary LEE; inf: L. LEE, father; pg:ln: 162:77

LEE, Stella; CF; b. 26 Oct 1896 in Ffx; father: Jas. LEE; occ: farmer; res: Ffx; mother: Lillie LEE; inf: Jas. LEE, father; pg:ln: 227:78

LEE, Thos.; WM; b. 22 Oct 1896 nr Bull Run PO; father: Thos. LEE; occ: farmer; res: nr Bull Run PO; mother: Caroline LEE; inf: father; pg:ln: 230:76

LEE, William; WM; b. 22 Feb 1882 in Falls Church; father: Jas. E. LEE; occ: farmer; res: Falls Church; mother: Mary LEE; inf: father; pg:ln: 134:33

LEE, Wm. W.; WM; b. 23 Dec 1890 in ___; father: Wm. D. LEE; occ: farmer; res: Ffx; mother: Emma E. LEE; inf: W. D. LEE, father; pg:ln: 186:69

LEEDS, Jno. W.; WM; b. 16 May 1894 in Ffx; father: Chas. T. LEEDS; occ: farmer; res: Ffx; mother: Mary V. LEEDS; inf: C. T. LEEDS, father; pg:ln: 218:73

LEIGH, ___; WF; b. 20 Nov 1887 in Ffx; father: Dr. Alfred LEIGH; occ: M. D.; res: Ffx; mother: M. M. LEIGH; inf: Dr. A. LEIGH, father; pg:ln: 162:83

LEIGH, Jas. S.; WM; b. 3 Feb 1889 in Ffx; father: Jas. S. LEIGH; occ: farmer; res: Ffx; mother: Annie LEIGH; inf: A. LEIGH, grand par.; pg:ln: 178:70

LEIGH, Karl; WM; b. 4 Feb 1887 in Ffx; father: Jas. S. LEIGH; occ: farmer; res: Ffx; mother: Annie LEIGH; inf: Jas. S. LEIGH, father; pg:ln: 162:84

LEMERICKS, Wallis Oto.; WM; b. 9 Dec 1889 in Ffx; father: W. LEMERICK[S]; occ: farmer; res: Ffx; mother: Emma LEMERICKS; inf: Wm. LIMERICKS, father; pg:ln: 182:55

LEONARD, Frank; WM; b. 18 Oct 1894 in Ffx; father: Jno. LEONARD; occ: farmer; res: Ffx; mother: Louisa LEONARD; inf: J. LEONARD, father; pg:ln: 218:72

LEWIS, ___; CF; b. 14 Mar 1896 in Ffx; father: Robt. LEWIS; occ: farmer; res: Ffx; mother: Isabella LEWIS; inf: Robt. LEWIS, father; pg:ln: 227:76

LEWIS, Clara Louisa; WF; b. 2 Sep 1892 nr Annandale; father: Wm. H. LEWIS; occ: farmer; res: nr Annandale; mother: Clara A. LEWIS; inf: father; pg:ln: 209:38

LEWIS, Clinton (twin); CM; b. 13 May 1890 in Ffx; father: Wesley LEWIS; occ: farmer; res: Ffx; mother: Susie LEWIS; inf: W. LEWIS, father; pg:ln: 190:63

LEWIS, Elberta; CF; b. 5 May 1894 in Ffx; father: Robt. LEWIS; occ: farmer; res: Ffx; mother: Isabella LEWIS; inf: Robt. LEWIS, father; pg:ln: 218:71

LEWIS, Ernest; WM; b. 9 Feb 1886 in Ffx; father: G. W. LEWIS; occ: farmer; res: Ffx; mother: Mary J. LEWIS; inf: G. W. LEWIS, father; pg:ln: 155:11

LEWIS, Fannie (twin); CF; b. 13 May 1890 in Ffx; father: Wesley LEWIS; occ: farmer; res: Ffx; mother: Susie LEWIS; inf: W. LEWIS, father; pg:ln: 190:64

LEWIS, Fred; CM; b. 5 Mar 1889 in Ffx; father: Wesley LEWIS; occ: farmer; res: Ffx; mother: Susan LEWIS; inf: W. LEWIS, father; pg:ln: 178:71

LEWIS, Georgie; CF; b. 18 Jun 1891 in Ffx; father: Wesley LEWIS; occ: farmer; res: Ffx; mother: Susie LEWIS; inf: W. LEWIS, father; pg:ln: 199:60

LEWIS, J. W.; CM; b. 29 Feb 1884 in Green Vale; father: Wesley LEWIS; occ: laborer; res: Green Vale; mother: Susan LEWIS; inf: father; pg:ln: 150:59

LEWIS, Jas.; CM; b. 14 Dec 1882 in Ffx; father: Wm. H. LEWIS; occ: ___; res: ___; mother: Mary LEWIS; inf: W. H. LEWIS, father; pg:ln: 137:46

LEWIS, John Arthur; WM; b. 19 Oct 1893 nr Clifton Sta.; father: H. R. LEWIS; occ: farmer; res: nr Clifton Sta.; mother: Cordelia LEWIS; inf: mother; pg:ln: 211:64

LEWIS, Joseph; CM; b. 15 Feb 1882 in Falls Church; father: Wesley LEWIS; occ: laborer; res: Falls Church; mother: Susan LEE; inf: father; pg:ln: 134:34

LEWIS, Kendel H.; WM; b. 16 Aug 1887 in ___; father: W. H. LEWIS; occ: farmer; res: Ffx; mother: Cora A. LEWIS; inf: W. H. LEWIS, father; pg:ln: 168:70

LEWIS, Laura; CF; b. 10 Apr 1889 in Ffx; father: Edwd. LEWIS; occ: farmer; res: Ffx; mother: Martha LEWIS; inf: E'd. LEWIS, father; pg:ln: 178:65

LEWIS, Laurence C.; WM; b. 1 Oct 1880 in Falls Church; father: J. Frank LEWIS; occ: clerk D.C.; res: Falls Church; mother: Alice T. LEWIS; inf: father; pg:ln: 124:40

LEWIS, Lottie; CF; b. 9 Jun 1892 nr Hayfield; father: Wm. H. LEWIS; occ: laborer; res: nr Hayfield; mother: Mary LEWIS; inf: father; pg:ln: 206:10

LEWIS, Michael; CM; b. 7 Jun 1889 in Ffx; father: Jarret LEWIS; occ: farmer; res: Ffx; mother: Cath'a. LEWIS; inf: J. LEWIS, father; pg:ln: 178:67

LEWIS, Michael; CM; b. 7 Jun 1890 in Ffx; father: Jarret LEWIS; occ: farmer; res: Ffx; mother: Kate LEWIS; inf: J. LEWIS, father; pg:ln: 191:66

LEWIS, Millie; CF; b. 17 Jan 1896 in Ffx; father: Wesley LEWIS; occ: farmer; res: Ffx; mother: Susie LEWIS; inf: Wesley LEWIS, father; pg:ln: 227:77

LEWIS, not named; CM; b. 22 Sep 1885 in Green Vale; father: Wesley LEWIS; occ: laborer; res: Green Vale; mother: Susan LEWIS; inf: father; pg:ln: 153:43

LEWIS, not named; WF; b. 3 Mar 1884 in Vienna; father: A. M. LEWIS; occ: farmer; res: Vienna; mother: ___ LEWIS; inf: father; pg:ln: 150:58

LEWIS, Ralph D.; WM; b. 5 Jun 1889 in Ffx; father: W. H. LEWIS; occ: farmer; res: Ffx; mother: Cora A. LEWIS; inf: W. H. LEWIS, father; pg:ln: 182:57

LEWIS, Rodger; CM; b. 20 Sep 1894 in Ffx; father: Wesley LEWIS; occ: farmer; res: Ffx; mother: Susie LEWIS; inf: W. LEWIS, father; pg:ln: 218:75

LEWIS, Rosa; CF; b. 11 Jul 1880 in Dranesville; father: Garrett LEWIS; occ: laborer; res: Dranesville; mother: Catherine LEWIS; inf: father; pg:ln: 125:41

LEWIS, Thomas W. (twin); CM; b. 3 Mar 1880 in Falls Church; father: Wesley LEWIS; occ: laborer; res: Falls Church; mother: Susan LEWIS; inf: father; pg:ln: 124:37

LEWIS, Wm. W. (twin); CM; b. 3 Mar 1880 in Falls Church; father: Wesley LEWIS; occ: laborer; res: Falls Church; mother: Susan LEWIS; inf: father; pg:ln: 124:36

LEWIS, Wm.; CM; b. 17 Jul 1896 nr Hayfield; father: Wm. LEWIS; occ: laborer; res: nr Hayfield; mother: Susan LEWIS; inf: mother; pg:ln: 231:80

LIGHTFOOT, Alva; WM; b. 4 Dec 1892 in Ffx; father: J. H. LIGHTFOOT; occ: farmer; res: Ffx; mother: Lillie LIGHTFOOT; inf: J. H. LIGHTFOOT, father; pg:ln: 203:63

LIGHTFOOT, Dollie; WF; b. 26 Jun 1890 in Ffx; father: Jos. H. LIGHTFOOT; occ: farmer; res: Ffx; mother: Lillie LIGHTFOOT; inf: J. H. LIGHTFOOT, father; pg:ln: 190:60

LIGHTFOOT, Maud; WF; b. 11 Dec 1887 in Ffx; father: S. H. LIGHTFOOT; occ: laborer; res: Ffx; mother: M. H. LIGHTFOOT; inf: S. H. LIGHTFOOT, father; pg:ln: 162:88

LIGHTFOOT, Samuel M.; WM; b. 16 Aug 1892 nr Pender; father: Samuel LIGHTFOOT; occ: carpenter; res: nr Pender; mother: Mildred LIGHTFOOT; inf: father; pg:ln: 208:16

LIMBRICK, Percy; WM; b. 22 Oct 1895 nr Lorton Sta.; father: Wm. LIMBRICK; occ: farmer; res: nr Lorton Sta.; mother: Emma LIMBRICK; inf: mother; pg:ln: 223:77

LINCKE, Louisa Virginia Alvina; WF; b. 4 May 1895 nr Lincolnia; father: Julius R. LINCKE; occ: farmer; res: nr Alex.; mother: Louisa LINCKE; inf: father; pg:ln: 223:73

LINTON, Chas. Edwd.; WM; b. 20 Dec 1890 in ___; father: John LINTON; occ: farmer; res: Ffx; mother: Sallie LINTON; inf: John LINTON, father; pg:ln: 186:68

LLOYD, Frances R.; WM; b. ___ Sep 1892 in Ffx; father: H. W. LLOYD; occ: farmer; res: Ffx; mother: Sarah E. LLOYD; inf: W. H. [H. W.?] LLOYD, father; pg:ln: 203:65

LLOYD, Franklin; WM; b. 9 Nov 1890 in ___; father: Jno. T. LLOYD; occ: laborer; res: Ffx; mother: Laura LLOYD; inf: J. T. LLOYD, father; pg:ln: 186:67

LLOYD, Grace; WF; b. 30 Mar 1891 nr Alexandria; father: J. H. LLOYD; occ: farmer; res: nr Alexandria; mother: Mildred LLOYD; inf: parents; pg:ln: 195:10

LLOYD, John; WM; b. 12 Aug 1892 nr Hayfield; father: John H. LLOYD; occ: farmer; res: nr Franconia; mother: Mildred LLOYD; inf: mother; pg:ln: 207:75

LLOYD, Maggie M.; WF; b. 24 Aug 1887 in Ffx; father: H. W. LLOYD; occ: farmer; res: Ffx; mother: Sarah E. LLOYD; inf: H. W. LLOYD, father; pg:ln: 162:76

LLOYD, Maggie; WF; b. 16 Oct 1895 nr Accotink; father: J. H. LLOYD; occ: farmer; res: nr Accotink; mother: Mildred LLOYD; inf: mother; pg:ln: 223:78

LOMAX, ___; CF; b. 8 Apr 1882 in Ffx; father: Inman LOMAX; occ: ___; res: ___; mother: Mary LOMAX; inf: I. LOMAX, father; pg:ln: 137:50

LOMAX, Basil; CM; b. 25 Jul 1890 in Ffx; father: Wm. Lewis LOMAX; occ: farmer; res: Ffx; mother: Eliza LOMAX; inf: Wm. L. LOMAX, father; pg:ln: 187:71

LOMAX, E. A.; CM; b. 2 Apr 1881 in Ffx; father: Inman LOMAX; occ: farmer; res: Ffx; mother: Mary LOMAX; inf: I. LOMAX, father; pg:ln: 132:27

LOMAX, J.; CM; b. 13 May 1880 in Ffx; father: Inman LOMAX; occ: farmer; res: Ffx; mother: Mary; inf: I. LOMAX, father; pg:ln: 128:54

LOMAX, Wm.; CM; b. 28 Sep 1885 in Ffx; father: Wm. L. LOMAX; occ: farmer; res: Ffx; mother: Jane LOMAX; inf: W. L. LOMAX, father; pg:ln: 157:38

LOVELACE, Bessie P.; WF; b. 5 Jan 1894 in Ffx; father: Henry LOVELACE; occ: farmer; res: Ffx; mother: Julia LOVELACE; inf: H. LOVELACE, father; pg:ln: 218:74

LOVELESS, ___; WM; b. 13 Nov 1890 in Ffx; father: Luther LOVELESS; occ: farmer; res: Ffx; mother: Eliza LOVELESS; inf: Luther LOVELESS, father; pg:ln: 191:65

LOVELESS, Bulah; WF; b. 29 Jul 1896 in Ffx; father: Nixon B. LOVELESS; occ: farmer; res: Ffx; mother: Mary LOVELESS; inf: N. B. LOVELESS, father; pg:ln: 227:73

LOVELESS, Carrie; WF; b. 27 Jun 1892 in Ffx; father: Henry LOVELESS; occ: farmer; res: Ffx; mother: Julia; inf: H. LOVELESS, father; pg:ln: 203:64

LOVELESS, Jno. S.; WM; b. 13 Nov 1889 in Ffx; father: Henry LOVELESS; occ: farmer; res: Ffx; mother: Julia LOVELESS; inf: H. LOVELESS, father; pg:ln: 178:72

LOVELESS, W. H.; WM; b. 6 Jul 1896 in Ffx; father: Henry LOVELESS; occ: farmer; res: Ffx; mother: Julia LOVELESS; inf: H. LOVELESS, father; pg:ln: 227:79

LOWE, Henry B.; WM; b. 11 Jan 1893 in ___; father: Henry F. LOWE; occ: ___; res: ___; mother: Hattie LOWE; inf: H. F. LOWE, father; pg:ln: 214:67

LOYD, Irene Mary; WF; b. 1 Jul 1885 in Falls Ch.; father: H. W. LOYD; occ: mechanic; res: Falls Ch.; mother: Mary E. LOYD; inf: father; pg:ln: 153:42

LUCAS, Augusta; CF; b. 15 Feb 1889 in Ffx; father: Henry LUCAS; occ: farmer; res: Ffx; mother: Lillie LUCAS; inf: H. LUCAS, father; pg:ln: 178:68

LUCAS, Kate; CF; b. 29 Apr 1887 in Ffx; father: Jarret LUCAS; occ: laborer; res: Ffx; mother: Caroline LUCAS; inf: J. LUCAS, father; pg:ln: 162:86

LUCAS, Logan; CM; b. 8 Mar 1888 in Ffx; father: Jesse LUCAS; occ: farmer; res: Ffx; mother: Amanda LUCAS; inf: J. LUCAS, father; pg:ln: 174:64

LUCAS, Malinda; CF; b. 5 Sep 1888 in Ffx; father: Townsend LUCAS; occ: farmer; res: Ffx; mother: Malinda LUCAS; inf: T. LUCAS, father; pg:ln: 174:63

LUCAS, Naaman G.; CM; b. 10 Sep 1891 in Ffx; father: Lee LUCAS; occ: farmer; res: Ffx; mother: Margt. LUCAS; inf: L. LUCAS, father; pg:ln: 199:58

LUCAS, Zebadee; CM; b. 20 Jul 1887 in Ffx; father: Henry LUCAS; occ: laborer; res: Ffx; mother: Lilly LUCAS; inf: H. LUCAS, father; pg:ln: 162:87

LUCKETT, Robt; CM; b. 6 Feb 1883 in Falls Church; father: Valentine LUCKETT; occ: laborer; res: Falls Church; mother: Mary LUCKETT; inf: father; pg:ln: 140:58

LUCKETT, Wallace; CM; b. 5 Mar 1886 in Prov.; father: Volentine LUCKETT; occ: laborer; res: Prov.; mother: Mary LUCKETT; inf: father; pg:ln: 158:29

LUDLOW, A. S.; WM; b. 30 Jul 1882 in Ffx; father: Daniel LUDLOW; occ: ___; res: ___; mother: Lizzie LUDLOW; inf: D. LUDLOW, father; pg:ln: 137:44

LUDLOW, Cleveland; WM; b. 10 Jun 1884 in Ffx; father: Danl. LUDLOW; occ: ___; res: ___; mother: Elizbt. LUDLOW; inf: Daniel LUDLOW, father; pg:ln: 147:47

LYLES, C. S.; WM; b. 13 Feb 1880 in Ffx; father: Fer'd. LYLES; occ: farmer; res: Ffx; mother: Frances; inf: F. LYLES, father; pg:ln: 128:56

LYLES, Chas. Julian; CM; b. 24 Dec 1891 nr Alexandria; father: Henry LYLES; occ: laborer; res: nr Alex.; mother: Hattie LYLES; inf: parent; pg:ln: 196:13

LYLES, Evaline; WF; b. 8 Aug 1892 nr Franconia Sta.; father: Geo. W. LYLES; occ: farmer; res: nr Franconia; mother: Emma J. LYLES; inf: mother; pg:ln: 207:76

LYLES, Irene; WF; b. 10 Aug 1883 in Ffx; father: Silas LYLES; occ: farmer; res: Ffx; mother: Harriet LYLES; inf: S. LYLES, father; pg:ln: 144:54

LYLES, Jane B.; CF; b. 9 Jun 1890 in Ffx; father: Henry LYLES; occ: laborer; res: Ffx; mother: Harriet LYLES; inf: Henry LYLES, father; pg:ln: 187:72

LYLES, Lillie; WF; b. 2 Apr 1890 in ___; father: Geo. W. LYLES; occ: farmer; res: Ffx; mother: Martha A. LYLES; inf: G. W. LYLES, father; pg:ln: 186:70

LYLES, Martha; WF; b. 8 Apr 1882 in Ffx; father: Geo. W. LYLES; occ: ___; res: ___; mother: Martha LYLES; inf: G. W. LYLES, father; pg:ln: 137:51

LYLES, Rebecca; WF; b. 13 Jun 1880 in Ffx; father: Silas LYLES; occ: farmer; res: Ffx; mother: Harriet; inf: Silas LYLES, father; pg:ln: 128:57

LYLES, Ruth Mable; WF; b. 18 Feb 1893 nr Springfield; father: George LYLES; occ: farmer; res: nr Springfield; mother: Emma J. LYLES; inf: mother; pg:ln: 211:68

LYNCH, C. E. (twin); WF; b. 25 Feb 1885 in Falls Ch.; father: W. N. LYNCH; occ: mechanic; res: Falls Ch.; mother: S. C. LYNCH; inf: father; pg:ln: 153:41

LYNCH, not named; WF; b. 16 Jan 1886 in Falls Ch.; father: W. N. LYNCH; occ: mechanic; res: Falls Ch.; mother: S. E. LYNCH; inf: father; pg:ln: 158:33

LYNCH, Stella; WF; b. 25 Dec 1883 in Falls Church; father: W. N. LYNCH; occ: mechanic; res: Falls Church; mother: S. E. LYNCH; inf: father; pg:ln: 140:59

LYNCH, W. H. (twin); WM; b. 25 Feb 1885 in Falls Ch.; father: W. N. LYNCH; occ: mechanic; res: Falls Ch.; mother: S. C. LYNCH; inf: father; pg:ln: 153:40

LYNN, Chas. Craig; WM; b. 21 Jan 1892 nr Sudley; father: Lewis LYNN; occ: farmer; res: nr Sudley; mother: Hannah LYNN; inf: father; pg:ln: 208:17

LYNN, Luther L.; WM; b. 10 Sep 1888 in Ffx; father: C. L. LYNN; occ: farmer; res: Ffx; mother: E. P. LYNN; inf: C. L. LYNN, father; pg:ln: 171:43

LYNN, Myrtle; WF; b. 10 Mar 1881 in Ffx; father: Thos. LYNN; occ: farmer; res: Ffx; mother: Betty LYNN; inf: T. LYNN, father; pg:ln: 132:26

LYNN, not named; WM; b. 15 Oct 1882 in Vienna; father: Clarence LYNN; occ: farmer; res: Vienna; mother: Ella LYNN; inf: father; pg:ln: 134:35

MABEN, Maggie; WF; b. 8 Dec 1887 in Ffx; father: Wm. MABEN; occ: mason; res: Ffx; mother: Eliza MABEN; inf: W. MABEN, father; pg:ln: 162:103

MABER, Nettie; WF; b. 1 Nov 1886 in Falls Ch.; father: William MABER; occ: mechanic; res: Falls Ch.; mother: Eliza MABER; inf: father; pg:ln: 159:39

MACHEN, Evelyn; WF; b. 25 Apr 1883 in Ffx; father: Jas. P. MACHEN; occ: farmer; res: Ffx; mother: Georgeana MACHEN; inf: J. P. MACHEN, father; pg:ln: 144:58

MACK, Jno. H.; CM; b. 5 Dec 1889 in Ffx; father: Henry MACK; occ: farmer; res: Ffx; mother: Mary MACK; inf: H. MACK, father; pg:ln: 182:67

MACK, Lulie Pearl; CF; b. 18 Nov 1892 nr Gunston; father: Henry MACK; occ: laborer; res: nr Gunston; mother: Mary MACK; inf: father; pg:ln: 206:11

MACK, Martha; CF; b. 15 Jan 1889 in Ffx; father: James MACK; occ: farmer; res: Ffx; mother: Lucretia MACK; inf: James MACK, father; pg:ln: 182:68

MACK, Miram; CF; b. 8 Sep 1895 nr Gunston Hall; father: Henry MACK; occ: laborer; res: nr Gunston Hall; mother: Mary MACK; inf: father; pg:ln: 223:94

MACK, not named (dead twins); CM; b. 15 Dec 1892 nr Gunston; father: James MACK; occ: laborer; res: nr Gunston; mother: LOUISA MACK; inf: father; pg:ln: 206:12

MACK, Rich'd. L.; CM; b. 1 Oct 1883 in Ffx; father: W. H. MACK; occ: farmer; res: Ffx; mother: Mary MACK; inf: W. H. MACK, father; pg:ln: 144:62

MACK, Robt. L.; CM; b. 17 May 1882 in Ffx; father: Henry MACK; occ: ___; res: ___; mother: Mary MACK; inf: H. MACK, father; pg:ln: 137:59

MACK, T. R. Y.; CF; b. 7 Aug 1884 in Prov.; father: J. E. MACK; occ: farmer; res: Prov.; mother: Eliza MACK; inf: father; pg:ln: 150:67

MaCRAE, Geo. A.; WM; b. 20 Jan 1883 in Falls Church; father: G. H. L. MaCRAE; occ: farmer; res: Falls Church; mother: Maggie MaCRAE; inf: father; pg:ln: 140:66

MAGARITY, Albert; WM; b. 1 Dec 1889 in Ffx; father: Albt. MAGARITY; occ: farmer; res: Ffx; mother: Massie MAGARITY; inf: A. MAGARITY, father; pg:ln: 179:81

MAGARITY, Francis; WM; b. 29 Dec 1881 in Vienna; father: Albert MAGARITY; occ: farmer; res: Vienna; mother: Mamie MAGARITY; inf: father; pg:ln: 131:40

MAGARITY, Hunter; WM; b. 13 Nov 1891 in Ffx; father: Albt. MAGARITY; occ: farmer; res: Ffx; mother: Mamie MAGARITY; inf: A. MAGARITY, father; pg:ln: 199:64

MAGARITY, Jas. L.; WM; b. 7 Apr 1882 in Lewinsville; father: Jos. W. MAGARITY; occ: farmer; res: Lewinsville; mother: Cath. E. MAGARITY; inf: father; pg:ln: 134:36

MAGARITY, Maggie C.; WF; b. 20 Apr 1887 in Ffx; father: J. L. MAGARITY; occ: farmer; res: Ffx; mother: Laura MAGARITY; inf: J. L. MAGARITY, father; pg:ln: 162:90

MAGARITY, Morrell; WM; b. 11 Jul 1896 in Ffx; father: J. S. MAGARITY; occ: farmer; res: Ffx; mother: Annie MAGARITY; inf: J. S. MAGARITY, father; pg:ln: 227:82

MAGNER, Joseph; WM; b. 20 Jun 1895 nr Burke Sta.; father: Peter MAGNER Jr.; occ: farmer; res: nr Burke Sta.; mother: Lucy MAGNER; inf: mother; pg:ln: 223:88

MAGNER, not named (dead); WM; b. 21 Mar 1893 nr Burke Sta; father:
Peter MAGNER; occ: farmer; res: nr Burke Sta; mother: Anne
MAGNER; inf: mother; pg:ln: 211:69

MAGNER, Phillip; WM; b. 6 Nov 1887 in ___; father: Patty MAGNER;
occ: R. Rd. laborer; res: Ffx; mother: Evaline MAGNER; inf: P.
MAGNER, father; pg:ln: 168:71

MAGRUDER, Mary; CF; b. 1 Oct 1891 in Ffx; father: Douglas
MAGRUDER; occ: farmer; res: Ffx; mother: Lucy MAGRUDER; inf:
D. MAGRUDER, father; pg:ln: 199:62

MAHAR, not named; WF; b. 16 May 1885 in Dranes.; father: Thos. S.
MAHAR; occ: farmer; res: Dranes.; mother: Mary MAHAR; inf:
father; pg:ln: 153:56

MAHAR, Vilarie; WF; b. 4 Dec 1889 in Ffx; father: Thos. MAHAR; occ:
farmer; res: Ffx; mother: Mary MAHAR; inf: T. MAHAR, father; pg:ln:
179:80

MAHORNEY, Chas. H.; WM; b. 5 Oct 1880 in Dranesville; father:
Rich'd. J. MAHORNEY; occ: farmer; res: Dranesville; mother: Annie
D. MAHORNEY; inf: father; pg:ln: 125:48

MAHORNEY, Clara; WF; b. 29 Feb 1887 in Ffx; father: B. MAHORNEY;
occ: farmer; res: Ffx; mother: Minnie MAHORNEY; inf: B.
MAHORNEY, father; pg:ln: 162:101

MAHORNEY, Ludo; WM; b. 10 Nov 1892 in Ffx; father: B. W.
MAHORNEY; occ: farmer; res: Ffx; mother: Minnie MAHORNEY; inf:
B. W. MAHORNEY, father; pg:ln: 204:72

MAJORS, Essy; CF; b. 8 Feb 1887 in Ffx; father: Wm. Henry MAJORS;
occ: butcher; res: Ffx; mother: Matilda MAJORS; inf: W. H.
MAJORS, father; pg:ln: 162:102

MAKELEY, Cassius; WM; b. 13 Sep 1883 in Ffx; father: Cash
MAKELEY; occ: farmer; res: Ffx; mother: Victorine MAKELEY; inf:
C. MAKELEY, father; pg:ln: 144:60

MAKLEY, Jas. R.; WM; b. 10 May 1885 in Ffx; father: Cash. E.
MAKLEY; occ: farmer; res: Ffx; mother: Victorine MAKLY; inf: C. E.
MAKLEY, father; pg:ln: 157:41

MALONEY, Julia Ayres; WF; b. 9 Jul 1896 in Fairfax Sta.; father: J. T.
MALONEY; occ: clerk; res: Fairfax Sta.; mother: Annie MALONEY;
inf: father; pg:ln: 231:81

MANCHESTER, Lucilla; WF; b. 20 Sep 1894 in Ffx; father: H. B.
MANCHESTER; occ: farmer; res: Ffx; mother: E. A. MANCHESTER;
inf: H. B. MANCHESTER, father; pg:ln: 219:86

MANKIN, Clinton E.; WM; b. 20 Jan 1885 in Falls Ch.; father: Chas. E.
MANKIN; occ: merchant; res: Falls Ch.; mother: V. A. MANKIN; inf:
father; pg:ln: 153:49

MANKIN, E. E.; WM; b. 7 Apr 1883 in Falls Church; father: C. E.
MANKIN; occ: merchant; res: Falls Church; mother: V. A. MANKIN;
inf: father; pg:ln: 140:62

MANKIN, Linda; WF; b. 30 May 1889 in Ffx; father: Chas. E. MANKIN;
occ: merchant; res: Ffx; mother: Linda MANKIN; inf: C. MANKIN,
father; pg:ln: 179:74

MANKIN, Morgan; WM; b. 18 Mar 1891 in Ffx; father: C. E. MANKIN; occ: farmer; res: Ffx; mother: V. A. MANKIN; inf: C. E. MANKIN, father; pg:ln: 199:68

MANLEY, not named; CF; b. 1 Jul 1896 in Chantilly; father: Thos. MANLEY; occ: laborer; res: Chantilly; mother: Etta MANLEY; inf: father; pg:ln: 231:92

MANLEY, not named; WM; b. 25 Feb 1892 in Ravensworth; father: ___; occ: ___; res: Ravensworth; mother: M. MANLEY; inf: Greenberry JOHNSTON; pg:ln: 209:36

MANLEY, Samuel; CM; b. 5 Sep 1892 nr Chantilly; father: Thos. MANLEY; occ: laborer; res: nr Chantilly; mother: Ella MANLEY; inf: mother; pg:ln: 206:26

MARCHE, Clara; WF; b. 12 Mar 1892 in Ffx; father: Jas. MARCHE; occ: farmer; res: Ffx; mother: Mary MARCHE; inf: J. MARCHE, father; pg:ln: 204:74

MARKS, Arch. C.; WM; b. 1 Jul 1885 in Ffx; father: Chas. R. MARKS; occ: farmer; res: Ffx; mother: Bettie MARKS; inf: C. R. MARKS, father; pg:ln: 157:43

MARKS, Minnie Ola; WF; b. 27 Sep 1887 in ___; father: Thos. MARKS; occ: R. Rd. laborer; res: Ffx; mother: Millie MARKS; inf: Thos. MARKS, father; pg:ln: 168:74

MARSHALL, Aaron (twin); CM; b. 11 Sep 1894 in Ffx; father: Frank MARSHALL; occ: farmer; res: Ffx; mother: Bessie MARSHALL; inf: Frank MARSHAL, father; pg:ln: 219:87

MARSHALL, Amasa (twin); CM; b. 11 Sep 1894 in Ffx; father: Frank MARSHALL; occ: farmer; res: Ffx; mother: Bessie MARSHALL; inf: Frank MARSHAL, father; pg:ln: 219:88

MARSHALL, Harry Lee; WM; b. 28 Jan 1892 nr Burke Sta.; father: Robert E. MARSHALL; occ: merchant; res: Burke Sta.; mother: Annie MARSHALL; inf: father. Middle name added to our records from Doctor's certificate. Harry Lee Marshall.; pg:ln: 209:52

MARSHALL, John; WM; b. 3 Aug 1890 in Ffx; father: G. W. MARSHALL; occ: R. Rd. man; res: Ffx; mother: Emma MARSHALL; inf: G. W. MARSHALL, father; pg:ln: 187:76

MARSHALL, Lewis; CM; b. 6 Nov 1889 in Ffx; father: Thos. MARSHALL; occ: farmer; res: Ffx; mother: Hattie MARSHALL; inf: T. MARSHALL, father; pg:ln: 182:69

MARSHALL, Mary Ellen; WF; b. 12 Aug 1895 nr Stoneleigh; father: Thos. T. MARSHALL; occ: farmer; res: nr Stoneleigh; mother: Charlotte I. MARSHALL; inf: father; pg:ln: 223:86

MARSHALL, Roy Armstead; WM; b. 14 Apr 1896 nr Occoquan; father: Thos. Thornton MARSHALL; occ: farmer; res: nr Occoquan; mother: Charlotte MARSHALL; inf: father; pg:ln: 231:87

MARSHALL, Wm. P.; WM; b. 28 Jun 1885 in Ffx; father: Chas. L. MARSHALL; occ: farmer; res: Ffx; mother: Salina MARSHALL; inf: C. L. MARSHALL, father; pg:ln: 157:39

MARTHERS, Fannie; WF; b. 21 Nov 1884 in Ffx; father: Armstead MARTHERS; occ: ___; res: ___; mother: Mary J. MARTHERS; inf: A. MARTHERS, father; pg:ln: 147:49

MARTHERS, not named; WM; b. 10 Jan 1884 in Ffx; father: Geo. W. MARTHERS; occ: ___; res: ___; mother: Nancy MARTHERS; inf: Geo. W. MARTHERS, father; pg:ln: 147:48

MARTIN, Agnes L.; WF; b. 21 Aug 1894 in Ffx; father: H. T. MARTIN; occ: farmer; res: Ffx; mother: Mary MARTIN; inf: H. T. MARTIN, father; pg:ln: 219:79

MARTIN, Alma; WF; b. 15 Jun 1881 in Ffx; father: Jno. S. MARTIN; occ: farmer; res: Ffx; mother: Sallie MARTIN; inf: Jno. S. MARTIN, father; pg:ln: 132:30

MARTIN, C. R.; WM; b. 21 Jun 1882 in Ffx; father: Jos. E. MARTIN; occ: ___; res: ___; mother: Jennie MARTIN; inf: J. E. MARTIN, father; pg:ln: 137:57

MARTIN, Frank Page; WM; b. 28 Oct 1887 in ___; father: Jno. S. MARTIN; occ: farmer; res: Ffx; mother: Sarah A. MARTIN; inf: Jno. S. MARTIN, father; pg:ln: 168:75

MARTIN, Jessie B.; CF; b. 9 Oct 1894 in Ffx; father: Mack MARTIN; occ: farmer; res: Ffx; mother: Josephine MARTIN; inf: M. MARTIN, father; pg:ln: 219:89

MARTIN, M.; WF; b. 3 Mar 1880 in Ffx; father: Jno. S. MARTIN; occ: farmer; res: Ffx; mother: Sallie; inf: J. S. MARTIN, father; pg:ln: 128:59

MARTIN, Mack; CM; b. 20 Jul 1886 in Prov.; father: Henry MARTIN; occ: laborer; res: Prov.; mother: Josephine MARTIN; inf: father; pg:ln: 159:40

MARTIN, Mack; WF; b. 10 Aug 1883 in Falls Church; father: Mack MARTIN; occ: laborer; res: Falls Church; mother: Martha MARTIN; inf: father; pg:ln: 140:65

MARTIN, Raymond; WM; b. 21 Sep 1884 in Ffx; father: Jno. S. MARTIN; occ: ___; res: ___; mother: Sallie MARTIN; inf: J. S. MARTIN, father; pg:ln: 147:50

MARTIN, W. L.; WM; b. 21 Jun 1882 in Ffx; father: W. L. MARTIN; occ: ___; res: ___; mother: Rosalie MARTIN; inf: W. L. MARTIN, father; pg:ln: 137:56

MARTIN, Walter J.; WM; b. 9 Oct 1885 in Ffx; father: Jno. S. MARTIN; occ: farmer; res: Ffx; mother: Sallie MARTIN; inf: J. S. MARTIN, father; pg:ln: 157:40

MARTIN, William; CM; b. 15 Aug 1884 in Falls Ch.; father: Mack MARTIN; occ: laborer; res: Falls Ch.; mother: Josephine MARTIN; inf: father; pg:ln: 150:65

MASON, Annie; CF; b. 20 May 1881 in Falls Church; father: George MASON; occ: laborer; res: Falls Church; mother: Josephine MASON; inf: father; pg:ln: 131:46

MASON, Ellen D.; WF; b. 24 Jul 1890 in Ffx; father: Jas. M. MASON; occ: farmer; res: Ffx; mother: M. T. MASON; inf: J. M. MASON, father; pg:ln: 191:71

MASON, Ethel L.; WF; b. 10 Oct 1886 [22 July line thru] in Ffx; father: J. P. H. MASON; occ: farmer; res: Ffx; mother: Anita C. MASON [Mary lined thru, Anita written over]; inf: J. P. H. MASON, father. Affidavit dated 4 Nov 1940 in Washington, VA: J. P. H. Mason and Anita Caldwell Millan were married at Woodville, Va Dec. 31, 1878. Ethel Louise Mason, daughter of J. P. H. Mason and his wife, Anita Caldwell Millan Mason, was born at Tamworth, Fairfax County, Va October 10th 1886. The entries made in the Millan Family Bible were made by Bettie A. Millan, sister of Anita Caldwell Mason. I am a sister of the aforesaid Anita Caldwell Mason and Bettie A. Millan, both being dead, and the Family Bible has been in my possession for a number of years. Signed Lucy Millan Stuart in Rappahannock Co. VA.; pg:ln: 155:13

MASON, J. P. H.; WM; b. 8 Apr 1893 nr Accotink; father: J. P. H. MASON; occ: mechanick; res: nr Accotink; mother: Etta C. MASON; inf: parent; pg:ln: 212:72

MASON, Lyle Millan; WM; b. 4 May 1891 nr Accotink; father: J. P. H. MASON; occ: mechanic; res: nr Accotink; mother: Annita Caldwell MASON; inf: parents; pg:ln: 195:12

MASON, Margt. T.; WF; b. 21 Feb 1882 in Ffx; father: B. R. MASON; occ: ___; res: ___; mother: E. H. MASON; inf: B. R. MASON, father; pg:ln: 137:55

MASON, Nellie Custus; WF; b. 22 Oct 1892 in Woodlawn; father: W. L. MASON; occ: farmer; res: Woodlawn; mother: Anna MASON; inf: mother; pg:ln: 207:78

MASON, Paul L.; CM; b. 6 May 1894 in Ffx; father: Geo. MASON; occ: farmer; res: Ffx; mother: Josephin MASON; inf: Geo. MASON, father; pg:ln: 219:90

MASON, Ralph O.; CM; b. 1 Oct 1896 in Ffx; father: Geo. MASON; occ: farmer; res: Ffx; mother: Josephin MASON; inf: Geo. MASON, father; pg:ln: 227:83

MASON, Rose; CF; b. 4 Jan 1892 in Ffx; father: Oscar MASON; occ: farmer; res: Ffx; mother: Isabela MASON; inf: O. MASON, father; pg:ln: 204:73

MASSEY, John; CM; b. 24 Feb 1882 in Falls Church; father: Alonzo MASSEY,; occ: laborer; res: Falls Church; mother: Jennie MASSEY; inf: father; pg:ln: 134:38

MASSIE, Jennie; CF; b. 9 Aug 1885 nr Falls Ch.; father: Alonzo MASSIE; occ: laborer; res: nr Falls Ch.; mother: Jennie MASSIE; inf: father; pg:ln: 153:48

MATEER, Jas. J.; WM; b. 28 Feb 1887 in Ffx; father: Jas. T. MATEER; occ: merchant; res: Ffx; mother: Olivia MATEER; inf: J. T. MATEER, father; pg:ln: 162:97

MATHERS, Iona Vane; WF; b. 2 Apr 1891 nr Clifton; father: Wm. H. MATHERS; occ: farmer; res: nr Clifton; mother: Jennie MATHERS; inf: parents; pg:ln: 194:15

MATHERS, Ruth; WF; b. 21 Jun 1895 nr Clifton Sta.; father: Wm. MATHERS; occ: farmer; res: nr Clifton Sta.; mother: Jennie MATHERS; inf: mother; pg:ln: 223:83

MATHEWS, ___; WM; b. 23 Sep 1889 in Ffx; father: A. MATHEWS; occ: farmer; res: Ffx; mother: Mary MATHEWS; inf: A. MATHEWS, father; pg:ln: 182:60

MATHEWS, Chas. M.; WM; b. 14 Aug 1882 in Ffx; father: Armstead MATHEWS; occ: ___; res: ___; mother: Mary J. MATHEWS; inf: A. MATHEWS, father; pg:ln: 137:53

MATHEWS, M. G.; WF; b. 11 Jul 1880 in Ffx; father: A. MATHEWS; occ: farmer; res: Ffx; mother: Mary; inf: A. MATHEWS, father; pg:ln: 128:64

MAY, WARNER; CM; b. 21 Jun 1882 in Ffx; father: Warner MAY; occ: ___; res: ___; mother: Dolly MAY; inf: Warner MAY, father; pg:ln: 137:58

MAYHUGH, Grace Mary; WF; b. 22 Nov 1896 in Clifton Sta.; father: Geo. L. MAYHUGH; occ: farmer; res: Clifton Sta.; mother: Harriet L. MAYHUGH; inf: father; pg:ln: 231:82

MAYLEY, James Henry; WM; b. 8 Apr 1896 nr Fairfax Sta.; father: John E. MAILEY; occ: farmer; res: nr Fairfax Sta.; mother: Mary C. MAILEY; inf: mother; pg:ln: 231:85

MAYO, William A.; CM; b. 13 Sep 1883 in Providence; father: Philip MAYO; occ: laborer; res: Providence; mother: Elizabeth MAYO; inf: father; pg:ln: 140:68

McCANN, Margaret; WF; b. 15 Feb 1895 nr Alexandria; father: Francis F. McCANN; occ: carpenter; res: nr Alex.; mother: Ellen McCANN; inf: mother; pg:ln: 223:91

McCANN, May Ellen; WF; b. 16 Jul 1896 nr Alex.; father: Francis T. McCANN; occ: stone cutter; res: nr Alex.; mother: Ellen McCANN; inf: mother; pg:ln: 231:88

McCARTY, Arthur W.; WM; b. 12 Jun 1894 in Ffx; father: Jno. E. McCARTY; occ: farmer; res: Ffx; mother: Beatrice McCARTY; inf: J. McCARTY, father; pg:ln: 218:78

McCAULEY, Ethel G.; WF; b. 27 Jun 1890 in Ffx; father: D. L. McCAULEY; occ: farmer; res: Ffx; mother: Rachael McCAULEY; inf: D. L. McCAULEY, father; pg:ln: 191:73

McCAULEY, Mary E.; WF; b. 7 Dec 1886 in Prov.; father: D. L. McCAULEY; occ: farmer; res: Prov.; mother: R. A. McCAULEY; inf: father; pg:ln: 159:44

McDANIEL, Archie L.; WM; b. 25 Dec 1896 in Ffx; father: Jas. McDANIEL; occ: farmer; res: Ffx; mother: Rose McDANIEL; inf: Jas. McDANIEL, father; pg:ln: 227:81

McDANIEL, Jesse S.; WM; b. 26 Oct 1892 in Ffx; father: Saml. McDANIEL; occ: farmer; res: Ffx; mother: Rose McDANIEL; inf: S. B. McDANIEL, father; pg:ln: 203:67

McDANIEL, Mariah Jane; CF; b. 27 Jul 1896 in Rosselen Sta.; father: Burwell McDANIEL; occ: laborer; res: nr Centreville; mother: Annie McDANIEL; inf: father; pg:ln: 231:93

McDONOUGH, Mary; WF; b. 13 May 1885 in Providence; father: Jno.
McDONOUGH; occ: farmer; res: Providence; mother: Mary
McDONOUGH; inf: father; pg:ln: 153:54

McGARITY, Lula; WF; b. 7 Jun 1890 in Ffx; father: Luther McGARITY;
occ: farmer; res: Ffx; mother: Laura McGARITY; inf: L. McGARITY,
father; pg:ln: 191:74

McGLINCEY, G. T.; WM; b. 8 Dec 1885 in Frying Pan; father: Geo.
McGLINCEY; occ: farmer; res: Frying Pan; mother: Martha
McGLINCEY; inf: father; pg:ln: 153:58

McINTOSH, Elmer; WM; b. 14 Mar 1894 in Ffx; father: L. L. McINTOSH;
occ: farmer; res: Ffx; mother: M. M. McINTOSH; inf: L. L.
McINTOSH, father; pg:ln: 219:82

McINTURF, Fre'd.; WM; b. 28 Feb 1894 in Ffx; father: Geo. F.
McINTURF; occ: farmer; res: Ffx; mother: Alice McINTURF; inf: G.
F. McINTURF, father; pg:ln: 219:84

McINTURFF, Mable; WF; b. 14 Sep 1891 in Ffx; father: Geo.
McINTURFF; occ: farmer; res: Ffx; mother: Alice McINTURFF; inf:
G. McINTURFF, father; pg:ln: 199:67

McKELLEGER, Jane; WF; b. 3 Dec 1884 in Seminary; father: William
McKELLEGER; occ: laborer; res: Seminary; mother: Ella
McKELLEGER; inf: father; pg:ln: 150:64

McKELLEGET, L. B. K.; WM; b. 14 May 1894 in Ffx; father: J. W.
McKELLEGET; occ: farmer; res: Ffx; mother: E. M. McKELLEGET;
inf: J. W. McKELLEGET, father; pg:ln: 219:85

McKELLET, Bessie; WF; b. 21 Apr 1889 in Ffx; father: Wm. McKELLET;
occ: farmer; res: Ffx; mother: Ellen McKELLET; inf: W. McKELLET,
father; pg:ln: 179:75

McKELLET, Bessie; WF; b. 27 Apr 1888 in Ffx; father: W. McKELLET;
occ: farmer; res: Ffx; mother: Ella McKELLET; inf: W. McKELLET,
father; pg:ln: 174:69

McKENZIE, David R.; CM; b. 12 Apr 1891 in Ffx; father: Lewis
McKENZIE; occ: farmer; res: Ffx; mother: Minnie McKENZIE; inf: L.
McKENZIE, father; pg:ln: 199:66

McKENZIE, Elizabt. J.; CF; b. 1 Nov 1896 in Ffx; father: Lewis
McKENZIE; occ: farmer; res: Ffx; mother: Minnie McKINZIE; inf: L.
McKENZIE, father; pg:ln: 227:85

McKENZIE, Lewis; CM; b. 15 Mar 1889 in Ffx; father: Lewis McKENZIE;
occ: farmer; res: Ffx; mother: Minnie McKENZIE; inf: L. McKENZIE,
father; pg:ln: 179:82

McKNIGHT, Harry; CM; b. 7 Jan 1889 in Ffx; father: Surl McKNIGHT;
occ: farmer; res: Ffx; mother: Mary McKNIGHT; inf: S. McKNIGHT,
father; pg:ln: 179:73

McKNIGHT, Horace; CM; b. 10 Feb 1892 in Ffx; father: Robt.
McKNIGHT; occ: janitor at Seminary; res: Ffx; mother: Susie
McKNIGHT; inf: Robt. McKNIGHT, father; pg:ln: 204:71

McKNIGHT, Willis; CM; b. 30 Aug 1885 in Seminary; father: R.
McKNIGHT; occ: laborer; res: Seminary; mother: S. McKNIGHT; inf:
father; pg:ln: 153:47

McKOWN, Geo.; WM; b. 7 Jan 1889 in Ffx; father: Math McKOWN; occ: farmer; res: Ffx; mother: Mary McKOWN; inf: M. McKOWN, father; pg:ln: 182:61

McLAIN, James Douglas; WM; b. 14 Jul 1895* nr Franconia; father: Donald McLAIN; occ: farmer; res: nr Franconia; mother: Lucy T. McLAIN*; inf: father; pg:ln: 223:90 [no indication what the * refers to]

McLANE, Fannie; WF; b. 17 Mar 1896 in Ffx; father: Timothy McLANE; occ: farmer; res: Ffx; mother: Mary McLANE; inf: T. McLANE, father; pg:ln: 227:86

McLEAN, Anna L.; WF; b. 29 Mar 1887 in ___; father: Donald McLEAN; occ: farmer; res: Ffx; mother: Lucy T. McLEAN; inf: D. McLEAN, father; pg:ln: 168:76

McLEAN, Anthony; WM; b. 25 Jun 1889 in Ffx; father: Donald McLEAN; occ: farmer; res: Ffx; mother: Lucy McLEAN; inf: D. McLEAN, father; pg:ln: 182:62

McLEAN, Willoughby Tebbs; WM; b. 23 Jun 1891 nr Alexandria; father: Donald McLEAN; occ: farmer; res: nr Alexandria; mother: Lucy T. McLEAN; inf: parents; pg:ln: 195:11

McLEOD, Manning; WM; b. 19 Mar 1883 in Providence; father: W. D. McLEOD; occ: physician; res: Providence; mother: Alice McLEOD; inf: father; pg:ln: 140:69

McMILLAN, Frankie; WF; b. 5 Feb 1894 in Ffx; father: J. R. McMILLAN; occ: farmer; res: Ffx; mother: Mary McMILLAN; inf: J. R. McMILLAN, father; pg:ln: 218:76

McMILLEN, A. C.; WM; b. 30 Sep 1887 in Ffx; father: W. W. McMILLEN; occ: farmer; res: Ffx; mother: P. M. McMILLEN; inf: W. W. McMILLEN, father; pg:ln: 162:98

McMULLEN, Judy; WF; b. 3 Aug 1892 nr Fairfax Sta.; father: Morion McMULLEN; occ: farmer; res: nr Fairfax Sta.; mother: Mary N. McMULLEN; inf: mother; pg:ln: 208:20

McMULLEN, Levi; WM; b. 19 Sep 1885 in Ffx; father: Levi McMULLEN; occ: farmer; res: Ffx; mother: C. W. McMULLEN; inf: L. McMULLEN, father; pg:ln: 157:44

McMULLEN, Rune; WM; b. 29 Dec 1889 in Ffx; father: M. F. McMULLEN; occ: farmer; res: Ffx; mother: M. A. McMULLEN; inf: M. F. McMULLEN, father; pg:ln: 182:65

McMULLIN, Lottie; WF; b. 28 Jan 1887 in ___; father: Marion McMULLEN; occ: carpenter; res: Ffx; mother: Mary McMULLEN; inf: M. McMULLEN, father; pg:ln: 168:78

McNIGHT, Harvey; CM; b. 20 Dec 1882 in Falls Church; father: Searls McNIGHT; occ: laborer; res: Falls Church; mother: Mary McNIGHT; inf: father; pg:ln: 134:39

MEEKIN, Dorothy [MACON written above]; WF; b. 2 Aug 1892 in Ffx; father: Edw'd. MEEKIN [MACON written above]; occ: farmer; res: Ffx; mother: E. B. MEEKIN [MACON written above]; inf: E. MEEKIN, father. Ct. Court of Richmond 4 Oct 1928: the order changing the name of Edward N. Meekins to Edward N. Macon was entered in this Court on 19 May 1903 in Order Book No. 37, page 107 and announced to the Army.; pg:ln: 203:66

MENTZEL, Fre'd.; WM; b. 16 Jul 1894 in Ffx; father: Jno. MENTZELL; occ: farmer; res: Ffx; mother: Laura MENTZEL; inf: J. MENTZELL, father; pg:ln: 218:77

MENTZEL, Perleanor; WF; b. 30 Aug 1896 in Ffx; father: Jno. MENTZEL; occ: farmer; res: Ffx; mother: Laura MENTZEL; inf: Jno. MENTZEL, father; pg:ln: 227:91

MENTZER, Hattie; WF; b. 24 Dec 1895 nr Centreville; father: Harvey MENTZER; occ: farmer; res: nr Centreville; mother: Lillie MENTZER; inf: father; pg:ln: 223:85

MERCER, not named (dead); WM; b. 14 Jan 1887 in ___; father: Walter S. MERCER; occ: farmer; res: Ffx; mother: Ida MERCER; inf: W. S. MERCER, father; pg:ln: 168:72

MERCHANT, Asberry B.; WM; b. 10 Jul 1896 in Fairfax Sta.; father: A. MERCHANT; occ: telegraph operator; res: Fairfax Sta.; mother: Hattee MERCHANT; inf: father; pg:ln: 231:89

MERCHANT, Edward; WM; b. 3 Oct 1890 in Ffx; father: J. E. MERCHANT; occ: farmer; res: Ffx; mother: Isabela MERCHANT; inf: J. E. MERCHANT, father; pg:ln: 187:82

MERO, Lucy; WF; b. 9 Aug 1895 nr Woodlawn; father: C. L. MERO; occ: farmer; res: nr Woodlawn; mother: Elizabeth MERO; inf: mother; pg:ln· 223:92

MERO, Percy Ashton; WM; b. 10 Jan 1895 in West End; father: J. W. MERO; occ: clerk; res: West End; mother: Ada E. MERO; inf: mother; pg:ln: 223:82

MERRY, Harry C.; WM; b. 20 Sep 1884 in Prov.; father: E. R. MERRY; occ: farmer; res: Prov.; mother: Eliza MERRY; inf: father; pg:ln: 150:66

MERRY, Hattie; CF; b. 15 Jul 1889 in Ffx; father: Jas. MERRY; occ: farmer; res: Ffx; mother: Kate MERRY; inf: Jas. MERRY, father; pg:ln: 179:85

MERRY, Jno. W.; WM; b. 1 Mar 1889 in Ffx; father: Geo. MERRY; occ: farmer; res: Ffx; mother: Martha MERRY; inf: Geo. MERRY, father; pg:ln: 179:84

MERRYMAN, ___ (dead); WF; b. 4 Jul 1889 in Ffx; father: San MERRYMAN; occ: farmer; res: Ffx; mother: Mary MERRYMAN; inf: S. MERRYMAN, father; pg:ln: 182:63

MERRYMAN, Harry L.; WM; b. 21 Jul 1884 in Ffx; father: Sanford MERRYMAN; occ: ___; res: ___; mother: Mary MERRYMAN; inf: S. MERRYMAN, father; pg:ln: 147:51

MERRYMAN, Hattie; WF; b. 11 Mar 1888 in Ffx; father: Sanford MERRYMAN; occ: laborer; res: Ffx; mother: Mary MERRYMAN; inf: S. MERRYMAN, father; pg:ln: 171:44

MERRYMAN, Henry; WM; b. 10 Sep 1890 in Ffx; father: Sanford MERRYMAN; occ: laborer; res: Ffx; mother: Mary MERRYMAN; inf: S. MERRYMAN, father; pg:ln: 187:80

MERRYMAN, Maggie May; WF; b. 15 Jul 1896 nr Springfield; father: Sanford MERRYMAN; occ: rail road hand; res: Springfield; mother: Mary MERRYMAN; inf: mother; pg:ln: 231:84

MIDDLETON, Benjn.; WM; b. __ Jun 1889 in Ffx; father: Brook MID[D]LETON; occ: farmer; res: Ffx; mother: Mary MID[D]LETON; inf: B. MID[D]LETON, father; pg:ln: 179:77

MIDDLETON, Emma; WF; b. 13 Aug 1891 in Ffx; father: Brook MIDDLETON; occ: farmer; res: Ffx; mother: Mary MIDDLETON; inf: B. MIDDLETON, father; pg:ln: 199:65

MIDDLETON, Harriett; WF; b. 24 Feb 1880 in Dranesville; father: G. H. MIDDLETON; occ: farmer; res: Dranesville; mother: Emma MIDDLETON; inf: father; pg:ln: 125:46

MIDDLETON, Hatty; WF; b. 24 Feb 1881 in Chantilly; father: M. H. MIDDLETON; occ: farmer; res: Chantilly; mother: Emma MIDDLETON; inf: father; pg:ln: 131:47

MIDDLETON, Mary; WF; b. 1 Sep 1885 in Dranes.; father: Brook MIDDLETON; occ: farmer; res: Dranes.; mother: Mary J. MIDDLETON; inf: father; pg:ln: 153:55

MILLARD, ___; WF; b. 5 Feb 1883 in Dranesville; father: Addison MILLARD; occ: farmer; res: Dranesville; mother: Emma MILLARD; inf: father; pg:ln: 140:72

MILLARD, Alfred; WM; b. 24 Mar 1889 in Ffx; father: A. B. MILLARD; occ: farmer; res: Ffx; mother: Emma MILLARD; inf: A. B. MILLARD, father; pg:ln: 179:76

MILLARD, Elsie; WF; b. 8 Jul 1896 in Ffx; father: E. E. MILLARD; occ: farmer; res: Ffx; mother: Edna MILLARD; inf: E. E. MILLARD, father; pg:ln: 227:89

MILLARD, Oscar; WM; b. 11 Nov 1887 in Ffx; father: A. B. MILLARD; occ: farmer; res: Ffx; mother: Emma MILLARD; inf: A. B. MILLARD, father; pg:ln: 162:100

MILLER, Carrie; CF; b. 8 Feb 1888 in Ffx; father: Jno. A. MILLER; occ: farmer; res: Ffx; mother: Lavina MILLER; inf: J. MILLER, father; pg:ln: 174:70

MILLER, Emma M.; WF; b. 2 Aug 1886 in Maple Wood; father: Henry MILLER; occ: farmer; res: Maple Wood; mother: Emma MILLER; inf: father; pg:ln: 159:70

MILLER, Frank M.; WM; b. 28 Oct 1882 in Falls Church; father: J. Frank MILLER; occ: Gov. Clerk; res: Falls Church; mother: Carrie V. MILLER; inf: father; pg:ln: 135:41

MILLER, Geo. B.; CM; b. 1 Jun 1885 in Falls Ch.; father: John MILLER; occ: laborer; res: Falls Ch.; mother: Jane MILLER; inf: father; pg:ln: 153:50

MILLER, Gordon S.; CM; b. 23 Oct 1884 in Seminary; father: Jno. A. MILER; occ: laborer; res: Seminary; mother: Louisa MILLER; inf: father; pg:ln: 150:62

MILLER, Jno. H.; CM; b. 15 Mar 1893 in Ffx; father: Jno. H. MILLER; occ: farmer; res: Ffx; mother: Jane MILLER; inf: Jno. H. MILLER, father; pg:ln: 215:73

MILLER, Josephus; CM; b. 24 Jul 1886 in Seminary; father: Jno. A.
MILLER; occ: farmer; res: Seminary; mother: L. MILLER; inf: father;
pg:ln: 159:37

MILLER, Mary E.; WF; b. 13 Feb 1888 in Ffx; father: Henry MILLER;
occ: farmer; res: Ffx; mother: Gertrude MILLER; inf: H. MILLER,
father; pg:ln: 174:67

MILLER, not named; CM; b. 21 Dec 1884 in Falls Church; father: John
MILLER; occ: laborer; res: Falls Church; mother: Jennie MILLER;
inf: father; pg:ln: 150:63

MILLER, Thomas; CM; b. 15 Mar 1880 in Falls Church; father: John
MILLER; occ: laborer; res: Falls Church; mother: Jane MILLER; inf:
father; pg:ln: 125:43

MILLER, W. C.; WM; b. 1 Nov 1881 in Ffx; father: Jno. R. MILLER; occ:
farmer; res: Ffx; mother: Cath. MILLER; inf: C. MILLER, mother;
pg:ln: 132:29

MILLNER, Clara; CF; b. 18 Apr 1887 in Ffx; father: Titus MILNER; occ:
farmer; res: Ffx; mother: Sela MILNER; inf: T. MILNER, father; pg:ln:
162:91

MILLS, H. H.; WM; b. 23 Aug 1881 in Germantown; father: A. T. MILLS;
occ: mechanic; res: Germantown; mother: Cornelia MILLS; inf:
mother; pg:ln: 131:43

MILLS, Joseph; WM; b. 16 Mar 1885 in Providence; father: L. F. MILLS;
occ: farmer; res: Providence; mother: Fannie MILLS; inf: father;
pg:ln: 153:52

MILLS, Lillian; WF; b. 29 Sep 1896 in Ffx; father: W. A. MILLS; occ:
farmer; res: Ffx; mother: Ella MILLS; inf: W. MILLS, father; pg:ln:
227:87

MILLS, M.; WF; b. 10 Aug 1880 in Ffx; father: G. MILLS; occ: farmer;
res: Ffx; mother: Jane; inf: Geo. MILLS, father; pg:ln: 128:61

MILNER, Arthur E.; CM; b. 28 Apr 1882 in near Viena; father: Titus
MILNER; occ: mechanic; res: near Viena; mother: Lydia MILNER;
inf: father; pg:ln: 134:40

MILNER, Thomas J.; CM; b. 15 Feb 1880 in Providence; father: Titus
MILNER; occ: mechanic; res: Providence; mother: Lydia MILNER;
inf: father; pg:ln: 125:44

MIMMS?, Margaret; CF; b. 1 Dec 1895 nr Gum Spring; father: Thos.
MIMMS?; occ: laborer; res: nr Gum Spring; mother: Cora MIMMS?;
inf: father; pg:ln: 223:95

MINOR, Andrew; CM; b. 15 Oct 1894 in Ffx; father: A. W. MINOR; occ:
farmer; res: Ffx; mother: Emma MINOR; inf: A. W. MINOR, father;
pg:ln: 219:91

MITCHELL, Geo. L.; WM; b. 20 Nov 1888 in Ffx; father: Jno. E.
MITCHELL; occ: R. R. agent; res: Ffx; mother: Cath. I. MITCHELL;
inf: J. E. MITCHELL, father; pg:ln: 171:46

MITCHELL, Hattie; WF; b. 20 Jan 1889 in Ffx; father: J. E. MITCHELL;
occ: R R agent; res: Ffx; mother: C. J. MITCHELL; inf: J. E.
MITCHELL, father; pg:ln: 182:66

MITCHELL, Hattie; WF; b. 30 Jan 1890 in Ffx; father: J. E. MITCHELL; occ: R. Rd. agent; res: Ffx; mother: Cath. MITCHELL; inf: J. E. MITCHELL, father; pg:ln: 187:75

MITCHELL, John (dead); WM; b. 9 Jul 1887 in ___; father: John MITCHELL; occ: R. Rd. agent; res: Ffx; mother: C. E. MITCHELL; inf: John MITCHELL, father; pg:ln: 168:80

MITCHELL, Maggie M.; WF; b. 12 Nov 1887 in ___; father: Albert MITCHELL; occ: farmer; res: Ffx; mother: Mamie MITCHELL; inf: Albert MITCHELL, father; pg:ln: 168:81

MITCHELL, Maud; WF; b. 5 Dec 1895 nr Fairfax C. H.; father: A. B. MITCHELL; occ: farmer; res: nr Fairfax C. H.; mother: Mamie MITCHELL; inf: father; pg:ln: 223:93

MITCHELL, W.; WM; b. 12 Dec 1880 in Ffx; father: J. E. MITCHELL; occ: farmer; res: Ffx; mother: Ida; inf: J. E. MITCHELL, father; pg:ln: 128:60

MOCK, Dennis; WM; b. 7 Dec 1882 in Ffx; father: G. R. MOCK; occ: farmer; res: Ffx; mother: Mary MOCK; inf: G. R. MOCK, father; pg:ln: 136:34

MOCK, Minnie; WF; b. 18 Oct 1896 in Ffx; father: E'd. MOCK; occ: farmer; res: Ffx; mother: Mary MOCK; inf: E'd. MOCK, father; pg:ln: 227:88

[MOCK], not named (dead); CF; b. 30 Mar 1881 in Dranesville; father: Edward MOCK; occ: laborer; res: Dranesville; mother: Eliz. A. MOCK; inf: mother; pg:ln: 131:42

MOHLER, ___ (dead); WM; b. 26 Jun 1888 in Ffx; father: C. J. MOHLER; occ: farmer; res: Ffx; mother: S. J. MOHLER; inf: C. J. MOHLER, father; pg:ln: 171:45

MOHLER, Cath'n. M.; WF; b. 27 Nov 1880 in Ffx; father: Jasper MOHLER; occ: farmer; res: Ffx; mother: Sallie J.; inf: Jasper MOHLER, father; pg:ln: 128:63

MOHLER, Daisy Allen; WF; b. 16 Jun 1892 nr Centreville; father: C. J. MOHLER; occ: farmer; res: nr Centreville; mother: Sallie J. MOHLER; inf: father; pg:ln: 208:19

MOHLER, Gracie H.; WF; b. 4 Mar 1890 in Ffx; father: C. J. MOHLER; occ: Postmaster; res: Ffx; mother: Sallie J. MOHLER; inf: C. J. MOHLER, father; pg:ln: 187:77

MOHLER, H. W.; WM; b. 12 Nov 1880 in Ffx; father: Jno. W. MOHLER; occ: farmer; res: Ffx; mother: M. E.; inf: J. W. MOHLER, father; pg:ln: 128:62

MOHLER, Josper Berton; WM; b. 27 Oct 1893 nr Centreville; father: C. J. MOHLER; occ: farmer; res: nr Centreville; mother: Sallie J. MOHLER; inf: mother; pg:ln: 211:71

MONCH, Florence Victoria; WF; b. 2 Feb 1893 nr Alex.; father: George MONCH; occ: farmer; res: nr Alex.; mother: Lola Virginia MONCH; inf: parent; pg:ln: 212:74

MONCH, Olevia [written as MOUNCH]; WF; b. 25 Dec 1893 nr Alex.; father: Wm. MONCH; occ: laborer; res: nr Alex.; mother: Ellen MONCH; inf: parent; pg:ln: 212:73

MONCURE, Frank P.; WM; b. 5 Nov 1889 in Ffx; father: W. P.
MONCURE; occ: physician; res: Ffx; mother: Mary MONCURE; inf:
W. P. MONCURE, father; pg:ln: 179:83

MONCURE, McCarty C.; WM; b. 1 Feb 1888 in Ffx; father: W. P.
MONCURE; occ: farmer; res: Ffx; mother: Mary J. MONCURE; inf:
W. P. MONCURE, father; pg:ln: 174:66

[MONCURE], not named (dead); WM; b. 10 Aug 1891 in Stafford C. H.;
father: R. M. MONCURE; occ: farmer; res: Potomac; mother: Laura
E. MONCURE; inf: parents; pg:ln: 195:25

MONEY, ___; WM; b. 25 Dec 1888 in Ffx; father: C. M. MONEY; occ:
farmer; res: Ffx; mother: Joanna MONEY; inf: C. M. MONEY, father;
pg:ln: 174:68

MONEY, Albt.; WM; b. 1 Jul 1896 in Ffx; father: Albt. MONEY; occ:
farmer; res: Ffx; mother: Nannie MONEY; inf: A. MONEY, father;
pg:ln: 227:80

MONEY, Elsie; WF; b. 10 Mar 1890 in Ffx; father: Albt. H. MONEY; occ:
farmer; res: Ffx; mother: Nannie MONEY; inf: A. H. MONEY, father;
pg:ln: 191:72

MONEY, Elsie; WF; b. 5 Jun 1893 in ___; father: H. A. MONEY; occ:
___; res: ___; mother: E. L. MONEY; inf: H. A. MONEY, father;
pg:ln: 214:70

MONEY, Estelle; WF; b. 25 Sep 1892 in Ffx; father: Albt. MONEY; occ:
farmer; res: Ffx; mother: Nannie MONEY; inf: A. MONEY, father;
pg:ln: 203:69

MONEY, Geo. Ashley; WM; b. 18 Mar 1887 in Ffx; father: Cornelius
MONEY; occ: farmer; res: Ffx; mother: Johanna MONEY; inf: C.
MONEY, father; pg:ln: 162:93

MONEY, Harry E.; WM; b. 3 Oct 1881 in Dranesville; father: Albert
MONEY; occ: farmer; res: Dranesville; mother: Nancy MONEY; inf:
father; pg:ln: 130:39

MONEY, James; WM; b. 9 May 1892 in Ffx; father: C. M. MONEY; occ:
farmer; res: Ffx; mother: Jane MONEY; inf: C. M. MONEY, father;
pg:ln: 203:70

MONEY, May E.; WF; b. 4 Feb 1887 in Ffx; father: H. H. MONEY; occ:
farmer; res: Ffx; mother: Ella MONEY; inf: H. H. MONEY, father;
pg:ln: 162:95

MONEY, not named; WF; b. 10 Oct 1883 in Dranesville; father: Albert
MONEY; occ: farmer; res: Dranesville; mother: M. MONEY; inf:
father; pg:ln: 140:67

MONEY, not named; WF; b. 4 Apr 1883 in Dranesville; father: J.
Thomas MONEY; occ: farmer; res: Dranesville; mother: Frances
MONEY; inf: father; pg:ln: 140:70

MONEY, not named; WM; b. 18 Mar 1886 in Prov.; father: Cornelius
MONEY; occ: farmer; res: Prov.; mother: J. MONEY; inf: father;
pg:ln: 159:42

MONEY, not named; WM; b. 3 Jan 1889 in Ffx; father: Jno. H. MONEY;
occ: farmer; res: Ffx; mother: Francis MONEY; inf: J. H. MONEY,
father; pg:ln: 179:78

MONEY, Ross; WM; b. 9 Mar 1880 in Dranesville; father: Cornelius MONEY; occ: farmer; res: Dranesville; mother: J. MONEY; inf: father; ρg:ln: 125:42

MONEY, Sarah Ann; WF; b. 15 Sep 1887 in Ffx; father: Albert MONEY; occ: farmer; res: Ffx; mother: Nancy MONEY; inf: Albert MONEY, father; pg:ln: 162:94

MONEY. R. Virginia; WF; b. 22 May 1885 in Providence; father: Cornelius MONEY; occ: farmer; res: Providence; mother: Joanna MONEY; inf: father; pg:ln: 153:53

MONROE, Catherine Rebecca; WF; b. 19 Jul 1895 nr Alexandria; father: James W. MONROE; occ: farmer; res: nr Alex.; mother: Mary MONROE; inf: mother; pg:ln: 223:89

MONROE, Clara; CF; b. 8 Nov 1889 in Ffx; father: Jno. MONROE; occ: farmer; res: Ffx; mother: Sarah MONROE; inf: J. MONROE, father; pg:ln: 179:79

MONROE, Grace; WF; b. 16 Jul 1896 nr Alex.; father: James W. MONROE; occ: farmer; res: nr Alex.; mother: Mary MONROE; inf: mother; pg:ln: 231:90

MONROE, Irene; CF; b. 25 Nov 1880 in Dranesville; father: John MONROE; occ: farmer; res: Dranesville; mother: Sarah J. MONROE; inf: father; pg:ln: 125:47

MONROE, Jas.; CM; b. 4 Jun 1894 in Ffx; father: Jno. MONROE; occ: farmer; res: Ffx; mother: Sarah MONROE; inf: Jno. T. MONROE, father; pg:ln: 219:92

MONROE, John; WM; b. 25 Aug 1881 in Herndon; father: Alfred C. MONROE; occ: laborer; res: Herndon; mother: Mary MONROE; inf: father; pg:ln: 131:45

MONROE, Wallis; WM; b. 23 May 1890 in Ffx; father: J. W. MONROE; occ: farmer; res: Ffx; mother: Mary MONROE; inf: J. W. MONROE, father; pg:ln: 187:83

MOODY, Ellis; WM; b. 5 Jun 1896 nr Lorton Sta.; father: John M. MOODY; occ: farmer; res: nr Lorton Sta.; mother: Eunice MOODY; inf: mother; pg:ln: 231:86

MOODY, not named; WM; b. 13 Mar 1895 nr Lorton Sta.; father: John MOODY; occ: farmer; res: nr Lorton Sta.; mother: Emma D. MOODY; inf: mother; pg:ln: 223:87

MOODY, Susan Elsie; WF; b. 31 Sep 1891 nr Lorton; father: John M. MOODY; occ: farmer; res: nr Lorton; mother: Dollie MOODY; inf: parents; pg:ln: 193:20

MOOE, Marshal; CM; b. 12 Sep 1888 in Ffx; father: Jas. MOOE; occ: farmer; res: Ffx; mother: Mary MOOE; inf: J. MOOE, father; pg:ln: 174:71

MOORE, Amanda; WF; b. 16 Mar 1883 in Mount Pleasant; father: Joseph MOORE; occ: laborer; res: Mount Pleasant; mother: Aga MOORE; inf: father; pg:ln: 140:64

MOORE, Katie; WF; b. 1 May 1896 nr Pender; father: Edward MOORE; occ: farmer; res: Pender; mother: Alice MOORE; inf: father; pg:ln: 231:83

MOORE, Maggie; CF; b. 1 Mar 1885 in Seminary; father: James
    MOORE; occ: mechanic; res: Seminary; mother: Mary MOORE; inf:
    father; pg:ln: 153:51
MOORE, Mary A.; WF; b. 16 Mar 1881 in Vienna; father: Wm. E.
    MOORE; occ: farmer; res: Vienna; mother: Sallie V. MOORE; inf:
    father; pg:ln: 130:38
MOORE, Milton; WM; b. 15 Dec 1890 in Ffx; father: Edw'd. MOORE;
    occ: farmer; res: Ffx; mother: Allie MOORE; inf: E. MOORE, father;
    pg:ln: 191:75
MOORE, Wallace; CM; b. 17 May 1886 in Seminary; father: Wallace
    MOORE; occ: mechanic; res: Seminary; mother: Mary MOORE; inf:
    father; pg:ln: 159:38
MOORE, Wallace; CM; b. 6 Apr 1883 in Seminary; father: Wallace
    MOORE; occ: laborer; res: Seminary; mother: Mollie MOORE; inf:
    father; pg:ln: 140:63
MORARITY, Bertha; CF; b. 4 Aug 1890 in Ffx; father: Tobe MORARITY;
    occ: laborer; res: Ffx; mother: Della MORARITY; inf: T. MORARITY,
    father; pg:ln: 187:73
MORELAND, Eva; WF; b. 6 Jul 1886 in Prov.; father: W. P.
    MORELAND; occ: farmer; res: Prov.; mother: E. MORELAND; inf:
    father; pg:ln: 159:43
MORGAN, Arthur; CM; b. 28 Jun 1887 in Ffx; father: Geo. MORGAN;
    occ: laborer; res: Ffx; mother: Martha MORGAN; inf: G. MORGAN,
    father; pg:ln: 162:92
MORGAN, Sina E.; CF; b. 17 May 1896 in Ffx; father: Nelson
    MORGAN; occ: farmer; res: Ffx; mother: Sarah MORGAN; inf:
    Nelson MORGAN, father; pg:ln: 227:84
MORIARTY, Frank; WM; b. 13 Jun 1894 in Ffx; father: Jno. W.
    MORIARTY; occ: farmer; res: Ffx; mother: Mary E. MORIARTY; inf:
    Jno. MORIARTY, father; pg:ln: 219:83
MORRIS, Frederick B.; WM; b. 26 Sep 1890 in Ffx; father: Chas. E.
    MORRIS; occ: farmer; res: Ffx; mother: Kate MORRIS; inf: Chas. E.
    MORRIS, father; pg:ln: 187:78
MORRIS, Jessie; WM; b. 16 Nov 1893 nr Colchester; father: Chs. E.
    MORRIS; occ: farmer; res: nr Colchester; mother: Mary C. MORRIS;
    inf: mother; pg:ln: 211:70
MORRIS, Virginia P.; WF; b. 27 Apr 1889 in Ffx; father: Chas. E.
    MORRIS; occ: farmer; res: Ffx; mother: Kate MORRIS; inf: C. E.
    MORRIS, father; pg:ln: 182:64
MORRIS, Walter Irving; WM; b. 12 Dec 1891 in Colchester; father:
    Chas. E. MORRIS; occ: farmer; res: Colchester; mother: Mary
    Catharine MORRIS; inf: parents; pg:ln: 193:21
MORRISON, Mary M.; WF; b. 3 Sep 1887 in Ffx; father: D. B.
    MORRISON; occ: farmer; res: Ffx; mother: L. H. MORRISON; inf: D.
    B. MORRISON, father; pg:ln: 162:99
MORRISON, Virginia; WF; b. 22 Nov 1886 in Falls CH.; father: Robt.
    MORRISON; occ: attorney; res: Falls CH.; mother: Ida MORRISON;
    inf: father; pg:ln: 159:41

MORTIMORE, Curtis S.; WM; b. 24 Feb 1881 in Bailey's X Roads;
father: Jno. T. MORTIMORE; occ: mechanic; res: Bailey's X Roads;
mother: Hannah H. MORTIMORE; inf: father; pg:ln: 131:41

MORTON, Jesse; CM; b. 2 Apr 1885 in Ffx; father: Jesse MORTON;
occ: farmer; res: Ffx; mother: Jennie MORTON; inf: J. MORTON,
father; pg:ln: 157:42

MORTON, Lulie; CF; b. ___ Feb 1882 in Ffx; father: Jesse MORTON;
occ: ___; res: ___; mother: Jennie MORTON; inf: J. MORTON,
father; pg:ln: 137:52

MORTON, Mary E.; CF; b. 7 Mar 1887 in ___; father: Samuel
MORTON; occ: laborer; res: Ffx; mother: Ellen MORTON; inf: Saml.
MORTON, father; pg:ln: 168:73

MORTON, William; CM; b. 5 Jun 1881 in Providence; father: Stephen
MORTON; occ: laborer; res: Providence; mother: Annie MORTON;
inf: father; pg:ln: 131:44

MORTON, Wm.; CM; b. 15 Nov 1883 in Ffx; father: Jesse MORTON;
occ: farmer; res: Ffx; mother: Agnes MORTON; inf: J. MORTON,
father; pg:ln: 144:61

MOSBY, Mattie; CF; b. 7 Sep 1880 in Vienna; father: John MOSBY;
occ: laborer; res: Vienna; mother: Maria MOSBY; inf: father; pg:ln:
125:45

MOUNT, Princis; CF; b. 22 Feb 1894 in Ffx; father: Lafayett MOUNT;
occ: farmer; res: Ffx; mother: Luella MOUNT; inf: L. MOUNT, father;
pg:ln: 219:80

MOXLEY, not named; WF; b. 1 Feb 1886 in Dranes.; father: W. A.
MOXLEY; occ: mcht.; res: Dranes.; mother: S. E. MOXLEY; inf:
father; pg:ln: 159:45

MOXLEY, not named; WM; b. 1 Jan 1885 in Dranes.; father: W. A.
MOXLEY; occ: merchant; res: Dranes.; mother: Susan E. MOXLEY;
inf: father; pg:ln: 153:57

MUDD, Lewis (twin); WM; b. 6 Jan 1887 in ___; father: Theopholus
MUDD; occ: farmer; res: Ffx; mother: Dorenda MUDD; inf: T. MUDD,
father; pg:ln: 168:77

MUDD, Mary Ellen; WF; b. 2 May 1890 in Ffx; father: Theophulus
MUDD; occ: laborer; res: Ffx; mother: Dora MUDD; inf: T. MUDD,
father; pg:ln: 187:81

MUDD, not named (twin); WM; b. 11 Jan 1892 in Village adj Alex.;
father: Theopelus MUDD; occ: ___; res: Village adj Alex.; mother:
Lorenda MUDD; inf: mother; pg:ln: 207:77

MUDD, not named (twin); WM; b. 11 Jan 1892 in Village adj Alex.;
father: Theopelus MUDD; occ: ___; res: Village adj Alex.; mother:
Lorenda MUDD; inf: mother; pg:ln: 207:77

MUDD, Robt. (twin); WM; b. 6 Jan 1887 in ___; father: Theopholus
MUDD; occ: farmer; res: Ffx; mother: Dorenda MUDD; inf: T. MUDD,
father; pg:ln: 168:77

MULHOLLAND, Chas. Alex.; WM; b. 25 Oct 1895 nr Centreville; father:
John MULHOLLAND; occ: farmer; res: nr Centreville; mother: Mary
Mildred MULHOLLAND; inf: mother; pg:ln: 223:84

MULHOLLAND, Jno.; WM; b. 20 Dec 1883 in Ffx; father: Jno.
MULHOLLAND; occ: farmer; res: Ffx; mother: Mary MULHOLLAND;
inf: Jno. MULHOLAND, father; pg:ln: 144:59

MULHOLLAND, John; WM; b. 21 Dec 1882 in Ffx; father: Jno.
MULHOLLAND; occ: ___; res: ___; mother: Mary MULHOLLAND;
inf: J. MULHOLLAND, father; pg:ln: 137:54

MULHOLLAND, Mary; WF; b. 26 Mar 1887 in ___; father: John
MULHOLLAND; occ: farmer; res: Ffx; mother: Mary MULHOLLAND;
inf: J. MULHOLLAND, father; pg:ln: 168:79

MULLEN, Annie; WF; b. 13 Dec 1894 in Ffx; father: An'd. MULLEN; occ:
farmer; res: Ffx; mother: A. L. MULLEN; inf: A. MULLEN, father;
pg:ln: 219:81

MUNCH, Henry; WM; b. 8 May 1890 in Ffx; father: Wm. MUNCH; occ:
farmer; res: Ffx; mother: Alice MUNCH; inf: Wm. MUNCH, father;
pg:ln: 187:79

MUNDLE, Jno. W.; CM; b. 2 Sep 1881 in Ffx; father: W. MUNDLE; occ:
farmer; res: Ffx; mother: Milly MUNDLE; inf: W. MUNDLE, father;
pg:ln: 132:28

MURNANE, Jno. A.; WM; b. 16 Apr 1891 in Ffx; father: Jas.
MURNANE; occ: farmer; res: Ffx; mother: Elizabt. MURNANE; inf: J.
MURNANE, father; pg:ln: 199:63

MURNANE, Jno. H.; WM; b. 16 Apr 1892 in Ffx; father: Jno.
MURNANE; occ: farmer; res: Ffx; mother: Elizabt. MURNANE; inf:
Jno. MURNANE, father; pg:ln: 203:68

MURPHY, Alcinda; WF; b. 8 Aug 1891 nr Springfield; father: Thos. H.
MURPHY; occ: farmer; res: nr Springfield; mother: Francis
MURPHY; inf: parents; pg:ln: 195:32

MURRAY, Emma C.; CF; b. 20 May 1890 in Ffx; father: Joshua
MURRAY; occ: stone mason; res: Ffx; mother: Evaline MURRAY;
inf: Joshua MURRAY, father; pg:ln: 187:74

MURRAY, Kate; CF; b. 8 Jun 1893 in ___; father: A. G. MURRAY; occ:
___; res: ___; mother: Mary MURRAY; inf: A. G. MURRAY, father;
pg:ln: 214:69

MURREY, Laura; CF; b. 15 Jul 1896 in Fairfax C. H.; father: Joshua
MURRY; occ: plasterer; res: Fairfax C. H.; mother: Emaline MURRY;
inf: father; pg:ln: 231:91

MUTERSBAUGH, Roanna; WF; b. 6 Oct 1882 in Lewinsville; father:
David MUTERSBAUGH; occ: farmer; res: Lewinsville; mother: Ellen
MUTERSBAUGH; inf: father; pg:ln: 134:37

MYERS, Anna; WF; b. 7 Sep 1883 in Dranesville; father: Thos. J.
MYERS; occ: farmer; res: Dranesville; mother: Catharine MYERS;
inf: father; pg:ln: 140:71

MYERS, Bertha; WF; b. 1 Sep 1896 in Ffx; father: T. J. MYERS; occ:
farmer; res: Ffx; mother: Mary MYERS; inf: T. J. MYERS, father;
pg:ln: 227:90

MYERS, Pearle V.; WF; b. 17 Apr 1887 in Ffx; father: Thos. J. MYERS;
occ: farmer; res: Ffx; mother: Kate V. MYERS; inf: T. J. MYERS,
father; pg:ln: 162:96

NAILOR, Leany; CF; b. 28 Apr 1885 in Ffx; father: Benj. NAILOR; occ: farmer; res: Ffx; mother: Mary NAILOR; inf: Benj. NAILOR, father; pg:ln: 157:45

NALLS, Bernice; WF; b. 22 Mar 1880 in Ffx; father: Burr NALLS; occ: farmer; res: Ffx; mother: Permelia B.; inf: B. NALLS, father; pg:ln: 128:65

NASH, Edward; CM; b. 16 Dec 1891 nr Accotink; father: Wm. NASH; occ: stone mason; res: nr Accotink; mother: Sarah NASH; inf: parent; pg:ln: 196:15

NASH, Harvie; CM; b. 29 Nov 1896 nr Accotink; father: Wm. NASH; occ: brick layer; res: Accotink; mother: Sarah NASH; inf: mother; pg:ln: 231:95

NASH, Lucy; CF; b. 22 Aug 1895 nr Accotink; father: Wm. NASH; occ: plasterer; res: nr Accotink; mother: Susan NASH; inf: mother; pg:ln: 223:97

NAYLOR, Dennis; CM; b. 20 Dec 1892 in Bull Run; father: Elijah NAYLOR; occ: blacksmith; res: Bull Run; mother: Suzannah NAYLOR; inf: mother; pg:ln: 206:27

NEAL, Joseph; CM; b. 11 May 1889 in Ffx; father: Joseph NEAL; occ: farmer; res: Ffx; mother: Ellen NEAL; inf: J. NEAL, father; pg:ln: 179:87

NEALE, Emma; CF; b. 1 Jul 1887 in Ffx; father: Joseph NEALE; occ: laborer; res: Ffx; mother: Ella NEALE; inf: J. NEALE, father; pg:ln: 163:105

NEIL, Mary Ella; CF; b. 1 Jun 1881 in Vienna; father: Joseph NEIL; occ: laborer; res: Vienna; mother: Ella NEIL; inf: father; pg:ln: 131:48

NELSON, Julia M.; WF; b. 9 May 1889 in Ffx; father: W. NELSON; occ: farmer; res: Ffx; mother: Julia NELSON; inf: Wm. NELSON, father; pg:ln: 182:70

NELSON, Mary; CF; b. 19 Mar 1884 in Seminary; father: ___ NELSON; occ: laborer; res: Seminary; mother: Mary NELSON; inf: father; pg:ln: 150:68

NELSON, Wm. Everett; WM; b. 30 Jun 1887 in ___; father: Wm. NELSON; occ: farmer; res: Ffx; mother: Julia NELSON; inf: Wm. NELSON, father; pg:ln: 168:82

NEWLAND, Gertrude; WF; b. 19 Nov 1891 in Ffx; father: S. R. NEWLAND; occ: farmer; res: Ffx; mother: B. NEWLAND; inf: S. R. NEWLAND, father; pg:ln: 200:69

NEWLON, Elsie; WF; b. 19 Nov 1886 in Fairfax; father: Sam R. NEWLON; occ: farmer; res: Fairfax; mother: L. NEWLON; inf: father; pg:ln: 159:47

NEWMAN, Ada; CF; b. 1 Jan 1887 in Ffx; father: Chas. NEWMAN; occ: laborer; res: Ffx; mother: Julia NEWMAN; inf: C. NEWMAN, father; pg:ln: 163:106

NEWMAN, Armstead; CM; b. 2 Nov 1880 in Dranesville; father: Charles NEWMAN; occ: farmer; res: Dranesville; mother: Julia NEWMAN; inf: father; pg:ln: 125:49

NEWMAN, Baby; WF; b. 13 Sep 1887 in Ffx; father: C. F. NEWMAN; occ: painter; res: Ffx; mother: Emma NEWMAN; inf: C. F. NEWMAN, father; pg:ln: 163:110

NEWMAN, Chas.; CM; b. 15 Mar 1890 in Ffx; father: Chas. H. NEWMAN; occ: farmer; res: Ffx; mother: Julia NEWMAN; inf: C. H. NEWMAN, father; pg:ln: 191:76

NEWMAN, Cornelius; CM; b. 13 Sep 1892 in Ffx; father: Chas. NEWMAN; occ: farmer; res: Ffx; mother: Julia NEWMAN; inf: Chas. NEWMAN, father; pg:ln: 204:75

NEWMAN, Hesther; CF; b. 15 Nov 1883 in Ffx; father: John NEWMAN; occ: farmer; ꜜes: Ffx; mother: Lillie NEWMAN; inf: Jno. NEWMAN, father; pg:ln: 144:64

NEWMAN, Lucy; CF; b. 10 Mar 1881 in Ffx; father: Oscar NEWMAN; occ: farmer; res: Ffx; mother: Mary NEWMAN; inf: Oscar NEWMAN, father; pg:ln: 132:31

NEWMAN, Mabel E.; WF; b. 2 May 1883 in Falls Church; father: Chas. F. NEWMAN; occ: mechanic; res: Falls Church; mother: Emma NEWMAN; inf: father; pg:ln: 141:73

NEWMAN, Margt. J.; CF; b. 5 May 1885 in Falls Ch.; father: Chas. F. NEWMAN; occ: mechanic; res: Falls Ch.; mother: E. J. NEWMAN; inf: father; pg:ln: 153:59

NEWMAN, Mary; CF; b. 5 Apr 1883 in Ffx; father: Oscar NEWMAN; occ: farmer; res: Ffx; mother: Mary NEWMAN; inf: O. NEWMAN, father; pg:ln: 144:63

NEWMAN, Nellie; WF; b. 27 Jan 1886 in Dranes.; father: Jno. NEWMAN; occ: farmer; res: Dranes.; mother: Georgie NEWMAN; inf: father; pg:ln: 159:46

NEWMAN, Robert; CM; b. 22 Mar 1895 nr Accotink; father: Jacob NEWMAN; occ: laborer; res: nr Accotink; mother: Louisa NEWMAN; inf: mother; pg:ln: 223:96

NEWTON, ___; WF; b. 2 Aug 1888 in Ffx; father: C. M. NEWTON; occ: tinner; res: Ffx; mother: Willie E. NEWTON; inf: C. M. NEWTON, father; pg:ln: 171:47

NEWTON, Henry H.; WM; b. 31 Jul 1881 in Ffx; father: Chas. M. NEWTON; occ: tinner; res: Ffx; mother: W. E. NEWTON; inf: C. M. NEWTON, father; pg:ln: 132:32

NEWTON, Jas. [Jos. written above]; WM; b. 13 Aug 1889 in Ffx; father: Walter NEWTON; occ: farmer; res: Ffx; mother: Virginia NEWTON; inf: W. NEWTON, father; pg:ln: 179:86

NEWTON, Viola; WF; b. 30 Jun 1891 in Ffx; father: Walter NEWTON; occ: farmer; res: Ffx; mother: Nora NEWTON; inf: W. NEWTON, father; pg:ln: 200:70

NICHOLS, Mary Elizabeth; WF; b. 16 Sep 1892 in Loudon Co.; father: C. W. NIC[H]OLS; occ: carpenter; res: West End; mother: Bertha NICHOLS; inf: father; pg:ln: 209:37

NICKENS, Moses; CM; b. 12 Feb 1887 in Ffx; father: M. NICKENS; occ: laborer; res: Ffx; mother: Amanda NICKINS; inf: M. NICKENS, father; pg:ln: 163:107

NICKINS, Richard; CM; b. 30 Jan 1891 in Washington DC; father: ___;
occ: ___; res: ___; mother: Sarah Ann NICKENS; inf: Lucus?
BELLFIELD, neighbor; pg:ln: 196:14

NICOLS, Minnie; WF; b. 27 Jun 1896 in Ffx; father: J. F. NICOLS; occ:
farmer; res: Ffx; mother: Annie NICOLS; inf: J. F. NICOLS, father;
pg:ln: 227:92

NIETZEY, Benj.; WM; b. 3 Nov 1896 nr Woodlawn; father: Wm.
NIETZEY; occ: farmer; res: nr Woodlawn; mother: Emma NIETZEY;
inf: mother; pg:ln: 231:94

NIGHT, Christian; WM; b. 17 Apr 1892 nr Mt. Vernon; father: Joseph
NIGHT; occ: farmer; res: nr Mt. Vernon; mother: Kate NIGHT; inf:
mother; pg:ln: 207:79

[NIGHTINGILL], not named (dead); WF; b. 20 Nov 1891 nr Alexandria;
father: Joseph NIGHTINGILL; occ: mechanic; res: nr Alexandria;
mother: Emma NIGHTINGILL; inf: parents; pg:ln: 195:13

NORMAN, Gertrude; CF; b. 28 Dec 1887 in Ffx; father: Isaac P.
NORMAN; occ: laborer; res: Ffx; mother: Hattie NORMAN; inf: I. P.
NEWMAN, father; pg:ln: 163:109

NORRIS, Ambrose; CM; b. 20 Mar 1882 in Providence; father: Ambrose
NORRIS; occ: laborer; res: Prov.; mother: Emily NORRIS; inf: father;
pg:ln: 135:42

NORRIS, Annie; CF; b. 25 Feb 1885 in Prov.; father: Ambrose NORRIS;
occ: laborer; res: Prov.; mother: Emma NORRIS; inf: father; pg:ln:
153:61

NORRIS, Gladdis; CF; b. 27 Sep 1894 in Ffx; father: Sandy NORRIS;
occ: farmer; res: Ffx; mother: Leatha NORRIS; inf: S. NORRIS,
father; pg:ln: 219:93

NORRIS, Irving; CM; b. 6 Nov 1887 in Ffx; father: Ambrose NORRIS;
occ: laborer; res: Ffx; mother: Emiley NORRIS; inf: A. NORRIS,
father; pg:ln: 163:104

NORRIS, W.; CM; b. 19 Dec 1889 in Ffx; father: Sandy NORRIS; occ:
farmer; res: Ffx; mother: Lenora NORRIS; inf: S. NORRIS, father;
pg:ln: 179:88

NORTHROP, Annie [Anna Amelia written above]; WF; b. 29 May 1887
in Ffx; father: Lewis L. NORTHROP; occ: salesman; res: Ffx;
mother: Nettie W. NORTHROP; inf: L. NORTHROP, father. Note:
Anna Amelia Northrup was born May 29, 1887, Falls Church Va
daughter of Lewis L. and Nettie W. Northrop. Carl Fredrick was born
May 13, 1885 of the same parents, same place. The occupation of
our father was salesman. He was travelling for a firm in Vermont.
Signed C. F. Northrup, Scout Executive; pg:ln: 163:108

NORTHROP, Caarroll [Carl Frederick written above]; WM; b. 13 May
1885 in Falls Ch.; father: Lewis L. NORTHROP; occ: hotel & livery
[salesman written above]; res: Falls Ch.; mother: Nettie W.
NORTHROP; inf: father. Note attached: Anna Amelia Northrup was
born May 29, 1887, Falls Church Va daughter of Lewis L. and Nettie
W. Northrop. Carl Fredrick was born May 13, 1885 of the same
parents, same place. The occupation of our father was salesman.

He was travelling for a firm in Vermont. Signed C. F. Northrup, Scout Executive; pg:ln: 153:60

NUCOMB, Mary Gertrude; WF; b. 9 Oct 1893 nr Fairfax Sta.; father: Edward NUCOMB; occ: rail roading; res: nr Fairfax Sta.; mother: Mary NUCOMB; inf: parent; pg:ln: 212:75

OKEEN, Thomas; WM; b. 28 Feb 1892 nr Burke Sta.; father: James OKEEN; occ: farmer; res: nr Burke Sta.; mother: Elizabeth OKEEN; inf: father; pg:ln: 209:53

OLIVER, not named; WM; b. 18 Mar 1885 in Prov.; father: E. E. OLIVER; occ: farmer; res: Prov.; mother: Marietta OLIVER; inf: father; pg:ln: 153:62

OLIVER, Alice; WF; b. 16 Jun 1887 in Ffx; father: E. E. OLIVER; occ: farmer; res: Ffx; mother: Mary E. OLIVER; inf: E. E. OLIVER, father; pg:ln: 163:111

OLIVER, Alvin E.; WM; b. 20 Jun 1892 in Ffx; father: Alvin OLIVER; occ: farmer; res: Ffx; mother: Fannie OLIVER; inf: A. OLIVER, father; pg:ln: 204:76

OLIVER, Bryan; WM; b. 15 Oct 1896 in Ffx; father: Jesse OLIVER; occ: farmer; res: Ffx; mother: Cora OLIVER; inf: J. OLIVER, father; pg:ln: 227:93

OLIVER, Edwin E.; WM; b. 28 Feb 1891 in Ffx; father: E. E. OLIVER; occ: farmer; res: Ffx; mother: M. R. OLIVER; inf: E. E. OLIVER, father; pg:ln: 200:71

OLIVER, Elsie M.; WF; b. 15 Aug 1894 in Ffx; father: Cornelius OLIVER; occ: farmer; res: Ffx; mother: Mary OLIVER; inf: C. OLIVER, father; pg:ln: 219:94

OLIVER, Geo.; WM; b. 30 Dec 1888 in Ffx; father: Calvin OLIVER; occ: farmer; res: Ffx; mother: Catharine OLIVER; inf: C. OLIVER, father; pg:ln: 175:73

OLIVER, Harry L.; WM; b. 29 Jun 1890 in Ffx; father: Jesse OLIVER; occ: farmer; res: Ffx; mother: Cora OLIVER; inf: J. OLIVER, father; pg:ln: 191:78

OLIVER, Inez; WF; b. 15 May 1893 in ___; father: Theo. OLIVER; occ: ___; res: ___; mother: Mary OLIVER; inf: Theo. OLIVER, father; pg:ln: 214:72

OLIVER, Irene; WF; b. 28 Aug 1890 in Ffx; father: Theodore OLIVER; occ: farmer; res: Ffx; mother: Mary C. OLIVER; inf: Theo. OLIVER, father; pg:ln: 191:79

OLIVER, Lee; WM; b. 9 May 1889 in Ffx; father: E. E. OLIVER; occ: farmer; res: Ffx; mother: M. R. OLIVER; inf: E. E. OLIVER, father; pg:ln: 179:89

OLIVER, Lucy; WF; b. 5 Feb 1893 in ___; father: E. E. OLIVER; occ: ___; res: ___; mother: M. R. OLIVER; inf: E. E. OLIVER, father; pg:ln: 214:71

OLIVER, Lura; WF; b. 23 Aug 1896 in Ffx; father: Chas. J. OLIVER; occ: farmer; res: Ffx; mother: Arabella OLIVER; inf: C. J. OLIVER, father; pg:ln: 227:94

OLIVER, Mamie Y.; WF; b. 13 Oct 1881 in Old Union; father: William T. OLIVER; occ: farmer; res: Old Union; mother: Eunice OLIVER; inf: father; pg:ln: 131:50

OLIVER, Mary A.; WF; b. 23 Sep 1883 in Herndon; father: Theodore OLIVER; occ: mechanic; res: Herndon; mother: Mary C. OLIVER; inf: father; pg:ln: 141:74

OLIVER, Merton J.; WM; b. 18 Aug 1888 in Ffx; father: Theodore OLIVER; occ: farmer; res: Ffx; mother: Mary C. OLIVER; inf: Theo. OLIVER, father; pg:ln: 175:74

OLIVER, not named; WM; b. 10 Nov 1882 in Providence; father: Lewis E. OLIVER; occ: mcht.; res: Prov.; mother: Lucretia OLIVER; inf: father; pg:ln: 135:43

[OLIVER], not named; WM; b. 11 Dec 1881 in Herndon; father: Jno. F. OLIVER; occ: mechanic; res: Herndon; mother: Mary OLIVER; inf: father; pg:ln: 131:49

OLIVER, Olive L.; WF; b. 9 Mar 1888 in Ffx; father: E. E. OLIVER; occ: farmer; res: Ffx; mother: M. R. OLIVER; inf: C. [E.?] OLIVER, father; pg:ln: 174:72

OLIVER, Ruth; WF; b. 8 Aug 1890 in Ffx; father: Calvin OLIVER; occ: farmer; res: Ffx; mother: Cath'e. OLIVER; inf: C. OLIVER, father; pg:ln: 191:77

OMEARER, Bessie A.; WF; b. 4 May 1880 in Falls Church; father: Albert B. OMEARER; occ: farmer; res: Falls Church; mother: Cath. A. OMEARER; inf: father; pg:ln: 125:50

OMEARER, Mildred V.; WF; b. 16 Feb 1884 in Providence; father: Albert OMEARER; occ: farmer; res: Providence; mother: Catharine OMEARER; inf: father; pg:ln: 150:69

OMEARER, Sinah; WF; b. 14 Dec 1880 in Falls Church; father: Valencia C. OMEARER; occ: mechanic; res: Falls Church; mother: Ida OMEARER; inf: father; pg:ln: 125:51

OMERA, Katie E.; WF; b. 5 Apr 1887 in Ffx; father: A. B. OMERA; occ: farmer; res: Ffx; mother: Catharine OMERA; inf: A. B. OMERA, father; pg:ln: 163:112

ORR, not named; WM; b. 12 Jul 1895 nr Alexandria; father: James ORR; occ: carpenter; res: nr Alexandria; mother: Esther ORR; inf: mother; pg:ln: 223:98

OTIS, Annie; WF; b. 14 Aug 1880 in Ffx; father: Jno. OTIS; occ: farmer; res: Ffx; mother: Iva; inf: Jno. OTIS, father; pg:ln: 128:66

OTIS, Fannie; WF; b. 29 Aug 1895 nr Clifton Sta; father: Harry OTIS; occ: farmer; res: nr Clifton Sta; mother: Adele OTIS; inf: mother; pg:ln: 224:138

OTTERBACK, ___; WF; b. 13 Aug 1881 in Ffx; father: B. L. OTTERBACK; occ: farmer; res: Ffx; mother: Sarah OTTERBACK; inf: B. L. OTTERBACK, father; pg:ln: 132:33

PADGETT, Wm. Mercer; WM; b. 4 Sep 1892 in Village adj Alex.; father: Wm. R. PADGETT; occ: farmer; res: nr Alex.; mother: Etta PADGETT; inf: mother; pg:ln: 207:82

PAGE, Jno. Richd.; WM; b. 29 Jun 1887 in Ffx; father: Henry PAGE; occ: farmer; res: Ffx; mother: M. C. PAGE; inf: H. PAGE, father; pg:ln: 163:117

PAGE, John; CM; b. 1 Dec 1881 in Falls Church; father: James PAGE; occ: laborer; res: Falls Church; mother: Chloe PAGE; inf: father; pg:ln: 131:54

PALLANT, Laura; WF; b. 12 Nov 1894 in Ffx; father: Geo. W. PALLANT; occ: farmer; res: Ffx; mother: Minnie PALLANT; inf: G. W. PALLANT, father; pg:ln: 219:97

PALLANT, Saul; WM; b. 17 Dec 1889 in Ffx; father: Geo. PALLANT; occ: farmer; res: Ffx; mother: Minnie PALLANT; inf: G. PALLANT, father; pg:ln: 179:90

PALLANT, Stephen T.; WM; b. 29 Apr 1892 in Ffx; father: Geo. PALLANT; occ: farmer; res: Ffx; mother: Minnie PALLANT; inf: Geo. PALLANT, father; pg:ln: 204:78

PALMER, ___; CM; b. 6 Nov 1890 in Ffx; father: Wm. PALMER; occ: farmer; res: Ffx; mother: Emma PALMER; inf: Wm. PALMER, father; pg:ln: 187:91

PALMER, Bell; WF; b. 7 Jul 1882 in Dranesville; father: Rich'd. H. PALMER; occ: farmer; res: Dranes.; mother: Susan D. PALMER; inf: father; pg:ln: 135:48

PALMER, Lettece McKinley; CF; b. 3 Nov 1896 nr Gunston; father: Wm. PALMER; occ: laborer; res: nr Gunston; mother: Emma N. PALMER; inf: mother; pg:ln: 231:104

PALMER, Mary Jane; CF; b. 20 Sep 1895 nr Gunston; father: Wm. PALMER; occ: laborer; res: nr Gunston; mother: Emma PALMER; inf: mother; pg:ln: 223:103

PALMER, W.; CM; b. 1 Nov 1889 in Ffx; father: W. PALMER; occ: farmer; res: Ffx; mother: Emma PALMER; inf: W. PALMER, father; pg:ln: 183:75

PANGLE, Fred. N.; WM; b. 18 Oct 1888 in Ffx; father: R. N. PANGLE; occ: farmer; res: Ffx; mother: Rebecca PANGLE; inf: R. N. PANGLE, father; pg:ln: 175:78

PARKER, Alice; CF; b. 15 Mar 1889 in Ffx; father: C. B. PARKER; occ: farmer; res: Ffx; mother: Silva PARKER; inf: C. B. PARKER, father; pg:ln: 183:72

PARKER, Annie B.; CF; b. 22 Apr 1896 in Ffx; father: Wesley PARKER; occ: farmer; res: Ffx; mother: Mary PARKER; inf: W. PARKER, father; pg:ln: 227:97

PARKER, Annie; CF; b. 26 Aug 1882 in Ffx; father: Cassius PARKER; occ: ___; res: ___; mother: Sylvia PARKER; inf: C. PARKER, father; pg:ln: 137:63

PARKER, Boby; CM; b. 11 Dec 1887 in Ffx; father: Jno. PARKER; occ: farmer; res: Ffx; mother: Sarah PARKER; inf: J. PARKER, father; pg:ln: 163:122

PARKER, Emma; CF; b. 19 Oct 1887 in Ffx; father: Page PARKER; occ: farmer; res: Ffx; mother: Matilda PARKER; inf: P. PARKER, father; pg:ln: 163:114

PARKER, Isaac; CM; b. 6 May 1880 in Providence; father: Henry PARKER; occ: laborer; res: Providence; mother: Harriet PARKER; inf: father; pg:ln: 125:60

PARKER, Jacob; CM; b. 6 May 1880 in Providence; father: Henry PARKER; occ: laborer; res: Providence; mother: Harriet PARKER; inf: father; pg:ln: 125:61

PARKER, Jessie; WF; b. 2 Oct 1891 nr Mt. Vernon; father: Lafayette PARKER; occ: farmer; res: nr Mt. Vernon; mother: Mary E. PARKER; inf: parents; pg:ln: 195:16

PARKER, Mamie; CF; b. 15 Oct 1886 in Ffx; father: Chas. PARKER; occ: farmer; res: Ffx; mother: Ann M. PARKER; inf: C. PARKER, father; pg:ln: 155:15

PARKER, Margaret; CF; b. 14 Jun 1882 in Falls Church; father: Henry PARKER; occ: laborer; res: Falls Church; mother: Harriet PARKER; inf: father; pg:ln: 135:45

PARKER, Maria; CF; b. 2 Oct 1884 in Falls Ch.; father: Henry PARKER; occ: laborer; res: Falls Ch.; mother: Harriet PARKER; inf: father; pg:ln: 150:72

PARKER, Martha; CF; b. 14 Apr 1885 in Ffx; father: Cash PARKER; occ: farmer; res: Ffx; mother: Sylva PARKER; inf: C. PARKER, father; pg:ln: 157:46

PARKER, Rose; CF; b. 10 Jul 1884 in Ffx; father: Chas. PARKER; occ: ___; res: ___; mother: Ann PARKER; inf: Chas. PARKER, father; pg:ln: 147:57

PARKER, Sallie; CF; b. 7 May 1880 in Ffx; father: Jno. PARKER; occ: farmer; res: Ffx; mother: Sarah; inf: Jno. PARKER, father; pg:ln: 128:68

PARKS, Jno. C.; CM; b. 1 Jun 1888 in Ffx; father: W. PARKS; occ: farmer; res: Ffx; mother: Maggie PARKE; inf: W. PARKS, father; pg:ln: 175:77

PARMER, Elizabeth; CF; b. 8 Jan 1891 nr Gunston; father: Wm. PARMER; occ: laborer; res: nr Gunston; mother: Emma PARMER; inf: parent; pg:ln: 196:17

PATTERSON, Fanny; WF; b. 29 Jan 1885 in Falls Church; father: J. B. PATTERSON; occ: clerk; res: Falls Church; mother: A. E. PATTERSON; inf: father; pg:ln: 153:63

PATTON, Charles; WM; b. 22 Dec 1880 in Chantilly; father: Joseph N. PATTON; occ: huckster; res: Chantilly; mother: Mary V. PATTON; inf: father; pg:ln: 125:56

PATTON, George; WM; b. 23 Jan 1887 in ___; father: J. N. PATTON; occ: farmer; res: Ffx; mother: Mollie PATTON; inf: J. N. PATTON, father; pg:ln: 168:88

PATTON, Jas. H.; WM; b. 6 Jul 1890 in Ffx; father: Jos. N. PATTON; occ: farmer; res: Ffx; mother: M. V. PATTON; inf: J. N. PATTON, father; pg:ln: 187:84

PATTON, Joseph; WM; b. 1 Dec 1892 nr Chantilly; father: Joseph PATTON [written as Josepph]; occ: farmer; res: nr Chantilly; mother: Mollie PATTON; inf: mother; pg:ln: 208:21

PATTON, William S.; WM; b. 27 Nov 1880 in Chantilly; father: John S. PATTON; occ: huckster; res: Chantilly; mother: Tacy A. PATTON; inf: father; pg:ln: 125:57

PAYNE, ___; WF; b. 12 Jun 1890 in Ffx; father: R. T. PAYNE; occ: mechanic; res: Ffx; mother: Lucretia PAYNE; inf: R. T. PAYNE, father; pg:ln: 187:85

PAYNE, Belle; WF; b. 3 Feb 1886 in Bailey's X Rds; father: M. P. PAYNE; occ: farmer; res: Bailey's X Rds; mother: Belle PAYNE; inf: father; pg:ln: 159:48

PAYNE, Benj.; CM; b. 18 Dec 1893 in Ffx; father: Benj. PAYNE; occ: farmer; res: ___; mother: Martha PAYNE; inf: B. PAYNE, father; pg:ln: 215:74

PAYNE, Betsey; CF; b. 15 Aug 1884 in Ffx; father: Albert PAYNE; occ: ___; res: ___; mother: Lucy PAYNE; inf: Albert PAYNE, father; pg:ln: 147:52

PAYNE, Clarence; WM; b. 7 Jul 1888 in Ffx; father: S. A. PAYNE; occ: farmer; res: Ffx; mother: A. S. PAYNE; inf: S. A. PAYNE, father; pg:ln: 171:51

PAYNE, E. L.; WF; b. 28 Oct 1880 in Ffx; father: R. T. PAYNE; occ: farmer; res: Ffx; mother: Lucretia; inf: R. T. PAYNE, father; pg:ln: 128:67

PAYNE, Edner H.; CF; b. 10 Jul 1896 in Ffx; father: W. PAYNE; occ: farmer; res: Ffx; mother: Lorinda PAYNE; inf: W. PAYNE, father; pg:ln: 227:98

PAYNE, F. L. Jr.; WM; b. 5 May 1881 in Bailey's X Roads; father: F. L. PAYNE Sr.; occ: farmer; res: Bailey's X Roads; mother: Mary E. PAYNE; inf: father; pg:ln: 131:57

PAYNE, Fre'd.; CM; b. 18 Jul 1893 in ___; father: W. PAYNE; occ: farmer; res: ___; mother: Laurinda PAYNE; inf: W. PAYNE, father; pg:ln: 215:79

PAYNE, Geo. E.; CM; b. 18 Dec 1882 in Falls Church; father: William PAYNE; occ: laborer; res: Falls Church; mother: Lorinda PAYNE; inf: father; pg:ln: 135:44

PAYNE, Henry; CM; b. 5 May 1889 in Ffx; father: Robt. PAYNE; occ: farmer; res: Ffx; mother: Georgiana PAYNE; inf: Robt. PAYNE, father; pg:ln: 183:71

PAYNE, Leannah Lewis; CF; b. 27 Aug 1892 nr Centreville; father: Albert PAYNE; occ: laborer; res: nr Centreville; mother: Louisa PAYNE; inf: mother; pg:ln: 206:28

PAYNE, Maggie J.; CF; b. 15 Jun 1887 in ___; father: Washington PAYNE; occ: laborer; res: Ffx; mother: Charity PAYNE; inf: Washington PAYNE, father; pg:ln: 168:86

PAYNE, Milton B.; WM; b. 11 Dec 1891 in Ffx; father: Milton PAYNE; occ: farmer; res: Ffx; mother: M. A. PAYNE; inf: M. PAYNE, father; pg:ln: 200:74

PAYNE, Nancy; WF; b. 3 May 1896 in Ffx; father: L. E. PAYNE; occ: mcht.; res: Ffx; mother: Violet V. PAYNE; inf: L. E. PAYNE, father; pg:ln: 227:100

PAYNE, not named; CM; b. 10 Mar 1880 in Falls Church; father: William PAYNE; occ: laborer; res: Falls Church; mother: Laura PAYNE; inf: father; pg:ln: 125:55

PAYNE, Ollie; WF; b. 20 Apr 1883 in Ffx; father: R. T. PAYNE; occ: farmer; res: Ffx; mother: Lucretia PETTIT [PAYNE]; inf: R. T. PAYNE, father; pg:ln: 144:66

PAYNE, Oscar L.; WM; b. 8 Apr 1890 in Ffx; father: S. A. PAYNE; occ: farmer; res: Ffx; mother: Augusta S. PAYNE; inf: S. A. PAYNE, father; pg:ln: 187:86

PAYNE, R. F.; WM; b. 10 Feb 1887 in ___; father: Robt. T. PAYNE; occ: carpenter; res: Ffx; mother: Lucretia PAYNE; inf: Robt. T. PAYNE, father; pg:ln: 168:85

PAYNE, Rachael; WF; b. 15 Apr 1895 nr Farr P.O.; father: Wm PAYNE; occ: farmer; res: nr Farr P.O.; mother: Cora PAYNE; inf: mother; pg:ln: 223:99

PAYNE, Ruth Ray; WF; b. 2 Dec 1883 in Falls Church; father: Saml. W. PAYNE; occ: farmer; res: Falls Church; mother: Mary P. PAYNE; inf: father; pg:ln: 141:75

PAYNE, Ruth; WF; b. 12 Jan 1896 in Ffx; father: Jno. D. PAYNE; occ: mcht.; res: Ffx; mother: Louisa PAYNE; inf: J. D. PAYNE, father; pg:ln: 227:99

PAYNE, Samuel; CM; b. 13 Dec 1884 in Falls Ch.; father: William PAYNE; occ: laborer; res: Falls Ch.; mother: L. PAYNE; inf: father; pg:ln: 150:70

PAYNE, Thornton; CM; b. 6 Jun 1888 in Ffx; father: Albert PAYNE; occ: laborer; res: Ffx; mother: Louisa PAYNE; inf: Albt. PAYNE, father; pg:ln: 171:50

PAYNE, Walter Benton; WM; b. 28 Sep 1881 in Munson's Hill; father: Samuel PAYNE; occ: farmer; res: Munson's Hill; mother: Mary PAYNE; inf: mother; pg:ln: 131:55

PAYNE, William; CM; b. 9 Jan 1887 in ___; father: Robt. PAYNE; occ: laborer; res: Ffx; mother: Georgianna PAYNE; inf: Robert PAYNE, father; pg:ln: 168:87

PAYNE, Wm. Jackson; WM; b. 21 Dec 1891 nr Clifton; father: R. F. PAYNE; occ: farmer; res: nr Clifton; mother: Lucretia PAYNE; inf: parents; pg:ln: 194:17

PAYTON, Geo. E. (twin); WM; b. 17 Jul 1885 in Ffx; father: G. D. PAYTON; occ: farmer; res: Ffx; mother: Zora PAYTON; inf: G. D. PAYTON, father; pg:ln: 157:47

PEACOCK, Annie E.; WF; b. 10 May 1880 in Dranesville; father: Naaman PEACOCK; occ: farmer; res: Dranesville; mother: Roberta PEACOCK; inf: father; pg:ln: 125:54

PEACOCK, Ever M.; WF; b. 12 Feb 1883 in Dranesville; father: Newman PEACOCK; occ: farmer; res: Dranesville; mother: Roberta PEACOCK; inf: father; pg:ln: 141:80

PEARSON, Clarence; WM; b. 22 Sep 1889 in Ffx; father: Robt. PEARSON; occ: farmer; res: Ffx; mother: Martha PEARSON; inf: Robt. PEARSON, father; pg:ln: 179:94

PEARSON, Hellen; WF; b. 25 Oct 1891 in Ffx; father: S. A. PEARSON; occ: farmer; res: Ffx; mother: Annie PEARSON; inf: S. A. PEARSON, father; pg:ln: 200:72

PEARSON, Jno. H.; WM; b. 11 Feb 1893 in Ffx; father: Robt. PEARSON; occ: farmer; res: ___; mother: Mattie PEARSON; inf: R. PEARSON, father; pg:ln: 215:76

PEARSON, Jno. W.; WM; b. 28 Aug 1893 in Ffx; father: S. A. PEARSON; occ: farmer; res: ___; mother: Annie PEARSON; inf: S. A. PEARSON, father; pg:ln: 215:75

PEARSON, Joshua; CM; b. 4 Nov 1892 in Ffx; father: Joshua PEARSON; occ: farmer; res: Ffx; mother: Carrie PEARSON; inf: J. PEARSON, father; pg:ln: 204:79

PEARSON, Josie; CF; b. 18 May 1880 in Providence; father: Richard PEARSON; occ: farmer; res: Providence; mother: Susan PEARSON; inf: father; pg:ln: 125:59

PEARSON, L. V.; WF; b. 16 May 1887 in Ffx; father: Jno. S. PEARSON; occ: farmer; res: Ffx; mother: Nancy PEARSON; inf: J. S. PEARSON, father; pg:ln: 163:115

PEARSON, Melvin; CM; b. 25 Jun 1889 in Ffx; father: Joshua PEARSON; occ: farmer; res: Ffx; mother: Carrie PEARSON; inf: J. PEARSON, father; pg:ln: 179:92

PEARSON, Morris; WM; b. 5 Jul 1887 in Ffx; father: Robt. PEARSON; occ: farmer; res: Ffx; mother: Matilda PEARSON; inf: Robt. PEARSON, father; pg:ln: 163:113

PEARSON, Oneatie; WF; b. 4 May 1892 in Ffx; father: Robt. PEARSON; occ: farmer; res: Ffx; mother: Mattie PEARSON; inf: R. PEARSON, father; pg:ln: 204:77

PEARSON, Sidney; WM; b. 25 Oct 1892 nr Accotink; father: H. A. PEARSON; occ: rail roading; res: nr Accotink; mother: Pollie PEARSON; inf: mother; pg:ln: 207:84

PECK, Jas. H.; WM; b. 6 Jul 1881 in Ffx; father: Harvie J. PECK; occ: farmer; res: Ffx; mother: Fannie PECK; inf: A. J. PECK, father; pg:ln: 132:36

PECK, Robert; WM; b. 13 Dec 1891 nr Alexandria; father: Harvie J. PECK; occ: farmer; res: nr Alexandria; mother: Elizabeth PECK; inf: parents; pg:ln: 195:14

PERRIGO, Annetta; WF; b. 2 May 1894 in Ffx; father: E. W. PERRIGO; occ: farmer; res: Ffx; mother: Rosa PERRIGO; inf: E. W. PERRIGO, father; pg:ln: 219:100

PERRIGO, Paul; WM; b. 30 Oct 1884 in Falls Ch.; father: Charles PERRIGO; occ: farmer; res: Falls Ch.; mother: J. A. PERRIGO; inf: father; pg:ln: 150:71

PERRIWIN, Emiley; CF; b. 1 Dec 1889 in Ffx; father: Moses PER[RI]WIN; occ: farmer; res: Ffx; mother: Martha PERRIWIN; inf: M. PER[RI]WIN, father; pg:ln: 183:74

PERRY, Eva M.; CF; b. 15 Feb 1893 in ___; father: Jno. H. PERRY; occ: farmer; res: ___; mother: Pink PERRY; inf: J. H. PERRY, father; pg:ln: 215:78

PETERSON, Jno. F.; CM; b. 20 Nov 1896 in Ffx; father: Rich'd.
PETERSON; occ: farmer; res: Ffx; mother: Millie PETERSON; inf: R.
PETERSON, father; pg:ln: 227:96

PETTETT, Archie; WM; b. 7 Oct 1891 nr Accotink; father: Silas D.
PETTETT; occ: farmer; res: nr Accotink; mother: Carrie PETTETT;
inf: parents; pg:ln: 195:17

PETTETT, Clara Bell; WF; b. 18 Jun 1896 nr Accotink; father: Silas
PETTETT; occ: farmer; res: Accotink; mother: Carrie Va PETTETT;
inf: father; pg:ln: 231:101

PETTETT, Mary Jane; WF; b. 16 Mar 1896 in Accotink; father: Edward
PETTETT; occ: farmer; res: Accotink; mother: Amelia PETTETT; inf:
father; pg:ln: 231:99

PETTETT, Nellie Remo; WF; b. 14 Sep 1896 nr Accotink; father:
Mortimer PETTETT; occ: farmer; res: Accotink; mother: Mamie
PETTETT; inf: father; pg:ln: 231:100

PETTIT, ___ (dead); WM; b. 5 May 1889 in Ffx; father: Thos. J.
PETTIT; occ: farmer; res: Ffx; mother: M. L. PETTIT; inf: T. J.
PETTIT, father; pg:ln: 179:93

PETTIT, Christopher; WM; b. 8 Jan 1880 in Ffx; father: Chas. PETTIT;
occ: farmer; res: Ffx; mother: Ella; inf: Chas. PETTIT, father; pg:ln:
128:73

PETTIT, Eddie; WM; b. 19 May 1883 in Ffx; father: Geo. W. PETTIT;
occ: farmer; res: Ffx; mother: Mary A. PETTIT; inf: G. W. PETTIT,
father; pg:ln: 144:65

PETTIT, Edna; WF; b. 18 Apr 1883 in Ffx; father: Joseph PETTIT; occ:
farmer; res: Ffx; mother: Lucy PETTIT; inf: Jos. PETTIT, father;
pg:ln: 144:67

PETTIT, Estella; WF; b. 18 Sep 1888 in Ffx; father: Thos. J. PETTIT;
occ: farmer; res: Ffx; mother: Mary E. PETTIT; inf: T. J. PETTIT,
father; pg:ln: 175:79

PETTIT, Goldie; WF; b. 13 Nov 1886 in Ffx; father: Norman PETTIT;
occ: farmer; res: Ffx; mother: Eva G. PETTIT; inf: N. PETTIT, father;
pg:ln: 155:14

PETTIT, Lottie; WF; b. 12 Feb 1880 in Ffx; father: Jas. PETTIT; occ:
farmer; res: Ffx; mother: Annie E.; inf: J. PETTIT, father; pg:ln:
128:72

PETTITT, Ada E.; WF; b. 15 May 1881 in Dranesville; father: David
PETTITT; occ: laborer; res: Dranesville; mother: Ada PETTIT; inf:
father; pg:ln: 131:51

PETTITT, Albert F.; WM; b. 28 Mar 1890 in Ffx; father: Chas. PETTITT;
occ: laborer; res: Ffx; mother: Mary PETTITT; inf: Chas. PETTITT,
father; pg:ln: 187:88

PETTITT, Arthur M.; WM; b. 18 Sep 1891 in Ffx; father: Henry E.
PETTITT; occ: farmer; res: Ffx; mother: Cora PETTITT; inf: H. E.
PETTITT, father; pg:ln: 200:78

PETTITT, Emma; WF; b. 15 Apr 1888 in Ffx; father: Jas. PETTITT; occ:
mechanic; res: Ffx; mother: Emma PETTITT; inf: Jas. PETTITT,
father; pg:ln: 171:49

PETTITT, Florence; WF; b. 7 Oct 1892 nr Woodlawn; father: Silos
    PETTITT; occ: farmer; res: nr Woodlawn; mother: Carrie PETTITT;
    inf: mother; pg:ln: 207:80
PETTITT, Frederick; WM; b. 24 Sep 1892 in C. H.; father: A. J.
    PETTITT; occ: blacksmith; res: C. H.; mother: Matilda PETTITT; inf:
    father; pg:ln: 208:31
PETTITT, Lewis; WM; b. 23 Oct 1893 nr Occoquan; father: Lorenzo
    PETTITT; occ: farmer; res: nr Occoquan; mother: Emma J.
    PETTITT; inf: parent; pg:ln: 212:76
PETTITT, Mary E.; WF; b. 12 Sep 1887 in ___; father: Charles
    PETTITT; occ: laborer; res: Ffx; mother: Mary Ellen PETTITT; inf:
    Charles PETTITT, father; pg:ln: 168:84
PETTITT, not named (dead); WM; b. 20 Feb 1892 nr Stoneleigh; father:
    James PETTITT; occ: farmer; res: nr Stoneleigh; mother: Elizabeth
    PETTITT; inf: mother; pg:ln: 209:54
PETTITT, not named; WF; b. 1 Dec 1892 nr Woodlawn; father: Lorenzo
    PETTITT; occ: farmer; res: nr Woodlawn; mother: Emma PETTITT;
    inf: mother; pg:ln: 207:81
PETTITT, Peyton M.; WM; b. 14 Apr 1887 in ___; father: A. J. PETTITT;
    occ: blacksmith; res: Ffx; mother: Matilda PETTITT; inf: Jackson
    PETTITT, father; pg:ln: 168:83
PETTITT, Wm. Isaac; WM; b. 10 Apr 1890 in Ffx; father: A. J. PETTITT;
    occ: blacksmith; res: Ffx; mother: Matilda PETTITT; inf: A. J.
    PETTITT, father; pg:ln: 187:87
PETTY, Edna V., WF; b. 26 May 1896 in West End; father: Willis F.
    PETTY; occ: glass blower; res: West End; mother: Anna Rebecca
    PETTY; inf: mother; pg:ln: 231:96
PEVERELL, Fannie L.; WF; b. 5 Nov 1887 in ___; father: George
    PEVERELL; occ: farmer; res: Ffx; mother: Fannie PEVERELL; inf:
    Geo. PEVERELL, father; pg:ln: 168:89
PEVERELL, Nellie; WF; b. 18 Dec 1883 in Ffx; father: L. PEVERELL;
    occ: farmer; res: Ffx; mother: Prudence PEVERELL; inf: L.
    PEVERELL, father; pg:ln: 144:68
PEYTON, Golden (twin); WM; b. 17 Jul 1885 in Ffx; father: G. D.
    PAYTON; occ: farmer; res: Ffx; mother: Zora PAYTON; inf: G. D.
    PAYTON, father; pg:ln: 157:48
PEYTON, Wm.; CM; b. 15 Sep 1889 in Ffx; father: Barney PEYTON;
    occ: farmer; res: Ffx; mother: Caroline PEYTON; inf: B. PEYTON,
    father; pg:ln: 183:73
PHENY, Thomas; CM; b. 24 Feb 1887 in Ffx; father: Thomas PHENY;
    occ: laborer; res: Ffx; mother: Amelia PHENY; inf: Thos. PHENY,
    father; pg:ln: 163:118
PHILIPS, Shuman; CM; b. 29 May 1893 in Ffx; father: Jno. PHILIPS;
    occ: farmer; res: ___; mother: Georgie PHILIPS; inf: Jno. PHILIPS,
    father; pg:ln: 215:77
PHILLIPS, not named; WF; b. 15 Apr 1883 in Providence Dist.; father:
    Chas. W. PHILLIPS; occ: farmer; res: Providence Dist.; mother: R.
    P. PHILLIPS; inf: father; pg:ln: 141:76

PHILLIPS, Rose; WF; b. 1 Apr 1881 in Providence; father: Chas. W. PHILLIPS; occ: farmer; res: Providence; mother: Roanna PHILLIPS; inf: father; pg:ln: 131:52

PIDGEON, Luther; WM; b. 1 Nov 1895 nr Woodlawn; father: Chas. M. PIDGEON; occ: farmer; res: nr Woodlawn; mother: Katie D. PIDGEON; inf: father; pg:ln: 223:100

PIERSON, A. G.; WM; b. 24 May 1881 in Ffx; father: A. J. PIERSON; occ: farmer; res: Ffx; mother: Bertie PIERSON; inf: A. J. PIERSON, father; pg:ln: 132:35

PIERSON, A.; WF; b. 28 Oct 1886 in Vienna; father: F. W. PIERSON; occ: farmer; res: Vienna; mother: A. PIERSON; inf: father; pg:ln: 159:49

PIERSON, Alice; CF; b. 29 Aug 1892 nr Burke Sta; father: Frank C. PEARSON; occ: farmer; res: nr Burke; mother: Annie M. PIERSON; inf: mother; pg:ln: 206:32

PIERSON, Annie; CF; b. 30 Jan 1896 nr Burke Sta.; father: Frank PIERSON; occ: laborer; res: nr Burke; mother: Annie PIERSON; inf: mother; pg:ln: 231:103

PIERSON, Charles Wm.; WM; b. 30 Jun 1891 in Wolf Run; father: David PIERSON; occ: farmer; res: Wolf Run; mother: Jane C. PIERSON; inf: parents; pg:ln: 194:16

PIERSON, Douglass; CM; b. 1 Jun 1895 nr Burke Sta; father: Douglas PIERSON; occ: laborer; res: nr Burke Sta; mother: Ada PIERSON; inf: father; pg:ln: 223:101

PIERSON, Florence; WF; b. 12 Sep 1887 in ___; father: Henry A. PIERSON; occ: farmer; res: Ffx; mother: Mary PIERSON; inf: H. A. PIERSON, father; pg:ln: 168:92

PIERSON, Henry N.,; WM; b. 5 Sep 1888 in Ffx; father: A. J. PIERSON; occ: farmer; res: Ffx; mother: Birtie PIERSON; inf: A. J. PIERSON, father; pg:ln: 171:48

PIERSON, John; CM; b. 15 Dec 1895 nr Burke Sta; father: ___; occ: ___; res: nr Burke Sta; mother: Mary Annie; inf: mother; pg:ln: 223:102

PIERSON, not named; WM; b. 26 Jul 1883 in Dranesville; father: Jno. S. PIERSON; occ: farmer; res: Dranesville; mother: Cath. V. PIERSON; inf: father; pg:ln: 141:78

PIERSON, Robert; CM; b. 15 May 1884 in Ffx; father: Joshua PIERSON; occ: ___; res: ___; mother: Martha PIERSON; inf: J. PIERSON, father; pg:ln: 147:53

PIERSON, Wm. E.; WM; b. 15 Oct 1884 in Ffx; father: Henry PIERSON; occ: ___; res: ___; mother: Mary V. PIERSON; inf: Henry PIERSON, father; pg:ln: 147:55

PINGREE?, Burton; WM; b. 7 Apr 1896 in Riverside Park; father: Frank PINGREE?; occ: merchant; res: Riverside Park; mother: Maggie E. PINGEE?; inf: father This was requested as 1896; pg:ln: 231:98

PINKETT, Gertrude; CF; b. 9 May 1887 in Ffx; father: Wesley PINKETT; occ: farmer; res: Ffx; mother: Eliza PINKETT; inf: W. PINKETT, father; pg:ln: 163:121

PINKETT, Roscoe D.; CM; b. 19 Dec 1891 in Ffx; father: Jno. P.
PINKETT; occ: farmer; res: Ffx; mother: C. B. PINKETT; inf: Jno. P.
PINKETT, father; pg:ln: 200:81

PINN, Hattie; CF; b. 24 Jan 1881 in Ffx; father: David PINN; occ:
farmer; res: Ffx; mother: Sallie PINN; inf: D. PINN, father; pg:ln:
132:34

PINN, Nellie E.; CF; b. 15 Oct 1884 in Ffx; father: David PINN; occ: ___;
res: ___; mother: Sallie F. PINN; inf: D. PINN, father; pg:ln: 147:54

PINN, Robert Davis; CM; b. 13 Mar 1892 nr Burnside Sta.; father: David
PINN; occ: laborer; res: nr Burnside Sta; mother: Sallie PINN; inf:
mother; pg:ln: 206:31

PIPER, not named; CM; b. 14 May 1883 in Dranesville; father: Harrison
PIPER; occ: laborer; res: Dranesville; mother: Elizabeth PIPER; inf:
father; pg:ln: 141:79

PITCHER, David L.; WM; b. 1 Sep 1880 in Dranesville; father: David L.
PITCHER; occ: farmer; res: Dranesville; mother: Susan PITCHER;
inf: father; pg:ln: 125:53

PITT, Susan Jane; WF; b. 7 Dec 1896 in Clifton Sta.; father: James H.
PITT; occ: huckster; res: Clifton Sta.; mother: Susan Jane PITT; inf:
father; pg:ln: 231:97

PLASKET, Annie; WF; b. 15 May 1880 in Ffx; father: Jno. PLASKET;
occ: farmer; res: Ffx; mother: Mary; inf: Jno. PLASKET, father; pg:ln:
128:69

PLASKET, Olive Pearl; WF; b. 12 Aug 1881 in Lebanon; father: C. W.
PLASKET; occ: mechanic; res: Lebanon; mother: Emma J.
PLASKET; inf: father; pg:ln: 131:53

PLITT, Kernelia; WF; b. 1 Dec 1894 in Ffx; father: Fre'd. PLITT; occ:
farmer; res: Ffx; mother: M. E. PLITT; inf: Fre'd. PLITT, father; pg:ln:
219:99

PLITT, Sabina; WF; b. 20 Feb 1889 in Ffx; father: Fred PLITT; occ:
farmer; res: Ffx; mother: Mary PLITT; inf: F. PLITT, father; pg:ln:
179:91

POLAND, Jas. W.; WM; b. 3 Apr 1894 in Ffx; father: Noble POLAND;
occ: farmer; res: Ffx; mother: Mary POLAND; inf: N. POLAND,
father; pg:ln: 219:96

POLEN, Rich'd. E.; WM; b. 2 Aug 1890 in Ffx; father: Noble POLEN;
occ: farmer; res: Ffx; mother: Mary C. POLEN; inf: N. POLEN,
father; pg:ln: 191:82

POLLARD, Malinda (twin); CF; b. 1 Jul 1889 in Ffx; father: Robt.
POLLARD; occ: farmer; res: Ffx; mother: Roberta POLLARD; inf: R.
POLLARD, father; pg:ln: 183:76

POLLARD, Rebecca (twin); CF; b. 1 Jul 1889 in Ffx; father: Robt.
POLLARD; occ: farmer; res: Ffx; mother: Roberta POLLARD; inf: R.
POLLARD, father; pg:ln: 183:77

POOL, Elizabeth; WF; b. 12 Dec 1882 in Dranesville; father: Joseph H.
POOL; occ: farmer; res: Dranes.; mother: Elizabeth POOL; inf:
father; pg:ln: 135:46

POOL, Mary; WF; b. 20 Jun 1882 in Dranesville; father: James H.
POOL; occ: farmer; res: Dranes.; mother: Laura E. POOL; inf:
father; pg:ln: 135:47

POOL, not named; WF; b. 26 Dec 1884 in Dranes.; father: Thos. L.
POOL; occ: farmer; res: Dranes.; mother: Mary E. POOL; inf: father;
pg:ln: 151:73

POOL, not named; WF; b. 4 Nov 1880 in Springvale; father: Joseph L.
POOL; occ: farmer; res: Springvale; mother: Mary K. POOL; inf:
father; pg:ln: 125:58

POOLE, Bertie; WF; b. 24 Apr 1881 in Dranesville; father: Thos. J.
POOLE; occ: farmer; res: Dranesville; mother: Harriet L. POOLE; inf:
father; pg:ln: 131:58

POOLE, Clyde H.; WM; b. 7 Aug 1891 in Ffx; father: J. H. POOLE; occ:
farmer; res: Ffx; mother: Laura A. POOLE; inf: J. H. POOLE, father;
pg:ln: 200:76

POOLE, Hattie; WF; b. 15 Jun 1890 in Ffx; father: Thos. J. POOLE; occ:
farmer; res: Ffx; mother: Hattie POOLE; inf: T. J. POOLE, father;
pg:ln: 191:81

POOLE, Isabel; WF; b. 26 Dec 1885 in Ash Grove; father: W. P.
POOLE; occ: farmer; res: Ash Grove; mother: Ella POOLE; inf:
father; pg:ln: 153:64

POOLE, Jno. E.; WM; b. 16 Jun 1887 in Ffx; father: Jno. H. POOLE;
occ: laborer; res: Ffx; mother: Laura A. POOLE; inf: J. H. POOLE,
father; pg:ln: 163:119

POOLE, Lizzie B.; WF; b. 3 Nov 1881 in Dranes.; father: Edwin W.
POOLE; occ: laborer; res: Dranes.; mother: Martha A. POOLE; inf:
father; pg:ln: 131:56

POOLE, not named; WM; b. 4 Mar 1883 in Dranesville; father: Jas. H.
POOLE; occ: farmer; res: Dranesville; mother: Laura A. POOLE; inf:
father; pg:ln: 141:77

POOLE, Stella; WF; b. 1 Oct 1888 in Ffx; father: Jos. L. POOLE; occ:
farmer; res: Ffx; mother: Mary C. POOLE; inf: J. L. POOLE, father;
pg:ln: 175:75

POPKINS, A. Lillian; WF; b. 5 Jan 1890 in Ffx; father: R. N. POPKINS;
occ: farmer; res: Ffx; mother: Laura POPKINS; inf: R. N. POPKINS,
father; pg:ln: 187:89

POPKINS, Earl Nelson; WM; b. 22 Dec 1893 nr Alex.; father: R. N.
POPKINS; occ: farmer; res: nr Alex.; mother: Laura POPKINS; inf:
parent; pg:ln: 212:77

POPKINS, Jane A.; WF; b. 30 Apr 1883 in Ffx; father: Rich'd.
POPKINS; occ: farmer; res: Ffx; mother: Laura POPKINS; inf: R.
POPKINS, father; pg:ln: 144:69

POPKINS, Thos. W.; WM; b. 5 Mar 1887 in ___; father: R. N.
POPKINS; occ: farmer; res: Ffx; mother: Laura POPKINS; inf: R. N.
POPKINS, father; pg:ln: 168:91

PORTER, Henry C.; WM; b. 17 Nov 1880 in Falls Church; father: Robert
S. PORTER; occ: farmer; res: Falls Church; mother: Camelia
PORTER; inf: father; pg:ln: 125:52

PORTER, Marion [Bray added above]; WM; b. 26 May 1896 in Ffx; father: R. S. PORTER; occ: farmer; res: Ffx; mother: M. B. PORTER; inf: R. S. PORTER, father. Middle name furnished by Marion Bray Porter Mch 31-30.; pg:ln: 227:95

PORTER, Robt. G.; WM; b. 22 Feb 1891 in Ffx; father: Robt. S. PORTER; occ: farmer; res: Ffx; mother: Nannie PORTER; inf: R. S. PORTER, father; pg:ln: 200:73

POTTER, Adalaid; WF; b. 22 Jun 1887 in Ffx; father: Charles POTTER; occ: farmer; res: Ffx; mother: Sarah E. POTTER; inf: C. POTTER, father; pg:ln: 163:120

POTTER, Benjamin; WM; b. 30 Oct 1891 in Telegraph Road; father: Edward POTTER; occ: farmer; res: Telegraph Rd.; mother: Eliza POTTER; inf: parents; pg:ln: 195:15

POTTER, Chas. W.; WM; b. 2 Sep 1888 in Ffx; father: Chas. POTTER; occ: farmer; res: Ffx; mother: Sara E. POTTER; inf: C. POTTER, father. Note: We find Chas. W. born to your parents on 2 Sep 1888. Were you given the name Chas. W. at birth and your name later changed to Wm. Henry? Applicant statement: My name was Charles William at birth, and later my parents added the name Henry, about thirty years ago I decided the name was too long, and discontinued using Charles. ; pg:ln: 175:76

POTTER, Frank; WM; b. 8 Apr 1887 in ___; father: Wm. POTTER; occ: farmer; res: Ffx; mother: Fannie POTTER; inf: Wm. POTTER, father; pg:ln: 168:90

POTTER, Henry; WM; b. 27 Nov 1892 nr Hayfield; father: Edward W. POTTER; occ: farmer; res: nr Hayfield; mother: Eliza POTTER; inf: mother; pg:ln: 207:83

POTTER, Paul (twin); WM; b. 20 Jul 1896 in Ffx; father: Chas. POTTER; occ: farmer; res: Ffx; mother: Sarah POTTER; inf: Chas. POTTER, father; pg:ln: 227:101

POTTER, Pearl (twin); WF; b. 20 Jul 1896 in Ffx; father: Chas. POTTER; occ: farmer; res: Ffx; mother: Sarah POTTER; inf: Chas. POTTER, father; pg:ln: 227:102

POWELL, Mamie; WF; b. 18 Apr 1891 in Ffx; father: Geo. W. POWELL; occ: farmer; res: Ffx; mother: Jennie POWELL; inf: G. W. POWELL, father; pg:ln: 200:79

POWELL, Mary D.; WF; b. 25 Sep 1891 in Ffx; father: Geo. C. POWELL; occ: farmer; res: Ffx; mother: Ann M. POWELL; inf: G. C. POWELL, father; pg:ln: 200:80

POWELL, Wm. B.; WM; b. 19 Jun 1891 in Ffx; father: Jno. W. POWELL; occ: farmer; res: Ffx; mother: Ada POWELL; inf: J. W. POWELL, father; pg:ln: 200:75

POWERS, Wm.; CM; b. 10 Nov 1896 nr Alex.; father: John POWERS; occ: laborer; res: nr Arcturas? P.O.; mother: Lillie POWERS; inf: mother; pg:ln: 231:105

PRESGRAVES, Hazle; WF; b. 10 Nov 1891 in Ffx; father: Wm. F. PRESGRAVES; occ: farmer; res: Ffx; mother: Jennie PRESGRAVES; inf: W. F. PRESGRAVES, father; pg:ln: 200:77

PRESGRAVES, Roy; WM; b. 4 Sep 1890 in Ffx; father: C. J.
PRESGRAVES; occ: farmer; res: Ffx; mother: Laura
PRESGRAVES; inf: C. J. PRESGRAVE[S], father; pg:ln: 191:80

PRESGRA'/ES, Thomas; WF; b. 12 Nov 1894 in Ffx; father: W. F.
PRESGRAVES; occ: farmer; res: Ffx; mother: Jennie
PRESGRAVES; inf: W. F. PRESGRAVES, father; pg:ln: 219:95

PROCTOR, ___; WF; b. 5 Mar 1887 in Ffx; father: Geo. H. PROCTOR;
occ: farmer; res: Ffx; mother: Laura V. PROCTOR; inf: G. H.
PROCTOR, father; pg:ln: 163:116

PROCTOR, Hilda; CF; b. 9 May 1891 nr Gum Spring; father: Henry
PROCTOR; occ: laborer; res: nr Gum Spring; mother: Ann
PROCTOR; inf: parent; pg:ln: 196:16

PULLMAN, ___ (dead); WF; b. 17 Feb 1882 in Ffx; father: P. R.
PULLMAN; occ: ___; res: ___; mother: Lillie A. PULLMAN; inf: P. R.
PULLMAN, father; pg:ln: 137:60

PULLMAN, Albert Wiley; WM; b. 14 Oct 1896 nr Alex.; father: Rosier
PULLMAN; occ: farmer; res: nr Alex.; mother: Mattee E. PULLMAN;
inf: father; pg:ln: 231:102

PULLMAN, Edna V.; WF; b. 14 Sep 1882 in Ffx; father: Oliver
PULLMAN; occ: ___; res: ___; mother: Virginia PULLMAN; inf: O.
PULLMAN, father; pg:ln: 137:62

PULLMAN, Edward; WM; b. 10 May 1882 in Ffx; father: Thos.
PULLMAN; occ: ___; res: ___; mother: S. E. PULLMAN; inf: T.
PULLMAN, father; pg:ln: 137:61

PULLMAN, Elmer L.; WM; b. 18 Oct 1890 in Ffx; father: Jas. T.
PULLMAN; occ: farmer; res: Ffx; mother: Lillie L. PULLMAN; inf: J.
T. PULLMAN, father; pg:ln: 187:90

PULLMAN, Florince Virginia; WF; b. 12 Sep 1892 nr West End; father:
Garbin PULLMAN; occ: ___; res: West End; mother: Mary L.
PULLMAN; inf: mother; pg:ln: 209:40

PULLMAN, Jas. L.; WM; b. 10 Apr 1880 in Ffx; father: Thos. PULLMAN;
occ: farmer; res: Ffx; mother: Sallie; inf: Thos. PULLMAN, father;
pg:ln: 128:71

PULLMAN, Mary A.; WF; b. 15 Jul 1884 in Ffx; father: Jos. PULLMAN;
occ: ___; res: ___; mother: Alice V. PULLMAN; inf: Jos. PULLMAN,
father; pg:ln: 147:56

PULLMAN, Willie; WM; b. 15 Sep 1880 in Ffx; father: O. PULLMAN;
occ: farmer; res: Ffx; mother: Mary; inf: O. PULLMAN, father; pg:ln:
128:70

PURCELL, Logan J.; WM; b. 5 Dec 1894 in Ffx; father: E. H. PURCELL;
occ: farmer; res: Ffx; mother: Mary PURCELL; inf: E. H. PURCELL,
father; pg:ln: 219:98

QUANDER, Annie E.; CF; b. 6 Feb 1887 in ___; father: Jas. E.
QUANDER; occ: farmer; res: Ffx; mother: Laura QUANDER; inf: J.
E. QUANDER, father; pg:ln: 168:93

QUANDER, Arbertha; CF; b. 26 Jul 1893 nr Woodlawn; father: James
QUANDER; occ: laborer; res: nr Woodlawn; mother: Leu? [Laura?]
QUANDER; inf: parent; pg:ln: 212:84

QUANDER, Hattie; CF; b. 16 Jan 1881 in Ffx; father: Jas. A.
QUANDER; occ: farmer; res: Ffx; mother: Amanda QUANDER; inf:
Jas. A. QUANDER, father; pg:ln: 132:38

QUANDER, Irene; CF; b. 1 Mar 1891 nr Woodlawn; father: Thos. H.
QUANDER; occ: farmer; res: nr Woodlawn; mother: Lucy
QUANDER; inf: parent; pg:ln: 196:18

QUANDER, Jackson; CM; b. 12 Jan 1885 in Ffx; father: Jas. E.
QUANDER; occ: farmer; res: Ffx; mother: Malinda QUANDER; inf: J.
E. QUANDER, father; pg:ln: 157:49

QUANDER, Jas. E.; CM; b. 6 Jan 1881 in Ffx; father: Jas. E.
QUANDER; occ: farmer; res: Ffx; mother: Laura QUANDER; inf: J.
E. QUANDER, father; pg:ln: 132:37

QUANDER, Jos. B.; CM; b. 10 Dec 1884 in Ffx; father: Chas.
QUANDER; occ: ___; res: ___; mother: Malinda QUANDER; inf:
Chas. QUANDER, father; pg:ln: 147:58

QUANDER, Sarah A.; CF; b. 6 Jul 1889 in Ffx; father: Jas. A.
QUANDER; occ: farmer; res: Ffx; mother: Malinda QUANDER; inf: J.
A. QUANDER, father; pg:ln: 183:78

QUIGG, Mary E.; WF; b. 16 Dec 1896 in Clifton Sta.; father: Lewis
QUIGG; occ: merchant; res: Clifton Sta.; mother: Mary E. QUIGG;
inf: father; pg:ln: 231:106

RAGAN, Timothy; WM; b. 18 Oct 1890 in Ffx; father: Daniel RAGAN;
occ: farmer; res: Ffx; mother: Kate RAGAN; inf: Daniel RAGAN,
father; pg:ln: 187:100

RAINEY, Rachel V.; WF; b. 13 Feb 1888 in Ffx; father: J. W. RAINEY;
occ: farmer; res: Ffx; mother: Sarah E. RAINEY; inf: J. W. RAINEY,
father; pg:ln: 171:53

RAMEY, Edgar; WM; b. 30 May 1894 in Ffx; father: Edgar L. RAMEY;
occ: farmer; res: Ffx; mother: Effie RAMEY; inf: E. L. RAMEY, father;
pg:ln: 219:101

RAMEY, M. A.; WF; b. 8 Jan 1884 in Seminary; father: W. L. RAMEY;
occ: student; res: Seminary; mother: Olevia RAMEY; inf: father;
pg:ln: 151:76

RAMEY, not named; WM; b. 8 Jan 1885 in Dranesville; father: J. W.
RAMEY; occ: farmer; res: Dranesville; mother: Josephine RAMEY;
inf: father; pg:ln: 154:73

RANDAL, Anna R.; CF; b. 5 Nov 1889 in Ffx; father: Henry RANDAL;
occ: farmer; res: Ffx; mother: Mary RANDAL; inf: H. RANDAL,
father; pg:ln: 183:84

RANDALL, Mary Alice; CF; b. 16 Jul 1892 nr Gum Spring; father: Henry
RANDALL; occ: laborer; res: Gum Spring; mother: Mary R.
RANDELL; inf: father; pg:ln: 206:13

RANDLE, Elizabt.; CF; b. 7 Oct 1886 in Ffx; father: Henry RANDLE;
occ: farmer; res: Ffx; mother: Nancy RANDLE; inf: H. RANDLE,
father; pg:ln: 155:18

RANEY, Clarence; WM; b. 4 Dec 1891 nr Lorton; father: J. W. RANEY;
occ: farmer; res: nr Lorton; mother: Sarah RANEY; inf: parents;
pg:ln: 193:23

RAY, Julian; WM; b. 3 May 1888 in Ffx; father: Samuel RAY; occ: farmer; res: Ffx; mother: Henrietta RAY; inf: Saml. RAY, father; pg:ln: 171:52

RA[Y]LEY, Mattie; WF; b. 18 May 1887 in Ffx; father: Thos. RAYLEY; occ: laborer; res: Ffx; mother: Jennie RAYLEY; inf: Thos. RALEY, father; pg:ln: 163:124

REA, Maggie; WF; b. 21 Mar 1880 in Ffx; father: Saml. REA; occ: farmer; res: Ffx; mother: Henrietta; inf: Saml. REA, father; pg:ln: 128:75

REA, Willie; WM; b. 15 Jun 1884 in Ffx; father: Samuel REA; occ: farmer; res: Ffx; mother: Henrietta REA; inf: S. REA, father; pg:ln: 148:62

REAGAN, Evaline; WF; b. 27 Mar 1895 nr Alexandria; father: Daniel REAGAN; occ: farmer; res: nr Alexandria; mother: Katie REAGAN; inf: mother; pg:ln: 223:106

RECTOR, Cleara; WF; b. 26 Aug 1896 nr Centreville; father: Jeff RECTOR; occ: farmer; res: nr Centreville; mother: Flora T. RECTOR; inf: father; pg:ln: 231:109

RECTOR, Flora T.; WF; b. 6 Apr 1890 in Ffx; father: J. F. RECTOR; occ: farmer; res: Ffx; mother: Flora T. RECTOR; inf: J. F. RECTOR, father; pg:ln: 187:96

RECTOR, Tilda Cornelia; WF; b. 29 Jul 1891 in Centreville; father: Jefferson F. RECTOR; occ: farmer; res: Centreville; mother: Flora Temple RECTOR; inf: parents; pg:ln: 194:19

REED, ___ (dead); WM; b. 18 Sep 1885 in West End; father: J. M. REED; occ: miller; res: West End; mother: S. REED; inf: father; pg:ln: 153:67

REID, ___; WM; b. 15 Jan 1887 in Ffx; father: Jos. S. REID; occ: laborer; res: Ffx; mother: Florence REID; inf: Jos. S. REID, father; pg:ln: 163:126

REID, Floyd F.; WM; b. 6 Nov 1882 in Dranesville; father: Jas. S. REID; occ: farmer; res: Dranes.; mother: F. J. REID; inf: father; pg:ln: 135:52

REID, Jas.; WM; b. 17 Nov 1892 in Ffx; father: Jas. M. REID; occ: farmer; res: Ffx; mother: Sallie REID; inf: J. M. REID, father; pg:ln: 204:83

REID, John L.; WM; b. 9 Aug 1880 in Dranesville; father: James S. REID; occ: carpenter; res: Dranesville; mother: Florence J. REID; inf: father; pg:ln: 125:66

REID, Laura; WF; b. __ Jun 1884 in Ffx; father: Chas. REID; occ: farmer; res: Ffx; mother: Mary F. REID; inf: Chas. REID, father; pg:ln: 148:61

REID, Lawrence M.; WM; b. 4 Sep 1887 in Ffx; father: James REID; occ: laborer; res: Ffx; mother: Alice REID; inf: J. REID, father; pg:ln: 163:125

REID, Lillie V.; WF; b. 27 Mar 1885 in Dranes.; father: Peter REID; occ: farmer; res: Dranes.; mother: Sarah E. REID; inf: father; pg:ln: 153:69

REID, Margie; WF; b. 8 Oct 1891 in Ffx; father: Thos. E. REID; occ: farmer; res: Ffx; mother: L. L. REID; inf: T. E. REID, father; pg:ln: 200:86

REID, Rose; WF; b. 1 Mar 1885 in Dranes.; father: C. H. REID; occ: merchant; res: Dranes.; mother: Annie REID; inf: father; pg:ln: 153:70

REMSBURG, Frank Eugine; WM; b. 13 May 1893 nr Clifton Sta.; father: F. REMSBURG; occ: farmer; res: nr Clifton Sta.; mother: Hettie REMSBURG; inf: parent; pg:ln: 212:79

RENNEY, Jno. E.; WM; b. 18 Aug 1880 in Ffx; father: Jno. RENNEY; occ: farmer; res: Ffx; mother: Elizabeth; inf: J. RENNEY, father; pg:ln: 129:79

RENNY, Julia; WF; b. 16 Aug 1888 in Ffx; father: Jno. H. RENNY; occ: farmer; res: Ffx; mother: Elizabth. RENNY; inf: Jno. H. RENNY, father; pg:ln: 171:55

RENNY, Walter; WM; b. 18 Nov 1887 in ___; father: Jno. H. RENNY; occ: farmer; res: Ffx; mother: Elizabeth RENNY; inf: J. H. RENNY, father; pg:ln: 168:94

RICE, Chas. W.; WM; b. 31 Mar 1881 in Bailey's X Roads; father: J. W. RICE; occ: farmer; res: Bailey's X Roads; mother: Ellen RICE; inf: father; pg:ln: 131:59

RICE, Frank W.; WM; b. 2 Nov 1891 nr Lee Chapel; father: H. D. RICE; occ: farmer; res: Pohick Rd.; mother: M. E. M. RICE; inf: parents; pg:ln: 193:24

RICE, Fre'd.; WM; b. 19 Feb 1893 in ___; father: R. A. RICE; occ: farmer; res: ___; mother: Hattie B. RICE; inf: R. A. RICE, father; pg:ln: 215:81

RICE, Ida E.; WF; b. 25 Oct 1883 in Falls Church; father: Jno. W. RICE; occ: farmer; res: Dranesville; mother: Ellen H. RICE; inf: father; pg:ln: 141:81

RICE, Jessie N.; WM; b. 9 Feb 1886 in Bailey's X Rds; father: J. W. RICE; occ: laborer; res: Bailey's X Rds; mother: E. J. RICE; inf: father; pg:ln: 159:52

RICE, Jessie N.; WM; b. 9 Mar 1885 in Baileys [X] Rds; father: J. W. RICE; occ: laborer; res: Baileys X Rds; mother: Ellen A. RICE; inf: father; pg:ln: 153:65

RICE, Laura V.; WF; b. 25 Oct 1893 in ___; father: J. W. RICE; occ: farmer; res: ___; mother: Clara V. RICE; inf: J. W. RICE, father; pg:ln: 215:82

RICE, Mary Eller.; WF; b. 2 Mar 1880 in Falls Church; father: John W. RICE; occ: farmer; res: Falls Church; mother: Ellen RICE; inf: father; pg:ln: 125:63

RICE, Nellie; WF; b. 27 Feb 1887 in ___; father: H. D. RICE; occ: farmer; res: Ffx; mother: Elizabeth RICE; inf: H. D. RICE, father; pg:ln: 168:96

RICE, Rena Eugenia [Frances lined thru]; WF; b. 31 Jul 1889 in Ffx; father: H. D. RICE; occ: farmer; res: Ffx; mother: Mary E. RICE; inf: H. D. RICE, father. Note of 15 Jul 1938: The name Frances Rice given the female child born July 31, 1889 to H. D. and Mary E. Rice was changed to Rena Eugenia Rice. Signed Mary E. Rice, mother; pg:ln: 183:80

RICE, Richard; WM; b. 19 Feb 1892 nr West End; father: Richard A. RICE; occ: farmer; res: nr West End; mother: Hattie B. RICE; inf: father; pg:ln: 209:39

RICHARDS, Edwd.; CM; b. 1 Dec 1889 in Ffx; father: Danl. RICHARDS; occ: farmer; res: Ffx; mother: Maggie RICHARDS; inf: D. RICHARDS, father; pg:ln: 179:96

RICHARDS, Geo. A.; WM; b. 28 Nov 1881 in Ffx; father: Henry RICHARDS; occ: farmer; res: Ffx; mother: Nancy RICHARDS; inf: H. RICHARDS, father; pg:ln: 133:40

RICHARDS, Henry T.; WM; b. 12 May 1881 in Ffx; father: Morgan RICHARDS; occ: farmer; res: Ffx; mother: Fannie RICHARDS; inf: Morgan RICHARDS, father; pg:ln: 133:41

RICHARDS, J. F.; WM; b. 15 Feb 1883 in Ffx; father: Morgan RICHARDS; occ: farmer; res: Ffx; mother: Fannie RICHARDS; inf: M. RICHARDS, father; pg:ln: 145:73

RICHARDS, Joseph; CM; b. 15 Sep 1885 in Ffx; father: Isaac RICHARDS; occ: farmer; res: Ffx; mother: Lucy RICHARDS; inf: Isaac RICHARDS, father; pg:ln: 157:51

RICHARDS, L.; CM; b. 10 Sep 1885 in Falls Church; father: D. RICHARDS; occ: laborer; res: Falls Church; mother: ___ RICHARD[S]; inf: father; pg:ln: 153:68

RICHARDS, M. J.; WF; b. 5 Jun 1880 in Ffx; father: Henry RICHARDS; occ: farmer; res: Ffx; mother: Nancy; inf: H. RICHARDS, father; pg:ln: 128:76

RICHARDS, Mary Ethel; WF; b. 27 Nov 1895 nr Annandale; father: Berkeley RICHARDS; occ: farmer; res: nr Annandale; mother: Sallie RICHARDS; inf: father; pg:ln: 223:105

RICHARDS, Mary F.; WF; b. 18 May 1880 in Falls Church; father: Saml. B. RICHARDS; occ: farmer; res: Falls Church; mother: Louisa RICHARDS; inf: father; pg:ln: 125:64

RICHARDS, Reuben; CM; b. 10 Jun 1884 in Ffx; father: Isaac RICHARDS; occ: farmer; res: Ffx; mother: Mary RICHARDS; inf: I. RICHARDS, father; pg:ln: 148:63

RICHARDSON, Mary B.; WF; b. 12 Dec 1889 in Ffx; father: F. W. RICHARDSON; occ: Clerk Co. Ct.; res: Ffx; mother: Milly RICHARDSON; inf: F. W. RICHARDSON, father; pg:ln: 179:95

RICHARDSON, Virginia F.; WF; b. 20 Mar 1891 in Ffx; father: F. W. RICHARDSON; occ: Clerk Co. Ct.; res: Ffx; mother: Milley L. RICHARDSON; inf: F. W. RICHARDSON, father; pg:ln: 200:82

RIED, Agnes; WF; b. 1 Jan 1887 in ___; father: Jas. M. RIED; occ: farmer; res: Ffx; mother: Sallie RIED; inf: J. M. REID, father; pg:ln: 168:97

RIED, Chas. H.; WM; b. 21 Dec 1888 in Ffx; father: C. H. RIED; occ: farmer; res: Ffx; mother: Annie RIED; inf: C. H. RIED, father; pg:ln: 175:84

RIED, Clara; CF; b. 3 Jan 1889 in Ffx; father: Simon RIED; occ: farmer; res: Ffx; mother: Cressie RIED; inf: S. RIED, father; pg:ln: 179:98

RIED, Dulsie; WF; b. 5 Oct 1896 nr Stoneleigh; father: Wm. P. RIED; occ: farmer; res: nr Stoneleigh; mother: Frances RIED; inf: father; pg:ln: 231:111

RIED, Eppa C.; WM; b. 31 May 1888 in Ffx; father: J. S. RIED; occ: farmer; res: Ffx; mother: Florence RIED; inf: J. S. RIED, father; pg:ln: 175:83

RIED, Ethel J.; WF; b. 11 Apr 1888 in Ffx; father: Jas. L. RIED; occ: farmer; res: Ffx; mother: Alice RIED; inf: J. L. RIED, father; pg:ln: 175:82

RIED, Lula; WF; b. 18 Nov 1890 in Ffx; father: Wm. P. RIED; occ: laborer; res: Ffx; mother: Francis RIED; inf: Wm. P. RIED, father; pg:ln: 187:93

RIED, Myrtle May; WF; b. 30 May 1889 in Ffx; father: W. P. RIED; occ: farmer; res: Ffx; mother: Frances RIED; inf: W. P. RIED, father; pg:ln: 183:81

RIED, Perry Coffer; WM; b. 9 Aug 1890 in Ffx; father: Robt. L. RIED; occ: laborer; res: Ffx; mother: Margaret RIED; inf: Robt. L. RIED, father; pg:ln: 187:92

RIED, Rose L.; WF; b. 30 May 1890 in Ffx; father: Thos. E. RIED; occ: farmer; res: Ffx; mother: Lilla RIED; inf: T. E. RIED, father; pg:ln: 191:84

RIGGLES, Claude E.; WM; b. 15 Feb 1882 in Ffx; father: Wm. L. RIGGLES; occ: ___; res: ___; mother: Katie RIGGLES; inf: W. L. RIGGLES, father; pg:ln: 137:65

RIGGLES, Hellen; WF; b. 1 Aug 1885 in Ffx; father: Wm. L. RIGGLES; occ: farmer; res: Ffx; mother: Kattie L. RIGGLES; inf: W. L. RIGGLES, father; pg:ln: 157:52

RIGGLES, Kate Pauline; WF; b. 12 Jan 1893 nr Fairfax Sta.; father: Wm. RIGGLES; occ: farmer; res: nr Fairfax Sta.; mother: Kate RIGGLES; inf: parent; pg:ln: 212:78

RIGGLES, Mary Ann; WF; b. 1 Nov 1891 nr Fairfax Sta.; father: W. L. RIGGLES; occ: farmer; res: Sangsters X Rods; mother: Kate Lewis RIGGLES; inf: parents; pg:ln: 193:22

RIGGLES, Naomi V.; WF; b. 22 Jun 1888 in Ffx; father: Wm. L. RIGGLES; occ: farmer; res: Ffx; mother: Kate L. RIGGLES; inf: Wm L. RIGGLES, father; pg:ln: 171:54

RIGGLES, Walter; WM; b. 5 Sep 1883 in Ffx; father: W. L. RIGGLES; occ: farmer; res: Ffx; mother: C. L. RIGGLES; inf: W. L. RIGGLES, father; pg:ln: 145:72

RIKER, Charlotte E.; WF; b. 13 Aug 1884 in Ffx; father: Geo. A. RIKER; occ: farmer; res: Ffx; mother: Fannie RIKER; inf: G. A. RIKER, father; pg:ln: 148:65

RIKER, Chas. Ross; WM; b. 5 Jul 1890 in Ffx; father: Geo. RIKER; occ: farmer; res: Ffx; mother: Theresa RIKER; inf: Geo. RIKER, father; pg:ln: 187:98

RILEY, Ernest; WM; b. 1 Sep 1896 nr Alex; father: James RILEY; occ: farmer; res: nr Alex; mother: Julia RILEY; inf: father; pg:ln: 231:110

RIPLEY, not named; WM; b. 14 Sep 1884 in Falls Church; father: E. H. RIPLEY; occ: Gov. clerk; res: Falls Church; mother: Mary RIPLEY; inf: father; pg:ln: 151:75

RISTON, Benj. Franklin; WM; b. 18 Jun 1892 nr Alex.; father: J. B. RISTON; occ: ___; res: nr Alex.; mother: Ada V. RISTON; inf: mother; pg:ln: 207:85

RISTON, Bertie V.; WF; b. 2 May 1889 in Ffx; father: Judah B. RISTON; occ: farmer; res: Ffx; mother: Ada RISTON; inf: J. B. RISTON, father. Note of 6/5/43 in Richmond Va: I have no knowledge of my middle initial as V. always May from my earliest memory. The date of my birth was always April 28 perhaps May 2 was the date is was recorded. I have filed my social security as Bertie May Riston. Clerk in Charge of Old Records: Applicant states that her middle name has always been May and she has always observed April 28 as her birthday.; pg:ln: 183:82

ROBERSON [ROBINSON], Carrie; CF; b. 4 Dec 1886 in West End; father: Newton ROBINSON; occ: laborer; res: West End; mother: Georgie ROBINSON; inf: father; pg:ln: 159:51

ROBERSON [ROBINSON], Essa; CF; b. 31 May 1886 in West End; father: Hanes ROBINSON; occ: laborer; res: West End; mother: Lizzie ROBINSON; inf: father; pg:ln: 159:50

ROBERSON, Jessie; CM; b. 1 Sep 1881 in Providence; father: James ROBERSON; occ: laborer; res: Providence; mother: Rose ROBERSON; inf: father; pg:ln: 131:60

ROBERSON, not named; CM; b. 8 Apr 1884 in Prov.; father: Wm. ROBERSON; occ: laborer; res: Prov.; mother: Sarah ROBERSON; inf: father; pg:ln: 151:77

ROBERSON, Willie; WM; b. 2 Apr 1883 in Ffx; father: Rich'd. ROBERSON; occ: farmer; res: Ffx; mother: Sanera ROBERSON; inf: R. ROBERSON, father; pg:ln: 145:70

ROBERTS, Margaret; WF; b. 11 Nov 1893 nr Accotink; father: Alfred ROBERTS; occ: farmer; res: nr Accotink; mother: Jane ROBERTS; inf: parent; pg:ln: 212:80

ROBERTS, Ridginal; CM; b. 5 Apr 1896 in C. H.; father: E. T. ROBERTS; occ: school teacher; res: C. H.; mother: Fannie R. ROBERTS; inf: father; pg:ln: 231:115

ROBERTSON, C. E.; WM; b. 22 Jan 1890 in Ffx; father: E. S. ROBERTSON; occ: farmer; res: Ffx; mother: T. A. ROBERTSON; inf: E. S. ROBERTSON, father; pg:ln: 187:94

ROBERTSON, Gertrude; WF; b. 6 Sep 1890 in Ffx; father: A. W. ROBERTSON; occ: farmer; res: Ffx; mother: Emma J. ROBERTSON; inf: A. W. ROBERTSON, father; pg:ln: 187:95

ROBEY, Eva May; WF; b. 5 Apr 1895 nr Clifton; father: Geo. ROBEY; occ: farmer; res: nr Clifton; mother: Cora L. ROBEY; inf: father; pg:ln: 223:104

ROBINSON see ROBERSON

ROBINSON, Amanda Jessie; CF; b. 18 Sep 1895 nr Centreville; father: Pearce ROBINSON; occ: farmer; res: nr Centreville; mother: Virginia ROBINSON; inf: father; pg:ln: 224:108

ROBINSON, Chas.; CM; b. 1 Jan 1887 in Ffx; father: Thos. ROBINSON; occ: laborer; res: Ffx; mother: Selena ROBINSON; inf: Thos. ROBINSON, father; pg:ln: 163:129

ROBINSON, Hattie Violet; WF; b. 20 Feb 1896 nr C. H.; father: Stafford ROBINSON; occ: farmer; res: nr C. H.; mother: Georgie ROBINSON; inf: father; pg:ln: 231:107

ROBINSON, Jno.; CM; b. 20 Mar 1882 in Ffx; father: Pen ROBINSON; occ: ___; res· ___; mother: Jane ROBINSON; inf: P. ROBINSON, father; pg:ln: 137:64

ROBINSON, Lucretia; CF; b. 4 Mar 1893 nr Bull Run; father: Thos. ROBINSON; occ: laborer; res: nr Bull Run; mother: Lottie ROBINSON; inf: parent; pg:ln: 212:85

ROBINSON, not named (dead); WM; b. 21 Aug 1896 nr Centreville; father: Joseph ROBINSON; occ: farmer; res: nr Centreville; mother: Maude ROBINSON; inf: father; pg:ln: 231:108

ROBINSON, Selena; CM; b. 3 Oct 1887 in Ffx; father: J. L. H. ROBINSON; occ: laborer; res: Ffx; mother: M. M. ROBINSON; inf: J. L. H. ROBINSON, father; pg:ln: 163:128

ROBINSON, W. H.; CM; b. 21 Mar 1885 in West End; father: Henry ROBINSON; occ: laborer; res: West End; mother: Lillie ROBINSON; inf: father; pg:ln: 153:66

ROBISON, Ann M. (twin); CF; b. 14 Jun 1880 in Ffx; father: Allen ROBISON; occ: farmer; res: Ffx; mother: Lucy; inf: Allen ROBISON, father; pg:ln: 128:78

ROBISON, Burnett; CM; b. 8 Oct 1887 in Ffx; father: Wm. ROBISON; occ: farmer; res: Ffx; mother: Sarah ROBISON; inf: W. ROBISON, father; pg:ln: 163:123

ROBISON, Cash; CM; b. 17 Apr 1884 in Ffx; father: Penn ROBINSON; occ: ___; res: ___; mother: Virginia ROBINSON; inf: Penn ROBISON, father; pg:ln: 147:59

ROBISON, Catha.; CF; b. 28 Dec 1889 in Ffx; father: Thos. ROBISON; occ: farmer; res: Ffx; mother: Celina ROBISON; inf: Thos. ROBISON, father; pg:ln: 179:97

ROBISON, Cora V.; CF; b. 7 Oct 1888 in Ffx; father: Douglas ROBINSON; occ: farmer; res: Ffx; mother: Matilda ROBISON; inf: D. ROBINSON, father; pg:ln: 175:80

ROBISON, Emma; WF; b. 12 Jan 1885 in Ffx; father: A. W. ROBISON; occ: farmer; res: Ffx; mother: Emma J. ROBISON; inf: A. W. ROBINSON, father; pg:ln: 157:53

ROBISON, Geo. R. (twin); CM; b. 14 Jun 1880 in Ffx; father: Allen ROBISON; occ: farmer; res: Ffx; mother: Lucy; inf: Allen ROBISON, father; pg:ln: 128:77

ROBISON, Jno.; CM; b. 18 Dec 1880 in Ffx; father: Tasco ROBISON; occ: farmer; res: Ffx; mother: Lettice; inf: T. ROBISON, father; pg:ln: 128:74

ROBISON, May; CF; b. 21 May 1886 in Ffx; father: Penn ROBISON; occ: farmer; res: Ffx; mother: Virginia ROBISON; inf: P. ROBISON, father; pg:ln: 155:16

ROBISON, Nettie; CF; b. 17 Jul 1891 in Ffx; father: Jno. ROBISON; occ: farmer; res: Ffx; mother: Julia ROBISON; inf: Jno. ROBISON, father; pg:ln: 200:85

ROBISON, Rich'd.; CM; b. 4 Sep 1892 in Ffx; father: Rich'd. ROBISON; occ: farmer; res: Ffx; mother: Annie ROBISON; inf: R. ROBISON, father; pg:ln: 204:80

ROBISON, Vivian; CF; b. 6 Jul 1894 in Ffx; father: W. H. ROBISON; occ: farmer; res: Ffx; mother: Sarah ROBISON; inf: W. H. ROBISON, father; pg:ln: 219:104

ROBY, Blanch; WF; b. 20 Mar 1894 in Ffx; father: Geo. D. ROBY; occ: farmer; res: Ffx; mother: Mattie ROBY; inf: G. D. ROBY, father; pg:ln: 219:103

ROBY, Edw'd.; WM; b. 26 Jun 1896 in Ffx; father: Geo. ROBY; occ: farmer; res: Ffx; mother: Mattie ROBY; inf: Geo. ROBY, father; pg:ln: 227:103

ROBY, Flora A.; WF; b. 16 Jan 1880 in Vienna; father: Manesseh ROBY; occ: laborer; res: Vienna; mother: Sarah E. ROBY; inf: father; pg:ln: 125:62

ROBY, Frank; WM; b. 14 Sep 1887 in Ffx; father: Wm. J. ROBY; occ: laborer; res: Ffx; mother: Mary E. ROBY; inf: Wm. J. ROBY, father; pg:ln: 163:127

ROBY, Harriet; WF; b. 11 Dec 1885 in Ffx; father: Geo. E. ROBY; occ: farmer; res: Ffx; mother: Emily ROBY; inf: G. E. ROBY, father; pg:ln: 157:50

ROBY, Harry; WM; b. 2 Oct 1896 in Ffx; father: W. ROBY; occ: farmer; res: Ffx; mother: Jennie ROBY; inf: W. ROBY, father; pg:ln: 227:106

ROBY, Lizzie May; WF; b. 15 Feb 1882 in Vienna; father: Manasseh ROBY; occ: mechanic; res: Vienna; mother: Sarah E. ROBY; inf: father; pg:ln: 135:50

ROBY, Mable; WF; b. 1 Oct 1891 in Ffx; father: Edgar ROBY; occ: farmer; res: Ffx; mother: Ella ROBY; inf: E. ROBY, father; pg:ln: 200:87

ROBY, Major; WM; b. 20 Dec 1883 in Ffx; father: Geo. ROBY; occ: farmer; res: Ffx; mother: Emily ROBY; inf: Geo. ROBY, father; pg:ln: 145:71

ROBY, Rich'd. L.; WM; b. 25 Jan 1883 in Herndon; father: W. T. ROBY; occ: merchant; res: Herndon; mother: Mary E. ROBY; inf: father; pg:ln: 141:83

ROCKWELL, Edith M.; WF; b. 13 Mar 1882 in Falls Church; father: Sam. H. ROCKWELL; occ: farmer; res: Falls Church; mother: Ellen M. ROCKWELL; inf: father; pg:ln: 135:49

ROCKWELL, Edith May; WF; b. 13 Mar 1881 in Falls Church; father: Hollister ROCKWELL; occ: farmer; res: Falls Church; mother: Ella ROCKWELL; inf: mother; pg:ln: 131:61

RODGERS, ___ (dead); WM; b. 12 Jun 1882 in Ffx; father: Levi
  RODGERS; occ: ___; res: ___; mother: Mgt. RODGERS; inf: L.
  RODGERS, father; pg:ln: 137:66
RODGERS, ___; WF; b. 13 May 1894 in Ffx; father: Geo. E.
  RODGERS; occ: farmer; res: Ffx; mother: Annie V. RODGERS; inf:
  Geo. E. RODGERS, father; pg:ln: 219:102
RODGERS, ___; WF; b. 20 Jun 1893 nr Springfield; father: Geo. W.
  RODGERS; occ: farmer; res: nr Hayfield; mother: Effie RODGERS;
  inf: parent; pg:ln: 212:82
RODGERS, Alice; WF; b. 4 Nov 1896 in Ffx; father: Geo. E.
  RODGERS; occ: farmer; res: Ffx; mother: Anna V. RODGERS; inf:
  G. E. RODGERS, father; pg:ln: 227:105
RODGERS, Dora; WF; b. 13 Apr 1896 nr Hayfield; father: Wm.
  RODGERS; occ: farmer; res: nr Hayfield; mother: Rebecca
  RODGERS; inf: father; pg:ln: 231:113
RODGERS, Elizabeth; WF; b. 10 Aug 1884 in Ffx; father: Robt.
  RODGERS; occ: farmer; res: Ffx; mother: Elizabeth RODGERS; inf:
  R. RODGERS, father; pg:ln: 148:64
RODGERS, Esther; WF; b. 18 Apr 1896 in Ffx; father: J. N. RODGERS;
  occ: farmer; res: Ffx; mother: Mary RODGERS; inf: J. N.
  RODGERS, father; pg:ln: 227:104
RODGERS, Eva Cleveland; WF; b. 18 Nov 1884 in Ffx; father: Henry
  RODGERS; occ: ___; res: ___; mother: Emma RODGERS; inf: H.
  RODGERS, father; pg:ln: 147:60
RODGERS, Geo. Clinton; WM; b. 7 Dec 1892 nr Hayfield; father: W. H.
  RODGERS Jr.; occ: farmer; res: nr Hayfield; mother: Rebecca
  RODGERS; inf: mother; pg:ln: 207:86
RODGERS, Guy T.; WM; b. 1 Oct 1888 in Ffx; father: J. N. RODGERS;
  occ: farmer; res: Ffx; mother: Mary E. RODGERS; inf: J. N.
  RODGERS, father; pg:ln: 175:81
RODGERS, Harvie; WM; b. 17 Dec 1886 in Ffx; father: Jno. M.
  RODGERS; occ: farmer; res: Ffx; mother: Mary RODGERS; inf: J.
  M. RODGERS, father; pg:ln: 155:17
RODGERS, James; WM; b. 27 Jul 1895 nr Woodlawn; father: James
  RODGERS; occ: farmer; res: nr Woodlawn; mother: Maggie
  RODGERS; inf: mother; pg:ln: 223:107
RODGERS, Lena M.; WF; b. 2 Apr 1892 nr Hayfield; father: Geo. W.
  RODGERS; occ: farmer; res: nr Hayfield; mother: Effie RODGERS;
  inf: mother; pg:ln: 207:87
RODGERS, Lillie Maud; WF; b. 21 Oct 1890 in Ffx; father: Geo. H.
  RODGERS; occ: farmer; res: Ffx; mother: Susan RODGERS; inf:
  Geo. H. RODGERS, father; pg:ln: 187:97
RODGERS, Lou T.; WF; b. 1 May 1891 in Ffx; father: Geo. E.
  RODGERS; occ: farmer; res: Ffx; mother: Annie V. RODGERS; inf:
  Geo. E. RODGERS, father; pg:ln: 200:83
RODGERS, Mary Lizzie; WF; b. 14 Mar 1896 in Hayfield; father: Arther
  RODGERS; occ: farmer; res: Hayfield; mother: Rosa RODGERS;
  inf: father; pg:ln: 231:114

RODGERS, Maud; WF; b. 15 Apr 1893 in ___; father: J. N. RODGERS; occ: farmer; res: ___; mother: M. E. RODGERS; inf: J. N. RODGERS, father; pg:ln: 215:80

RODGERS, Milton; WM; b. 6 Dec 1890 in Ffx; father: Jno. M. RODGERS; occ: farmer; res: Ffx; mother: Sarah RODGERS; inf: Jno. M. RODGERS, father; pg:ln: 187:99

RODGERS, Nettie; WF; b. 12 Oct 1889 in Ffx; father: W. H. RODGERS; occ: farmer; res: Ffx; mother: Rebecca RODGERS; inf: W. H. RODGERS, father; pg:ln: 183:83

RODGERS, not named (dead); WF; b. 7 Jun 1887 in ___; father: Levi RODGERS; occ: farmer; res: Ffx; mother: Margaret RODGERS; inf: Levi RODGERS, father; pg:ln: 168:95

RODGERS, Pearl; WF; b. 21 Apr 1893 nr Hayfield; father: John M. RODGERS; occ: farmer; res: nr Hayfield; mother: Sarah E. RODGERS; inf: parent; pg:ln: 212:81

RODGERS, Raymond; WM; b. 20 Mar 1893 nr Hayfield; father: Richard RODGERS; occ: farmer; res: nr Hayfield; mother: Emaline RODGERS; inf: parent; pg:ln: 212:83

RODGERS, Theodore; WM; b. 12 Sep 1881 in Ffx; father: Jas. E. RODGERS; occ: farmer; res: Ffx; mother: Magt. RODGERS; inf: J. E. RODGERS, father; pg:ln: 133:42

ROGERS, Dolly Fairfax; WF; b. 21 Aug 1884 in Prov.; father: J. N. ROGERS; occ: farmer; res: Prov.; mother: M. E. ROGERS; inf: father; pg:ln: 151:78

ROGERS, E. M.; WM; b. 17 Aug 1886 in Lewinsville; father: J. N. RODGERS; occ: farmer; res: Lewinsville; mother: M. E. ROGERS; inf: father; pg:ln: 159:53

ROGERS, Hammond [Harman RODGERS lined thru]; WM; b. 27 Mar 1891 in Ffx; father: J. N. ROGERS [RODGERS lined thru]; occ: farmer; res: Ffx; mother: Mary ROGERS [RODGERS lined thru]; inf: J. N. ROGERS, father; pg:ln: 200:84

ROGERS, Mary; WF; b. 9 Jan 1883 in Lewinsville; father: J. N. ROGERS; occ: farmer; res: Lewinsville; mother: M. E. ROGERS; inf: father; pg:ln: 141:82

ROGERS, Robert; WM; b. 28 May 1891 nr Hayfield; father: W. H. ROGERS; occ: farmer; res: nr Hayfield; mother: Rebecca ROGERS; inf: parents; pg:ln: 195:18

ROLLINS, Annie L.; WF; b. 5 Jan 1885 in Dranes.; father: Lewis F. ROLLINS; occ: farmer; res: Dranes.; mother: Carrie ROLLINS; inf: father; pg:ln: 153:71

ROLLINS, Minnie; WF; b. 20 Nov 1888 in Ffx; father: Lewis F. ROLLINS; occ: farmer; res: Ffx; mother: Carrie ROLLINS; inf: L. F. ROLLINS, father; pg:ln: 175:85

ROSE, Alice; WF; b. 2 Jun 1892 in Ffx; father: Jas. H. ROSE; occ: farmer; res: Ffx; mother: Summer ROSE; inf: J. H. ROSE, father; pg:ln: 204:82

ROSE, Amanda M.; WF; b. 23 Mar 1896 in Ffx; father: J. H. ROSE; occ: farmer; res: Ffx; mother: S. M. ROSE; inf: J. H. ROSE, father; pg:ln: 227:107

ROSS, Eula; WF; b. 21 Jan 1891 nr Chantilly; father: J. T. ROSS; occ: farmer; res: nr Chantilly; mother: Susie B. ROSS; inf: parents; pg:ln: 194:18

ROWELL, Edw'd.; WM; b. 7 Aug 1890 in Ffx; father: A. E. ROWELL; occ: farmer; res: Ffx; mother: Clara ROWELL; inf: A. E. ROWELL, father; pg:ln: 191:83

ROWLEY, Chas. Joseph; WM; b. 5 Nov 1896 in Accotink; father: Wm. ROWLEY; occ: retired U. S. Soldier; res: Accotink; mother: Mary ROWLEY; inf: father; pg:ln: 231:112

ROWZEE, Edwin E.; WM; b. 4 Jun 1882 in Dranesville; father: Geo. A. ROWZEE; occ: mcht.; res: Dranes.; mother: Annie L. ROWZEE; inf: father; pg:ln: 135:51

ROWZEE, John A.; WM; b. 19 Apr 1880 in Dranesville; father: W. S. ROWZEE; occ: farmer; res: Dranesville; mother: C. W. ROWZEE; inf: father; pg:ln: 125:65

ROWZEE, not named; WF; b. 12 Dec 1882 in Dranesville; father: W. S. ROWZEE; occ: mcht.; res: Dranes.; mother: Clara W. ROWZEE; inf: father; pg:ln: 135:53

ROWZEE, not named; WF; b. 2 Dec 1885 in Dranes.; father: Wm. S. ROWZEE; occ: merchant; res: Dranes.; mother: Clara ROWZEE; inf: father; pg:ln: 153:72

ROWZIE, Ruben R.; WM; b. 15 Jul 1892 in Ffx; father: W. S. ROWZIE; occ: farmer; res: Ffx; mother: P. W. ROWZIE; inf: W. S. ROWZIE, father; pg:ln: 204:81

ROY, Jane E.; CF; b. 13 Mar 1887 in Ffx; father: Richd. ROY; occ: laborer; res: Ffx; mother: Jane ROY; inf: Richd. ROY, father; pg:ln: 163:130

ROY, not named; CF; b. 13 Sep 1884 nr Seminary; father: Richard ROY; occ: laborer; res: nr Seminary; mother: Lucy ROY; inf: father; pg:ln: 151:74

RUCKER, Marvin; WM; b. 6 Jan 1881 in Ffx; father: E. T. RUCKER; occ: M.D.; res: Ffx; mother: Ann C. RUCKER; inf: E. T. RUCKER, father; pg:ln: 132:39

RYAN, Robt. H.; WM; b. 21 Aug 1889 in Ffx; father: H. S. RYAN; occ: farmer; res: Ffx; mother: Isabella RYAN; inf: H. S. RYAN, father; pg:ln: 183:79

SADLIER, John; CM; b. 21 Feb 1880 in Ffx; father: Jas. E. SADLIER; occ: farmer; res: Ffx; mother: Julia A.; inf: J. E. SADLIER, father; pg:ln: 129:85

SAFFER, Rachael; WF; b. 5 Nov 1887 in Ffx; father: Wm. F. SAFFER; occ: farmer; res: Ffx; mother: Elizabt. SAFFER; inf: Wm. F. SAFFER, father; pg:ln: 163:133

SANDERS, Annie N.; WF; b. 18 Jun 1887 in Ffx; father: Henderson SANDERS; occ: laborer; res: Ffx; mother: Laura SANDERS; inf: H. SAUNDERS, father; pg:ln: 164:152

SANDERS, Earl D.; WM; b. 16 Sep 1892 in Ffx; father: W. B.
SANDERS; occ: farmer; res: Ffx; mother: Rosetta SANDERS; inf: B.
W. [W. B.?] SAUNDERS, father; pg:ln: 204:91

SANDERS, J. A.; WM; b. 10 Oct 1889 in Ffx; father: Jno. F. SANDERS;
occ: farmer; res: Ffx; mother: G. A. SANDERS; inf: J. F. SANDERS,
father; pg:ln: 179:105

SANDERS, Maude; WF; b. 8 Sep 1883 in Dranesville; father:
Henderson SANDERS; occ: farmer; res: Dranesville; mother: Susan
SANDERS; inf: father; pg:ln: 141:93

SANDERS, not named; WF; b. 29 Oct 1882 in Walters Mill; father:
Harrison SANDERS; occ: farmer; res: Walters Mill; mother: Mary C.
SANDERS; inf: father; pg:ln: 135:57

SANDERS, Stacy; WM; b. 6 Apr 1886 in Dranes.; father: Jno. F.
SANDERS; occ: mcht.; res: Dranes.; mother: Georgianna
SANDERS; inf: father; pg:ln: 159:60

SANDERS Virginia; WF; b. 16 Dec 1882 in Dranesville; father: Jno. F.
SANDERS; occ: mcht.; res: Dranes.; mother: Georgia SANDERS;
inf: father; pg:ln: 135:55

SANFORD, Eva L.; WF; b. 9 Jan 1896 in Ffx; father: Douglas
SANFORD; occ: farmer; res: Ffx; mother: Mary SANFORD; inf: D.
SANFORD, father; pg:ln: 228:111

SAULS, Robert A.; WM; b. 25 Aug 1886 in Fairfax; father: N. W.
SAULS; occ: mechanic; res: Fairfax; mother: Mary C. SAULS; inf:
father; pg:ln: 159:57

SAULSBERRY, Fax; WM; b. 15 Dec 1892 in Ffx; father: J. E.
SAULSBERRY; occ: farmer; res: Ffx; mother: Alice SAULSBERRY;
inf: J. E. SAULSBERRY, father; pg:ln: 204:87

SAUNDERS, Otto L; WM; b. 5 Oct 1891 nr Centreville; father: D. Lee
SAUNDERS; occ: farmer; res: nr Centreville; mother: Martha E.
SAUNDERS; inf: parents; pg:ln: 194:21

SAUNDERS, Stacy; WM; b. 6 Apr 1887 in Ffx; father: Jno. F.
SAUNDERS; occ: farmer; res: Ffx; mother: Georgia SAUNDERS;
inf: J. F. SAUNDERS, father; pg:ln: 163:135

SCHEURMAN, Martha; WF; b. 3 Apr 1887 in Ffx; father: T. A. J.
SCHEURMAN; occ: farmer; res: Ffx; mother: Barbara
SCHEURMAN; inf: T. A. J. SCHEURMAN, father; pg:ln: 164:140

SCHNEIDER, Jacob; WM; b. 7 Mar 1890 in Ffx; father: George
SCHNEIDER; occ: farmer; res: Ffx; mother: Barbara SCHNEIDER;
inf: G. SCHNEIDER, Father; pg:ln: 187:101

SCHNIEDER, ___ (dead); WM; b. 10 Aug 1888 in Ffx; father: Geo.
SCHNIEDER; occ: farmer; res: Ffx; mother: Barbara SCHNIEDER;
inf: Gec. SCHNIEDER, father; pg:ln: 171:63

SCOTT, Emma; WF; b. 20 Aug 1881 in Falls Church; father: Edgar
SCOTT; occ: farmer; res: Falls Church; mother: Lavinia SCOTT; inf:
father; pg:ln: 131:66

SCOTT, Estella; CF; b. 3 Jan 1892 in Ffx; father: Jas. A. SCOTT; occ:
farmer; res: Ffx; mother: Emma SCOTT; inf: J. A. SCOTT, father;
pg:ln: 204:90

SCOTT, Eva Bell; CF; b. 18 Dec 1891 in Germantown; father: Abram
SCOTT; occ: laborer; res: Germantown; mother: Willie Ann SCOTT;
inf: parent; pg:ln: 196:29

SCOTT, F.; CF; b. 1 Jan 1883 in Falls Church; father: Jas. A. SCOTT;
occ: farmer; res: Falls Church; mother: Charlotte SCOTT; inf: father;
pg:ln: 141:84

SCOTT, Gersie [Gussie?]; CF; b. 29 Nov 1892 nr Sudley; father:
Nathan SCOTT; occ: laborer; res: nr Sudley; mother: Ella SCOTT;
inf: mother; pg:ln: 206:29

SCOTT, Gussie; CF; b. 5 Jan 1895 in Bull Run; father: Nathan SCOTT;
occ: farmer; res: Bull Run; mother: Ella SCOTT; inf: father; pg:ln:
224:115

SCOTT, Loren; CM; b. 13 Jan 1890 in Ffx; father: James SCOTT; occ:
farmer; res: Ffx; mother: Emma SCOTT; inf: J. SCOTT, father; pg:ln:
191:85

SCOTT, Maggie M.; WF; b. 27 Aug 1888 in Ffx; father: Chas. E.
SCOTT; occ: farmer; res: Ffx; mother: Martha SCOTT; inf: C. E.
SCOTT, father; pg:ln: 175:89

SCOTT, Oceola; CF; b. 8 Mar 1893 nr Fairfax C. H.; father: Abram
SCOTT; occ: laborer; res: nr Fairfax C. H.; mother: Willie A. SCOTT;
inf: parent; pg:ln: 212:88

SCOTT, T. J.; CM; b. 8 Apr 1886 in Falls Ch.; father: Jas. A. SCOTT;
occ: mcht.; res: Falls Ch.; mother: E. V. SCOTT; inf: father; pg:ln:
159:55

SCOTT, T. J.; WM; b. 22 Sep 1882 in Ffx; father: J. R. SCOTT; occ:
___; res: ___; mother: Annie SCOTT; inf: J. R. SCOTT, father; pg:ln:
137:67

SCOTT, W. A.; WM; b. 8 Aug 1886 in Ffx; father: W. H. SCOTT; occ:
farmer; res: Ffx; mother: Ann V. SCOTT; inf: W. H. SCOTT, father;
pg:ln: 155:19

SCOTT, W. S. H.; WM; b. 23 Jun 1880 in ___; father: John SCOTT;
occ: farmer; res: Ffx; mother: Annie; inf: Jno. SCOTT, father; pg:ln:
129:93

SEATON, ___ (dead); WM; b. 1 Sep 1891 in Ffx; father: Geo. W.
SEATON; occ: farmer; res: Ffx; mother: May SEATON; inf: G. W.
SEATON, father; pg:ln: 200:95

SEATON, Estella; WF; b. 14 Nov 1893 in ___; father: Geo. W.
SEATON; occ: farmer; res: ___; mother: Fannie SEATON; inf: G. W.
SEATON, father; pg:ln: 215:83

SEATON, Estella; WF; b. 14 Sep 1892 in Ffx; father: Geo. W. SEATON;
occ: farmer; res: Ffx; mother: Fannie SEATON; inf: G. W. SEATON,
father; pg:ln: 204:86

SEATON, Nettie V.; WF; b. 2 Jul 1891 in Ffx; father: Hiram SEATON;
occ: farmer; res: Ffx; mother: Laura SEATON; inf: H. SEATON,
father; pg:ln: 200:90

SELECMAN, Raymond; WM; b. 15 Nov 1887 in Ffx; father: Thos. H.
SELECMAN; occ: farmer; res: Ffx; mother: Georgia SELECMAN; inf:
T. H. SELECMAN, father; pg:ln: 169:102

SELECMAN, Silas U.; WM; b. 2 Feb 1880 in ___; father: Thos. H.
SELECMAN; occ: farmer; res: Ffx; mother: Georgian; inf: ___; pg:ln:
129:89

SELF, Florence; WF; b. 10 Sep 1894 in Ffx; father: Robt. SELF; occ:
farmer; res: Ffx; mother: Ellen SELF; inf: Robt. SELF, father; pg:ln:
219:107

SELF, Jno. A.; WM; b. 14 May 1890 in Ffx; father: Robt. SELF; occ:
farmer; res: Ffx; mother: Ellen C. SELF; inf: R. SELF, father; pg:ln:
191:89

SELF, not named; WF; b. 15 Aug 1885 in Lewinsville; father: Robert
SELF; occ: laborer; res: Lewinsville; mother: Ellenn SELF; inf:
father; pg:ln: 154:76

SELVA, Georgiana; CF; b. 6 Nov 1892 in Ffx; father: Jno. SELVA; occ:
farmer; res: Ffx; mother: Mary SELVA; inf: J. SELVA, father; pg:ln:
204:96

SELVA, Lewis; CM; b. 3 Dec 1891 in Ffx; father: John SELVA; occ:
farmer; res: Ffx; mother: Mary SELVA; inf: Jno. SELVA, father;
pg:ln: 200:96

SEMONS, Pearl Irene; WF; b. 22 Sep 1891 nr Ravensworth; father:
Wm. SEMONS; occ: Rail Rd. hand; res: nr Ravensworth; mother:
Ida SEMONS; inf: parents; pg:ln: 195:19

SENNIE?, Leo Carroll; WM; b. 23 Jun 1895 nr Pohick Church; father: H.
H. SENNIE?; occ: farmer; res: nr Pohick Church; mother: Maggie E.
SENNIE?; inf: father; pg:ln: 224:111

SETPHIN, Mary; WF; b. 5 May 1892 nr Clifton; father: John H.
SETPHIN; occ: farmer; res: nr Clifton; mother: Catharine SETPHIN;
inf: mother; pg:ln: 208:22

SEVERARY, not named; CM; b. 6 Feb 1884 in Ffx; father: Jno.
SEVERARY; occ: farmer; res: Ffx; mother: Mary SEVERARY; inf:
Jno. SEVERARY, father; pg:ln: 148:68

SEWALL, Marie Alice; WF; b. 15 Oct 1887 in Ffx; father: J. P. SEWALL;
occ: farmer; res: Ffx; mother: Mary E. SEWALL; inf: J. P. SEWALL,
father; pg:ln: 164:145

SEWALL, Wilber W.; WM; b. 18 Oct 1889 in Ffx; father: J. P. SEWALL;
occ: farmer; res: Ffx; mother: M. C. SEWALL; inf: J. P. SEWALL,
father; pg:ln: 180:110

SHANKS, Effie; WF; b. 30 Jun 1896 in Ffx; father: G. P. SHANKS; occ:
farmer; res: Ffx; mother: Dolly E. SHANKS; inf: G. P. SHANKS,
father; pg:ln: 228:115

SHARPER, Mary E.; CF; b. 8 Jul 1887 in Ffx; father: Sanford
SHARPER; occ: farmer; res: Ffx; mother: Mary SHARPER; inf: S.
SHARPER, father; pg:ln: 163:137

SHARPER, not named; CM; b. 9 May 1886 in Kenmore; father: Sam. H.
SHARPER; occ: mechanic; res: Kenmore; mother: Millie SHARPER;
inf: father; pg:ln: 159:59

SHAW, Fannie; WF; b. 24 Aug 1882 in Clouds Mill; father: Jno. T.
SHAW; occ: miller; res: Clouds Mill; mother: Ida R. SHAW; inf:
father; pg:ln: 135:60

SHAWE, Ina; WF; b. 15 Nov 1888 in Ffx; father: James SHAWE; occ:
    laborer; res: Ffx; mother: Lillie SHAWE; inf: J. SHAWE, father; pg:ln:
    171:62
SHAWEN, Ninna; WF; b. 6 Sep 1892 in Ffx; father: Chas. SHAWEN;
    occ: farmer; res: Ffx; mother: Rosa SHAWEN; inf: C. SHAWEN,
    father; pg:ln: 204:89
SHAWEN, Walter; WM; b. 12 Feb 1894 in Ffx; father: Chas. SHAWEN;
    occ: farmer; res: Ffx; mother: Rosabel SHAWEN; inf: Chas.
    SHAWEN, father; pg:ln: 219:109
SHELTON, ___; CF; b. 3 Jul 1881 in Ffx; father: W. SHELTON; occ:
    farmer; res: Ffx; mother: Milly SHELTON; inf: W. SHELTON, father;
    pg:ln: 133:50
SHELTON, Haywood (dead); CM; b. 21 Oct 1889 in Ffx; father: Watkin
    SHELTON; occ: farmer; res: Ffx; mother: Milly SHELTON; inf: W.
    SHELTON, father; pg:ln: 183:89
SHEPHERD, Alice; WF; b. 10 Sep 1887 in Ffx; father: Saml.
    SHEPHERD; occ: fisherman; res: Ffx; mother: Alice SHEPHERD;
    inf: S. SHEPHERD, father; pg:ln: 169:106
SHEPHERD, Bessie; WF; b. 17 Sep 1881 in Ffx; father: John
    SHEPHERD; occ: farmer; res: Ffx; mother: Bettie SHEPHERD; inf:
    Jno. SHEPHERD, father; pg:ln: 133:46
SHEPHERD, Charles; WM; b. 30 Nov 1893 nr Accotink; father: Chs.
    SHEPHERD; occ: fisherman; res: nr Accotink; mother: Jennie
    SHEPHERD; inf: parent; pg:ln: 212:90
SHEPHERD, Elenor; WF; b. 17 Jul 1881 in Ffx; father: James
    SHEPHERD; occ: farmer; res: Ffx; mother: Mary SHEPHERD; inf:
    Jas. SHEPHERD, father; pg:ln: 133:47
SHEPHERD, Gertie; WF; b. 9 Jan 1891 nr Accotink; father: Chas.
    SHEPHERD; occ: farmer; res: nr Accotink; mother: Jane
    SHEPHERD; inf: parents; pg:ln: 195:21
SHEPHERD, Harry; WM; b. 9 Jun 1889 in Ffx; father: Chas.
    SHEPHERD; occ: farmer; res: Ffx; mother: Jane SHEPHERD; inf: C.
    SHEPHERD, father; pg:ln: 183:91
SHEPHERD, Herbert Grey; WM; b. 26 Oct 1892 nr Accotink; father:
    Silos SHEPHERD; occ: farmer; res: Accotink; mother: Annie
    SHEPHERD; inf: mother; pg:ln: 207:90
SHEPHERD, John; CM; b. 21 Nov 1887 in Ffx; father: Williard
    SHEPHERD; occ: laborer; res: Ffx; mother: Mary SHEPHERD; inf:
    Willard SHEPHERD, father; pg:ln: 169:107
SHEPHERD, Lillie May; WF; b. 9 Jun 1892 nr Accotink; father: Samuel
    SHEPHERD; occ: fisherman; res: Accotink; mother: Alice
    SHEPHERD; inf: mother; pg:ln: 207:89
SHEPHERD, Maud; WF; b. 1 Oct 1885 in Ffx; father: Jas. SHEPHERD;
    occ: farmer; res: Ffx; mother: Jane SHEPHERD; inf: Jas.
    SHEPHERD, father; pg:ln: 157:54
SHEPHERD, May; CF; b. 1 May 1894 in Ffx; father: Douglas
    SHEPHERD; occ: farmer; res: Ffx; mother: Lydia SHEPHERD; inf:
    D. SHEPHERD, father; pg:ln: 219:112

SHEPHERD, Mollie; WF; b. 27 Oct 1890 in Ffx; father: Silas
  SHEPHERD; occ: farmer; res: Ffx; mother: Annie SHEPHERD; inf:
  S. SHEPHERD, father; pg:ln: 187:103
SHEPHERD, not named; CF; b. 15 Sep 1884 in Cloud's. Mill; father:
  Brown SHEPHERD; occ: laborer; res: Cloud's. Mill; mother:
  Georgianna SHEPHERD; inf: father; pg:ln: 151:84
SHEPHERD, not named; WM; b. 11 Dec 1892 nr Accotink; father: Chs.
  SHEPHERD; occ: farmer; res: nr Accotink; mother: Jane V.
  SHEPHERD; inf: mother; pg:ln: 207:91
SHEPHERD, Walter; WM; b. 2 Mar 1880 in ___; father: R. H.
  SHEPHERD; occ: farmer; res: Ffx; mother: Mary; inf: R. H.
  SHEPHERD, father; pg:ln: 129:90
SHERMAN, Caroline; WF; b. 6 Oct 1881 in Ash Grove; father: Franklin
  SHERMAN; occ: farmer; res: Ash Grove; mother: Caroline M. C. A.
  SHERMAN; inf: father; pg:ln: 131:63
SHERMAN, James; WM; b. 6 May 1890 in Ffx; father: Franklin
  SHERMAN; occ: farmer; res: Ffx; mother: Caroline SHERMAN; inf:
  F. SHERMAN, father; pg:ln: 191:87
SHERMAN, Jno. H.; WM; b. 22 Dec 1887 in Ffx; father: Franklin
  SHERMAN; occ: farmer; res: Ffx; mother: Caroline SHERMAN; inf:
  F. SHERMAN, father; pg:ln: 164:147
SHERMAN, Miriam; WF; b. 8 Jan 1880 in Ash Grove; father: Franklin
  SHERMAN; occ: farmer; res: Providence; mother: C. M. C. A.
  SHERMAN; inf: father; pg:ln: 125:68
SHERMAN, Theodore F.; WF; b. 9 Sep 1883 in Ash Grove; father:
  Franklin SHERMAN; occ: farmer; res: Ash Grove; mother: ___
  SHERMAN; inf: father; pg:ln: 141:87
SHERWOOD, ___; WF; b. 11 Feb 1880 in Ffx; father: Frank
  SHERWOOD; occ: farmer; res: Ffx; mother: Sarah; inf: F.
  SHERWOOD, father; pg:ln: 129:84
SHERWOOD, Jesse; WM; b. 24 Dec 1881 in Ffx; father: Frank
  SHERWOOD; occ: farmer; res: Ffx; mother: Sarah SHERWOOD;
  inf: F. SHERWOOD, father; pg:ln: 133:51
SHERWOOD, Joseph; WM; b. 18 Jan 1891 in Warrenton Pike; father:
  L. F. SHERWOOD; occ: farmer; res: nr Warrenton Pike; mother:
  Sarah SHERWOOD; inf: parents; pg:ln: 194:20
SHERWOOD, Josephine; WF; b. 7 Aug 1883 in Providence Dist.;
  father: R. J. SHERWOOD; occ: farmer; res: Providence Dist.;
  mother: M. B. SHERWOOD; inf: father; pg:ln: 141:91
SHERWOOD, Luther; WM; b. 5 Jan 1884 in Ffx; father: Frank
  SHERWOOD; occ: farmer; res: Ffx; mother: Sarah SHERWOOD;
  inf: F. SHERWOOD, father; pg:ln: 148:67
SHERWOOD, Thos.; WM; b. 25 Jun 1892 nr Fairfax C. H.; father: Frank
  SHERWOOD; occ: gardener; res: nr Fairfax C. H.; mother: Sarah
  SHERWOOD; inf: father; pg:ln: 208:23
SHIPMAN, Geo.; WM; b. 4 Jul 1894 in Ffx; father: Steven SHIPMAN;
  occ: farmer; res: Ffx; mother: Mary SHIPMAN; inf: S. SHIPMAN,
  father; pg:ln: 219:110

SHIPMAN, Henrietta; WF; b. 5 Aug 1887 in Ffx; father: Stephen SHIPMAN; occ: farmer; res: Ffx; mother: Mary E. SHIPMAN; inf: S. SHIPMAN, father; pg:ln: 164:148

SHIPMAN, Lucy T.; WF; b. 15 Oct 1882 in Lewinsville; father: Mason SHIPMAN; occ: farmer; res: Lewinsville; mother: Caroline SHIPMAN; inf: father; pg:ln: 135:58

SHIPMAN, R. E. Lee; WM; b. 13 Mar 1889 in Ffx; father: Stephen SHIPMAN; occ: farmer; res: Ffx; mother: Mary E. SHIPMAN; inf: S. SHIPMAN, father; pg:ln: 179:107

SHIPMAN, S. P.; WM; b. 8 Jun 1893 in ___; father: S. P. SHIPMAN; occ: farmer; res: ___; mother: H. R. SHIPMAN; inf: S. P. SHIPMAN, father; pg:ln: 215:86

SHIPMAN, Sarah; WF; b. 6 Dec 1891 in Ffx; father: Stephen SHIPMAN; occ: farmer; res: Ffx; mother: Mary SHIPMAN; inf: S. SHIPMAN, father; pg:ln: 200:88

SHIPMAN, W. N.; CM; b. 19 Jul 1896 in Ffx; father: S. E. SHIPMAN; occ: farmer; res: Ffx; mother: Mary SHIPMAN; inf: S. E. SHIPMAN, father; pg:ln: 228:113

SHIPMAN, Willard T.; WM; b. 23 Dec 1884 in Prov.; father: Stephen E. SHIPMAN; occ: farmer; res: Prov.; mother: Mary SHIPMAN; inf: father; pg:ln: 151:81

SHIRLEY, A. S.; CM; b. 19 Jul 1891 in Ffx; father: A. T. SHIRLEY; occ: farmer; res: Ffx; mother: Martha SHIRLEY; inf: A. T. SHIRLEY, father; pg:ln: 200:98

SHIRLEY, Jos. R.; CM; b. 22 Dec 1893 in ___; father: Arch. T. SHIRLEY; occ: farmer; res: ___; mother: Martha SHIRLEY; inf: A. T. SHIRLEY, father; pg:ln: 215:92

SHORTER, Bertha; CF; b. 9 Nov 1889 in Ffx; father: Henry SHORTER; occ: farmer; res: Ffx; mother: Eva M. SHORTER; inf: H. SHORTER, father; pg:ln: 183:90

SHORTER, Catherine; CF; b. 1 Oct 1880 in Providence; father: Edward SHORTER; occ: laborer; res: Providence; mother: Charity SHORTER; inf: father; pg:ln: 125:69

SHORTER, Jarret; CM; b. 23 May 1891 in Sheridans Point; father: Henry SHORTER; occ: fisherman; res: Sheridans Point; mother: Eva Ann SHORTER; inf: parent; pg:ln: 196:19

SHREEVE, Dora M.; WF; b. 31 Jan 1893 in ___; father: B. B. SHREEVE; occ: farmer; res: ___; mother: Dora L. SHREEVE; inf: B. B. SHREEVE, father; pg:ln: 215:84

SHREEVE, Pearle; WF; b. 24 Sep 1891 in Ffx; father: B. R. SHREEVES; occ: farmer; res: Ffx; mother: Ida SHREEVE; inf: B. R. SHREEVE, father; pg:ln: 200:89

SHREEVE, Rust; WF; b. 20 Feb 1892 in Ffx; father: B. B. SHREEVE; occ: farmer; res: Ffx; mother: Dora SHREEVE; inf: B. B. SHREEVE, father; pg:ln: 204:85

SHREVE, Carroll V.; WM; b. 16 Mar 1884 in Fairfax; father: Wm. H. SHREVE; occ: farmer; res: Fairfax; mother: ___ SHREVE; inf: father; pg:ln: 151:82

SHREVE, Co[r]nelia A.; WF; b. 14 Nov 1884 in Falls Church; father: John SHREVE; occ: farmer; res: Falls Church; mother: Laura SHREVE; inf: father; pg:ln: 151:83

SHREVE, Earnest; WM; b. 10 Nov 1885 nr Falls Church; father: Robert SHREVE; occ: farmer; res: nr Falls Church; mother: Anna SHREVE; inf: father; pg:ln: 154:74

SHREVE, Gracie; WF; b. 5 May 1886 in Falls Church; father: Robt. H. SHREVE; occ: farmer; res: Falls Church; mother: Annah SHREVE; inf: father; pg:ln: 159:58

SHREVE, not named (dead); WM; b. 9 Mar 1882 in Falls Church; father: Jno. W. SHREVE; occ: farmer; res: Falls Ch; mother: Laura J. SHREVE; inf: father; pg:ln: 135:78

SHREVE, R. F.; WM; b. 14 Aug 1882 in Falls Church; father: J. Frank SHREVE; occ: farmer; res: Falls Church; mother: Martha SHREVE; inf: father; pg:ln: 135:59

SHUGARS, Cassie; WF; b. 2 Aug 1893 in ___; father: Jas. SHUGARS; occ: farmer; res: ___; mother: Cassie SHUGARS; inf: J. SHUGARS, father; pg:ln: 215:88

SHYBOLD, Magdaline; WF; b. 13 May 1892 in Ffx; father: Jno. SHYBOLD; occ: farmer; res: Ffx; mother: Maggie SHYBOLD; inf: Jno. SHYBOLD, father; pg:ln: 204:98

SIMIS, Joseph; CM; b. 9 Sep 1885 in Herndon; father: Henry SIMIS; occ: mechanic; res: Herndon; mother: Annie SIMIS; inf: father; pg:ln: 154:78

SIMMS, ___ (twin); CM; b. 15 Feb 1883 in Ffx; father: Wm. SIMMS; occ: farmer; res: Ffx; mother: Mary E. SIMMS; inf: W. SIMMS, father; pg:ln: 145:76

SIMMS, ___ (twin, dead); CF; b. 15 Feb 1883 in Ffx; father: Wm. SIMMS; occ: farmer; res: Ffx; mother: Mary E. SIMMS; inf: W. SIMMS, father; pg:ln: 145:77

SIMMS, Algerney (twin); WM; b. 22 Feb 1895 nr Franconia; father: Samuel SIMMS; occ: farmer; res: nr Franconia; mother: Sarah Jane SIMMS; inf: mother; pg:ln: 224:114

SIMMS, Bessie; WF; b. 8 Sep 1891 nr Hayfield; father: Daniel SIMMS; occ: farmer; res: nr Hayfield; mother: Bessie SIMMS; inf: parents; pg:ln: 195:20

SIMMS, Frank; WM; b. 1 Feb 1881 in Ffx; father: Craven SIMMS; occ: farmer; res: Ffx; mother: Rose SIMMS; inf: C. SIMMS, father; pg:ln: 133:44

SIMMS, Henry; CM; b. 16 Feb 1896 in Ffx; father: Geo. T. SIMMS; occ: farmer; res: Ffx; mother: Julia SIMMS; inf: G. T. SIMMS, father; pg:ln: 228:119

SIMMS, Maggie; CF; b. 5 Jun 1894 in Ffx; father: Geo. SIMMS; occ: farmer; res: Ffx; mother: Julia SIMMS; inf: Geo. SIMMS, father; pg:ln: 219:105

SIMMS, Mary; CF; b. 1 Aug 1887 in Ffx; father: Daniel SIMMS; occ: farmer; res: Ffx; mother: Martha SIMMS; inf: D. SIMMS, father; pg:ln: 164:139

SIMMS, not named; WM; b. 5 Jan 1887 in Ffx; father: Craven SIMMS; occ: farmer; res: Ffx; mother: Rosina SIMMS; inf: Craven SIMMS, father; pg:ln: 169:105

SIMMS, Rebecca; CF; b. 15 Jun 1890 in Ffx; father: Chas. THOMPSON; occ: farmer; res: Ffx; mother: Rebecca SIMMS; inf: R. SIMMS, mother; pg:ln: 191:92

SIMMS, Rollin Ashley (twin); WM; b. 22 Feb 1895 in Hayfield; father: Geo. W. SIMMS; occ: farmer; res: Hayfield; mother: Albina W. SIMMS; inf: mother; pg:ln: 224:113

SIMONS, Benj.; CM; b. 4 Jul 1881 in Ffx; father: Wesley SIMONS; occ: farmer; res: Ffx; mother: Elizabt. SIMONS; inf: W. SIMONS, father; pg:ln: 133:52

SIMPSON, Edith V.; WF; b. 8 Sep 1891 nr Clifton; father: Edward SIMPSON; occ: farmer; res: nr Clifton; mother: Susie SIMPSON; inf: parents; pg:ln: 194:22

SIMPSON, Effie; WF; b. 6 Sep 1892 in Village adj Alex.; father: Wm. G. SIMPSON; occ: ___; res: Village adj Alex.; mother: Hettie SIMPSON; inf: father; pg:ln: 207:88

SIMPSON, Eva; WF; b. 12 Dec 1880 in Ffx; father: Geo. C. SIMPSON; occ: farmer; res: Ffx; mother: Mary M.; inf: G. C. SIMPSON, father; pg:ln: 129:81

SIMPSON, Geo. Edwd.; WM; b. 21 Feb 1889 in Ffx; father: G. C. SIMPSON; occ: farmer; res: Ffx; mother: Nina SIMPSON; inf: G. C. SIMPSON, father; pg:ln: 183:88

SIMPSON, James Bruce; WM; b. 30 Dec 1892 nr Lee Chapel; father: James H. SIMPSON; occ: farmer; res: nr Lee Chapel; mother: Ellen M. SIMPSON; inf: mother; pg:ln: 209:55

SIMPSON, Leola; WF; b. 28 Jun 1887 in Ffx; father: M. E. SIMPSON; occ: farmer; res: Ffx; mother: R. F. SIMPSON; inf: M. E. SIMPSON, father; pg:ln: 164:150

SIMPSON, Mitchell; WM; b. 17 May 1893 nr Fairfax Sta.; father: Geo. C. SIMPSON; occ: farmer; res: nr Fairfax Sta.; mother: Mary M. SIMPSON; inf: parent; pg:ln: 212:86

SIMPSON, Rosa; WF; b. 11 Jun 1888 in Ffx; father: Henry C. SIMPSON; occ: mechanic; res: Ffx; mother: Annie SIMPSON; inf: H. C. SIMPSON, father; pg:ln: 171:57

SIMPSON, W. H.; WM; b. 4 Dec 1881 in Ffx; father: Geo. C. SIMPSON; occ: farmer; res: Ffx; mother: Mary SIMPSON; inf: G. C. SIMPSON, father; pg:ln: 133:49

SIMS, Mary; CF; b. 5 Oct 1883 in Dranesville; father: Henry SIMS; occ: mechanic; res: Dranesville; mother: Annie SIMS; inf: father; pg:ln: 141:97

SINKFIELD, Sarah; CF; b. 17 Jan 1887 in Ffx; father: Richd. SINKFIELD; occ: farmer; res: Ffx; mother: Julia SINKFIELD; inf: R. SINKFIELD, father; pg:ln: 163:138

SISSON, Edith; WF; b. 16 May 1891 nr Fairfax C. H.; father: Samuel SISSON; occ: farmer; res: Braddock Rd.; mother: Cora V. SISSON; inf: parents; pg:ln: 193:25

SISSON, Edward; WM; b. 11 Apr 1895 nr Fairfax C. H.; father: Samuel
SISSON; occ: farmer; res: nr Fairfax C. H.; mother: Cora L. SISSON
[initial F. lined out]; inf: father; pg:ln: 224:109

SKILLMAN, ___; WF; b. 22 Dec 1896 in Ffx; father: J. B. SKILLMAN;
occ: farmer; res: Ffx; mother: Annie SKILLMAN; inf: J. B.
SKILLMAN, father; pg:ln: 228:114

SKILLMAN, Maud; WF; b. 7 Jun 1880 in ___; father: W. SKILLMAN;
occ: farmer; res: Ffx; mother: Sarah E.; inf: W. SKILLMAN, father;
pg:ln: 129:87

SKINNER, ___; WM; b. 24 Apr 1883 in Dranesville; father: A. J.
SKINNER; occ: farmer; res: Dranesville; mother: Helen S.
SKINNER; inf: father; pg:ln: 141:94

SKINNER, not named (dead); WF; b. 23 Sep 1882 in Langley; father:
Robt. SKINNER; occ: farmer; res: Langley; mother: Ida SKINNER;
inf: father; pg:ln: 135:79

SKINNER, not named; WF; b. 5 Jul 1887 in Ffx; father: Sylvester
SKINNER; occ: farmer; res: Ffx; mother: Kate SKINNER; inf:
Sylvester SKINNER, father; pg:ln: 169:104

SLACK, Helena H.; WF; b. 19 Oct 1887 in Ffx; father: Stanly J. SLACK;
occ: farmer; res: Ffx; mother: Gertrude SLACK; inf: S. J. SLACK,
father; pg:ln: 163:136

SLADE, Cook; WM; b. 17 Jul 1891 in Ffx; father: C. F. SLADE; occ:
farmer; res: Ffx; mother: S. E. SLADE; inf: C. F. SLADE, father;
pg:ln: 200:94

SLADE, Elizabt.; WF; b. 25 Dec 1890 in Ffx; father: Cook F. SLADE;
occ: farmer; res: Ffx; mother: Sarah E. SLADE; inf: C. F. SLADE,
father; pg:ln: 191:86

SLAUGHTER, Julian; WM; b. 24 Aug 1887 in Ffx; father: Richd.
SLAUGHTER; occ: farmer; res: Ffx; mother: Rosa SLAUGHTER; inf:
R. SLAUGHTER, father; pg:ln: 164:143

SLAYTON, Dollie; WF; b. 17 Apr 1887 in Ffx; father: Wm. S. SLAYTON;
occ: farmer; res: Ffx; mother: Julia SLAYTON; inf: Wm. S.
SLAYTON, father; pg:ln: 169:103

SLAYTON, Flora; WF; b. 15 Apr 1881 in Ffx; father: Willie SLAYTON;
occ: farmer; res: Ffx; mother: Julia SLAYTON; inf: W. SLAYTON,
father; pg:ln: 133:53

SLAYTON, Roswell; WM; b. 19 Oct 1882 in Ffx; father: Wm. SLAYTON;
occ: ___; res: ___; mother: Julia SLAYTON; inf: Wm. SLAYTON,
father; pg:ln: 137:76

SLAYTON, Roy; WM; b. 12 Apr 1889 in Ffx; father: W. S. SLAYTON;
occ: farmer; res: Ffx; mother: Julia SLAYTON; inf: W. S. SLAYTON,
father; pg:ln: 183:86

SMARR, Charles McC.; WM; b. 4 Sep 1887 in Ffx; father: Charles
SMARR; occ: farmer; res: Ffx; mother: Osie SMARR; inf: Chas.
SMARR, father; pg:ln: 169:101

SMITH, ___ (dead); CM; b. 11 Nov 1882 in Ffx; father: Harrison SMITH;
occ: ___; res: ___; mother: Matilda SMITH; inf: H. SMITH, father;
pg:ln: 137:68

SMITH, ___; WM; b. 21 Mar 1887 in Ffx; father: Jno. H. SMITH; occ: farmer; res: Ffx; mother: Elizabt. SMITH; inf: J. H. SMITH, father; pg:ln: 163:134

SMITH, Alfred T.; WM; b. 28 Feb 1889 in Ffx; father: Henry SMITH; occ: farmer; res: Ffx; mother: Bell SMITH; inf: H. SMITH, father; pg:ln: 179:102

SMITH, Annie E.; CF; b. 28 Jan 1888 in Ffx; father: W. SMITH; occ: farmer; res: Ffx; mother: Annie E. SMITH; inf: W. SMITH, father; pg:ln: 175:92

SMITH, Annie; WF; b. 15 Aug 1889 in Ffx; father: W. SMITH; occ: farmer; res: Ffx; mother: Annie SMITH; inf: W. SMITH, father; pg:ln: 179:101

SMITH, Bertha; WF; b. 10 Oct 1890 in Ffx; father: W. SMITH; occ: farmer; res: Ffx; mother: Marianna SMITH; inf: W. SMITH, father; pg:ln: 191:88

SMITH, Carrie; WF; b. 15 May 1889 in Ffx; father: Jno. H. SMITH; occ: farmer; res: Ffx; mother: E. B. SMITH; inf: J. H. SMITH, father; pg:ln: 179:100

SMITH, Chester L.; WM; b. 14 Jun 1882 nr C. H.; father: S. Ernest SMITH; occ: mcht.; res: nr C. H.; mother: Ellen J. SMITH; inf: father; pg:ln: 135:56

SMITH, Chester; CM; b. 31 Jul 1896 in Ffx; father: Benj. SMITH; occ: farmer; res: Ffx; mother: Rose SMITH; inf: B. SMITH, father; pg:ln: 227:108

SMITH, Elizabeth; CF; b. 27 Dec 1888 in Ffx; father: Chas. SMITH; occ: farmer; res: Ffx; mother: Jemima SMITH; inf: Chas. SMITH, father; pg:ln: 171:64

SMITH, Eva; WF; b. 4 Apr 1885 in Prov.; father: Geo. W. SMITH; occ: farmer; res: Prov.; mother: Mary E. SMITH; inf: father; pg:ln: 154:77

SMITH, Florence R.; WF; b. 31 Jan 1884 in Vienna; father: Henry SMITH; occ: farmer; res: Vienna; mother: Belle SMITH; inf: father; pg:ln: 151:80

SMITH, Gertrude; WF; b. 19 Oct 1891 in Ffx; father: J. H. SMITH; occ: farmer; res: Ffx; mother: Lela SMITH; inf: J. H. SMITH, father; pg:ln: 200:91

SMITH, Golder; CM; b. 24 Nov 1890 in Ffx; father: Saml. D. SMITH; occ: farmer; res: Ffx; mother: Jennie SMITH; inf: S. D. SMITH, father; pg:ln: 191:91

SMITH, Hattie B.; CF; b. 12 Aug 1880 in Dranesville; father: William SMITH; occ: laborer; res: Dranesville; mother: Annie E. SMITH; inf: father; pg:ln: 125:67

SMITH, Ida M.; CF; b. 12 Oct 1881 in Dranesville; father: William SMITH; occ: laborer; res: Dranesville; mother: Annie E. SMITH; inf: father; pg:ln: 131:67

SMITH, Jesse LeRoy (twin); WM; b. 23 Sep 1883 in Oakton; father: S. E. SMITH; occ: merchant; res: Oakton; mother: E. G. SMITH; inf: father; pg:ln: 141:95

SMITH, Jno. H.; CM; b. 26 Jul 1884 in Bailey's X Road; father: Andrew SMITH; occ: laborer; res: Bailey's X Road; mother: Sarah SMITH; inf: father; pg:ln: 151:79

SMITH, Linton; WM; b. 9 Jun 1886 in Seminary; father: Alexis SMITH; occ: farmer; res: Seminary; mother: Mary SMITH; inf: father; pg:ln: 159:54

SMITH, Margery Louise (twin); WF; b. 23 Sep 1883 in Oakton; father: S. E. SMITH; occ: merchant; res: Oakton; mother: E. G. SMITH; inf: father; pg:ln: 141:96

SMITH, Mary; CF; b. 23 Oct 1891 in Ffx; father: Saml. D. SMITH; occ: farmer; res: Ffx; mother: Jennie SMITH; inf: S. D. SMITH, father; pg:ln: 200:97

SMITH, Maurice; WM; b. 4 Jun 1893 in ___; father: W. SMITH; occ: farmer; res: ___; mother: Mirian SMITH; inf: W. SMITH, father; pg:ln: 215:90

SMITH, Owen; WM; b. 28 Jun 1889 in Ffx; father: W. SMITH; occ: farmer; res: Ffx; mother: Marian SMITH; inf: W. SMITH, father; pg:ln: 179:103

SMITH, Sidney; WM; b. 7 Jul 1880 in Seminary; father: Alexis SMITH; occ: merchant; res: Falls Church; mother: Mary SMITH; inf: father; pg:ln: 125:72

SMITH, Warren; WM; b. 22 Nov 1886 in Dranes.; father: William SMITH; occ: farmer; res: Dranes.; mother: M. W. SMITH; inf: father; pg:ln: 159:61

SMOOT, James; WM; b. 13 Dec 1890 in Ffx; father: G. W. SMOOT; occ: farmer; res: Ffx; mother: Jennie SMOOT; inf: G. W. SMOOT, father; pg:ln: 187:104

SMOOT, Jno. D.; WM; b. 3 Mar 1883 in Lewinsville; father: W. S. SMOOT; occ: farmer; res: Lewinsville; mother: Jane SMOOT; inf: father; pg:ln: 141:90

SNIDER, Daisy; WF; b. 28 Apr 1885 in Dranes.; father: E. T. SNIDER; occ: farmer; res: Dranes.; mother: Martha SNIDER; inf: father; pg:ln: 154:79

SNIDER, Turner F.; WM; b. 28 Jan 1890 in Ffx; father: E. F. SNIDER; occ: farmer; res: Ffx; mother: Martha SNIDER; inf: E. F. SNIDER, father; pg:ln: 191:95

SNIDER, Turner; WM; b. 20 Jan 1891 in Ffx; father: E. T. SNIDER; occ: farmer; res: Ffx; mother: Martha SNIDER; inf: E. T. SNIDER, father; pg:ln: 200:92

SNOOK, Nettie R.; WF; b. 29 Sep 1889 in Ffx; father: C. W. SNOOK; occ: farmer; res: Ffx; mother: Mollie SNOOK; inf: C. W. SNOOK, father; pg:ln: 180:109

SNYDER, Cora L.; CF; b. 1 Dec 1884 in Ffx; father: Grandison SNYDER; occ: farmer; res: Ffx; mother: Emma SNYDER; inf: G. SNYDER, father; pg:ln: 148:70

SNYDER, Olaf E.; WM; b. 14 Aug 1896 in Ffx; father: Chas. SNYDER; occ: farmer; res: Ffx; mother: Eva SNYDER; inf: Chas. SNYDER, father; pg:ln: 228:117

SOONS, Agnes; WF; b. 28 Feb 1890 in Ffx; father: Geo. SOONS; occ: farmer; res: Ffx; mother: Catharine SOONS; inf: Geo. SOONS, father; pg:ln: 187:105

SOONS, Geo. L. D.; WM; b. 17 May 1892 in Alexandria; father: Geo. SOONS; occ: ___; res: West End; mother: Catharine SOONS; inf: mother; pg:ln: 209:42

SORRELL, Cora (twin); WF; b. 14 Jul 1892 in Ffx; father: J. F. SORRELL; occ: farmer; res: Ffx; mother: Laura SORRELL; inf: J. F. SORRELL, father; pg:ln: 204:94

SORRELL, Dora (twin); WF; b. 14 Jul 1892 in Ffx; father: J. F. SORRELL; occ: farmer; res: Ffx; mother: Laura SORRELL; inf: J. F. SORRELL, father; pg:ln: 204:95

SORRELL, Jno. F.; WM; b. 12 Apr 1889 in Ffx; father: Jno. F. SORRELL; occ: farmer; res: Ffx; mother: Laura SORRELL; inf: J. F. SORRELL, father; pg:ln: 179:106

SOVEREIGN, Geo. R.; WM; b. 7 Sep 1883 in Providence Dist.; father: B. SOVEREIGN; occ: farmer; res: Providence Dist.; mother: Lula SOVEREIGN; inf: father; pg:ln: 141:92

SPAULDING, Emma A.; WF; b. 3 Jun 1880 in Providence; father: R. C. SPAULDING; occ: plasterer; res: Providence; mother: Sarah H. SPAULDING; inf: father; pg:ln: 125:70

SPAULDING, R. C.; WM; b. 18 Aug 1894 in Ffx; father: R. C. SPAULDING; occ: farmer; res: Ffx; mother: M. E. SPAULDING; inf: R. C. SPAULDING, father; pg:ln: 219:108

SPEER, Celia B.; WF; b. 29 Sep 1887 in Ffx; father: C. H. SPEER; occ: farmer; res: Ffx; mother: S. A. SPEER; inf: C. H. SPEER, father; pg:ln: 164:149

SPEER, G. E.; WM; b. 26 Oct 1892 in Ffx; father: D. E. SPEER; occ: farmer; res: Ffx; mother: Mary SPEER; inf: D. E. SPEER, father; pg:ln: 204:88

SPEER, not named; WF; b. 28 Aug 1883 in Providence Dist.; father: C. H. SPEER; occ: farmer; res: Providence Dist.; mother: Sarah A. SPEER; inf: father; pg:ln: 141:88

SPEER, W.; WM; b. 3 May 1889 in Ffx; father: C. H. SPEER; occ: farmer; res: Ffx; mother: Sarah SPEER; inf: C. H. SPEER, father; pg:ln: 179:99

SPICER, Verona A.; WF; b. 18 Feb 1887 in Ffx; father: Alvah SPICER; occ: farmer; res: Ffx; mother: Almeda SPICER; inf: A. SPICER, father; pg:ln: 164:142

SPINDLE, Agnis; WF; b. 21 Nov 1880 in ___; father: Robt. L. SPINDLE; occ: farmer; res: Ffx; mother: Virginia; inf: R. L. SPINDLE, father; pg:ln: 129:86

SPITTLE, Rena; WF; b. 3 Mar 1890 in Ffx; father: Matthew SPITTLE; occ: farmer; res: Ffx; mother: Susan SPITTLE; inf: M. SPITTLE, father; pg:ln: 187:102

SPRINGMAN, Albt.; WM; b. 14 Feb 1889 in Ffx; father: G. W. SPRINGMAN; occ: farmer; res: Ffx; mother: Louisa SPRINGMAN; inf: G. W. SPRINGMAN, father; pg:ln: 183:85

SPRINGMAN, Jno. Guy; WM; b. 13 Aug 1888 in Ffx; father: J. M.
SPRINGMAN; occ: merchant; res: Ffx; mother: Emma J.
SPRINGMAN; inf: J. M. SPRINGMAN, father; pg:ln: 171:60

SPRINGMAN, Leonard; WM; b. 1 Oct 1893 nr Stoneleigh; father: G. W.
SPRINGMAN; occ: farmer; res: nr Stoneleigh; mother: Louisa
SPRINGMAN; inf: parent; pg:ln: 212:87

SPRINGMAN, Mabel; WF; b. 20 Oct 1888 in Ffx; father: Geo. W.
SPRINGMAN; occ: farmer; res: Ffx; mother: Louisa SPRINGMAN;
inf: Geo. W. SPRINGMAN, father; pg:ln: 171:61

STAATS, Guy L.; WM; b. 6 Oct 1896 in Ffx; father: Jas. STAATS; occ:
farmer; res: Ffx; mother: Tinie STAATS; inf: Jas. STAATS, father;
pg:ln: 228:116

STAMBAUGH, Annie M.; WF; b. 17 May 1896 in Ffx; father: Geo.
STAMBAUGH; occ: Gov. clerk; res: Ffx; mother: Alice
STAMBAUGH; inf: Geo. STAMBAUGH, father; pg:ln: 228:112

STARR, Mary; CF; b. 15 Sep 1892 in Ffx; father: Wash'n. STARR; occ:
farmer; res: Ffx; mother: Eva STARR; inf: W. STARR, father; pg:ln:
204:97

STARRIN, Arthur; WM; b. 4 Jun 1889 in Ffx; father: Albt. STAR[R]IN;
occ: farmer; res: Ffx; mother: Mary STARRIN; inf: A. STARRIN,
father; pg:ln: 179:108

STEARNS, Chas. M.; WM; b. 10 Jul 1883 in Falls Church; father: Jno.
M. STEARNS; occ: farmer; res: Falls Church; mother: Melinda
STEARNS; inf: father; pg:ln: 141:85

STEEL, Lottie; WF; b. __ Nov 1880 in ___; father: Jno. T. STEEL; occ:
farmer; res: Ffx; mother: Ida; inf: J. T. STEEL, father; pg:ln: 129:88

STEELE, Anna M.; WF; b. 25 Feb 1884 in Ffx; father: Jno. W. STEELE;
occ: farmer; res: Ffx; mother: Mary STEELE; inf: J. W. STEELE,
father; pg:ln: 148:69

STEELE, Frederick; WM; b. 8 Oct 1892 nr Burke Sta.; father: Edgar
STEELE; occ: farmer; res: nr Burke Sta.; mother: Ruth C. STEELE;
inf: motner; pg:ln: 209:56

STEELE, Geo. R.; WM; b. 21 Jul 1881 in Ffx; father: Jno. W. STEELE;
occ: farmer; res: Ffx; mother: Mary STEELE; inf: J. W. STEELE,
father; pg:ln: 133:48

STEELE, Harvey; WM; b. 10 Feb 1882 in Ffx; father: Edgar STEELE;
occ: ___; res: ___; mother: R. C. STEELE; inf: E. STEELE, father;
pg:ln: 137:72

STEELE, Lee; WM; b. 7 Jul 1880 in Ffx; father: Edgar STEELE; occ:
farmer; res: Ffx; mother: R. C.; inf: E. STEELE, father. Attached
note: applicant states that the date of his birth is July 5, 1880.; pg:ln:
129:80

STEELE, Richd. E.; WM; b. 3 Jul 1885 in Ffx; father: Edgar STEELE;
occ: farmer; res: Ffx; mother: R. C. STEELE; inf: E. STEELE, father;
pg:ln: 157:55

STEELE, Susie A.; WF; b. 2 Mar 1882 in Ffx; father: Jno. T. STEELE;
occ: ___; res: ___; mother: A. V. STEELE; inf: Jno. T. STEELE,
father; pg:ln: 137:71

STEER, not named; WM; b. 28 Aug 1881 in near C. H.; father: Chas. H.
SPEER; occ: farmer; res: near C. H.; mother: Sarah A. SPEER; inf:
father; pg:ln: 131:62

STEWART, Alice E.; WF; b. 30 Oct 1893 in ___; father: Jno. R.
STEWART; occ: farmer; res: ___; mother: Elizabt. STEWART; inf: J.
R. STEWART, father; pg:ln: 215:89

STEWART, Alice; CF; b. 14 Jun 1884 in Falls Ch.; father: William
STEWART; occ: laborer; res: Falls Ch.; mother: Adaline STEWART;
inf: father; pg:ln: 151:85

STEWART, Annie L.; WF; b. 6 Feb 1888 in Ffx; father: G. W.
STEWART; occ: farmer; res: Ffx; mother: A. L. STEWART; inf: G.
W. STEWART, father; pg:ln: 175:86

STEWART, Elizabeth; WF; b. 21 Jan 1885 in Prov.; father: J. R.
STEWART; occ: farmer; res: Prov.; mother: Elizabeth STEWART;
inf: father; pg:ln: 154:75

STEWART, Everit E.; CM; b. 12 Oct 1890 in Ffx; father: Frank
STEWART; occ: farmer; res: Ffx; mother: Carrie STEWART; inf: F.
STEWART, father; pg:ln: 191:94

STEWART, Harvey E.; CM; b. 12 Dec 1887 in Ffx; father: Frank
STEWART; occ: laborer; res: Ffx; mother: Carrie STEWART; inf: F.
STEWART, father; pg:ln: 164:151

STEWART, Jane S.; CF; b. 25 Jun 1882 in Falls Church; father: William
STEWART; occ: laborer; res: Falls Church; mother: Adaline
STEWART; inf: father; pg:ln: 135:54

STEWART, Jno. R. J.; WM; b. 9 Sep 1888 in Ffx; father: Jno. R.
STEWART; occ: farmer; res: Ffx; mother: E. C. STEWART; inf: J. R.
STEWART, father; pg:ln: 175:87

STEWART, Lettese; CF; b. 3 Dec 1893 in ___; father: Frank
STEWART; occ: farmer; res: ___; mother: Carrie STEWART; inf: F.
STEWART, father; pg:ln: 215:91

STEWART, Magdaline; WF; b. 30 May 1893 in ___; father: W.
STEWART; occ: farmer; res: ___; mother: Adline STEWART; inf: W.
STEWART, father; pg:ln: 215:85

STEWART, Maggie; WF; b. 1 Jun 1881 in Ffx; father: A. T. STEWART;
occ: farmer; res: Ffx; mother: Annie STEWART; inf: A. T.
STEWART, father; pg:ln: 133:43

STEWART, Maria L.; WF; b. 31 Jan 1892 in Ffx; father: Chas.
STEWART; occ: farmer; res: Ffx; mother: Mary STEWART; inf: C.
STEWART, father; pg:ln: 204:84

STEWART, Mary E.; WF; b. 23 Mar 1887 in Ffx; father: Chas. D. N.
STEWART; occ: farmer; res: Ffx; mother: Emily STEWART; inf: C.
D. N. STEWART, father; pg:ln: 163:132

STEWART, Rose; WF; b. 16 Apr 1887 in Ffx; father: Jno. R.
STEWART; occ: farmer; res: Ffx; mother: Elizabt. STEWART; inf: J.
R. STEWART, father; pg:ln: 163:131

STILES, Wm. Edward; WM; b. 13 May 1893 nr Stoneleigh; father: John
P. STILES; occ: farmer; res: nr Stoneleigh; mother: Catharine V.
STILES; inf: parent; pg:ln: 212:89

STONE, Agness; WF; b. 24 Aug 1896 nr Stoneleigh; father: J. C.
STONE; occ: farmer; res: nr Stoneleigh; mother: Ella STONE; inf:
father; pg:ln: 232:118

STONE, Conrad; WM; b. 25 Nov 1883 in Ffx; father: Thos. K. STONE;
occ: farmer; res: Ffx; mother: Marie STONE; inf: T. K. STONE,
father; pg:ln: 145:74

STONE, Effie; WF; b. 8 Sep 1882 in Ffx; father: Jas. E. STONE; occ:
___; res: ___; mother: Sarah C. STONE; inf: J. E. STONE, father;
pg:ln: 137:74

STONE, Francis; WM; b. 28 Mar 1887 in Ffx; father: T. K. STONE; occ:
farmer; res: Ffx; mother: Massie STONE; inf: T. K. STONE, father;
pg:ln: 169:100

STONE, Hobert Mc.; WM; b. 11 Feb 1896 in Ffx; father: M. H. STONE;
occ: farmer; res: Ffx; mother: Dora STONE; inf: M. M. STONE,
father; pg:ln: 228:109

STONE, Maggie May (twin); WF; b. 29 Feb 1880 in Ffx; father: Thos. K.
STONE; occ: farmer; res: Ffx; mother: Mary; inf: T. K. STONE,
father; pg:ln: 129:82

STONE, Manie Lee (twin); WF; b. 29 Feb 1880 in Ffx; father: Thos. K.
STONE; occ: farmer; res: Ffx; mother: Mary; inf: T. K. STONE,
father; pg:ln: 129:83

STONE, not named (dead); CF; b. 20 May 1886 in Fairfax; father: M. H.
STONE; occ: farmer; res: Fairfax; mother: Dora STONE; inf: father;
pg:ln: 159:56

STONE, Sangster; CM; b. 20 Apr 1887 in Ffx; father: Milton STONE;
occ: farmer; res: Ffx; mother: Dora STONE; inf: M. STONE, father;
pg:ln: 164:144

STONE, Willis; WM; b. 22 Sep 1891 nr Farr P.O.; father: Rob L.
STONE; occ: farmer; res: nr Farr P.O.; mother: M. V. STONE; inf:
parents; pg:ln: 193:27

STONEBURNER, Grace; WF; b. 17 Oct 1891 in Ffx; father: T. R.
STONEBURNER; occ: farmer; res: Ffx; mother: Rebecca
STONEBURNER; inf: T. R. STONEBURNER, father; pg:ln: 200:93

STONEBURNER, Minnie; WF; b. 9 Jun 1894 in Ffx; father: David E.
STONEBURNER; occ: farmer; res: Ffx; mother: Ada
STONEBURNER; inf: D. E. STONEBURNER, father; pg:ln: 219:111

STONEBURNER, Myrtle; WF; b. 14 Apr 1896 in Ffx; father: D. E.
STONEBURNER; occ: blacksmith; res: Ffx; mother: Ada
STONEBURNER; inf: D. E. STONEBURNER, father; pg:ln: 228:110

STORM, Adelia; WF; b. 25 May 1890 in Ffx; father: J. A. STORM; occ:
farmer; res: Ffx; mother: S. A. STORM; inf: J. A. STORM, father;
pg:ln: 191:90

STORM, Henry A.; WM; b. 29 Sep 1881 in Lewinsville; father: J. A.
STORM; occ: farmer; res: Lewinsville; mother: Sarah STORM; inf:
father; pg:ln: 131:65

STORM, Johnathan C.; WM; b. 29 Sep 1883 in Lewinsville; father: J. A.
STORM; occ: farmer; res: Lewinsville; mother: Sarah STORM; inf:
father; pg:ln: 141:89

STOTTS, ___; CM; b. 13 Nov 1890 in Ffx; father: Frank STOTTS; occ: farmer; res: Ffx; mother: Maggie STOTTS; inf: F. STOTTS, father; pg:ln: 191:93

STOTTS, Chas.; CM; b. 5 Jun 1884 in Ffx; father: Samuel STOTTS; occ: farmer; res: Ffx; mother: Jennie STOTTS; inf: S. STOTTS, father; pg:ln: 148:66

STOTTS, Lottie; CF; b. 25 Sep 1890 in Ffx; father: Samuel STOTTS; occ: farmer; res: Ffx; mother: Jennie STOTTS; inf: Saml. STOTTS, father; pg:ln: 188:109

STOTTS, Robert; CM; b. 10 Aug 1896 nr Clifton Sta; father: Samuel STOTTS; occ: farmer; res: nr Clifton Sta; mother: Jennie STOTTS; inf: father This registration was requested as 1896.; pg:ln: 231:116

STOUT, Surnella; WF; b. __ Aug 1880 in ___; father: Saml. STOUT; occ: farmer; res: Ffx; mother: Mary; inf: S. STOUT, father; pg:ln: 129:92

STOUT, W. G.; WM; b. 1 Aug 1881 in Ffx; father: W. H. STOUT; occ: farmer; res: Ffx; mother: Rebecca STOUT; inf: W. H. STOUT, father; pg:ln: 133:45

STOY, Susan; WF; b. 15 Feb 1888 in Ffx; father: Chas. STOY; occ: farmer; res: Ffx; mother: P. A. STOY; inf: C. STOY, father; pg:ln: 175:90

STRANGE, Annie; CF; b. 28 Dec 1894 in Ffx; father: Geo. STRANGE; occ: farmer; res: Ffx; mother: Ida STRANGE; inf: Geo. STRANGE, father; pg:ln: 219:113

STRINGFELLOW, Jno. M.; WM; b. 27 Mar 1883 in Seminary; father: Frank STRINGFELLOW; occ: minister; res: Seminary; mother: Emma STRINGFELLOW; inf: father; pg:ln: 141:86

STRUDER, ___; WF; b. 5 Dec 1880 in ___; father: Geo. W. STRUDER; occ: farmer; res: Ffx; mother: Martha; inf: G. W. STRUDER, father; pg:ln: 129:91

STRUDER, Chas. L.; WM; b. 1 Mar 1882 in Ffx; father: Victor STRUDER; occ: ___; res: ___; mother: Adelia STRUDER; inf: V. STRUDER, father; pg:ln: 137:75

STRUHS, Ethel; WF; b. 17 Mar 1892 in Ffx; father: M. C. STHRUS [STRUHS[; occ: farmer; res: Ffx; mother: Fannie STHRUS [STRUHS]; inf: M. C. STHRUS [STRUHS], father; pg:ln: 204:92

STRUHS, Myrtle B.; WF; b. 23 Sep 1894 in Ffx; father: Martin C. STRUHS; occ: farmer; res: Ffx; mother: Fannie STRUHS; inf: M. C. STRUHS, father; pg:ln: 219:106

STRUTT, Herbert; WM; b. 12 Dec 1895 in Mt. Vernon (Gale); father: Christian STRUTT; occ: laborer; res: Mt. Vernon (Gale); mother: Sadie STRUTT; inf: mother; pg:ln: 224:112

STUART, ___ (dead); WM; b. 5 Jul 1888 in Ffx; father: W. STUART; occ: farmer; res: Ffx; mother: G. STUART; inf: W. STUART, father; pg:ln: 175:88

STUDDS, Carroll; WM; b. 13 Nov 1895 in West End; father: John F. STUDDS; occ: farmer; res: West End; mother: Amanda STUDDS; inf: father; pg:ln: 224:110

STUDDS, George; WM; b. 1 Jan 1892 in West End; father: Wm.
STUDDS; occ: ___; res: West End; mother: Mary Jane STUDDS;
inf: mother; pg:ln: 209:41

STUDDS, Harry; WM; b. 9 Mar 1890 in Ffx; father: Jno. F. STUDDS;
occ: farmer; res: Ffx; mother: Amanda STUDDS; inf: J. F. STUDDS,
father; pg:ln: 188:107

STUDDS, Nellie; WF; b. 15 Feb 1891 in West End; father: D. A.
STUDDS; occ: dairyman; res: West End; mother: Sarah E.
STUDDS; inf: parents; pg:ln: 195:33

STUDDS, not named; WM; b. 11 Mar 1883 in Ffx; father: D. A.
STUDDS; occ: farmer; res: Ffx; mother: Sarah STUDDS; inf: D. A.
STUDDS, father; pg:ln: 145:78

STUDDS, Sarah; WF; b. 17 Sep 1885 in Ffx; father: D. A. STUDDS;
occ: farmer; res: Ffx; mother: Sallie STUDDS; inf: D. A. STUDDS,
father; pg:ln: 157:56

STYLES, Grace; CF; b. 19 Mar 1896 in Ffx; father: Wash't. STYLES;
occ: farmer; res: Ffx; mother: Eva STYLES; inf: W. STYLES, father;
pg:ln: 228:118

SULLIVAN, Ritta; WF; b. 20 Jan 1882 in Ffx; father: T. J. SULLIVAN;
occ: ___; res: ___; mother: L. SULLIVAN; inf: T. J. SULLIVAN,
father; pg:ln: 137:70

SUMMERS, Lewis; CM; b. 10 May 1893 in ___; father: Dorsey
SUMERS; occ: farmer; res: ___; mother: Elsie SUMERS; inf: D.
SUMERS, father; pg:ln: 215:87

SUTHERLAND, J. W.; WM; b. 20 May 1882 in Ffx; father: Jno.
SUTHERLAND; occ: ___; res: ___; mother: Ellen SUTHERLAND;
inf: J. SUTHERLAND, father; pg:ln: 137:73

SUTHERLIN, ___; WM; b. 1 May 1890 in Ffx; father: Jas. B.
SUTHERLIN; occ: laborer; res: Ffx; mother: Mary SUTHERLIN; inf:
J. B. SUTHERLIN, father; pg:ln: 188:108

SUTHERLIN, ___; WM; b. 20 Mar 1888 in Ffx; father: Jas. B.
SUTHERLIN; occ: farmer; res: Ffx; mother: Rosa SUTHERLIN; inf:
J. B. SUTHERLIN, father; pg:ln: 171:56

SUTHERLIN, Edna (twin); WF; b. 15 Jul 1888 in Ffx; father: Wm. Thos.
SUTHERLIN; occ: farmer; res: Ffx; mother: Fannie SUTHERLIN; inf:
Wm. T. SUTHERLIN, father; pg:ln: 171:59

SUTHERLIN, Emily May; WF; b. 29 Oct 1891 nr Burke Sta.; father: Wm.
F. SUTHERLIN; occ: farmer; res: Middle Run; mother: Fannie
SUTHERLIN; inf: parents; pg:ln: 193:26

SUTHERLIN, Eva (twin); WF; b. 15 Jul 1888 in Ffx; father: Wm. Thos.
SUTHERLIN; occ: farmer; res: Ffx; mother: Fannie SUTHERLIN; inf:
Wm. T. SUTHERLIN, father; pg:ln: 171:58

SUTHERLIN, Major; WM; b. 8 Oct 1883 in Ffx; father: Jno.
SUTHERLIN; occ: farmer; res: Ffx; mother: Ellen SUTHERLIN; inf:
Jno. SUTHERLIN, father; pg:ln: 145:75

SWART, Asa Irving; WM; b. 20 Nov 1887 in Ffx; father: J. H. SWART;
occ: farmer; res: Ffx; mother: Florence SWART; inf: J. H. SWART,
father; pg:ln: 164:146

SWART, Blanche N.; WF; b. 17 Sep 1880 in Germantown; father: John
H. SWART; occ: farmer; res: Providence; mother: Florence SWART;
inf: father; pg:ln: 125:71

SWART, Florence Elizabeth; WF; b. 18 Mar 1895 nr Fairfax C. H.;
father: John H. SWART; occ: farmer; res: nr Fairfax C. H.; mother:
Florence SWART; inf: father; pg:ln: 224:116

SWART, M. B.; WF; b. 25 May 1882 in Ffx; father: Jno. H. SWARTZ;
occ: ___; res: ___; mother: Florence SWARTZ; inf: J. H. SWARTZ,
father; pg:ln: 137:69

SWART, Mollie; WF; b. 10 Nov 1890 in Ffx; father: John SWART; occ:
R Rd Brakeman; res: Ffx; mother: Martha SWART; inf: Jno.
SWART, father; pg:ln: 187:106

SWART, Stacy Stirling; WM; b. 18 Feb 1891 nr Fairfax C. H.; father:
John H. SWART; occ: farmer; res: nr Fairfax C. H.; mother:
F[l]orence SWART; inf: parents; pg:ln: 194:02

SWAYZEE, Everett William [W. E. lined thru]; WM; b. 14 Feb 1893 in
___; father: E. E. SWAYZEE; occ: farmer; res: ___; mother: Jennie
SWAYZEE; inf: E. E. SWAYZEE, father. Birth certificate of Everett
William Swayze b. 14 Feb 1893. Father E. E. Swayze of Chantilly
Va age 29 b. Warren Co. NJ, farmer. Mother Jennie Reid of
Chantilly, age 34, b. Prince Wm. Co. Va, housekeeper in own
house.; pg:ln: 215:93

SWEENY, Albert; WM; b. 25 Apr 1881 in near C. H.; father: A. A.
SWEENY; occ: farmer; res: near C. H.; mother: Sarah J. SWEENY;
inf: father; pg:ln: 131:64

SWETNAM, ___; WM; b. 20 Jul 1889 in Ffx; father: E. R. SWETNAM;
occ: merchant; res: Ffx; mother: Mary SWETNAM; inf: E. R.
SWETNAM, father; pg:ln: 183:87

SWETNAM, E. F.; WF; b. 19 Nov 1887 in Ffx; father: C. F. SWETNAM;
occ: merchant; res: Ffx; mother: Jennie SWETNAM; inf: C. F.
SWETNAM, father; pg:ln: 169:99

SWETNAM, Lizzie; WF; b. 15 Sep 1887 in Ffx; father: E. R. SWETNAM;
occ: merchant; res: Ffx; mother: Mollie SWETNAM; inf: E. R.
SWETNAM, father; pg:ln: 169:98

SWINK, Archie W.; WM; b. 7 Sep 1887 in Ffx; father: Z. T. SWINK; occ:
farmer; res: Ffx; mother: Julia A. SWINK; inf: Z. T. SWINK, father;
pg:ln: 164:141

SWINK, Farley; WM; b. 16 Jun 1889 in Ffx; father: Z. T. SWINK; occ:
farmer; res: Ffx; mother: Julia SWINK; inf: Z. T. SWINK, father;
pg:ln: 179:104

SWINK, Jno. E.; WM; b. 1 Oct 1888 in Ffx; father: E. F. SWINK; occ:
farmer; res: Ffx; mother: Carrie H. SWINK; inf: E. F. SWINK, father;
pg:ln: 175:91

SWINK, Lillie M.; WF; b. 21 Aug 1892 in Ffx; father: Z. T. SWINK; occ:
farmer; res: Ffx; mother: Julia SWINK; inf: Z. T. SWINK, father;
pg:ln: 204:93

SWITNAM, Chas. F.; WM; b. 19 Sep 1896 in Burke Sta; father: Chas. F.
SWITNAM; occ: merchant; res: Burke Sta; mother: Jennee
SWITNAM; inf: father; pg:ln: 232:117

TALBERT, Chas. E.; WM; b. 24 Jan 1886 in Ffx; father: Horace
TALBERT; occ: farmer; res: Ffx; mother: Myra V. TALBERT; inf: H.
TALBERT, father; pg:ln: 155:21

TALBOT, Frank; WM; b. 23 Apr 1880 in ___; father: W. T. TALBOT;
occ: farmer; res: Ffx; mother: Elizabt.; inf: W. TALBOT, father; pg:ln:
129:94

TALBOT, Jas. W.; WM; b. 3 Nov 1882 in Ffx; father: Jas. R. TALBOT;
occ: ___; res: ___; mother: Margt. TALBOT; inf: J. R. TALBOT,
father; pg:ln: 138:81

TALBOT, Robt. T.; WM; b. 10 Aug 1880 in ___; father: Jas. R. TALBOT;
occ: farmer; res: Ffx; mother: Margt.; inf: J. R. TALBOT, father;
pg:ln: 129:95

TATE, ___ (dead); CM; b. 9 Apr 1889 in Ffx; father: Robt. TATE; occ:
farmer; res: Ffx; mother: Sarah TATE; inf: Robt. TATE, father; pg:ln:
183:95

TATE, Carrie; CF; b. 9 Dec 1896 in Masons Neck; father: Robert TATE;
occ: laborer; res: Masons Neck; mother: Sarah TATE; inf: mother;
pg:ln: 232:127

TATE, Edith May; CF; b. 30 Dec 1896 in Masons Neck; father: ___; occ:
___; res: ___; mother: Edith TATE; inf: mother; pg:ln: 232:126

TATE, not named; CM; b. 9 Oct 1887 in Ffx; father: Robt. TATE; occ:
laborer; res: Ffx; mother: Sarah TATE; inf: Robt. TATE, father; pg:ln:
169:110

TATE, Walter; CM; b. 26 Jan 1896 in Masons Neck; father: ___; occ:
___; res: ___; mother: Charlotte TATE; inf: mother; pg:ln: 232:125

TAUBERSMIDT, Annie L.; WM; b. 2 Dec 1885 in Bailey's X Rds; father:
Geo. TAUBERSMIDT; occ: farmer; res: Bailey's X Rds; mother: Eva
M. TAUBERSMIDT; inf: father; pg:ln: 154:83

TAYLOR, Alice; WF; b. 27 Mar 1884 in Ffx; father: Jas. E. TAYLOR;
occ: farmer; res: Ffx; mother: Mary TAYLOR; inf: J. E. TAYLOR,
father; pg:ln: 148:74

TAYLOR, Amelia; CF; b. 25 May 1890 in Ffx; father: Joseph TAYLOR;
occ: farmer; res: Ffx; mother: Lavenia TAYLOR; inf: Jos. TAYLOR,
father; pg:ln: 192:96

TAYLOR, Annie; WF; b. 13 Aug 1887 in Ffx; father: Jas. E. TAYLOR;
occ: farmer; res: Ffx; mother: Mary TAYLOR; inf: J. E. TAYLOR,
father; pg:ln: 169:113

TAYLOR, Benjamin; CM; b. 14 Dec 1883 in Providence Dist.; father:
Joseph TAYLOR; occ: laborer; res: Providence Dist.; mother:
Lavinia TAYLOR; inf: father; pg:ln: 141:98

TAYLOR, Bessie; WF; b. 8 Jan 1891 nr Accotink; father: John N.
TAYLOR; occ: farmer; res: nr Accotink; mother: Sallie TAYLOR; inf:
parents; pg:ln: 195:24

TAYLOR, Edw'd.; WM; b. 7 Nov 1883 in Ffx; father: Jno. H. TAYLOR; occ: farmer; res: Ffx; mother: Mary L. TAYLOR; inf: J. H. TAYLOR, father; pg:ln: 145:80

TAYLOR, Effie M.; WF; b. 2 Feb 1883 in Ffx; father: Jas. E. TAYLOR; occ: farmer; res: Ffx; mother: Mary TAYLOR; inf: J. E. TAYLOR, father; pg:ln: 145:82

TAYLOR, Effie; WF; b. 24 Apr 1888 in Ffx; father: Jas. E. TAYLOR; occ: farmer; res: Ffx; mother: Mary TAYLOR; inf: J. E. TAYLOR, father; pg:ln: 171:66

TAYLOR, Eliza; CF; b. 10 Nov 1880 in ___; father: W. H. TAYLOR; occ: farmer; res: Ffx; mother: Annie; inf: W. H. TAYLOR, father; pg:ln: 129:96

TAYLOR, Harry; WM; b. 25 Mar 1892 nr Fairfax C. H.; father: R. A. TAYLOR; occ: farmer; res: nr Fairfax C. H.; mother: Mary TAYLOR; inf: father; pg:ln: 208:32

TAYLOR, J. F.; WM; b. 11 Sep 1882 in Ffx; father: Saml. TAYLOR; occ: ___; res: ___; mother: Alice J. TAYLOR; inf: S. J. TAYLOR, father; pg:ln: 137:77

TAYLOR, J. S.; CM; b. 13 Jun 1890 in Ffx; father: Jas. TAYLOR; occ: farmer; res: Ffx; mother: Julia TAYLOR; inf: Jas. TAYLOR, father; pg:ln: 192:97

TAYLOR, Joshua P.; WM; b. 6 May 1889 in Ffx; father: J. P. TAYLOR; occ: farmer; res: Ffx; mother: Ida TAYLOR; inf: J. P. TAYLOR, father; pg:ln: 183:92

TAYLOR, Julia; WF; b. 4 Apr 1895 nr Fairfax C. H.; father: Robert A. TAYLOR; occ: farmer; res: Fairfax C. H.; mother: Mary TAYLOR; inf: father; pg:ln: 224:126

TAYLOR, Leroy Smith; WM; b. 3 Nov 1890 in Ffx; father: J. P. TAYLOR; occ: farmer; res: Ffx; mother: Ida L. TAYLOR; inf: J. P. TAYLOR, father; pg:ln: 188:113

TAYLOR, Lewis F.; WM; b. 24 Jul 1890 in Ffx; father: Geo. TAYLOR; occ: farmer; res: Ffx; mother: Georgian TAYLOR; inf: G. TAYLOR, father; pg:ln: 192:100

TAYLOR, Lottie; CF; b. 6 Feb 1896 in Ffx; father: Robt. TAYLOR; occ: farmer; res: Ffx; mother: Cora TAYLOR; inf: Robt. TAYLOR, father; pg:ln: 228:123

TAYLOR, Mamie; WF; b. 5 Oct 1885 in Ffx; father: Jno. M. TAYLOR; occ: farmer; res: Ffx; mother: Cora TAYLOR; inf: J. M. TAYLOR, father; pg:ln: 157:60

TAYLOR, Martha Ellen; WF; b. 20 May 1895 nr Burke Sta.; father: James E. TAYLOR; occ: farmer; res: nr Burke Sta.; mother: Mary TAYLOR; inf: father; pg:ln: 224:119

TAYLOR, Mary E.; WF; b. 1 May 1889 in Ffx; father: Jno. H. TAYLOR; occ: farmer; res: Ffx; mother: Lillie TAYLOR; inf: J. H. TAYLOR, father; pg:ln: 180:118

TAYLOR, Mary E.; WF; b. 10 Apr 1889 in Ffx; father: Jas. E. TAYLOR; occ: farmer; res: Ffx; mother: Mary TAYLOR; inf: J. E. TAYLOR, father; pg:ln: 183:98

TAYLOR, Maud (twin); WF; b. 14 Aug 1884 in Ffx; father: Chas. F.
  TAYLOR; occ: farmer; res: Ffx; mother: Eglantine TAYLOR; inf: C.
  F. TAYLOR, father; pg:ln: 148:72
TAYLOR, Myron (twin); WM; b. 14 Aug 1884 in Ffx; father: Chas. F.
  TAYLOR; occ: farmer; res: Ffx; mother: Eglantine TAYLOR; inf: C.
  F. TAYLOR, father; pg:ln: 148:73
TAYLOR, Naoma; WF; b. 29 May 1892 nr Burke Sta.; father: James E.
  TAYLOR; occ: farmer; res: nr Burke Sta.; mother: Mary TAYLOR;
  inf: mother; pg:ln: 209:57
[TAYLOR], not named (dead); CF; b. __ Dec 1891 nr Gum Spring;
  father: Edmond TAYLOR; occ: laborer; res: nr Gum Spring; mother:
  Cornelia TAYLOR; inf: parent; pg:ln: 196:21
[TAYLOR], not named (dead); WM; b. 3 Jan 1885 in Ffx; father: Wm.
  TAYLOR; occ: farmer; res: Ffx; mother: Mary TAYLOR; inf: Wm.
  TAYLOR, father; pg:ln: 157:57
TAYLOR, not named; WF; b. 16 Jan 1882 in Providence; father: Geo. P.
  TAYLOR; occ: farmer; res: Prov.; mother: Georgianna TAYLOR; inf:
  father; pg:ln: 135:64
TAYLOR, Pamola; WF; b. 27 Jul 1895 nr Centreville; father: W. W.
  TAYLOR; occ: farmer; res: nr Centreville; mother: Pamola TAYLOR;
  inf: father; pg:ln: 224:117
TAYLOR, Pearl Hester; WF; b. 30 Feb 1893 nr Fairfax C. H.; father: J.
  P. TAYLOR; occ: farmer; res: nr Fairfax C. H.; mother: Edna L.
  TAYLOR; inf: parent; pg:ln: 212:91
TAYLOR, Thomas; CM; b. 8 Nov 1887 in Ffx; father: Moses TAYLOR;
  occ: laborer; res: Ffx; mother: Pollie TAYLOR; inf: Moses TAYLOR,
  father; pg:ln: 169:114
TAYLOR, Thos. Braxton; CM; b. 24 Sep 1895 in Gum Spring; father:
  Samuel TAYLOR; occ: laborer; res: Gum Spring; mother: Rachael
  TAYLOR; inf: father; pg:ln: 224:128
TAYLOR, Wm. McKinley; WM; b. 30 Nov 1896 nr Burke Sta; father:
  James TAYLOR; occ: farmer; res: nr Burke Sta; mother: Luticia
  TAYLOR; inf: father; pg:ln: 232:121
TEBBS, Lucy Virginia; CF; b. 6 Jun 1895 nr Pender; father: Chas. H.
  TEBBS; occ: laborer; res: nr Pender; mother: Fannie TEBBS; inf:
  father; pg:ln: 224:125
TERRELL, Amanda; CF; b. 28 Jun 1882 in Seminary; father: William
  TERRELL; occ: laborer; res: Seminary; mother: B. TERRELL; inf:
  mother; pg:ln: 135:61
TERRELL, Beatrice; CF; b. 19 Mar 1890 in Ffx; father: Wilson
  TERRELL; occ: farmer; res: Ffx; mother: Fannie TERRELL; inf: W.
  TERRELL, father; pg:ln: 192:101
TERRELL, Bertie; CF; b. 24 Jan 1884 in Seminary; father: William
  TERRELL; occ: gardener; res: Seminary; mother: B. TERRELL; inf:
  father; pg:ln: 151:87
TERRELL, Clarence; CM; b. 20 Dec 1889 in Ffx; father: W. TERRELL;
  occ: farmer; res: Ffx; mother: Burna TERRELL; inf: W. TERRELL,
  father; pg:ln: 180:119

TERRELL, Florence; CF; b. 20 Oct 1887 in Ffx; father: Jake TERRELL; occ: farmer; res: Ffx; mother: Harriet TERRELL; inf: J. TERRELL, father; pg:ln: 164:155

TERRELL, Harvey T. (twin); WM; b. 27 Sep 1882 [15th lined thru] in Ffx; father: Eugene J. TERRELL [E. E. lined thru]; occ: farmer; res: Ffx; mother: Ella TERRELL; inf: Eugene TERRELL, father. Note of 20 Jan 1832 in Prince George Co. Md: I, Eugene I. Tyrrell, father of Irving Tyrrell, swear that said Irving Tyrrell was born September 27, 1882. He was born in Lee District, Fairfax Co. Va. Second note: In reply to your letter of August 26, 1835, please be advised that I am a twin brother of Harvey T., and that the correct spelling of my given name is Irving and not Erving. Attached hereto is a sworn statement made by my father giving as the date of my birth September 27, 1882 and not September 15th as indicated by your records. Signed Irving Eugene Tyrell, RFD, Lorton, Va.; pg:ln: 138:78

TERRELL, Henry C.; WM; b. 11 Mar 1896 nr Colchester; father: Eugene TERRELL; occ: farmer; res: nr Colchester; mother: Mary Ellen TERRELL; inf: father; pg:ln: 232:124

TERRELL, Irving Eugene (twin) [given name E. lined thru]; WM; b. 27 Sep 1882 [15th lined thru] in Ffx; father: Eugene J. TERRELL [E. E. lined thru]; occ: ___; res: ___; mother: Ella TERRELL; inf: Eugene TERRELL, father. Note of 20 Jan 1832 in Prince George Co. Md: I, Eugene I. Tyrrell, father of Irving Tyrrell, swear that said Irving Tyrrell was born September 27, 1882. He was born in Lee District, Fairfax Co. Va. Second note: In reply to your letter of August 26, 1835, please be advised that I am a twin brother of Harvey T., and that the correct spelling of my given name is Irving and not Erving. Attached hereto is a sworn statement made by my father giving as the date of my birth September 27, 1882 and not September 15th as indicated by your records. Signed Irving Eugene Tyrell, RFD, Lorton, Va.; pg:ln: 138:79

TERRELL, Minty; CF; b. 27 Nov 1887 in Ffx; father: Wm. TERRELL; occ: farmer; res: Ffx; mother: Jane TERRELL; inf: Wm. TERRELL, father; pg:ln: 164:156

TERRELL, Richd.; CM; b. 11 Oct 1887 in Ffx; father: Wilson TERRELL; occ: laborer; res: Ffx; mother: Fannie TERRELL; inf: Wilson TERRELL, father; pg:ln: 164:166

TERRET, Nellie; WF; b. 17 Aug 1889 in Ffx; father: Thos. TERRET; occ: farmer; res: Ffx; mother: Mary TERRET; inf: Thos. TERRETT, father; pg:ln: 180:117

TERRETT, Eva; WF; b. 25 Dec 1880 in Seminary; father: Thomas TERRETT; occ: farmer; res: Falls Church; mother: Mary C. TERRETT; inf: father. For date of this birth see photostat attached to page 66 [see TERRETT, Nellie L.]; pg:ln: 125:75

TERRETT, Gibson J.; WM; b. 20 Nov 1882 nr Falls Ch.; father: Gibson A. TERRETT; occ: farmer; res: nr Falls Ch.; mother: J. T. TERRETT; inf: father; pg:ln: 135:65

TERRETT, Joseph G.; WM; b. 10 Sep 1881 in Falls Church; father:
    Gibson A. TERRETT; occ: farmer; res: Falls Church; mother:
    Victoria T. TERRETT; inf: father; pg:ln: 131:70

TERRETT, M. Grace; WF; b. 23 Jan 1884 in Bailey's X Roads; father:
    Thomas TERRETT; occ: farmer; res: Bailey's X Roads; mother:
    Mary TERRETT; inf: father; pg:ln: 151:86

THIRMES?, Paul Peter; WM; b. 26 Nov 1893 nr Newington; father: John
    M. THIRMES?; occ: painter; res: nr Newington; mother: Alice Ann
    THIRMES; inf: parent; pg:ln: 212:93

THOMAS Everett; CM; b. 19 May 1886 in Falls Ch.; father: Geo.
    THOMAS; occ: mechanic; res: Falls Ch.; mother: Kate THOMAS; inf:
    father; pg:ln: 159:64

THOMAS, Alta; WF; b. 6 Jan 1896 in Ffx; father: M. E. THOMAS; occ:
    farmer; res: Ffx; mother: Minnie THOMAS; inf: M. E. THOMAS,
    father; pg:ln: 228:121

THOMAS, Ella; CF; b. 15 Aug 1887 in Ffx; father: Geo. W. THOMAS;
    occ: laborer; res: Ffx; mother: Kate THOMAS; inf: G. W. THOMAS,
    father; pg:ln: 164:153

THOMAS, Geo. R.; CM; b. 19 Dec 1881 in Providence; father: Thomas
    THOMAS; occ: laborer; res: Providence; mother: Martha THOMAS;
    inf: father; pg:ln: 131:71

THOMAS, Lillie; CF; b. 16 Jan 1882 in Falls Church; father: Geo. W.
    THOMAS; occ: mechanic; res: Falls Church; mother: Kate
    THOMAS; inf: father; pg:ln: 135:63

THOMAS, Lucy J.; CF; b. 9 Feb 1885 in Prov.; father: Thomas
    THOMAS; occ: laborer; res: Prov.; mother: Mary THOMAS; inf:
    father; pg:ln: 154:84

THOMAS, not named; CF; b. 3 May 1884 in Dranes.; father: Clinton
    THOMAS; occ: laborer; res: Dranes.; mother: Scynthia THOMAS;
    inf: father; pg:ln: 151:96

[THOMAS], not named; WF; b. 5 Aug 1885 in Ffx; father: P. P.
    THOMAS; occ: farmer; res: Ffx; mother: Bettie THOMAS; inf: P. P.
    THOMAS, father; pg:ln: 157:59

THOMAS, Preston; CM; b. 17 Aug 1896 nr Accotink; father: Geo.
    THOMAS; occ: blacksmith; res: nr Accotink; mother: Nancy
    THOMAS; inf: father; pg:ln: 232:128

THOMAS, Sherman; WM; b. 14 Nov 1887 in Ffx; father: Jno. P.
    THOMAS; occ: farmer; res: Ffx; mother: Lou THOMAS; inf: J. P.
    THOMAS, father; pg:ln: 169:117

THOMAS, Tolbert; CM; b. 1 Sep 1891 in Ffx; father: Geo. W. THOMAS;
    occ: farmer; res: Ffx; mother: Kate THOMAS; inf: Geo. W. THOMAS,
    father; pg:ln: 200:100

THOMAS, William C.; CM; b. 5 Mar 1891 nr Accotink; father: George
    THOMAS; occ: laborer; res: nr Accotink; mother: Nancy THOMAS;
    inf: parent; pg:ln: 196:22

THOMAS, Wm. W.; CM; b. 15 Jun 1884 in Falls Church; father: Geo. W.
    THOMAS; occ: mechanic; res: Falls Church; mother: Kate
    THOMAS; inf: father; pg:ln: 151:90

THOMPSON, ___; WF; b. 15 Aug 1890 in Ffx; father: Elisha
THOMPSON; occ: farmer; res: Ffx; mother: Mary V. THOMPSON;
inf: Elisha THOMPSON, father; pg:ln: 192:108

THOMPSON, ___; WM; b. 15 Jul 1890 in Ffx; father: F. M.
THOMPSON; occ: farmer; res: Ffx; mother: Gertrude THOMPSON;
inf: F. M. THOMPSON, father; pg:ln: 192:106

THOMPSON, ___; WM; b. 20 Feb 1890 in Ffx; father: Jno. H.
THOMPSON; occ: farmer; res: Ffx; mother: Mary THOMPSON; inf:
Jno. H. THOMPSON, father; pg:ln: 192:99

THOMPSON, ___; WM; b. 20 May 1892 in Ffx; father: J. M.
THOMPSON; occ: farmer; res: Ffx; mother: Lucy THOMPSON; inf:
J. M. THOMPSON, father; pg:ln: 204:102

THOMPSON, ___; WM; b. 9 Jul 1890 in Ffx; father: J. M. THOMPSON;
occ: farmer; res: Ffx; mother: Lucy J. THOMPSON; inf: J. M.
THOMPSON, father; pg:ln: 192:109

THOMPSON, A. G.; WM; b. 14 Nov 1890 in Ffx; father: W. H.
THOMPSON; occ: farmer; res: Ffx; mother: Julia THOMPSON; inf:
W. H. THOMPSON, father; pg:ln: 192:98

THOMPSON, A. T.; WM; b. 2 Nov 1889 in Ffx; father: Alfred
THOMPSON; occ: farmer; res: Ffx; mother: Annie THOMPSON; inf:
A. THOMPSON, father; pg:ln: 180:121

THOMPSON, Ada G.; WF; b. 14 Nov 1888 in Ffx; father: Winfield
THOMPSON; occ: farmer; res: Ffx; mother: Sara THOMPSON; inf:
W. THOMPSON, father; pg:ln: 175:95

THOMPSON, Albert Lewis; WM; b. 20 Aug 1895 nr Pender; father:
Lewis THOMPSON; occ: carpenter; res: nr Pender; mother: Carrie
THOMPSON; inf: father; pg:ln: 224:118

THOMPSON, Albert V.; WM; b. 26 Jun 1887 in Ffx; father: Albert
THOMPSON; occ: farmer; res: Ffx; mother: E. V. THOMPSON; inf:
A. THOMPSON, father; pg:ln: 164:159

THOMPSON, Alice; WF; b. 19 Sep 1887 in Ffx; father: Edward
THOMPSON; occ: farmer; res: Ffx; mother: Ida THOMPSON; inf:
Edward THOMPSON, father; pg:ln: 164:161

THOMPSON, Benj. F.; WM; b. 27 Oct 1881 in Dranes.; father: Lewis E.
THOMPSON; occ: mechanic; res: Dranes.; mother: Emma
THOMPSON; inf: father; pg:ln: 131:69

THOMPSON, C. L.; WM; b. 29 May 1888 in Ffx; father: Willis
THOMPSON; occ: farmer; res: Ffx; mother: Lillie THOMPSON; inf:
W. THOMPSON, father; pg:ln: 175:97

THOMPSON, Celia; WF; b. 8 Sep 1891 in Ffx; father: W. W.
THOMPSON; occ: farmer; res: Ffx; mother: Annie THOMPSON; inf:
W. W. THOMPSON, father; pg:ln: 200:103

THOMPSON, Chas. B.; WM; b. 13 Sep 1892 in Ffx; father: Isaiah
THOMPSON; occ: farmer; res: Ffx; mother: Mary C. THOMPSON;
inf: Isaiah THOMPSON, father; pg:ln: 204:104

THOMPSON, Clide (twin); WM; b. 3 Feb 1883 in Dranesville; father:
Dan. THOMPSON; occ: farmer; res: Dranesville; mother: Alice V.
THOMPSON; inf: father; pg:ln: 141:101

THOMPSON, David; WM; b. 23 Aug 1888 in Ffx; father: H.
THOMPSON; occ: farmer; res: Ffx; mother: Madge THOMPSON;
inf: H. THOMPSON, father; pg:ln: 171:68

THOMPSON, Dorris; WF; b. 10 Feb 1893 in ___; father: Arthur
THOMPSON; occ: farmer; res: ___; mother: L. THOMPSON; inf: A.
THOMPSON, father; pg:ln: 215:94

THOMPSON, Edith; WF; b. 3 Mar 1884 in Falls Church; father: S. E.
THOMPSON; occ: mechanic; res: Falls Church; mother: Florence
THOMPSON; inf: father; pg:ln: 151:89

THOMPSON, Edwd. S.; WM; b. 23 Oct 1889 in Ffx; father: Ed.
THOMPSON; occ: farmer; res: Ffx; mother: Ida THOMPSON; inf: E.
THOMPSON, father; pg:ln: 180:112

THOMPSON, Eppa V.; WM; b. 7 Jul 1887 in Ffx; father: Mortimer
THOMPSON; occ: farmer; res: Ffx; mother: Florence THOMPSON;
inf: M. THOMPSON, father; pg:ln: 169:116

THOMPSON, Florence; WF; b. 12 Feb 1894 in Ffx; father: Lewis E.
THOMPSON; occ: farmer; res: Ffx; mother: Emsie THOMPSON; inf:
L. E. THOMPSON, father; pg:ln: 219:115

THOMPSON, Gean; WF; b. 20 Sep 1893 in ___; father: Winfield
THOMPSON; occ: farmer; res: ___; mother: S. J. THOMPSON; inf:
Winfield THOMPSON, father; pg:ln: 215:96

THOMPSON, Geo. C.; WM; b. 24 Jul 1884 in Falls Church; father: Geo.
M. THOMPSON; occ: Gov. Dept.; res: Falls Church; mother: Nettie
THOMPSON; inf: father; pg:ln: 151:88

THOMPSON, Grace; WF; b. 17 Jul 1894 in Ffx; father: J. Y.
THOMPSON; occ: farmer; res: Ffx; mother: Lula THOMPSON; inf: J.
Y. THOMPSON, father; pg:ln: 220:122

THOMPSON, Hallee; WF; b. 12 Aug 1894 in Ffx; father: J. M.
THOMPSON; occ: farmer; res: Ffx; mother: Lucy J. THOMPSON;
inf: J. M. THOMPSON, father; pg:ln: 219:116

THOMPSON, Harvie; WM; b. 1 Oct 1892 in Ffx; father: Edw'd.
THOMPSON; occ: farmer; res: Ffx; mother: Ida THOMPSON; inf:
E'd. THOMPSON, father; pg:ln: 205:106

THOMPSON, Hattie L.; WF; b. 7 Jun 1894 in Ffx; father: Alfred H.
THOMPSON; occ: farmer; res: Ffx; mother: A. L. THOMPSON; inf:
A. H. THOMPSON, father; pg:ln: 220:123

THOMPSON, Howard; WM; b. 8 Sep 1890 in Ffx; father: Mortimore
THOMPSON; occ: farmer; res: Ffx; mother: Florence THOMPSON;
inf: M. THOMPSON, father; pg:ln: 192:102

THOMPSON, Irene; WF; b. 14 May 1891 in Ffx; father: W. S.
THOMPSON; occ: farmer; res: Ffx; mother: Ida THOMPSON; inf: W.
S. THOMPSON, father; pg:ln: 200:102

THOMPSON, J. M.; WM; b. 27 Mar 1892 in Ffx; father: Arch.
THOMPSON; occ: farmer; res: Ffx; mother: Lucy THOMPSON; inf:
Arch THOMPSON, father; pg:ln: 205:105

THOMPSON, Jane (dead); WF; b. 15 Apr 1890 in Ffx; father: Daniel
THOMPSON; occ: farmer; res: Ffx; mother: Elizabt. THOMPSON;
inf: D. THOMPSON, father; pg:ln: 188:115

THOMPSON, Jane; WF; b. 25 Jun 1881 in Ffx; father: R. S.
THOMPSON; occ: farmer; res: Ffx; mother: Mary J. THOMPSON;
inf: R. S. THOMPSON, father; pg:ln: 133:54

THOMPSON, Jesse; CM; b. 8 Mar 1891 in Ffx; father: Wm.
THOMPSON, occ: farmer; res: Ffx; mother: Bettie THOMPSON; inf:
Wm. THOMPSON, father; pg:ln: 200:101

THOMPSON, Jno. J.; WM; b. 2 Oct 1890 in Ffx; father: Isaiah
THOMPSON; occ: farmer; res: Ffx; mother: Mary C. THOMPSON;
inf: Isaiah THOMPSON, father; pg:ln: 192:107

THOMPSON, John Thomas; WM; b. 25 Sep 1891 nr Clifton; father:
Wm. H. THOMPSON; occ: laborer; res: nr Clifton; mother: Madge
THOMPSON; inf: parents; pg:ln: 194:23

THOMPSON, Kate; CF; b. 12 Sep 1894 in Ffx; father: Alfred
THOMPSON; occ: farmer; res: Ffx; mother: Sophia THOMPSON;
inf: A. THOMPSON, father; pg:ln: 220:127

THOMPSON, Kile (twin); WM; b. 3 Feb 1883 in Dranesville; father: Dan.
THOMPSON; occ: farmer; res: Dranesville; mother: Alice V.
THOMPSON; inf: father; pg:ln: 141:102

THOMPSON, Lesley; WM; b. 16 Apr 1889 in Ffx; father: Daniel
THOMPSON; occ: farmer; res: Ffx; mother: Alice THOMPSON; inf:
Danl. THOMPSON, father; pg:ln: 180:115

THOMPSON, Lillean; WF; b. 14 Feb 1894 in Ffx; father: Edw'd. E.
THOMPSON; occ: farmer; res: Ffx; mother: Ida THOMPSON; inf: E.
E. THOMPSON, father; pg:ln: 219:117

THOMPSON, Lola; WF; b. 8 Oct 1889 in Ffx; father: F. A. THOMPSON;
occ: farmer; res: Ffx; mother: Catharine THOMPSON; inf: F. A.
THOMPSON, father; pg:ln: 180:113

THOMPSON, Lucretia; WF; b. 21 Aug 1880 in Dranesville; father:
Joseph THOMPSON; occ: farmer; res: Dranesville; mother: ___
THOMPSON; inf: father; pg:ln: 125:79

THOMPSON, Lula Cecil; WF; b. 10 Apr 1892 nr Pender; father: Lewis
THOMPSON; occ: carpenter; res: nr Pender; mother: Carrie
THOMPSON; inf: mother; pg:ln: 208:24

THOMPSON, Malvina; CF; b. 10 Jun 1885 in Falls Ch.; father: Wm.
THOMPSON; occ: laborer; res: Falls Ch.; mother: Maria
THOMPSON; inf: father; pg:ln: 154:81

THOMPSON, Margaret; WF; b. 22 Apr 1896 in Sideburn Sta.; father: B.
F. THOMPSON; occ: farmer; res: Sideburn Sta.; mother: Laura C.
THOMPSON; inf: father; pg:ln: 232:123

THOMPSON, Marion; WF; b. 18 Oct 1890 in Ffx; father: Arthur
THOMPSON; occ: farmer; res: Ffx; mother: Laura THOMPSON; inf:
A. THOMPSON, father; pg:ln: 192:105

THOMPSON, Mary E.; WF; b. 19 May 1896 nr Alex.; father: Daniel D.
THOMPSON; occ: farmer; res: nr Alex.; mother: Elizabeth E.
THOMPSON; inf: father; pg:ln: 232:119

THOMPSON, Max W.; WM; b. 27 Jan 1893 in ___; father: Mortimer
THOMPSON; occ: farmer; res: ___; mother: Florence THOMPSON;
inf: Mortimer THOMPSON, father; pg:ln: 215:95

THOMPSON, Millard; WF; b. 1 Feb 1894 in Ffx; father: not known; occ: farmer; res: Ffx; mother: Jane THOMPSON; inf: Ed. McCOY, friend; pg:ln: 219:114

THOMPSON, Minnie; WF; b. 11 Dec 1887 in Ffx; father: Willis THOMPSON; occ: farmer; res: Ffx; mother: L. B. THOMPSON; inf: Willis THOMPSON, father; pg:ln: 164:164

THOMPSON, not named; WF; b. 9 Aug 1893 in ___; father: W. W. THOMPSON; occ: farmer; res: ___; mother: Annie THOMPSON ; inf: W. W. THOMPSON, father; pg:ln: 215:98

THOMPSON, Ora; WF; b. 22 Sep 1887 in Ffx; father: Wilson THOMPSON; occ: farmer; res: Ffx; mother: Mary THOMPSON; inf: Wilson THOMPSON, father; pg:ln: 164:160

THOMPSON, R. E.; WM; b. 13 Jul 1889 in Ffx; father: W. S. THOMPSON; occ: farmer; res: Ffx; mother: Ida B. THOMPSON; inf: W. S. THOMPSON, father; pg:ln: 180:116

THOMPSON, R. H.; WM; b. 13 Jan 1893 in ___; father: J. Y. THOMPSON; occ: farmer; res: ___; mother: Lulu THOMPSON; inf: J. Y. THOMPSON, father; pg:ln: 215:97

THOMPSON, Rosa Alice; WF; b. 18 Nov 1887 in Ffx; father: Wm. T. THOMPSON; occ: farmer; res: Ffx; mother: Louisa THOMPSON; inf: W. T. THOMPSON, father; pg:ln: 164:163

THOMPSON, Roy; WM; b. 9 Sep 1894 in Ffx; father: Jasper THOMPSON; occ: farmer; res: Ffx; mother: Cordelia THOMPSON; inf: J. THOMPSON, father; pg:ln: 220:121

THOMPSON, Stacy Leon [Stanley lined thru]; WM; b. 13 Jul 1891 in Ffx; father: E. E. THOMPSON; occ: farmer; res: Ffx; mother: Ida THOMPSON; inf: E. E. THOMPSON, father. Note of 17 Feb 1944 Herndon: A full list of all the children born to Edward Ellsworth Thompson and Ida Mabel Thompson with their correct birth dates. Parents Edward Ellsworth Thompson deceased; mother Ida Mabel Thompson, maiden name Pettitt. Allie Ellen Thompson 4 Dec 1887; Edward Stanley Thompson 23 Oct 1889 deceased; Stacy Leon Thompson 13 Jul 1891; Harvey Clifton Thompson 24 Oct 1892; Sarah Lillian Thompson 14 Feb 1894; Acie Ross Thompson 9 Aug 1896; Edith May Thompson 6 Dec 1898; William Henry Thompson 4 Jan 1901; Nellie Catherine Thompson 23 Oct 1903; Mildred Emma Thompson 12 Jan 1906; Everett Quentin Thompson 22 Sep 1908.; pg:ln: 200:104

THOMPSON, Theresa; WF; b. 14 Jul 1895 in Hollin Hall; father: Egbert THOMPSON; occ: farmer; res: Hollin Hall; mother: Mary THOMPSON; inf: father; pg:ln: 224:122

THOMPSON, Viola; WF; b. 2 Oct 1888 in Ffx; father: Isaiah THOMPSON; occ: farmer; res: Ffx; mother: Mary THOMPSON; inf: Isaiah THOMPSON, father; pg:ln: 175:98

THOMPSON, W. A.; WM; b. 28 May 1888 in Ffx; father: Harrison THOMPSON; occ: farmer; res: Ffx; mother: Florence THOMPSON; inf: H. THOMPSON, father; pg:ln: 175:96

THOMPSON, W. A.; WM; b. 8 Dec 1889 in Ffx; father: W. W.
THOMPSON; occ: farmer; res: Ffx; mother: Annie THOMPSON; inf:
W. W. THOMPSON, father; pg:ln: 180:114

THOMPSON, W. S.; CM; b. 22 Nov 1888 in Ffx; father: W.
THOMPSON; occ: farmer; res: Ffx; mother: Rachel THOMPSON;
inf: W. THOMPSON, father; pg:ln: 175:94

THOMPSON, Walter E.; WM; b. 8 May 1887 in Ffx; father: Lewis E.
THOMPSON; occ: farmer; res: Ffx; mother: Emsie THOMPSON; inf:
L. E. THOMPSON, father; pg:ln: 164:162

THOMPSON, Walter; CM; b. 20 Jun 1887 in Ffx; father: Wm.
THOMPSON; occ: farmer; res: Ffx; mother: Bettie THOMPSON; inf:
W. THOMPSON, father; pg:ln: 164:157

THOMPSON, Willis C.; WM; b. 8 May 1892 in Ffx; father: Willis
THOMPSON; occ: farmer; res: Ffx; mother: Lillie THOMPSON; inf:
Willis THOMPSON, father; pg:ln: 204:103

THORN, Ruth Annetta; WF; b. 17 Sep 1887 in Ffx; father: Jacob M.
THORN; occ: farmer; res: Ffx; mother: Mary E. THORNE; inf: J. M.
THORN, father; pg:ln: 164:154

THORNE Sarah V. C.; WF; b. 19 Nov 1882 in Falls Church; father: J. M.
THORNE; occ: nurseryman; res: Falls Church; mother: Mary E.
THORNE; inf: father; pg:ln: 135:62

THORNE, Geo. Kendall; WM; b. 20 Jun 1880 in Falls Church; father:
Jacob M. THORNE; occ: nurseryman; res: Falls Church; mother:
Mary E. THORNE; inf: father; pg:ln: 125:73

THORNE, Milton Martelle; WM; b. 3 Aug 1885 in Falls Ch.; father: J. M.
THORNE; occ: nurseryman; res: Falls Ch.; mother: Mary E.
THORNE; inf: father; pg:ln: 154:80

THORNTON, Katie; CF; b. 1 Jun 1891 in Huntley; father: John
THORNTON; occ: laborer; res: Huntley; mother: Anna THORNTON;
inf: parent; pg:ln: 196:20

THORNTON, Mary F.; WF; b. 28 Sep 1888 in Ffx; father: Wm. H.
THORNTON; occ: farmer; res: Ffx; mother: Mary THORNTON; inf:
Wm. H. THORNTON, father; pg:ln: 171:67

TIBBS, Caroline; CF; b. 8 Oct 1887 in Ffx; father: Thomas TIBBS; occ:
laborer; res: Ffx; mother: Annie TIBBS; inf: Thos. TIBBS, father;
pg:ln: 169:109

TIBBS, Massie; CM; b. 2 Jun 1889 in Ffx; father: Thos. TIBBS; occ:
farmer; res: Ffx; mother: Anna TIBBS; inf: Thos. TIBBS, father;
pg:ln: 183:94

TILLETT, Louisa; WF; b. 13 Sep 1895 nr Fort Washington; father:
Robert TILLETT; occ: farmer; res: nr Fort Washington; mother:
Carrie TILLETT; inf: father; pg:ln: 224:121

TINNER, Chas.; CM; b. 1 May 1891 in Ffx; father: Wm. TINNER; occ:
farmer; res: Ffx; mother: Viney TINNER; inf: Wm. TINNER, father;
pg:ln: 200:99

TINNER, Everett; CM; b. 21 Jan 1896 in Ffx; father: J. B. TINNER; occ:
farmer; res: Ffx; mother: C. V. TINNER; inf: J. B. TINNER, father;
pg:ln: 228:126

TINNER, Frances; CF; b. 22 Mar 1886 in Prov.; father: Chas. T.
TINNER; occ: mechanic; res: Prov.; mother: Eliza TINNER; inf:
father; pg:ln: 159:63

TINNER, Guy; CM; b. 19 Dec 1894 in Ffx; father: Chas. TINNER; occ:
farmer; res: Ffx; mother: Louisa TINNER; inf: Chas. TINNER, father;
pg:ln: 220:126

TOBIN, Kate T.; WF; b. 9 Dec 1894 in Ffx; father: K. G. TOBIN; occ:
farmer; res: Ffx; mother: N. E. TOBIN; inf: K. G. TOBIN, father;
pg:ln: 220:125

TODD, Martha E. H.; WF; b. 20 Nov 1887 in Ffx; father: Jno. T. TODD;
occ: farmer; res: Ffx; mother: Margaret TODD; inf: Jno. T. TODD,
father; pg:ln: 169:115

TOLBERT, Annie; WF; b. 19 Aug 1890 in Ffx; father: Silas TOLBERT;
occ: farmer; res: Ffx; mother: Elizabt. TOLBERT; inf: S. TOLBERT,
father; pg:ln: 188:116

TOLBERT, Bessie V.; WF; b. 20 Feb 1890 in Ffx; father: Horris
TOLBERT; occ: farmer; res: Ffx; mother: Virginia TOLBERT; inf: H.
TOLBERT, father; pg:ln: 188:114

TOLBERT, Caroline; WF; b. 1 Jun 1889 in Ffx; father: Jas. TOLBERT;
occ: farmer; res: Ffx; mother: Margt. TOLBERT; inf: Jas. TOLBERT,
father; pg:ln: 183:96

TOLBERT, Eva S.; WF; b. 7 Jan 1890 in Ffx; father: Jas. N. TOLBERT;
occ: farmer; res: Ffx; mother: Sophia TOLBERT; inf: J. N.
TOLBERT, father; pg:ln: 188:112

TOLBERT, Eva; WF; b. 19 Jul 1891 nr Accotink; father: Alfred
TOLBERT; occ: farmer; res: nr Accotink; mother: Catharine
TOLBERT; inf: parents; pg:ln: 195:22

TOLBERT, Gladys [written as TALBOT]; WF; b. 22 Feb 1893 in ___;
father: T. M. TOLBERT; occ: farmer; res: ___; mother: A. K.
TOLBERT; inf: T. M. TOLBERT, father; pg:ln: 215:101

TORREYSON, Howard L.; WM; b. 12 Jun 1884 in Prov.; father: William
TORREYSON; occ: farmer; res: Prov.; mother: Jennie
TORREYSON; inf: father; pg:ln: 151:93

TORREYSON, Mary; WF; b. 11 Jul 1880 in Langley; father: Henry A.
TORREYSON; occ: farmer; res: Langley; mother: Emma J.
TORREYSON; inf: father; pg:ln: 126:81

TORRISON, Geo. W.; WM; b. 20 May 1883 in Providence Dist.; father:
Henry A. TORRISON; occ: mechanic; res: Providence Dist.; mother:
Emma TORRISON; inf: father; pg:ln: 141:99

TORRISON, Jno. F.; WM; b. 7 Sep 1885 in F. B. Pike; father: Wm.
TORRISON; occ: farmer; res: F. B. Pike; mother: Jennie
TORRISON; inf: father; pg:ln: 154:82

TRACEY, Rich'd. N.; WM; b. 25 Feb 1884 in Dranes.; father: Jno. W.
TRACEY; occ: mechanic; res: Dranes.; mother: Margt. E. TRACEY;
inf: father; pg:ln: 151:95

TRAMEL, Robt.; WM; b. 8 Feb 1896 in Ffx; father: Robt. H. TRAMEL;
occ: farmer; res: Ffx; mother: Mary TRAMELL; inf: R. H. TRAMELL,
father; pg:ln: 228:120

TRAMELL, ___; WF; b. 15 Nov 1890 in Ffx; father: Chas. TRAMELL;
    occ: farmer; res: Ffx; mother: Margt. TRAMELL; inf: Chas.
    TRAMELL, father; pg:ln: 192:104
TRAMELL, Cora; WF; b. 17 Jan 1883 in Ffx; father: Wm. H. TRAMELL;
    occ: farmer; res: Ffx; mother: Fannie TRAMELL; inf: W. H.
    TRAMELL, father; pg:ln: 145:79
TRAMELL, Hattie; WF; b. 11 May 1892 in Ffx; father: Lewis TRAMELL;
    occ: farmer; res: Ffx; mother: Amanda TRAMELL; inf: L. TRAMELL,
    father; pg:ln: 204:100
TRAMELL, Henry E.; WM; b. 17 Jul 1894 in Ffx; father: R. B.
    TRAMELL; occ: farmer; res: Ffx; mother: Jennet TRAMELL; inf: R.
    B. TRAMELL, father; pg:ln: 220:124
TRAMELL, Irene; WF; b. 8 Sep 1896 in Ffx; father: Wash't. TRAMELL;
    occ: farmer; res: Ffx; mother: Olevia TRAMELL; inf: W. TRAMELL,
    father; pg:ln: 228:123
TRAMELL, J. Edward; WM; b. 5 Sep 1887 in Ffx; father: L. F.
    TRAMELL; occ: laborer; res: Ffx; mother: Amanda TRAMELL; inf: L.
    F. TRAMELL, father; pg:ln: 164:167
TRAMELL, Myrtle V.; WF; b. 21 Oct 1888 in Ffx; father: Washington
    TRAMELL; occ: farmer; res: Ffx; mother: Virginia TRAMELL; inf: W.
    TRAMELL, father; pg:ln: 175:93
TRAMELL, Raymond; WM; b. 15 May 1892 in Ffx; father: Ruben
    TRAMELL; occ: farmer; res: Ffx; mother: Jannett TRAMELL; inf: R.
    TRAMELL, father; pg:ln: 204:99
TRAMELL, Robt.; WM; b. 9 Mar 1894 in Ffx; father: L. T. TRAMELL;
    occ: farmer; res: Ffx; mother: Amanda TRAMEL; inf: L. T.
    TRAMELL, father; pg:ln: 220:119
TRAMELL, Rosa N.; WF; b. 1 May 1886 in Ffx; father: W. H. TRAMELL;
    occ: farmer; res: Ffx; mother: Elvira TRAMELL; inf: W. H. TRAMELL,
    father; pg:ln: 155:20
TRAMELL, Roy L.; WM; b. 10 Mar 1894 in Ffx; father: Robt. TRAMELL;
    occ: farmer; res: Ffx; mother: Emma TRAMELL; inf: Robt.
    TRAMELL, father; pg:ln: 220:118
TRAMILL, Rebecca Moss; WF; b. 16 Jan 1891 in Blue Spring; father:
    Wm. H. TRAMILL; occ: farmer; res: Blue Spring; mother: Fannie
    TRAMILL; inf: parents; pg:ln: 194:24
TRAMMEL, Jos. F.; WM; b. 28 May 1886 in Langley; father: Wash
    TRAMMELL; occ: farmer; res: Langley; mother: Virginia
    TRAMMELL; inf: father; pg:ln: 159:65
TRAMMELL, Bertha; WF; b. 9 Sep 1884 in F. C. Dis.; father: Phillip
    TRAMMEL; occ: farmer; res: F. C. Dis.; mother: Elizabeth
    TRAMMELL; inf: father; pg:ln: 151:91
TRAMMELL, Bertie L.; WF; b. 7 Jan 1880 in Dranesville; father: Chas.
    W. TRAMMELL; occ: farmer; res: Dranesville; mother: Mariah P.
    TRAMMELL; inf: father; pg:ln: 125:76
TRAMMELL, Ethel; WF; b. 15 Jun 1884 in Prov.; father: Wash.
    TRAMMEL; occ: farmer; res: Prov.; mother: Eugenia TRAMMELL;
    inf: father; pg:ln: 151:92

TRAMMELL, Hardy C.; WM; b. 28 Jul 1880 in Dranesville; father:
James D. TRAMMELL; occ: farmer; res: Dranesville; mother: Mary
J. TRAMMELL; inf: father; pg:ln: 125:80

TRAMMELL, Rebecca Moss; WF; b. 3 Aug 1892 nr Pleasant Valley;
father: Wm. H. TRAMMELL; occ: farmer; res: nr Pleasant Valley;
mother: Fannie TRAMMELL; inf: mother; pg:ln: 208:25

TRAMMELL, Thos. W.; WM; b. 9 Mar 1880 in Dranesville; father: Lewis
T. TRAMMELL; occ: blacksmith; res: Dranesville; mother: Amanda
TRAMMELL; inf: father; pg:ln: 125:74

TRICE, Ethel J.; WF; b. 24 Jul 1883 in Ffx; father: Luther R. TRICE;
occ: farmer; res: Ffx; mother: Mary A. TRICE; inf: L. R. TRICE,
father; pg:ln: 145:81

TRICE, Grover Cleveland; WM; b. 8 Nov 1884 in Ffx; father: L. R.
TRICE; occ: farmer; res: Ffx; mother: Mary A. TRICE; inf: L. R.
TRICE, father; pg:ln: 148:71

TRICE, Sadie B.; WF; b. 5 Sep 1888 in Ffx; father: L. R. TRICE; occ:
farmer; res: Ffx; mother: Mary A. TRICE; inf: L. R. TRICE, father;
pg:ln: 171:65

TRICKET, Alfred B.; WM; b. 13 Aug 1893 in ___; father: G. W.
TRICKETT; occ: farmer; res: ___; mother: A. L. TRICKETT; inf: G.
W. TRICKETT, father; pg:ln: 215:99

TRICKET, Geo. W.; WM; b. 1 May 1892 in Ffx; father: Geo. W.
TRICKET; occ: farmer; res: Ffx; mother: America TRICKET; inf: G.
W. TRICKET, father; pg:ln: 204:101

TRICKETT, Eva; WF; b. 9 Aug 1887 in Ffx; father: Geo. W. TRICKETT;
occ: farmer; res: Ffx; mother: America TRICKETT; inf: Geo.
TRICKETT, father; pg:ln: 164:165

TRICKETT, Gladys; WF; b. 17 Jun 1889 in Ffx; father: Geo. W.
TRICKET; occ: farmer; res: Ffx; mother: America TRICKET; inf: G.
W. TRICKET, father; pg:ln: 180:111

TRIPLET, Dunbar B.; WM; b. 28 Jun 1889 in Ffx; father: J. Everet
TRIPLET; occ: farmer; res: Ffx; mother: Olive D. TRIPLET; inf: J. E.
TRIPLET, father; pg:ln: 183:97

TRIPLETT, Francis J.; WM; b. 20 Oct 1887 in Ffx; father: J. Everet
TRIPLETT; occ: farmer; res: Ffx; mother: Olive D. TRIPLETT; inf: J.
E. TRIPLETT, father; pg:ln: 169:111

TRIPLETT, Geo. Archibald; WM; b. 30 Nov 1893 nr Franconia; father:
Everett TRIPLETT; occ: farmer; res: nr Franconia; mother: Olevia D.
TRIPLETT; inf: parent; pg:ln: 212:92

TRIPLETT, Mary Lindsey; WF; b. 10 Jun 1891 in Rolling Road; father:
Everett TRIPLETT; occ: farmer; res: Rolling Rd.; mother: Olive
TRIPLETT; inf: parents; pg:ln: 195:23

TROTH, Annie R.; WF; b. 29 Jul 1887 in Ffx; father: Geo. H. TROTH;
occ: merchant; res: Ffx; mother: Emma V. TROTH; inf: Geo. H.
TROTH, father; pg:ln: 169:112

TROTH, Geo.; WM; b. 11 Dec 1885 in Ffx; father: Geo. H. TROTH; occ:
farmer; res: Ffx; mother: Emma V. TROTH; inf: G. H. TROTH,
father; pg:ln: 157:58

TROTH, Martha R.; WF; b. 20 Jul 1882 in Ffx; father: Frank W. TROTH; occ: ___; res: ___; mother: Martha W. TROTH; inf: F. W. TROTH, father; pg:ln: 138:80

TRUMBLE, Clara Tracy; WF; b. 5 Mar 1890 in Ffx; father: Saml. T. TRUMBLE; occ: farmer; res: Ffx; mother: Ellen TRUMBLE; inf: S. TRUMBLE, father; pg:ln: 188:111

TRUMBULL, Roberta; WF; b. 7 Nov 1895 nr Burke Sta.; father: Robert TRUMBULL; occ: farmer; res: nr Burke Sta.; mother: Nora TRUMBULL; inf: father; pg:ln: 224:120

TRUMBULL, Royal Robert; WM; b. 20 Jan 1896 nr Ravensworth; father: Robert L. TRUMBULL; occ: farmer; res: nr Ravensworth; mother: Elinora TRUMBULL; inf: mother; pg:ln: 232:122

TUCKER, ___; WM; b. 15 Oct 1888 in Ffx; father: Jno. P. TUCKER; occ: farmer; res: Ffx; mother: M. F. TUCKER; inf: Jno. P. TUCKER, father; pg:ln: 175:99

TUCKER, ___; WM; b. 23 Sep 1883 in Dranesville; father: Jno. P. TUCKER; occ: farmer; res: Dranesville; mother: Maria F. TUCKER; inf: father; pg:ln: 141:100

TUCKER, B. A..; WF; b. 4 Apr 1880 in Springvale; father: John P. TUCKER; occ: farmer; res: Dranesville; mother: Mariah T. TUCKER; inf: father; pg:ln: 125:77

TUCKER, Clarence E.; WM; b. 11 Sep 1884 in Dranes.; father: Geo. W. TUCKER; occ: farmer; res: Dranes.; mother: ___ TUCKER; inf: father; pg:ln: 151:94

TUCKER, Lillian; WF; b. 15 Oct 1887 in Ffx; father: M. T. TUCKER; occ: laborer; res: Ffx; mother: Mary L. TUCKER; inf: M. T. TUCKER, father; pg:ln: 169:108

TUCKER, not named; WF; b. 31 Dec 1881 in Spring Vale; father: Jno. P. TUCKER; occ: farmer; res: Spring Vale; mother: Maria T. TUCKER; inf: father; pg:ln: 131:68

TUCKER, Phebe E.; WF; b. 1 Jun 1890 in Ffx; father: Jno. P. TUCKER; occ: farmer; res: Ffx; mother: Fannie TUCKER; inf: J. P. TUCKER, father; pg:ln: 192:103

TUCKER, Zella; WF; b. 4 Apr 1893 in ___; father: Jno. P. TUCKER; occ: farmer; res: ___; mother: Maria TUCKER; inf: J. P. TUCKER, father; pg:ln: 215:100

TURBERVILL, H. L.; WF; b. 4 Jul 1881 in Ffx; father: G. R. TURBERVILL; occ: farmer; res: Ffx; mother: Addie TURBERVILL; inf: G. R. TURBERVILL, father; pg:ln: 133:55

TURLEY, ___; CF; b. 5 Sep 1889 in Ffx; father: W. TURLEY; occ: farmer; res: Ffx; mother: Maggie TURLEY; inf: W. TURLEY, father; pg:ln: 183:93

TURLEY, Lee; CM; b. 13 Nov 1881 in Ffx; father: W. TURLEY; occ: farmer; res: Ffx; mother: Molly TURLEY; inf: W. TURLEY, father; pg:ln: 133:57

TURLEY, Vida; CF; b. 6 Apr 1891 in Fairfax C. H.; father: Wm. T. TURLEY; occ: laborer; res: Fairfax C. H.; mother: Mollie TURLEY; inf: parent; pg:ln: 196:30

TURNER, Alice D. T.; WF; b. 10 Jan 1890 in Ffx; father: ___ TURNER; occ: farmer; res: Ffx; mother: Ida Estell TURNER; inf: I. E. TURNER, mother; pg:ln: 188:117

TURNER, Elsie; WF; b. 16 Jun 1894 in Ffx; father: W. TURNER; occ: farmer; res: Ffx; mother: Bessie TURNER; inf: W. TURNER, father; pg:ln: 220:120

TURNER, Elsie; WF; b. 25 Mar 1896 in Reading Pa; father: Geo. W. TURNER; occ: spoke turner; res: nr Alex.; mother: Ida TURNER; inf: father; pg:ln: 232:120

TURNER, Geo.; CM; b. 10 Jun 1896 in Ffx; father: Chas. TURNER; occ: farmer; res: Ffx; mother: Mittie TURNER; inf: Chas. TURNER, father; pg:ln: 228:124

TURNER, Hannah E.; WF; b. 28 Oct 1880 in Springvale; father: James TURNER; occ: farmer; res: Dranesville; mother: Rebecca TURNER; inf: father; pg:ln: 125:78

TURNER, Harry; CM; b. __ Jan 1889 in Ffx; father: Wilson TURNER; occ: farmer; res: Ffx; mother: Sallie TURNER; inf: W. TURNER, father; pg:ln: 180:120

TURNER, Ivy; WF; b. 12 Jun 1896 in Ffx; father: W. TURNER; occ: farmer; res: Ffx; mother: Bessie TURNER; inf: W. TURNER, father; pg:ln: 228:122

TURNER, John; WM; b. 14 Jan 1887 in Ffx; father: Wm. R. TURNER; occ: farmer; res: Ffx; mother: Sallie TURNER; inf: W. R. TURNER, father; pg:ln: 164:158

TYERS, Marshall E.; WM; b. 19 Oct 1890 in Ffx; father: Geo. E. TYERS; occ: farmer; res: Ffx; mother: Maggie TYERS; inf: Geo. E. TYERS, father; pg:ln: 188:110

TYLER, Carrie; WF; b. 15 Aug 1895 nr Accotink; father: M. W. TYLER; occ: farmer; res: nr Accotink; mother: Anna E. TYLER; inf: father; pg:ln: 224:124

TYLER, Clarence G.; CM; b. 8 Jan 1892 in Ffx; father: W. H. TYLER; occ: farmer; res: ___; mother: Sarah TYLER; inf: W. H. TYLER, father; pg:ln: 205:107

TYLER, Lottie; WF; b. 13 Jul 1881 in Ffx; father: Danl. TYLER; occ: farmer; res: Ffx; mother: Julia TYLER; inf: D. TYLER, father; pg:ln: 133:56

TYLER, Mary Dulin; WF; b. 14 Nov 1895 nr Franconia; father: Wm. TYLER; occ: farmer; res: nr Franconia; mother: Mary C. TYLER; inf: father; pg:ln: 224:123

TYLER, William; CM; b. 31 Dec 1886 in Prov.; father: Reuben TYLER; occ: laborer; res: Prov.; mother: B. TYLER; inf: father; pg:ln: 159:62

TYRRELL, Conrad; WM; b. 27 Aug 1884 in Ffx; father: Eugene TERRELL; occ: farmer; res: Ffx; mother: Mary E. TYRRELL; inf: E. TYRRELL, father; pg:ln: 148:75

URON, W. S.; WM; b. 6 Sep 1889 in Ffx; father: Saml. T. URON; occ: farmer; res: Ffx; mother: Clara S. URON; inf: S. T. URON, father; pg:ln: 180:122

Van NUYS, Margaret LaGrange [originally written as Van NAYS, Margaret]; WF; b. 22 Sep 1895 [23-1894 written above] in Arcturus? P.O.; father: Wm. Van NUYS [originally written as Van NAY]; occ: farmer; res: Arcturus?; mother: Ida Van NUYS [originally written as Van NAYS]; inf: mother; pg:ln: 224:130

Van NUYS, Margaret LaGrange; WF; b. 23 Sep 1894 in Ffx; father: Wm. Van NUYS; occ: farmer; res: Ffx; mother: Ida Van NUYS; inf: mother See 1895 line 130; pg:ln: 220:131 1/2

VANDEVENTER, Albt. M.; WM; b. 17 Oct 1890 in Ffx; father: M. G. VANDEVENTER; occ: farmer; res: Ffx; mother: Bessie VANDEVENTER; inf: M. G. VANDEVENTER, father; pg:ln: 192:110

VANDYKE, John H.; WM; b. 5 Jan 1880 in Lewinsville; father: Frank R. VANDYKE; occ: farmer; res: Vienna; mother: Nellie VANDYKE; inf: father; pg:ln: 126:82

VANDYKE, Margaret L.; WF; b. 27 Feb 1883 in Lewinsville; father: R. F. VANDYKE; occ: mechanic; res: Lewinsville; mother: Nellie VANDYKE; inf: father; pg:ln: 141:103

VANHORN, Goldie M.; WF; b. 18 Dec 1894 in Ffx; father: Edw'd. VANHORN; occ: farmer; res: Ffx; mother: A. E. VANHORN; inf: E. VANHORN, father; pg:ln: 220:129

VANHORN, Mary H.; WF; b. 8 Jan 1887 in Ffx; father: Edwd. VANHORN; occ: laborer; res: Ffx; mother: A. E. VANHORN; inf: E. VANHORN, father; pg:ln: 164:168

VEITCH, Cora; WF; b. 12 Apr 1892 in Ffx; father: W. H. VEITCH; occ: farmer; res: ___; mother: M. E. VEITCH; inf: W. H. VEITCH, father; pg:ln: 205:108

VENNEY, Bertha; CF; b. 26 Feb 1894 in Ffx; father: Cornelius VENEY; occ: farmer; res: Ffx; mother: Lydia VENEY; inf: C. VENNEY, father; pg:ln: 220:131

VERMILYA, Raymond; WM; b. 12 Feb 1896 in Gunston; father: H. W. VERMILYA; occ: farmer; res: Gunston; mother: Hattee VERMILYA; inf: mother; pg:ln: 232:130

VIOLET, Bertha McBride; WF; b. 17 Oct 1889 in Ffx; father: Milton F. VIOLET; occ: farmer; res: Ffx; mother: Annie VIOLET; inf: Milton F. VIOLET, father; pg:ln: 183:100

VIOLET, Claud R.; WM; b. 4 Jan 1888 in Ffx; father: Milton F. VIOLET; occ: farmer; res: Ffx; mother: Annie VIOLET; inf: M. F. VIOLET, father; pg:ln: 171:69

VIOLET, Cleone E.; WF; b. 17 Feb 1889 in Ffx; father: Chas. A. VIOLET; occ: farmer; res: Ffx; mother: Anna VIOLET; inf: Chas. VIOLET, father; pg:ln: 183:99

VIOLET, Edith Josephine; WF; b. 14 May 1892 nr Lorton Sta.; father: Milton VIOLET; occ: farmer; res: nr Lorton Sta.; mother: Annie VIOLET; inf: father; pg:ln: 209:58

VIOLET, Frederick Lee; WM; b. 27 Jun 1888 in Ffx; father: Chas. A. VIOLET; occ: farmer; res: Ffx; mother: Anna N. VIOLET; inf: Chas. A. VIOLET, father; pg:ln: 171:71

VIOLET, George Elmer; WM; b. 5 Apr 1891 nr Lorton; father: Chas. A. VIOLET; occ: farmer; res: nr Lorton; mother: Annie VIOLET; inf: parents; pg:ln: 193:28

VIOLET, Milton Ellis; WM; b. 21 May 1895 nr Lorton Sta.; father: Milton VIOLET; occ: farmer; res: Lorton Sta.; mother: Annie VIOLET; inf: mother; pg:ln: 224:129

VIOLET, Richard; WM; b. 19 Mar 1888 in Ffx; father: Napoleon S. VIOLET; occ: farmer; res: Ffx; mother: Lula VIOLET; inf: N. S. VIOLET, father; pg:ln: 171:70

VIOLETT, Cleone; WF; b. 5 Feb 1890 in Ffx; father: Chas. A. VIOLETT; occ: farmer; res: Ffx; mother: Annie N. VIOLETT; inf: C. A. VIOLETT, father; pg:ln: 188:118

VIRTS, Edna T.; WF; b. 6 Aug 1896 in Ffx; father: J. E. L. VIRTS; occ: farmer; res: Ffx; mother: H. M. VIRTS; inf: J. E. L. VIRTS, father; pg:ln: 228:127

VIRTS, Jennie; WF; b. 14 Dec 1894 in Ffx; father: Jacob VIRTS; occ: farmer; res: Ffx; mother: Hettie VIRTS; inf: J. VIRTS, father; pg:ln: 220:128

VISEY, Neil; WM; b. 24 Jul 1896 nr Lorton Sta; father: H. B. VISEY; occ: farmer; res: nr Lorton Sta; mother: Lillie VISEY; inf: father; pg:ln: 232:129

[VOIGT], not named; WF; b. 4 Oct 1891 nr Clifton; father: Augustine VOIGT; occ: farmer; res: Boothlet Farm; mother: Mary Alberta VOIGT; inf: parents; pg:ln: 194:25

VONHERBULIS, Walter; WM; b. 1 Jan 1894 in Ffx; father: Albt. O. VONHERBULIS; occ: farmer; res: Ffx; mother: Amelia VONHERBULIS; inf: A. O. VONHERBULIS, father; pg:ln: 220:130

VORHEES, Bertha B.; WF; b. 8 Sep 1887 in Ffx; father: J. M. VORHEES; occ: farmer; res: Ffx; mother: Ella VORHEES; inf: J. M. VORHEES, father; pg:ln: 164:169

WAINES, W. H.; CM; b. 4 Mar 1891 in Ffx; father: Henson WAINES; occ: farmer; res: Ffx; mother: Harriet WAINES; inf: H. WAINES, father; pg:ln: 201:113

WAINES, W.; CM; b. 21 Jul 1896 in Ffx; father: Henson WAINES; occ: farmer; res: Ffx; mother: Harriet WAINES; inf: H. WAINES, father; pg:ln: 228:132

WAINS, Seth; CM; b. 1 Nov 1882 in Providence; father: Benj. WAINS; occ: laborer; res: Prov.; mother: Frances WAINS; inf: father; pg:ln: 135:70

WAIT, Katie J.; WF; b. 20 Dec 1880 in ___; father: W. F. WAIT; occ: farmer; res: Ffx; mother: Jenney; inf: W. F. WAIT, father; pg:ln: 129:98

WAIT, not named; WM; b. 30 Dec 1882 in Providence; father: E. S. WAIT; occ: farmer; res: Prov.; mother: Elizabeth WAIT; inf: father; pg:ln: 135:68

WAKEFIELD, Lowell; WM; b. 24 Mar 1884 in Annandale; father: E. W. WAKEFIELD; occ: farmer; res: Annandale; mother: M. R. WAKEFIELD; inf: father; pg:ln: 151:104

WAKEFIELD, Minnie L.; WF; b. 17 Jun 1893 in Ffx; father: M. M.
WAKEFIELD; occ: farmer; res: Ffx; mother: Lola M. WAKEFIELD;
inf: M. M. WAKEFIELD, father; pg:ln: 216:109

WALKER, ___; WM; b. 29 Dec 1887 in ___; father: R. F. WALKER; occ:
farmer; res: Ffx; mother: Annie M. WALKER; inf: R. F. WALKER,
father; pg:ln: 165:173

WALKER, Alcinda; CF; b. 20 Dec 1889 in Ffx; father: W. WALKER; occ:
farmer; res: Ffx; mother: Alcinda WALKER; inf: W. WALKER, father;
pg:ln: 180:126

WALKER, Annie E.; WF; b. 7 Jun 1889 in Ffx; father: Geo. C. WALKER;
occ: farmer; res: Ffx; mother: Sarah E. WALKER; inf: G. C.
WALKER, father; pg:ln: 180:124

WALKER, Bertha R.; WF; b. 18 Aug 1880 in Providence; father: Wm. T.
WALKER; occ: farmer; res: Providence; mother: Margaret WALKER;
inf: father; pg:ln: 126:86

WALKER, Blanch; WF; b. 7 Jun 1887 in ___; father: J. H. WALKER;
occ: farmer; res: Ffx; mother: Ada WALKER; inf: J. H. WALKER,
father; pg:ln: 165:179

WALKER, Ella; WF; b. 4 Nov 1889 in Ffx; father: Jas. H. WALKER; occ:
farmer; res: Ffx; mother: Virginia WALKER; inf: J. H. WALKER,
father; pg:ln: 180:125

WALKER, Emory A.; WM; b. 25 Apr 1887 in ___; father: Geo. C.
WALKER; occ: farmer; res: Ffx; mother: Sarah E. WALKER; inf:
Geo. C. WALKER, father; pg:ln: 165:174

WALKER, Grace; WF; b. 5 Oct 1884 in Prov.; father: Jno. W. WALKER;
occ: farmer; res: Prov.; mother: Ada WALKER; inf: father; pg:ln:
151:98

WALKER, Henry L.; CM; b. 29 Sep 1891 in Ffx; father: Wm. WALKER;
occ: farmer; res: Ffx; mother: A. C. WALKER; inf: W. WALKER,
father; pg:ln: 201:117

WALKER, J. E.; CF; b. 19 Jul 1893 in ___; father: W. WALKER; occ:
farmer; res: ___; mother: Alcinda WALKER; inf: W. WALKER, father;
pg:ln: 215:106

WALKER, Jno. H.; CM; b. 15 Apr 1896 in Ffx; father: W. WALKER; occ:
farmer; res: Ffx; mother: Alcinda WALKER; inf: W. WALKER, father;
pg:ln: 228:134

WALKER, Jno. T.; CM; b. 28 Nov 1893 in ___; father: Jno. WALKER;
occ: farmer; res: ___; mother: Annie WALKER; inf: Jno. WALKER,
father; pg:ln: 215:102

WALKER, Lola B.; WF; b. 30 Apr 1893 in Ffx; father: C. W. WALKER;
occ: farmer; res: ___; mother: Rosa B. WALKER; inf: Chas.
WALKER, father; pg:ln: 205:115

WALKER, Margt.; WF; b. 26 Jan 1896 in Ffx; father: J. D. WALKER;
occ: clergyman; res: Ffx; mother: Margt. WALKER; inf: J. D.
WALKER, father; pg:ln: 228:137

WALKER, Mary J.; WF; b. 5 Jun 1880 in Dranesville; father: Geo. C.
WALKER; occ: farmer; res: Dranesville; mother: Sarah E. WALKER;
inf: father; pg:ln: 126:85

WALKER, Matilda; CF; b. 20 Apr 1883 in Falls Church; father: William
WALKER; occ: laborer; res: Falls Church; mother: Louisa WALKER;
inf: father; pg:ln: 141:107

WALKER, Minnie; WF; b. 8 Aug 1894 in Ffx; father: Rich'd. F. WALKER;
occ: farmer; res: Ffx; mother: Annie WALKER; inf: R. F. WALKER,
father; pg:ln: 220:133

WALKER, Nora; WF; b. 15 Nov 1892 in Ffx; father: Jno. WALKER; occ:
farmer; res: ___; mother: Ada WALKER; inf: Jno. WALKER, father;
pg:ln: 205:109

WALKER, not named; CM; b. 7 Nov 1882 in Falls Church; father: Gabe.
WALKER; occ: laborer; res: Falls Church; mother: Maria WALKER;
inf: father; pg:ln: 135:71

WALKER, not named; WM; b. 17 Feb 1883 in Dranesville; father: R. F.
WALKER; occ: farmer; res: Dranesville; mother: Annie M. WALKER;
inf: father; pg:ln: 142:115

WALKER, Orra Lee; WF; b. 25 Nov 1882 in Frying Pan; father: Geo. C.
WALKER; occ: farmer; res: Frying Pan; mother: Sarah E. WALKER;
inf: father; pg:ln: 135:66

WALKER, Vera M.; WF; b. 26 Oct 1889 in Ffx; father: Stephen
WALKER; occ: farmer; res: Ffx; mother: Julia A. WALKER; inf: S.
WALKER, father; pg:ln: 180:123

WALKER, Virginia; WF; b. 20 Apr 1894 in Ffx; father: Jas. H. WALKER;
occ: farmer; res: Ffx; mother: Virginia WALKER; inf: J. H. WALKER,
father; pg:ln: 220:136

WALKER, Wilber S.; WM; b. 4 May 1888 in Ffx; father: J. H. WALKER;
occ: farmer; res: Ffx; mother: J. C. WALKER; inf: J. H. WALKER,
father; pg:ln: 175:105

WALKER, Wm. S.; CM; b. 15 Apr 1884 in Bailey's X Roads; father:
William WALKER; occ: laborer; res: Bailey's X Roads; mother:
Louisa WALKER; inf: father; pg:ln: 151:97

WALL, Darwin A.; WM; b. 11 Jun 1888 in Ffx; father: Jas. A. WALL; occ:
farmer; res: Ffx; mother: Gertrude WALL; inf: J. A. WALL, father;
pg:ln: 175:101

WALL, Ethel G.; WF; b. 8 May 1890 in Ffx; father: Jas. A. WALL; occ:
farmer; res: Ffx; mother: G. L. WALL; inf: J. A. WALL, father; pg:ln:
192:116

WALL, Guy M.; WM; b. 14 Sep 1892 in Ffx; father: Jas. A. WALL; occ:
farmer; res: ___; mother: G. L. WALL; inf: J. A. WALL, father; pg:ln:
205:114

WALL, Minnie M.; WF; b. 8 Feb 1887 in ___; father: J. A. WALL; occ:
farmer; res: Ffx; mother: Gertrude WALL; inf: J. A. WALL, father;
pg:ln: 165:177

WALTERS, ___ (twin); WM; b. 1 Jul 1891 in Ffx; father: G. F. M.
WALTERS; occ: farmer; res: Ffx; mother: Katie WALTERS; inf: G. F.
M. WALTERS, father; pg:ln: 201:107

WALTERS, ___ (twin); WM; b. 1 Jul 1891 in Ffx; father: G. F. M.
WALTERS; occ: farmer; res: Ffx; mother: Katie WALTERS; inf: G. F.
M. WALTERS, father; pg:ln: 201:108

WALTERS, ___; WF; b. 14 Mar 1888 in Ffx; father: L. N. WALTERS; occ: farmer; res: Ffx; mother: L. J. WALTERS; inf: J. [L.?] N. WALTERS, father; pg:ln: 175:102

WALTERS, Alfred G.; WM; b. 17 Jun 1888 in Ffx; father: C. C. WALTERS; occ: farmer; res: Ffx; mother: Annie L. WALTERS; inf: C. C. WALTERS, father; pg:ln: 175:104

WALTERS, Alice H.; WF; b. 11 Mar 1886 in Langley; father: A. B. WALTERS; occ: farmer; res: Langley; mother: A. W. WALTERS; inf: father; pg:ln: 159:68

WALTERS, Geo. M.; WM; b. 19 Oct 1890 in Ffx; father: U. S. WALTERS; occ: farmer; res: Ffx; mother: Hattie WALTERS; inf: U. S. WALTERS, father; pg:ln: 192:114

WALTERS, Henry N.; WM; b. 16 Jun 1888 in Ffx; father: Ulysses S. WALTERS; occ: farmer; res: Ffx; mother: Hattie WALTERS; inf: U. S. WALTERS, father; pg:ln: 176:108

WALTERS, Marian O.; WF; b. 5 Jan 1883 in Providence Dist.; father: C. C. WALTERS; occ: farmer; res: Providence Dist.; mother: Annie WALTERS; inf: father; pg:ln: 142:110

WALTERS, Marion F.; WM; b. 15 May 1892 in Ffx; father: Jno. WALTERS; occ: farmer; res: ___; mother: Eliza WALTERS; inf: Jno. WALTERS, father; pg:ln: 205:113

WALTERS, not named; WM; b. 1 Sep 1884 in Langley; father: Julian WALTERS; occ: farmer; res: Langley; mother: Martha WALTERS; inf: father; pg:ln: 151:102

WALTERS, S. W.; WM; b. 21 Jul 1883 in Providence Dist.; father: Lucien WALTERS; occ: farmer; res: Providence Dist.; mother: Lenora WALTERS; inf: father; pg:ln: 142:111

WALTERS, W. H.; WM; b. 6 Jun 1888 in Ffx; father: G. F. WALTERS; occ: farmer; res: Ffx; mother: C. H. WALTERS; inf: G. F. WALTERS, father; pg:ln: 175:103

WALTON, Andrew; WM; b. 17 Nov 1889 in Ffx; father: J. N. WALTON; occ: farmer; res: Ffx; mother: Va. WALTON; inf: J. N. WALTON, father; pg:ln: 180:129

WALTON, Jas. H.; WM; b. 5 Sep 1883 in Providence Dist.; father: J. N. WALTON; occ: farmer; res: Providence Dist.; mother: V. A. WALTON; inf: father; pg:ln: 142:114

WALTON, Julian N.; WM; b. 27 Aug 1885 in Prov.; father: J. N. WALTON; occ: farmer; res: Providence; mother: V. A. WALTON; inf: father; pg:ln: 154:86

WANSER, Mary; CF; b. 1 Dec 1891 in Ffx; father: Jos. WANSER; occ: farmer; res: Ffx; mother: Fannie WANSER; inf: Jos. WANSER, father; pg:ln: 201:118

WANSEY, Joseph; CM; b. 6 Jun 1889 in Ffx; father: Joseph WANSEY; occ: farmer; res: Ffx; mother: Fannie WANSEY; inf: J. WANSEY, father; pg:ln: 180:132

WAPLE, Jarret; WM; b. 13 Apr 1881 in Waples Mill; father: Jno. H. WAPLE; occ: miller; res: Waples Mill; mother: Isabella WAPLE; inf: father; pg:ln: 131:74

WAPLE, Minnie BELL; WF; b. 18 Mar 1883 in Providence Dist.; father: Jno. H. WAPLE; occ: miller; res: Providence Dist.; mother: Isabel WAPLE; inf: father; pg:ln: 142:112

WAPLE, Morselle; WM; b. 25 Mar 1892 in Ffx; father: Jno. H. WAPLE; occ: farmer; res: ___; mother: Isabela WAPLE; inf: J. H. WAPLE, father; pg:ln: 205:110

WAPLE, Randolph; WM; b. 28 Oct 1887 in ___; father: J. H. WAPLE; occ: farmer; res: Ffx; mother: Isabell WAPLE; inf: J. H. WAPLE, father; pg:ln: 165:178

WAPLE, Richd. H.; WM; b. 20 May 1890 in Ffx; father: Jno. H. WAPLE; occ: farmer; res: Ffx; mother: Isabella WAPLE; inf: J. H. WAPLE, father; pg:ln: 192:113

WARD, Ader; CF; b. 30 Apr 1883 in Ffx; father: Geo. WARD; occ: farmer; res: Ffx; mother: Ellen WARD; inf: Geo. WARD, father; pg:ln: 145:86

WARD, Phillip O.; WM; b. 26 Feb 1882 in Ffx; father: Wm. R. WARD; occ: ___; res: ___; mother: Susie WARD; inf: Wm. R. WARD, father; pg:ln: 138:84

WARD, Sarah R.; WF; b. 12 Apr 1883 in Ffx; father: W. R. WARD; occ: farmer; res: Ffx; mother: Susan WARD; inf: W. R. WARD, father; pg:ln: 145:85

WARD, Wilson; CM; b. 1 Jul 1893 in ___; father: Geo. WARD; occ: farmer; res: ___; mother: Ellin WARD; inf: G. WARD, father; pg:ln: 215:107

WARNER, Charlotte; CF; b. 7 Apr 1896 in Ffx; father: Grant WARNER; occ: farmer; res: Ffx; mother: Annie WARNER; inf: G. WARNER, father; pg:ln: 228:131

WARNER, Grant; CM; b. 5 Feb 1894 in Ffx; father: Grant WARNER; occ: farmer; res: Ffx; mother: Mary WARNER; inf: Grant WARNER, father; pg:ln: 220:144

WARNER, Jas. E.; CM; b. 8 Aug 1893 in ___; father: Grant WARNER; occ: farmer; res: ___; mother: Hattie WARNER; inf: G. WARNER, father; pg:ln: 215:104

WARNER, Robt.; CM; b. 25 Apr 1896 in Ffx; father: Robt. WARNER; occ: farmer; res: Ffx; mother: Ida WARNER; inf: Robt. WARNER, father; pg:ln: 228:133

WARNER, Susie; CF; b. 5 Nov 1892 in Ffx; father: Henry WARNER; occ: farmer; res: ___; mother: Rebecca WARNER; inf: H. WARNER, father; pg:ln: 205:118

WASHINGTON Auther; CM; b. 20 Nov 1880 in ___; father: Jno. WASHINGTON; occ: farmer; res: Ffx; mother: Sarah; inf: J. WASHINGTON, father; pg:ln: 129:99

WASHINGTON, Annie; CF; b. 29 Mar 1891 in Alexandria; father: Simon WASHINGTON; occ: blacksmith; res: nr Langston; mother: Gussie WASHINGTON; inf: parent; pg:ln: 197:09

WASHINGTON, Arthur W.; CM; b. 8 Jun 1882 in Providence; father: George WASHINGTON; occ: farmer; res: Prov.; mother: Sallie WASHINGTON; inf: father; pg:ln: 135:67

WASHINGTON, Delia; CF; b. 4 Apr 1894 in Ffx; father: Geo.
WASHINGTON; occ: farmer; res: Ffx; mother: Ceilia
WASHINGTON; inf: G. WASHINGTON, father; pg:ln: 220:145
WASHINGTON, Jno. S.; CM; b. 1 Oct 1894 in Ffx; father: Geo.
WASHINGTON; occ: farmer; res: Ffx; mother: Mary WASHINGTON;
inf: G. WASHINGTON, father; pg:ln: 220:140
WASHINGTON, Maggie; CF; b. 7 Jun 1884 in Ffx; father: W.
WASHINGTON; occ: farmer; res: Ffx; mother: Cornelia
WASHINGTON; inf: W. WASHINGTON, father; pg:ln: 148:77
WASHINGTON, Mamie; CF; b. 5 Jul 1890 in Ffx; father: John
WASHINGTON; occ: farmer; res: Ffx; mother: Mary WASHINGTON;
inf: Jno. WASHINGTON, father; pg:ln: 188:119
WASHINGTON, Minnie; CF; b. 14 Nov 1887 in Ffx; father: Simon
WASHINGTON; occ: laborer; res: Ffx; mother: Queen
WASHINGTON; inf: Simon WASHINGTON, father; pg:ln: 169:125
WASHINGTON, Simon; CM; b. 3 Jun 1893 nr Fairfax Sta.; father:
Simon WASHINGTON; occ: blacksmith; res: nr Fairfax Sta.; mother:
Queen WASHINGTON; inf: parent; pg:ln: 212:94
WATKINS, Clara (twin); WF; b. 11 Jul 1888 in Ffx; father: J. D.
WATKINS; occ: merchant; res: Ffx; mother: Lizzie WATKINS; inf: J.
D. WATKINS, father; pg:ln: 172:72
WATKINS, Claudia (twin); WF; b. 11 Jul 1888 in Ffx; father: J. D.
WATKINS; occ: merchant; res: Ffx; mother: Lizzie WATKINS; inf: J.
D. WATKINS, father; pg:ln: 172:73
WATKINS, Frank; WM; b. 25 Aug 1885 in Ffx; father: Geo. D.
WATKINS; occ: farmer; res: Ffx; mother: Ella WATKINS; inf: G. D.
WATKINS, father; pg:ln: 157:67
WATKINS, not named; WM; b. 21 Jan 1886 in Oakton; father: E. W.
WATKINS; occ: farmer; res: Oakton; mother: M. E. WATKINS; inf:
father; pg:ln: 159:67
[WATKINS], not named; WM; b. 28 Mar 1891 nr Fairfax Sta.; father:
Wm. R. WATKINS; occ: farmer; res: nr Fairfax Sta.; mother: Kate
WATKINS; inf: parents; pg:ln: 194:26
WATKINS, Oceola; WF; b. 30 Apr 1884 in Prov.; father: W. B.
WATKINS; occ: farmer; res: Prov.; mother: Catharine WATKINS; inf:
father; pg:ln: 151:103
WATKINS, Rezin L.; WM; b. 7 Oct 1888 in Ffx; father: W. B. WATKINS;
occ: farmer; res: Ffx; mother: Kate WATKINS; inf: W. B. WATKINS,
father; pg:ln: 172:74
WATSON, John; WM; b. 10 Sep 1893 nr Fairfax C. H.; father: James
WATSON; occ: farmer; res: nr Fairfax C. H.; mother: Emma
WATSON; inf: parent; pg:ln: 212:97
WATT, Egbert F.; WM; b. 8 May 1889 in Ffx; father: Wm. WATT; occ:
farmer; res: Ffx; mother: Elizabt. WATT; inf: W. WATT, father; pg:ln:
183:102
WATT, Elizabeth E. Fitzhugh; WF; b. 23 Apr 1896 nr Ravensworth;
father: Wm. WATT; occ: farmer; res: nr Ravensworth; mother:
Elizabeth WATT; inf: mother; pg:ln: 232:135

WATTS, ___ (dead); CF; b. 8 Mar 1894 in Ffx; father: Robt. WATTS; occ: farmer; res: Ffx; mother: Maggie WATTS; inf: Robt. WATTS, father; pg:ln: 220:143

WATTS, Lizzie; CF; b. 12 Mar 1892 in Ffx; father: Robt. WATTS; occ: farmer; res: ___; mother: Maggie WATTS; inf: R. WATTS, father; pg:ln: 205:116

WAY, Paul H.; WM; b. 2 May 1882 in Ffx; father: N. S. WAY; occ: ___; res: ___; mother: Esther WAY; inf: N. S. WAY, father; pg:ln: 138:85

WAYNES, Esther L.; CF; b. 13 Mar 1888 in Ffx; father: Benjn. WAYNES; occ: farmer; res: Ffx; mother: Margt. WAYNES; inf: B. WAYNES, father; pg:ln: 176:109

WAYNES, Louisa L.; CF; b. 8 Jan 1887 in ___; father: Benjn. WAYNES; occ: farmer; res: Ffx; mother: Margaret WAYNES; inf: Benjn. WAYNES, father; pg:ln: 165:180

WAYNES, Ruth A.; CF; b. 15 Jun 1884 in Prov.; father: Benj. WAYNES; occ: farmer; res: Prov.; mother: Margt. WAYNES; inf: father; pg:ln: 151:100

WEADON, Ernest Daniel; WM; b. 14 May 1896 nr Bone Mill; father: Chas. WEADON; occ: laborer; res: nr Bone Mill; mother: Martha WEADON; inf: mother; pg:ln: 232:136

WEAVER, ___; CM; b. 13 Apr 1896 in Ffx; father: Wash't. WEAVER; occ: farmer; res: Ffx; mother: Lavenia WEAVER; inf: W. WEAVER, father; pg:ln: 228:129

WEAVER, Ethel; CF; b. 16 May 1896 nr Chantilly; father: Robert WEAVER; occ: laborer; res: nr Chantilly; mother: Leticia WEAVER; inf: mother; pg:ln: 232:132

WEAVER, M.; CF; b. 1 May 1893 in ___; father: Frank WEAVER; occ: farmer; res: Ffx; mother: Nellie WEAVER; inf: F. WEAVER, father; pg:ln: 216:115

WEAVER, Mary; WF; b. 6 May 1886 in Ffx; father: Jno. B. WEAVER; occ: farmer; res: Ffx; mother: Elvira WEAVER; inf: J. B. WEAVER, father; pg:ln: 155:22

WEAVER, Ose D.; CF; b. 20 Sep 1889 in Ffx; father: Wash WEAVER; occ: farmer; res: Ffx; mother: Lavinia WEAVER; inf: W. WEAVER, father; pg:ln: 180:130

WEAVER, Phoebe B.; WF; b. 26 Nov 1890 in Ffx; father: Jno. B. WEAVER; occ: farmer; res: Ffx; mother: Elmira WEAVER; inf: J. B. WEAVER, father; pg:ln: 188:122

WEAVER, Phoebe Bell; WF; b. 26 Nov 1891 in Fairfax C. H.; father: John B. WEAVER; occ: ___; res: Fairfax C. H.; mother: Elvira WEAVER; inf: parents; pg:ln: 194:03

WEAVER, Sidney; CM; b. 17 Sep 1892 in Ffx; father: Wash. WEAVER; occ: farmer; res: ___; mother: Lavena WEAVER; inf: W. WEAVERS, father; pg:ln: 205:111

WEAVER, Susannah; CF; b. 3 Mar 1891 in Ffx; father: Frank WEAVER; occ: farmer; res: Ffx; mother: Nellie WEAVER; inf: Frank WEAVER, father; pg:ln: 201:109

WEAVER, Walter M.; CM; b. 15 Sep 1887 in ___; father: Washington
WEAVER; occ: farmer; res: Ffx; mother: Louisa WEAVER; inf: W.
WEAVER, father; pg:ln: 165:171

WEBB, ___ (dead); CM; b. 20 Mar 1891 in Ffx; father: Thos. WEBB;
occ: farmer; res: Ffx; mother: Jennie WEBB; inf: Thos. WEBB,
father; pg:ln: 201:115

WEBB, Ada; CF; b. 2 Jan 1888 in Ffx; father: David WEBB; occ: farmer;
res: Ffx; mother: Rose WEBB; inf: D. WEBB, father; pg:ln: 175:107

WEBB, Dolly V.; CF; b. 8 Jun 1882 in Providence; father: David WEBB;
occ: farmer; res: Prov.; mother: Rose WEBB; inf: father; pg:ln:
135:69

WEBB, French; CM; b. 8 May 1884 in Prov.; father: David WEBB; occ:
farmer; res: Prov.; mother: Rose WEBB; inf: father; pg:ln: 151:101

[WEBB], not named (dead); CM; b. 26 May 1885 in Ffx; father: Carter
WEBB; occ: farmer; res: Ffx; mother: Nancy WEBB; inf: C. WEBB,
father; pg:ln: 157:66

WEBB, Robert; CM; b. 8 May 1892 nr Mt. Vernon; father: Carter WEBB;
occ: farmer; res: nr Mt. Vernon; mother: Delsy WEBB; inf: father;
pg:ln: 206:14

WEBB, W. H.; CM; b. 15 Nov 1889 in Ffx; father: Carter WEBB; occ:
farmer; res: Ffx; mother: Dorcas WEBB; inf: C. WEBB, father; pg:ln:
183:105

WEIHLE, Gladdie; WF; b. 4 Oct 1893 in ___; father: J. R. WEIHLE; occ:
farmer; res: Ffx; mother: Mariana WEIHLE; inf: J. R. WEIHLE,
father; pg:ln: 216:111

WELLS, ___; WF; b. 4 Nov 1883 in Ffx; father: Jacob WELLS; occ:
farmer; res: Ffx; mother: Ann E. WELLS; inf: J. WELLS, father; pg:ln:
145:87

WELLS, Alice (twin); WF; b. 3 Nov 1891 in Ffx; father: Edwd. WELLS;
occ: farmer; res: Ffx; mother: Mary E. WELLS; inf: Edwd. WELLS,
father; pg:ln: 201:105

WELLS, Bertie (twin); WF; b. 3 Nov 1891 in Ffx; father: Edwd. WELLS;
occ: farmer; res: Ffx; mother: Mary E. WELLS; inf: Edwd. WELLS,
father; pg:ln: 201:106

WELLS, Danl. A.; WM; b. 18 Nov 1886 in Falls Church; father: Jno. A.
WELLS; occ: mechanic; res: Falls Church; mother: Estella WELLS;
inf: father; pg:ln: 159:69

WELLS, Henry; WM; b. 25 Jan 1885 in Falls Ch.; father: Jno. H.
WELLS; occ: mechanic; res: Falls Ch.; mother: Estella WELLS; inf:
father; pg:ln: 154:88

WELLS, Jesse R.; WM; b. 9 Nov 1891 in Ffx; father: Jno. H. WELLS;
occ: farmer; res: Ffx; mother: E. M. WELLS; inf: J. H. WELLS, father;
pg:ln: 201:111

WELLS, Jno. R.; WM; b. 23 Feb 1894 in Ffx; father: Jno. H. WELLS;
occ: farmer; res: Ffx; mother: Estella WELLS; inf: J. H. WELLS,
father; pg:ln: 220:137

WELLS, Lawrence; WM; b. 18 Oct 1887 in Ffx; father: J. H. WELLS; occ: farmer; res: Ffx; mother: Elizabeth WELLS; inf: J. H. WELLS, father; pg:ln: 165:170

WELLS, Leander Brenan James; WM; b. 31 Mar 1895 nr Centreville; father: Thos. J. WELLS; occ: laborer; res: nr Centreville; mother: Louisa WELLS; inf: mother; pg:ln: 223:74

WELLS, Leon; WM; b. 1 Dec 1896 in Ffx; father: Jno. H. WELLS; occ: farmer; res: Ffx; mother: Susie WELLS; inf: J. H. WELLS, father; pg:ln: 228:135

WELLS, Mary E.; WF; b. 27 Mar 1884 in Prov.; father: Jas. A. WELLS; occ: farmer; res: Prov.; mother: Millie H. WELLS; inf: father; pg:ln: 151:99

WELLS, Pirs? Joseph Sam; WM; b. 20 Oct 1893 nr Centreville; father: Thos. WELLS; occ: laborer; res: nr Centreville; mother: Fannie WELLS; inf: parent; pg:ln: 212:98

WESLEY, Cornelia; CF; b. 10 Aug 1888 in Ffx; father: Chas. WESLEY; occ: farmer; res: Ffx; mother: Millie WESLEY; inf: C. WESLEY, father; pg:ln: 175:106

WEST, Adolphus E.; WM; b. 1 Jul 1892 in West End; father: Geo. J. WEST; occ: dairyman; res: West End; mother: Mary E. WEST; inf: mother; pg:ln: 209:43

WEST, David A.; CM; b. 5 Jun 1889 in Ffx; father: Geo. WEST; occ: farmer; res: Ffx; mother: Mary E. WEST; inf: Geo. WEST, father; pg:ln: 184:110

WHALEN, Walter; WM; b. 13 Feb 1884 in Ffx; father: M. F. WHALEN; occ: farmer; res: Ffx; mother: Roxann WHALEN; inf: M. F. WHALEN, father; pg:ln: 148:79

WHALEY, Lucy Fitzhugh; WF; b. 10 Aug 1893 nr Chantilly; father: Everett WHALEY; occ: farmer; res: nr Chantilly; mother: Fannie F. WHALEY; inf: parent; pg:ln: 212:99

WHALEY, Mary Bird; WF; b. 8 Jan 1891 nr Centreville; father: E. B. WHALEY; occ: farmer; res: nr Centreville; mother: Fannie C. WHALEY; inf: parents; pg:ln: 194:27

WHALEY, not named; WM; b. 20 Feb 1887 in Ffx; father: F. M. WHALEY; occ: farmer; res: Ffx; mother: Eleanor WHALEY; inf: F. M. WHALEY, father; pg:ln: 169:120

WHALEY, Rosie; WF; b. 25 Jul 1892 nr Chantilly; father: Everett WHALEY; occ: farmer; res: nr Chantilly; mother: Fannie WHALEY; inf: mother; pg:ln: 208:26

WHEELER, Laura; CF; b. 9 Dec 1892 in Ffx; father: Jno. WHEELER; occ: farmer; res: ___; mother: Harriet WHEELER; inf: Jno. WHEELER, father; pg:ln: 205:117

WHITE, Edward; CM; b. 18 May 1887 in ___; father: Woodson WHITE; occ: farmer; res: Ffx; mother: Alice WHITE; inf: W. WHITE, father; pg:ln: 165:175

WHITE, Georgie; WF; b. 28 Sep 1896 in Ffx; father: T. H. WHITE; occ: butcher, res: Ffx; mother: M. A. WHITE; inf: T. H. WHITE, father; pg:ln: 228:136

WHITE, Jno. W.; CM; b. 24 Nov 1894 in Ffx; father: Henry WHITE; occ: farmer; res: Ffx; mother: Liberta WHITE; inf: H. WHITE, father; pg:ln: 220:135

WHITE, Rich'd. H.; CM; b. 23 May 1893 in ___; father: Henry WHITE; occ: farmer; res: Ffx; mother: Lebertha WHITE; inf: H. WHITE, father; pg:ln: 216:112

WHITENBERGER, Percy; WM; b. 28 Oct 1891 in Ffx; father: Henry WHITENBERGER; occ: farmer; res: Ffx; mother: Cath. WHITENBERGER; inf: H. WHITENBERGER, father; pg:ln: 201:110

WHITFIELD, B.; CM; b. 11 Jun 1891 in Ffx; father: Geo. WHITFIELD; occ: farmer; res: Ffx; mother: Adonia WHITFIELD; inf: Geo. WHITFIELD, father; pg:ln: 201:119

WHITFIELD, Della; CF; b. 2 Feb 1889 in Ffx; father: Geo. WHITFIELD; occ: farmer; res: Ffx; mother: Mary WHITFIELD; inf: G. WHITFIELD, father; pg:ln: 180:133

WHITFIELD, Laura M.; CF; b. 5 Oct 1893 in ___; father: Geo. WHITFIELD; occ: farmer; res: ___; mother: Dora WHITFIELD; inf: G. WHITFIELD, father; pg:ln: 215:105

WILAS, Eva; WF; b. 26 Jul 1895 nr Alexandria; father: Wm. WILAS; occ: farmer; res: nr Alex.; mother: Mary WILAS; inf: mother; pg:ln: 224:131

WILDBOAR, Edith F.; WF; b. 25 Dec 1884 in Ffx; father: F. S. WILDBOAR; occ: farmer; res: Ffx; mother: Sarah A. WILDBOAR; inf: F. S. WILDBOAR, father; pg:ln: 148:78

WILEY, Clarence; WM; b. 29 Jun 1891 in Ffx; father: H. C. WILEY; occ: farmer; res: Ffx; mother: Hattie WILEY; inf: H. C. WILEY, father; pg:ln: 201:112

WILEY, Edith; WF; b. 20 Jun 1887 in Ffx; father: Robert WILEY; occ: farmer; res: Ffx; mother: Mary E. WILEY; inf: Robt. WILEY, father; pg:ln: 169:118

WILEY, John; WM; b. 16 Aug 1895 in Mason's Neck; father: M. WILEY; occ: fisherman; res: Mason's Neck; mother: Annie WILEY; inf: mother; pg:ln: 224:133

WILEY, Pauline; WF; b. 8 Oct 1896 in Ffx; father: H. C. WILEY; occ: farmer; res: Ffx; mother: H. A. WILEY; inf: H. C. WILEY, father; pg:ln: 228:138

WILKERSON, Frank; CM; b. 22 Mar 1894 in Ffx; father: Sandy WILKERSON; occ: farmer; res: Ffx; mother: Mary WILKERSON; inf: S. WILKERSON, father; pg:ln: 220:134

WILKERSON, Henry; CM; b. 24 Jul 1896 in Ffx; father: Sandy WILKERSON; occ: farmer; res: Ffx; mother: Mary WILKERSON; inf: S. WILKERSON, father; pg:ln: 228:128

WILKERSON, not named; CF; b. 13 Mar 1883 in Falls Church; father: Newton WILKERSON; occ: laborer; res: Falls Church; mother: Eliza WILKERSON; inf: father; pg:ln: 141:108

WILKINSON, Chas. K.; WM; b. 21 Aug 1895 nr Mt. Vernon; father: Chas. WILKINSON; occ: farmer; res: nr Mt. Vernon; mother: Mary A. WILKINSON; inf: mother; pg:ln: 224:132

WILLIAMS, ___ (dead); CF; b. 20 Jan 1889 in Ffx; father: Rezin
WILLIAMS; occ: farmer; res: Ffx; mother: Nancy WILLIAMS; inf: R.
WILLIAMS, father; pg:ln: 180:127

WILLIAMS, ___; CM; b. 29 Dec 1890 in Ffx; father: Resin WILLIAMS;
occ: farmer; res: Ffx; mother: Nancy WILLIAMS; inf: R. WILLIAMS,
father; pg:ln: 192:115

WILLIAMS, ___; WF; b. 28 Apr 1894 in Ffx; father: Moses T.
WILLIAMS; occ: farmer; res: Ffx; mother: Sarah WILLIAMS; inf:
Moses WILLIAMS, father; pg:ln: 220:132

WILLIAMS, Bertie; WF; b. 17 Jan 1885 in Dranes.; father: Moses F.
WILLIAMS; occ: laborer; res: Dranes.; mother: Sarah WILLIAMS; inf:
father; pg:ln: 154:87

WILLIAMS, Blanche; CF; b. 28 Mar 1895 nr Woodlawn; father: James
WILLIAMS; occ: farmer; res: nr Woodlawn; mother: Hattie
WILLIAMS; inf: father; pg:ln: 224:137

WILLIAMS, Burr; CM; b. 8 Dec 1894 in Ffx; father: Burr WILLIAMS; occ:
farmer; res: Ffx; mother: Ann WILLIAMS; inf: B. WILLIAMS, father;
pg:ln: 220:142

WILLIAMS, Catharine F. (twin); CF; b. 29 May 1883 in Falls Church;
father: Henry WILLIAMS; occ: farmer; res: Falls Church; mother:
Harriet WILLIAMS; inf: father; pg:ln: 141:104

WILLIAMS, Charlotte; CF; b. 10 Jun 1883 in Falls Church; father:
Robert WILLIAMS; occ: laborer; res: Falls Church; mother: Lucy
WILLIAMS; inf: father; pg:ln: 141:106

WILLIAMS, Chas. H.; CM; b. 9 Dec 1889 in Ffx; father: Uriah
WILLIAMS; occ: farmer; res: Ffx; mother: Malinda WILLIAMS; inf:
Uriah WILLIAMS, father; pg:ln: 184:108

WILLIAMS, Chas. P.; CM; b. 14 Feb 1885 in Falls Ch.; father: Ashton
WILLIAMS; occ: laborer; res: Falls Ch.; mother: Alice WILLIAMS; inf:
father; pg:ln: 154:89

WILLIAMS, Clarra; WF; b. 30 Apr 1888 in Ffx; father: Moses WILLIAMS;
occ: farmer; res: Ffx; mother: Sarah WILLIAMS; inf: M. WILLIAMS,
father; pg:ln: 175:100

WILLIAMS, Elizabeth; CF; b. 6 Sep 1890 in Ffx; father: Morris
WILLIAMS; occ: farmer; res: Ffx; mother: Lucy WILLIAMS; inf: M.
WILLIAMS, father; pg:ln: 188:120

WILLIAMS, Emma; WF; b. 8 Nov 1880 in Dranesville; father: Fielder
WILLIAMS; occ: farmer; res: Dranesville; mother: Elizabeth
WILLIAMS; inf: father; pg:ln: 126:84

WILLIAMS, Ethel; CF; b. 5 Jul 1889 in Ffx; father: Ashton WILLIAMS;
occ: farmer; res: Ffx; mother: Alice WILLIAMS; inf: A. WILLIAMS,
father; pg:ln: 180:128

WILLIAMS, Eva; CF; b. 1 Feb 1890 in Ffx; father: Lawrence H.
WILLIAMS; occ: farmer; res: Ffx; mother: Elizabt. WILLIAMS; inf: L.
H. WILLIAMS, father; pg:ln: 188:121

WILLIAMS, Frank; CM; b. 15 May 1881 in Dranesville; father: Rezin
WILLIAMS; occ: laborer; res: Dranesville; mother: Nancy WILLIAMS;
inf: father; pg:ln: 131:72

WILLIAMS, Gabriel; CM; b. 26 Dec 1893 nr Woodlawn; father:
Lawrence WILLIAMS; occ: laborer; res: nr Woodlawn; mother:
Elizabeth WILLIAMS; inf: parent; pg:ln: 212:96

WILLIAMS, Gabriel; CM; b. 4 Jan 1895 in Gum Spring; father: Lawrence
WILLIAMS; occ: laborer; res: Gum Spring; mother: Elizabeth
WILLIAMS; inf: father; pg:ln: 224:135

WILLIAMS, Geo. W.; CM; b. 2 Jan 1885 in Bailey's X Roads; father:
Robert WILLIAMS; occ: laborer; res: Bailey's X Roads; mother: Lucy
WILLIAMS; inf: father; pg:ln: 154:90

WILLIAMS, Herbert; CM; b. 15 Jul 1893 in ___; father: Zack WILLIAMS;
occ: farmer; res: Ffx; mother: Lizzie WILLIAMS; inf: Z. WILLIAMS,
father; pg:ln: 216:113

WILLIAMS, Jas. E.; CM; b. 1 Jan 1891 in Ffx; father: Jas. E. WILLIAMS;
occ: farmer; res: Ffx; mother: Adlade WILLIAMS; inf: J. E.
WILLIAMS, father; pg:ln: 201:116

WILLIAMS, Jesse; CM; b. 1 Dec 1896 in Ffx; father: Zack WILLIAMS;
occ: farmer; res: Ffx; mother: Lizzie WILLIAMS; inf: Z. WILLIAMS,
father; pg:ln: 228:130

WILLIAMS, Jno. R.; CM; b. 5 Mar 1889 in Ffx; father: Dock WILLIAMS;
occ: farmer; res: Ffx; mother: Lucinda WILLIAMS; inf: D. WILLIAMS,
father; pg:ln: 184:107

WILLIAMS, Lewis; CM; b. 22 Jun 1895 in Mason's Neck; father: Lewis
WILLIAMS; occ: farmer; res: Mason's Neck; mother: Sylvia
WILLIAMS; inf: father; pg:ln: 224:136

WILLIAMS, Ludwell; CM; b. 1 Dec 1883 in Dranesville; father: Rezin
WILLIAMS; occ: laborer; res: Dranesville; mother: Nancy WILLIAMS;
inf: father; pg:ln: 142:117

WILLIAMS, M. Louise; WF; b. 21 Aug 1880 in Providence; father:
Franklin WILLIAMS; occ: farmer; res: Vienna; mother: ___
WILLIAMS; inf: father; pg:ln: 126:83

WILLIAMS, Mary J.; CF; b. 8 Jun 1887 in Ffx; father: Lewis WILLIAMS;
occ: laborer; ·res: Ffx; mother: Sylvia WILLIAMS; inf: Lewis
WILLIAMS, father; pg:ln: 169:124

WILLIAMS, Mary; CF; b. 3 Jan 1887 in ___; father: R. WILLIAMS; occ:
farmer; res: Ffx; mother: Mary WILLIAMS; inf: R. WILLIAMS, father;
pg:ln: 165:172

WILLIAMS, Milton (twin); CM; b. 30 Jul 1895 in Mason's Neck; father:
Uriah WILLIAMS; occ: laborer; res: Mason's Neck; mother: Malinda
WILLIAMS; inf: father. The index shows a record of the birth of Uriah
Milton Williams 30 Jul 1894. colored, parents Uriah & Malinda.
Note: As your name Uriah Milton & later changed to Hugh Uriah
WILLIAMS? We would like information before we issue a birth
certificate. Chrisen Uriah Hugh and later changed to Hugh Uriah,
my twin brother is named Jesse Milton. The reason of lateness of
reply my oldest sister Mary Frances Hughes were away as to know
truth had to wait her return.; pg:ln: 224:134

WILLIAMS, not named (twin, dead); CF; b. 29 May 1883 in Falls
    Church; father: Henry WILLIAMS; occ: farmer; res: Falls Church;
    mother: Harriet WILLIAMS; inf: father; pg:ln: 141:105

[WILLIAMS], not named; CM; b. 27 Oct 1885 in Ffx; father: Jas. K.
    WILLIAMS; occ: farmer; res: Ffx; mother: Ann WILLIAMS; inf: J. K.
    WILLIAMS, father; pg:ln: 157:63

WILLIAMS, Rebecca; CF; b. 26 May 1885 in Ffx; father: Lewis
    WILLIAMS; occ: farmer; res: Ffx; mother: Maria WILLIAMS; inf: L.
    WILLIAM[S], father; pg:ln: 157:65

WILLIAMS, Richard W.; CM; b. 6 Jun 1891 in Belmont Bay; father:
    Lewis WILLIAMS; occ: laborer; res: Belmont Bay; mother: Sarah
    WILLIAMS; inf: parent; pg:ln: 196:23

WILLIAMS, Robert W.; CM; b. 31 Dec 1893 nr Woodlawn; father: H. L.
    WILLIAMS; occ: laborer; res: nr Woodlawn; mother: Charity
    WILLIAMS; inf: parent; pg:ln: 212:95

WILLIAMS, Robt E.; CM; b. 16 Dec 1886 in Falls Church; father: Robt.
    WILLIAMS; occ: laborer; res: Falls Church; mother: Lucy WILLIAMS;
    inf: fathɘr; pg:ln: 159:66

WILLIAMS, Roland R.; CM; b. 6 Jul 1889 in Ffx; father: Lewis
    WILLIAMS; occ: farmer; res: Ffx; mother: Sylvia WILLIAMS; inf:
    Lewis WILLIAMS, father; pg:ln: 184:109

WILLIAMS, Sadie; CF; b. 11 Dec 1894 in Ffx; father: Ashton WILLIAMS;
    occ: farmer; res: Ffx; mother: Annie WILLIAMS; inf: A. WILLIAMS,
    father; pg:ln: 220:138

WILLIAMS, Thos. E.; CM; b. 3 May 1891 in Ffx; father: Thos.
    WILLIAMS; occ: farmer; res: Ffx; mother: Matilda WILLIAMS; inf:
    Thos. WILLIAMS, father; pg:ln: 201:114

WILLIAMS, Uriah (twin); CM; b. 30 Jul 1895 in Mason's Neck; father:
    Uriah WILLIAMS; occ: laborer; res: Mason's Neck; mother: Malinda
    WILLIAMS; inf: father The index shows a record of the birth of Uriah
    Milton Williams 30 Jul 1894. colored, parents Uriah & Malinda.
    Note: As your name Uriah Milton & later changed to Hugh Uriah
    WILLIAMS? We would like information before we issue a birth
    certificate. Chrisen Uriah Hugh and later changed to Hugh Uriah,
    my twin brother is named Jesse Milton. The reason of latness of
    reply my oldest sister Mary Frances Hughes were away as to know
    truth had to wait her return.; pg:ln: 224:134

WILLIAMS, Virgie; CF; b. 24 Dec 1894 in Ffx; father: Robt. WILLIAMS;
    occ: farmer; res: Ffx; mother: Lucy WILLIAMS; inf: Robt. WILLIAMS,
    father; pg:ln: 220:139

WILLIAMS, Zadie; CF; b. 15 Dec 1890 in Ffx; father: Henry WILLIAMS;
    occ: farmer; res: Ffx; mother: Laura WILLIAMS; inf: H. WILLIAMS,
    father; pg:ln: 192:112

WILLIAMSON, Daisy Bell; WF; b. 13 Oct 1896 nr Pohick Ch.; father:
    John T. WILLIAMSON; occ: fisherman; res: nr Pohick Ch.; mother:
    Laura WILLIAMSON; inf: mother; pg:ln: 232:134

WILLIAMSON, Mark; WM; b. 8 Apr 1887 in Ffx; father: J. R. WILLIAMSON; occ: blacksmith; res: Ffx; mother: Mary WILLIAMSON; inf: J. R. WILLIAMSON, father; pg:ln: 169:123

WILLIAMSON, Martha; WF; b. 12 Aug 1889 in Ffx; father: Jno. R. WILLIAMSON; occ: farmer; res: Ffx; mother: Mary WILLIAMSON; inf: J. R. WILLIAMSON, father; pg:ln: 183:101

WILLIAMSON, Rebecca; WF; b. 21 Oct 1882 in Ffx; father: D. WILLIAMSON; occ: ___; res: ___; mother: Mary WILLIAMSON; inf: D. WILLIAMSON, father; pg:ln: 138:86

WILMOTH, Mary Ireane [initial M. lined thru]; WF; b. 13 Mar 1893 in ___; father: H. C. WILMOTH; occ: farmer; res: Ffx; mother: Mary Ireane WILMOTH [initial W. lined thru]; inf: H. C. WILMOTH, father. Note: This is to certify that Mary Ireane Wilmoth was born in Vienna, Fairfax County, Virginia on 13 Mar 1893. Father's name Henry C. Wilmoth. Mother's name before marriage, Mary Ireane Groves. Signed Henry C. Wilmoth, father.; pg:ln: 216:110

WILSON, Fred; WM; b. 9 Aug 1888 in Ffx; father: Z. P. WILSON; occ: laborer; res: Ffx; mother: Gertrude WILSON; inf: Z. P. WILSON, father; pg:ln: 172:76

WILSON, Manda D.; WF; b. 5 Feb 1887 in Ffx; father: C. V. WILSON; occ: farmer; res: Ffx; mother: Ida WILSON; inf: C. V. WILSON, father; pg:ln: 169:121

WILSON, Maud L.; WF; b. 16 Aug 1888 in Ffx; father: C. B. WILSON; occ: laborer; res: Ffx; mother: Nannie WILSON; inf: C. B. WILSON, father; pg:ln: 172:75

WINSTON, Clarence Jay; WM; b. 31 May 1891 nr Alexandria; father: W. H. WINSTON; occ: carpenter; res: West End; mother: A. E. WINSTON; inf: parents; pg:ln: 195:34

WINZELL, Virgie J.; WF; b. 11 Dec 1883 in Dranesville; father: Geo. W. WINZELL; occ: farmer; res: Dranesville; mother: Carrie M. WINZELL; inf: father; pg:ln: 142:118

WOOD, Ella B.; CF; b. 12 Jun 1892 nr Accotink; father: Isaac WOOD; occ: laborer; res: nr Accotink; mother: Laura WOOD; inf: father; pg:ln: 206:15

WOOD, Georgia; CF; b. 21 Dec 1894 in Ffx; father: Douglas WOOD; occ: farmer; res: Ffx; mother: Minnie WOOD; inf: D. WOOD, father; pg:ln: 220:141

WOOD, Manda A.; CF; b. 13 Jun 1893 in ___; father: Douglas WOOD; occ: farmer; res: ___; mother: Matilda WOOD; inf: D. WOOD, father; pg:ln: 215:108

WOOD, Matilda; CF; b. 15 Nov 1889 in Ffx; father: Isaac WOOD; occ: farmer; res: Ffx; mother: Laura WOOD; inf: I. WOOD, father; pg:ln: 183:106

WOOD, W.; CM; b. 22 Oct 1889 in Ffx; father: Douglas WOOD; occ: farmer; res: Ffx; mother: Matilda WOOD; inf: D. WOOD, father; pg:ln: 180:134

WOODARD, Annie E.; WF; b. 14 Nov 1889 in Ffx; father: Geo.
WOODARD; occ: farmer; res: Ffx; mother: Alice WOODARD; inf: G.
WOODARD, father; pg:ln: 180:131

WOODDEN, Henry; CM; b. 16 Mar 1890 in Ffx; father: Thos.
WOODDEN; occ: farmer; res: Ffx; mother: Ellen WOODDEN; inf:
Thos. WOODDEN, father; pg:ln: 192:111

WOODSON, Flora; CF; b. 15 Feb 1892 in Ffx; father: Thos.
WOODSON; occ: farmer; res: ___; mother: Ellen WOODSON; inf:
Thos. WOODSON, father; pg:ln: 205:112

WOODYARD, Harry; WM; b. 4 Dec 1889 in Ffx; father: R. W.
WOODYARD; occ: farmer; res: Ffx; mother: Mary WOODYARD; inf:
R. W. WOODYARD, father; pg:ln: 183:104

WOODYARD, Irene; WF; b. 20 Sep 1896 nr Alex; father: Wm.
WOODYARD; occ: laborer; res: Cameron; mother: Silma
WOODYARD; inf: mother; pg:ln: 232:133

WOODYARD, Jas P.; WF; b. 12 Jun 1888 in Ffx; father: J. P.
WOODYARD; occ: farmer; res: Ffx; mother: M. V. WOODYARD; inf:
M. V. WOODYARD, mother; pg:ln: 172:77

WOODYARD, Lillie E.; WF; b. 15 Mar 1882 in Ffx; father: Lewis
WOODYARD; occ: ___; res: ___; mother: Emma WOODYARD; inf:
L. WOODYARD, father; pg:ln: 138:83

WOODYARD, Nettie M.; WF; b. 1 Apr 1885 in Ffx; father: Jas. P.
WOODYARD; occ: farmer; res: Ffx; mother: Mary V. WOODYARD;
inf: J. P. WOODYARD, father; pg:ln: 157:61

WOODYARD, Osa; WM; b. 19 Apr 1883 in Ffx; father: I. F.
WOODYARD; occ: farmer; res: Ffx; mother: Elvira WOODYARD; inf:
I. F. WOODYARD, father; pg:ln: 145:83

WOODYARD, Pearle V.; WF; b. 3 Feb 1885 in Ffx; father: Isaac F.
WOODYARD; occ: farmer; res: Ffx; mother: Elvira WOODYARD; inf:
I. F. WOODYARD, father; pg:ln: 157:64

WOODYARD, Sudie M.; WF; b. 4 Mar 1892 nr Fairfax Sta.; father: Isaac
F. WOODYARD; occ: farmer; res: nr Fairfax Sta.; mother: Elvira
WOODYARD; inf: father; pg:ln: 209:59

WOODYARD, W.; WM; b. 21 Mar 1893 in ___; father: W. H.
WOODYARD; occ: farmer; res: ___; mother: August. WOODYARD;
inf: W. H. WOODYARD, father; pg:ln: 215:103

WOOSTER, Chas.; WM; b. 30 Mar 1883 in Ffx; father: F. WOOSTER
Jr.; occ: farmer; res: Ffx; mother: Ella WOOSTER; inf: F. WOOSTER
Jr., father; pg:ln: 145:84

WOOSTER, Edith D.; WF; b. 6 Sep 1889 in Ffx; father: Frank
WOOSTER Jr.; occ: farmer; res: Ffx; mother: Ella WOOSTER; inf: F.
WOOSTER Jr., father; pg:ln: 183:103

WOOSTER, Luella; WF; b. 4 Jul 1887 in Ffx; father: Beauregard
WOOSTER; occ: farmer; res: Ffx; mother: Mary WOOSTER; inf: B.
WOOSTER, father; pg:ln: 169:119

WOOSTER, Rebecca J.; WF; b. 13 Aug 1880 in ___; father: Bogue
WOOSTER; occ: farmer; res: Ffx; mother: Mary; inf: B. WOOSTER,
father; pg:ln: 129:100

WORTHINGTON, Elizabeth; WF; b. 25 Mar 1883 in Seminary; father:
Geo. Y. WORTHINGTON; occ: merchant; res: Seminary; mother: W.
T. WORTHINGTON; inf: father; pg:ln: 142:109

WRENN, Alice V.; WF; b. 1 Nov 1881 in Prov.; father: Wm. H. WRENN;
occ: farmer; res: Prov.; mother: Annie WRENN; inf: father; pg:ln:
131:73

WRENN, E. G.; WM; b. 27 Oct 1885 in Ffx; father: Albt. WRENN; occ:
farmer; res: Ffx; mother: Hannah WRENN; inf: A. WRENN, father;
pg:ln: 157:62

WRENN, Elcon; WM; b. 28 Jan 1890 in Ffx; father: G. H. WRENN; occ:
farmer; res: Ffx; mother: Laura WRENN; inf: G. H. WRENN, father;
pg:ln: 192:117

WRENN, Jennie E.; WF; b. 5 Jun 1887 in Ffx; father: W. C. WRENN;
occ: merchant; res: Ffx; mother: Susan L. WRENN; inf: W. C.
WRENN, father; pg:ln: 169:122

WRENN, Mattie; WF; b. 28 May 1883 in Providence Dist.; father: W. H.
WRENN; occ: farmer; res: Providence Dist.; mother: Annie WRENN;
inf: father; pg:ln: 142:113

WRENN, Otha; WF; b. 30 Nov 1883 in Dranesville; father: G. H.
WRENN; occ: farmer; res: Dranesville; mother: Laura C. WRENN;
inf: father; pg:ln: 142:116

WRENN, Rufus; WM; b. 21 Apr 1893 in ___; father: G. H. WRENN; occ:
farmer; res: Ffx; mother: Laura WRENN; inf: G. H. WRENN, father;
pg:ln: 216:114

WRENN, Ruth; WF; b. 4 Jul 1887 in ___; father: J. O. WRENN; occ:
farmer; res: Ffx; mother: Lula WRENN; inf: J. O. WRENN, father;
pg:ln: 165:176

WRENN, Vernor; WM; b. 16 Sep 1885 in Chantilly; father: W. C.
WRENN; occ: farmer; res: Chantilly; mother: Susan WRENN; inf:
father; pg:ln: 154:85

WRIGHT, Anderson A.; CM; b. 7 Aug 1882 in Ffx; father: Anderson
WRIGHT; occ: ___; res: ___; mother: Willie Ann WRIGHT; inf: A.
WRIGHT, father; pg:ln: 138:82

WRIGHT, Clarence; CM; b. 16 Oct 1896 nr Burke Sta; father: Henry
WRIGHT; occ: laborer; res: nr Burke; mother: Martha WRIGHT; inf:
mother; pg:ln: 232:131

WRIGHT, Donia A.; CF; b. 10 May 1888 in Ffx; father: Anderson
WRIGHT; occ: farmer; res: Ffx; mother: W. A. WRIGHT; inf: A.
WRIGHT, father; pg:ln: 172:78

WRIGHT, Susetta; CF; b. 27 May 1880 in ___; father: Anderson
WRIGHT; occ: farmer; res: Ffx; mother: Willann; inf: A. WRIGHT,
father; pg:ln: 129:97

WRIGHT, William; CF; b. 25 Sep 1884 in Ffx; father: Anderson
WRIGHT; occ: farmer; res: Ffx; mother: Willann WRIGHT; inf: A.
WRIGHT, father; pg:ln: 148:76

YATES, Frances; WF; b. 18 May 1892 nr Chantilly; father: J. W.
YATES; occ: farmer; res: Chantilly; mother: Sarah YATES; inf:
father; pg:ln: 208:27

YOUNG, A. O.; WM; b. 4 Sept 1894 in Ffx; father: W. F. YOUNG; occ: farmer; res: Ffx; mother: S. V. YOUNG; inf: W. F. YOUNG, father; pg:ln: 220:146

YOUNG, Annie M.; CF; b. 20 Jul 1883 in Seminary; father: James YOUNG; occ: laborer; res: Seminary; mother: Harriett YOUNG; inf: father; pg:ln: 142:119

YOUNG, Emiley; WF; b. 14 Jan 1881 in Ffx; father: Jas. P. YOUNG; occ: farmer; res: Ffx; mother: Elizabt. YOUNG; inf: J. P. YOUNG, father; pg:ln: 133:58

YOUNG, James; CM; b. 29 Aug 1892 in Ffx; father: Jas. YOUNG; occ: farmer; res: ___; mother: Harriet YOUNG; inf: J. YOUNG, father; pg:ln: 205:119

YOUNG, Jesse; WM; b. 25 Jun 1893 in ___; father: Jno. W. YOUNG; occ: farmer; res: Ffx; mother: Annie YOUNG; inf: J. W. YOUNG, father; pg:ln: 216:116

YOUNG, W. T.; WM; b. 8 Dec 1892 in Ffx; father: W. F. YOUNG; occ: farmer; res: ___; mother: S. V. YOUNG; inf: W. F. YOUNG, father; pg:ln: 205:120

YOUNG, Waddie; CF; b. 7 Nov 1892 nr Mt. Vernon; father: Harry YOUNG; occ: laborer; res: nr Mt. Vernon; mother: Hannah YOUNG; inf: father; pg:ln: 206:16

YOUNT, Ephraim C.; WM; b. 5 Nov 1882 in Dranesville; father: Ephraim YOUNT; occ: farmer; res: Dranes.; mother: Laura R. YOUNT; inf: father; pg:ln: 135:72

YOUNT, Morris A.; WM; b. 5 Oct 1880 in Herndon; father: Ephriam M. YOUNT; occ: farmer; res: Herndon; mother: Laura R. YOUNT; inf: father; pg:ln: 126:87

ZIMMERMAN, Frank; WF; b. 2 Apr 1896 nr Mt. Vernon; father: Chas ZIMMERMAN; occ: farmer; res: nr Mt. Vernon; mother: Mary ZIMMERMAN; inf: mother; pg:ln: 232:137

INDEX
Different Surnames

Other Heritage Books by Patricia B. Duncan:

1850 Fairfax County and Loudoun County, Virginia Slave Schedule

1850 Fauquier County, Virginia Slave Schedule

1860 Loudoun County, Virginia Slave Schedule

Clarke County, Virginia Death Register, 1853-1896, with Birth Records, 1855-1856, Entered on Death Register

Clarke County, Virginia Marriages, 1836-1886

Clarke County, Virginia Marriages, 1887-1925

Clarke County, Virginia Will Book Abstracts: Books A-I (1836-1904) and 1A-3C (1841-1913)

Fairfax County, Virginia Birth Register, 1853-1879

Fairfax County, Virginia Birth Register, 1880-1896

Fauquier County, Virginia, Birth Register, 1853-1880

Fauquier County, Virginia, Birth Register, 1881-1896

Fauquier County, Virginia, Marriage Register, 1854-1882

Fauquier County, Virginia, Marriage Register, 1883-1906

Fauquier County, Virginia Death Register, 1853-1896

Hunterdon County, New Jersey 1895 State Census, Part I: Alexandria-Junction

Hunterdon County, New Jersey 1895 State Census, Part II: Kingwood-West Amwell

Genealogical Abstracts from The Lambertville Press, *Lambertville, New Jersey: 4 November 1858 (Vol. 1, Number 1) to 30 October 1861 (Vol. 3, Number 155)*

Genealogical Abstracts from The Democratic Mirror *and* The Mirror, *1857-1879, Loudoun County, Virginia*

Genealogical Abstracts from The Mirror, *1880-1890, Loudoun County, Virginia*

Genealogical Abstracts from The Mirror, *1891-1899, Loudoun County, Virginia*

Genealogical Abstracts from The Mirror, *1900-1919, Loudoun County, Virginia*

Genealogical Abstracts from The Telephone, *1881-1888, Loudoun County, Virginia*

Genealogical Abstracts from The Telephone, *1889-1896, Loudoun County, Virginia*

Jefferson County, [West] Virginia Death Register, 1853-1880

Jefferson County, West Virginia Death Register, 1881-1903

Jefferson County, Virginia 1802-1813 Personal Property Tax Lists

Jefferson County, Virginia 1814-1824 Personal Property Tax Lists

Jefferson County, Virginia 1825-1841 Personal Property Tax Lists

1810-1840 Loudoun County, Virginia Federal Population Census Index

1860 Loudoun County, Virginia Federal Population Census Index

1870 Loudoun County, Virginia Federal Population Census Index

Abstracts from Loudoun County, Virginia Guardian Accounts: Books A-H, 1759-1904

Abstracts of Loudoun County, Virginia Register of Free Negroes, 1844-1861

Index to Loudoun County, Virginia Land Deed Books A-Z, 1757-1800

Index to Loudoun County, Virginia Land Deed Books 2A-2M, 1800-1810

Index to Loudoun County, Virginia Land Deed Books 2N-2U, 1811-1817

Index to Loudoun County, Virginia Land Deed Books 2V-3D, 1817-1822

Index to Loudoun County, Virginia Land Deed Books 3E-3M, 1822-1826

Index to Loudoun County, Virginia Land Deed Books 3N-3V, 1826-1831

Index to Loudoun County, Virginia Land Deed Books 3W-4D, 1831-1835

Index to Loudoun County, Virginia Land Deed Books 4E-4N, 1835-1840

Index to Loudoun County, Virginia Land Deed Books 4O-4V, 1840-1846

Loudoun County, Virginia Birth Register, 1853-1879

Loudoun County, Virginia Birth Register, 1880-1896

Loudoun County, Virginia Clerks Probate Records
Book 1 (1904-1921) and Book 2 (1922-1938)

(With Elizabeth R. Frain) *Loudoun County, Virginia Marriages after 1850,*
Volume 1, 1851-1880

Loudoun County, Virginia Partially Proven Deeds

Loudoun County, Virginia 1800-1810 Personal Property Taxes

Loudoun County, Virginia 1826-1834 Personal Property Taxes

Loudoun County, Virginia Will Book Abstracts, Books A-Z, Dec. 1757-Jun. 1841

Loudoun County, Virginia Will Book Abstracts, Books 2A-3C, Jun. 1841-Dec. 1879
and Superior Court Books A and B, 1810-1888

Loudoun County, Virginia Will Book Index, 1757-1946

Genealogical Abstracts from The Brunswick Herald, *Brunswick, Maryland:*
Mar. 6 1891-Dec. 28 1894

Genealogical Abstracts from The Brunswick Herald, *Brunswick, Maryland:*
Jan. 4 1895-Dec. 30 1898

Genealogical Abstracts from The Brunswick Herald, *Brunswick, Maryland:*
Jan. 6 1899-Dec. 26 1902

Genealogical Abstracts from The Brunswick Herald, *Brunswick, Maryland:*
Jan. 2 1903-June 29 1906

Genealogical Abstracts from The Brunswick Herald, *Brunswick, Maryland:*
July 6 1906-Feb. 25 1910

CD: *Loudoun County, Virginia Personal Property Tax List, 1782-1850*